AF600135

THE NEW CHURCH LAW ON MATRIMONY

DISSERTATION

Submitted to the Faculty of Sacred Sciences at the Catholic University of America in partial fulfillment of requirements for the Doctorate in Canon Law.

BY THE

REV. JOSEPH J. C. PETROVITS, J.C.L., S.T.D.

OF THE DIOCESE OF HARRISBURG

PHILADELPHIA

JOHN JOSEPH McVEY

1919

INTRODUCTION.

The promulgation of the New Code of Canon Law has not only revolutionized ecclesiastical discipline but has become an epoch-making factor of far-reaching consequences. By codifying its laws the Church has simplified, facilitated, and stabilized the study of a very important ecclesiastical science, and has afforded an access to a permanent and authentic source which, besides serving as a guide, will constitute the basis of Church government. The systematic presentation of the various canons contained in the New Code is of signal assistance to the student, but the terseness of the language in which they are couched and the scientific and technical terminology employed, must of necessity give rise to some difficulties. These difficulties have been anticipated by the Supreme Legislator and a remedy was applied by establishing a Sacred Congregation, or rather *Commission,* whose exclusive purpose is to render authentic decisions in doubts arising in connection with the interpretation of the various canons. This *Commission* has already exercised its function by promulgating authentic declarations and interpretations in doubts submitted for solution. Some of these decisions concern the subject which forms the burden of this work.

The subject of matrimony, as viewed in the light of the New Code of Canon Law, has undergone many changes, some of them fundamental, others again less significant. With regard to its importance the subject cannot be overemphasized. Its comprehensiveness is admitted by all who are engaged in the sacred ministry.

The principles directly or indirectly connected with it are many, their application is very consequential. Some of the 133 canons, within whose compass the main discipline of the Church on this subject (exclusive of some specific dispensations, and matrimonial trials) is comprised, embody a discipline entirely new, others again either implicitly or explicitly modify or abrogate the former law. To explain the canons mentioned above all the available sources on which the author could draw were limited to the former discipline of the Church as reflected in the *Corpus Iuris,* in the numerous decisions of the various Sacred Congregations, in the works of accepted and approved authors, and to the mere wording in which the matrimonial legislation is couched. This limitation is due to the fact that the present law is of very recent origin, the interpretations thus far suggested fragmentary, hastily compiled and necessarily inadequate, and the times unfavorable to serious and extensive research, to publication, and to the procuring of works, if there be any, on the subject treated in this book. These facts will explain why the author was not in a position to advance authorities for some of his statements regarding certain opinions he has espoused in the interpretation of canons containing a law either entirely new or modified when compared with the former discipline. Though the author guarded his statements as much as possible, the seeming obscurity and indefiniteness prevailing in some canons constrain him to say that some of his opinions in this, what may be styled a pioneer-work, are only tentative and provisional.

These facts, when viewed cumulatively, the author hopes, will constitute a sufficient ground for asking indulgence and leniency on the part of those whose critical acumen is better equipped than his own to discern any flaws or incorrect statements which might have crept into his work for want of more adequate comprehension of the law each canon is intended to enforce.

As time advances, whatever inaccuracies may be contained in this work the author hopes to correct after the meaning of certain canons has been clarified, either by authentic decisions emanating from the "*Commissio*" or by interpretations advanced by canonists whose opinions are of weight. In the meantime, the author hopes that his work will be of some assistance to the shepherds of souls who, owing to their many-sided duties, cannot spare the time consumed in research such as is required of one who wishes to give a fairly comprehensive interpretation of the scope of each canon legislating on matrimony.

In conclusion the author wishes to retract any and all statements which are not strictly in accord with the law contained in the New Code. He submits all his opinions to the decision of the Church and will welcome all criticism.

AUTHOR.

CATHOLIC UNIVERSITY OF AMERICA, WASHINGTON, D. C.

On Ascension Day, May 29, 1919.

TABLE OF CONTENTS.

CHAPTER I.

Preliminary Notions of Marriage.

CHAPTER II.

Espousals.

CHAPTER III.

Transactions Preceding the Celebration of Marriage.

CHAPTER IV.

Matrimonial Impediments.

CHAPTER V.

Impedient Impediments.

CHAPTER VI.

Diriment Impediments.

CHAPTER VII.

Matrimonial Consent.

CHAPTER VIII.

The Form to be Observed in the Celebration of Marriage.

CHAPTER IX.

CHAPTER X.

Time and Place of Marriage.

CHAPTER XI.

The Effects of Marriage.

CHAPTER XII.

The Separation of Consorts.

CHAPTER XIII.

The Validation of Marriage.

CHAPTER XIV.

ERRATA.

Page 6, line 16, "reception" should read "making."

Page 6, line 26, "anathemizes" should read "anathematizes."

Page 8, line 16, "is a source" should read "is the source."

Page 9, line 19, "sacrament of marriage" should read "sacrament of matrimony."

Page 10, line 8, "anathemizes" should read "anathematizes."

Page 14, line 8, "in the performance in" should read "in the performance of."

Page 23, line 22, "intimated" should read "intimidated."

Page 25, line 6, "it sway" should read "its way."

Page 31, line 32, "to the mere civil effects" should read "over the mere civil effects."

Page 34, line 7, "Bishop" should read "Ordinary."

Page 35, line 16, "texts" should read "text."

Page 40, line 19, "certain subject" should read "certain subjects."

Page 50, line 19, "sixteenth" should read "fourteenth."

Page 50, line 20, "fourteenth" should read "twelfth."

Page 63, line 18, "hope" should read "fear."

Page 73, line 11, "Gieran" should read "Gearin."

Page 80, line 11, "grades" should read "grade."

Page 86, line 28, "Gieran" should read "Gearin."

Page 117, line 1, "diffamation" should read "defamation."

Page 122, line 21, "Romal Missal" should read "Roman Missal."

Page 123, line 15, "*scandale remoto*" should read "*scandalo remoto.*"

Page 162, line 9, "baptists" should read "Baptists."

Page 169, line 31, "diffamation" should read "defamation."

Page 175, line 16, "unforseen" should read "unforeseen."

Page 196, line 13, "anathemizes" should read "anathematizes."

Page 222, line 1, "burden to repair" should read "burden of repairing."

Page 225, line 10, "desirous to establish" should read "desirous of establishing."

The New Church Law on Matrimony.

CHAPTER I.

Preliminary Notions of Marriage.
(Canons 1012-1016.)

I. Marriage in General.

1. The word matrimony is a compound derived from two Latin words, namely, *matris munium,* meaning the office of the mother. The burdens inherent in gestation, the pain accompanying parturition and the numerous anxieties subsequent to child-birth, being indicative of the most intimate relationship between mother and child, are generally adduced as the reason why the word mother in preference to that of father has been embodied in the name of this sacrament.[1]

2. Matrimony may be considered as a mere contract or as a contract elevated to the dignity of a sacrament. It is a mere contract between two unbaptized persons. It becomes a contract invested with sacramental dignity between two baptized persons.[2] The former does not differ from the latter essentially. The sacrament of matrimony is a contract retaining all the character-

[1] "Cum puer adhuc infans existat, propter quod magis materno indiget solatio, quam paterno, sibique (matri) ante partum onerosus, dolorosus in partu, post partum laboriosus fuisse noscatur ac ex hoc legitima coniunctio maris et feminae magis matrimonium quam patrimonium nuncupatur. (Decr. Gregorii IX, *Lib. III, tit. XXXIII; De conversione infidelium, cap. II.*)

[2] Cod. Iur. Can., Can. 1012, §1.

istics it enjoys by virtue of natural law, and becoming supernaturalized by sanctifying grace, this grace being calculated not only to perfect the union of the Christian couple but also to promote the end of this union in a special manner. Since, however, by virtue of the supervening grace, there is an accidental difference between the natural contract and the matrimonial contract, it will be necessary to treat them individually.

II. Marriage as a Mere Natural Contract.

(Canon 1012.)

3. Marriage may be taken in a twofold sense, *viz.,* marriage *in fieri,* and marriage *in facto esse.* The former is a contract in which a qualified man and woman mutually oblige themselves to an indissoluble union in which by mutual consent each becomes a partial co-principle in the procreation of offspring. The indissoluble union, or the marriage bond thus arising, is called marriage *in facto esse.*

4. The leading modern theologians as well as those of the past are practically unanimous in teaching that marriage is a real bi-lateral contract imposing an obligation on the contracting parties by virtue of commutative justice.[3] This needs no proof. It is obvious that the parties concerned form the material object of the contract, while its formal object is the particular mode of life arising therefrom. In this mode of life the contracting parties mutually oblige themselves not only to render those things and to perform those duties which are essential to the very nature of such special contract, but also to abstain from everything incompatible with its nature.

[3] For the adversaries of this opinion see WERNZ, *De matrimonio,* n. 30. Rome, 1904.

5. It must be borne in mind that marriage, aside from its sacramental dignity, is, by its very nature, something holy.[4] Therefore, the contract from which it springs is of a superior order,[5] and, in a certain sense, may be qualified as religious.[6]

6. Hence it differs from other contracts in several respects. Its material object in the New Law must be only one man and one woman. Other contracts may be valid even by virtue of unilateral obligation, arising on the part of only one of the contracting parties. The distinctive characteristic of the matrimonial contract is that it binds either both parties or neither one of them.[7] Neither the civil authority, nor the contracting parties themselves possess as much right over the matrimonial contract as is ceded to them over mere civil contracts. Finally, the duration and the firmness of the matrimonial contract do not depend on the contracting parties, for, even in the case of only a ratified marriage, the contract is not rescindable at their will. This difference between the matrimonial contract and other contracts is founded on the religious character of the former, which, even among the unbaptized, in a wide sense, symbolizes the sacred and indissoluble union existing between Christ and His Church.[8]

7. Since marriage is a real bilateral contract, in order that it may be valid, it must possess all the essential characteristics requisite for a binding contract, *viz.*, it must be entered into with a true, free, mutual, simultaneous, and externally expressed consent by two qualified individuals. This qualification presupposes a physical aptitude for the act of procreation, freedom

[4] "Sit sua vi, sua natura, sua sponte sacrum" (ENCYCL. *"Arcanum" Leonis XIII Acta*, vol. II, p. 23).

[5] GASPARRI, *De Matrimonio*, n. 202. Paris, 1891.

[6] WERNZ, *op. cit.*, n. 37.

[7] S. THOMAS, *Suppl. IIIae*, p., q. XLVII, a. 4. c.

[8] *Gen.* II, 23, 24.

from diriment impediment prohibitive by natural or divine law, and a sufficient foreknowledge of the future responsibilities. It also implies a mutual willingness to comply with those essentials which constitute the primary and the secondary end of marriage. The contracting parties must conform to the civil law regulating such contracts, and introduced by the legitimate authority to which they are subject.

8. The essence of the marriage *in fieri* consists in the manifestation of mutual consent to the matrimonial bond. This implies a mutual exclusive and perpetual right which each of the contracting parties yields over the body of the other for the purpose of procreation and education of children. The essence of the marriage *in facto esse* consists in the conjugal union (*ligamen*).[9] The actual consummation of marriage, and community of shelter, of table and bed, pertain only to the integrity of the matrimonial contract, not to its essence.[10]

9. A question may now arise as to the legitimate authority over the matrimonial contracts of unbaptized persons. It is manifest that an infidel, not being a subject of the Catholic Church, can only indirectly be affected by Canon Law, *viz.,* when he enters into marriage with a baptized person, regardless of whether the baptism was administered in the Catholic Church or outside of it. It cannot be presumed, however, that so sacred an institution as marriage was left to the whims and caprices of individuals. It is certain that in the Old Covenant marriage was regulated by civil authority, whose duty it is to safeguard the interests and welfare of society. These considerations lead one to infer that the legitimately constituted

[9] GASPARRI, *op. cit.,* nn. 206, 207.

[10] WERNZ, *op. cit.,* n. 36; SCHMALZGRUEBER, *De matrimonio,* tit. I, sec. II, n. 256; GASPARRI, *op. cit.,* n. 859.

civil authority may rightly exercise the function of guardian over the matrimonial contracts of infidels, this permission being granted to it not by virtue of natural law, but by virtue of transferred right. This opinion is confirmed by the principle that things of natural law ought to be interpreted by positive law.[11]

10. We are confronted here with a much mooted question whose settlement was effected by the new legislation. The Roman Curia always acted on the opinion just mentioned, and it may rightly be called the more common opinion of the leading canonists and theologians.[12] Consequently, two unbaptized persons who are subject to the laws of two different states cannot contract a valid marriage, if either of them is disqualified by a diriment impediment of his state.[13] In case a dispensation is granted in behalf of the Catholic party, but the unbaptized party labors under a diriment impediment imposed by the civil law, the marriage is null. This conclusion is drawn from the nature of the matrimonial contract, for whose validity the absolute competency of both parties is required. When the Church grants a dispensation it is to be presumed that the contemplated marriage will be contracted with a person who does not labor under an impediment. The canonical dispensation does not render competent the unbaptized party whom the civil law disqualifies for a just reason.[14]

III. Marriage as a Contract and Sacrament.

(Canon 1012.)

11. Matrimony is a sacrament conferring a special

[11] D'ANNIBALE, *Summa Theol. Moralis*, vol. III, n. 425. Romae, 1892.
[12] WERNZ, *op. cit.*, nn. 80, 81; COD. IUR. CAN., Can. 1036, §3.
[13] WERNZ, *op. cit.*, n. 40.
[14] GASPARRI, *op. cit.*, n. 297.

supernatural grace to enable two united Christians to discharge faithfully their conjugal obligations. This supernatural assistance is not confined to the duties which the contracting parties owe to each other. It extends over the whole sphere of the primary and secondary ends of marriage, including the procreation and the mental, physical and moral training of their children.

12. It is certain that the matrimonial contract between two baptized persons is invested with the dignity of a sacrament.[15] The Sacred Scriptures, together with tradition containing the practically unanimous teaching handed down by the Fathers of the Church, furnish the dogmatic theologian with ample evidence to convince any unbiased inquirer on this point. The valid reception of a marriage contract between Christians necessitates the simultaneous reception of the sacrament of matrimony; the contract being inseparably united with the sacrament. This proposition can be proved, whether it is viewed dogmatically or historically. The various texts taken from the Holy Scripture,[16] the testimony of the Fathers,[17] the definitions of various Councils,[18] the testimony of ancient Rituals,[19] and iconographic documents [20] have finally culminated in the first canon formulated by the Council of Trent which anathemizes those who assert that matrimony is not one of the seven sacraments instituted by Christ to give a special grace.[21]

[15] Cod. Iur. Can., Can. 1012.
[16] *Matt.* XIX, 6; *Eph.* V, 26-32.
[17] See text cited by De Smet, *op. cit.*, n. 99.
[18] *II. Lateran Council* (1139), Mansi, vol. 21, col. 532; *Council of Verona* (1184), *loc. cit.*, vol. 22, col. 477; *Council of Florence* (1438), *loc. cit.*, vol. 31a, col. 1058.
[19] Martène, *De Antiquis Ecc. Ritibus,* lib. I, p. II, p. 614; Rotomagi, 1700.
[20] Martigny, *Dictionnaire . . . ,* art., *Mariage Chrétien,* p. 446.
[21] Sessio XXIV, *de sacramento matrimonii,* can. I.

13. Pope Pius IX condemned the proposition which holds that the sacrament of matrimony can be dissociated from the contract,[22] and Leo XIII declares the two inseparable.[23] Therefore, the matrimonial contract of unbaptized persons is a natural contract; that of baptized persons supernatural. It is not the nature but only the order of the contract that undergoes a change by virtue of the sacramental grace.[24] The distinction between the sacrament and the matrimonial contract has a foundation *in re,* but *in se* the two cannot be disunited. To the Church alone has been committed the administration of sacred things. Therefore, the opinion which establishes an ontological distinction between the sacrament and the matrimonial contract (in one and the same union) the latter to be regulated by the state and the former by the Church, must be stigmatized as heretical.[25]

14. St. Thomas concludes that the sacramental grace of matrimony is a necessary postulate of the principle that whenever God bestows on a man the right to use a certain thing, He simultaneously gives him a special help for the exercise of that right. In matrimony man by divine institution receives the right of ownership over the body of his consort with a view to the procreation (which implies also the education) of children. Consequently, he receives also a particular grace without which such a duty cannot be adequately discharged.[26]

15. Furthermore, since there are different degrees of perfection in the physical life as well as in the spiritual life, provision must be made for both. From this principle St. Thomas establishes a proof in favor

[22] DENZINGER, *Ench.,* n. 1766.
[23] *Leonis XIII Acta,* vol. II, p. 25; ENCYC. *"Arcanum Divina."*
[24] *Council of Trent,* Sessio XXIV, *Doctrina de sacr. matrimonii.*
[25] For the refutation of these errors see DE SMET, *op. cit.,* n. 103.
[26] ST. THOMAS, *Suppl. IIIae, p.,* q. XLII, a. III, c.

of the sacramental character of the marriage contract by an argument adduced on the ground of congruity. The sacrament of matrimony, he says, is calculated to perfect the spiritual life of man in a manner analogous to that in which it perfects him in the physical life. The natural propagation of species is effected by matrimony both in the spiritual and in the physical life, since it is not only a sacrament but also an office of nature.[27]

16. There being only a conceptional distinction between the matrimonial contract and the sacrament, Christians who enter into a marriage contract thereby (*eo ipso*) receive the sacrament, while those who would expressly exclude the sacrament would fail to make even a valid contract.

17. Baptism is a source from which springs the sacramental character of the marriage contract. Therefore, the valid marriage contract of two unbaptized persons becomes a sacrament the moment they are baptized. The grace of this sacrament is not divided into two parts and thus conferred on the two contracting parties. As they are considered two in one flesh, so the two derive benefit from one sacrament, whose undivided supernatural grace penetrates into all the avenues of their conjugal life. We do not subscribe to the opinion which admits the reception of the sacrament of matrimony by the baptized party though the other consort may be an infidel. The new legislation does not favor such a one-sided reception of the sacrament.[28] In such case the realization of the sacramental grace is prevented, because one of the contracting parties, not being baptized, does not possess the right to receive it. If this inference were incorrect, then the bond of matrimony would be much stronger on the

[27] St. Thomas, *p. III*, q. LXV, a. I, c.
[28] Cod. Iur. Can., Can. 1012.

side of the baptized party than on the other side, an affirmation which involves a contradiction.[29] This statement is further corroborated by the fact that the sacrament of matrimony, after the marriage has once been consummated, is absolutely indissoluble. But if one of two infidel consorts becomes converted, even if the marriage is subsequently consummated, the conjugal bond may still be dissolved, by Pauline privilege, provided the infidel party refuses to cohabit peaceably.[30]

18. The ministers of the sacrament of matrimony are the two contracting parties. They receive the sacrament provided they are both baptized. The incompetency incurred by one of the parties on account of infidelity is not removed even by a dispensation of disparity of worship. Such dispensation does indeed permit the Catholic party to contract marriage with an infidel, but it cannot qualify the latter to administer to himself the sacrament of marriage. An infidel is not under the jurisdiction of the Church. He lacks that distinguishing, indelible character which paves the way for the reception of other sacraments. This character is communicated only by the sacrament of Baptism, which the Council of Florence (1438) designates as *"vitae spiritualis ianua."*[31]

19. The precept concerning procreation regards the community as such, not every individual without exception.[32] Its principal end is the general good of the race as a whole, not the individual good as a part. The design of nature is promoted sufficiently, as long as there are enough individuals who of their own volition undertake the office of perpetuating mankind. There-

[29] WERNZ, *op. cit.*, n. 44.
[30] COD. IUR. CAN., Can. 1124.
[31] EUGENIUS IV, Bulla *"Exultate Deo,"* MANSI, vol. 31a. col. 1056.
[32] ST. THOMAS, *IIa-IIae*, q. CL, a. II, ad 2.

fore, celibacy and virginity are not in conflict with the demands of the natural law. St. Thomas with an argument from analogy endeavors to prove their permissibility. But he does not content himself with merely reconciling them with natural law, he goes further when he points out the particular benefit accruing from them to mankind.[33] The Sacred Scripture exalts them as a higher calling [34] and the Council of Trent anathemizes those who contradict the teaching of St. Paul on this question.[35]

20. Right to marriage is founded on natural law. No authority, civil or religious, may deprive man absolutely of this right, unless that same natural law disqualifies him. The denial of such a right does not militate against impediments established by legitimate human or civil authority. Such authority, as a rule, does not go any further than to declare one incompetent on the grounds of natural law, or to forbid his marriage with a determined person, or to invalidate it for reasons suggested by the welfare of society.

21. The same contracting parties are the active and the passive subjects of the sacrament of matrimony. As active agents they are the ministers of the sacrament, and they are free to enter into a matrimonial contract, provided there is no obstacle between them interfering with its lawfulness or validity. As passive agents they become the recipients of the sacramental grace, if they are baptized; provided their contract is not invalidated by an impediment arising from natural, divine, or canon law.

22. The contracting parties do not necessarily have to present themselves before the parish priest in order to enter into a matrimonial contract. The present

[33] *Loc. cit.*, q. CLII, a. II, ad 1.
[34] *I Cor.* VII, 8, 32, 34, 38.
[35] Sessio XXIV, *De sacramento matr.*, Can. X.

legislation gives an express approval to the old custom of contracting marriages by proxy, or by procurator [36] or interpreter.[37] The same explicit approval is not given to marriages to be contracted by means of a letter. It may be legitimately inferred, therefore, that this very ancient custom [38] is not to be retained. The new legislation prescribes certain conditions in order that the marriage contracted by proxy or procurator may be accepted as valid even in the eyes of the Church.

23. In order that a proxy may validly contract marriage in the name of another, not only his integrity but also the authenticity of the mandate must be unquestioned.[39] The person represented as well as the second party to the contract must be determined. The document must be signed by the authorizer (*mandans*) and countersigned by either the parish priest or the Ordinary of the place in which the commission is given; or by a priest delegated by either of them, or, as a minimum requirement, by two reliable witnesses. If the *mandans* does not know how to write, this fact is to be noted in the authorizing document, and the signature of additional witness is required. Failure to comply with this proviso would invalidate the whole transaction.[40]

24. If the *mandans* revoked his authorization or became demented before the proxy contracted the contemplated marriage in his name, the marriage is invalid though neither the procurator nor the other contracting party was aware of the revocation of the authorization or of the mental derangement of the *man-*

[36] Cod. Iur. Can., Can. 1089; Can., 1091; Can., 1088, §1; Schmalzgrüber, *op. cit.*, tit. I, nn. 251 ff.

[37] Cod. Iur. Can., Can. 1090.

[38] Schmalzgrüber, *op. cit., loc. cit.*, nn. 254 ff.

[39] Cod. Iur. Can., Can. 1091.

[40] *Op. cit.*, Can. 1089, §2.

dans. For the validity of the marriage it is required that the procurator should himself execute the commission entrusted to his care.[41] Therefore he has no power to subdelegate. In the past with the explicit permission of the *mandans* the procurator was allowed to acquit himself of the task committed to him, *sive per se, sive per alium.* It would seem that the tenor of this canon does not deprive the *mandans* of the faculty to invest his representative with the right of subdelegation in case the latter cannot execute the mandate in person. Such authorization cannot be presumed on the part of the proxy; it must be given expressly by the *mandans.* The procurator who is positively authorized to select another in case of inability to fulfill the undertaken mission, becomes only a conditional procurator, if he has actually transferred his task to another. The title of procuratorship in that case is transmitted to the one who is appointed by means of subdelegation. The subdelegated procurator is not permitted to choose a substitute in his own place without the explicit consent of the *mandans.* It is preferable that the proxy should be of the same sex as the person represented.

25. If the consent of the person represented (*mandans*) virtually continued at the time his proxy contracted a marriage in his name, then the contract was valid as soon as the other party to the contract gave the proper consent.[42] The subsequent ratification of the marriage is only an accidental ceremony allowed by the Church for the display of greater solemnity.

26. A marriage by proxy should not be permitted without a justifying cause. If time permits, the assistance of the parish priest at such marriages should be

[41] *Op. cit.*, Can. 1089, §4.
[42] GASPARRI, *op. cit.*, nn. 834-839.

preceded by the asking of permission from the Ordinary.[43]

Marriage by proxy or by interpreter is a real sacrament. If the *mandans* specified certain conditions and instructed the procurator that their fulfillment is a *conditio sine qua non,* the contract is null and void unless they are verified.[44] The procurator, being only a representative, need not be in the state of grace, but the party represented by him should be free from mortal sin at the time the contract is made.[45]

27. The form of the sacrament of matrimony is the mutual acceptance by the contracting parties of the transfer of ownership over their respective bodies. This mutual acceptance, or form of the sacrament, indicates the matter of the same sacrament, namely, the mutual transfer of such ownership expressed by the contracting parties in some sensible way.

The intimate connection existing between the matrimonial contract and the sacrament, requires that the contracting parties be also the ministers of the sacrament. They produce the sacrament, whether they are aware of it or not, as long as they mean to do what the Church does or what Christ intended. Consequently, the office of the priest, though his presence may be a *conditio sine qua non* of validity, is only that of an authorized witness.

28. Most of the effects of the marriage contract are the same, whether it is made by baptized or unbaptized persons. The former, however, in addition to the general effects, participate in those superadded effects which are produced by virtue of the sacramental grace. By the effects in a cumulative sense, we understand the rights, the duties and the privileges to which the

[43] COD. IUR. CAN., Can. 1091.
[44] WERNZ, *op. cit.*, nn. 832, 833.
[45] GASPARRI, *op. cit.*, n. 740.

consent (*sacramentum tantum*) gives rise for the welfare of the consorts, of the offspring and of society.

From the consent or sensible sign springs the conjugal bond (*res et sacramentum*) which gives the right to the husband and wife to become one common principle in the procreation and rearing of children. Another effect is the sacramental grace communicated to the baptized consorts as an aid in the performance in their onerous duties.

Some of these effects are so intrinsically connected with the matrimonial contract that they are inseparable from its essence, namely, the unity and indissolubility of the marriage tie, the legitimacy of the children, etc. Other effects may be separable from it, like cohabitation under one roof.[46] The effects may be extrinsic, affecting the contract merely accidentally, as, for instance, the matrimonial impediments. The effects may be supernatural or natural.

IV. Ends of Marriage.

(Canons 1013 and 1014.)

29. The Codex of Pius X declares[47] that the primary end of marriage consists in the procreation and education of children, its secondary end in mutual help and in remedy for concupiscence. The essential characteristics of matrimony are unity and indissolubility, which to a Christian marriage communicate a special stability by reason of the sacrament. The following pages will be devoted to the explanation of these propositions.

30. Nature demands the continuance of the human race. It is extremely doubtful whether unlimited, uncontrolled promiscuity would sufficiently promote this

[46] Wernz, *op. cit.*, n. 50.
[47] Cod. Iur. Can., Can. 1013.

end of nature. Cronin[48] adduces several reasons in his attempt to prove that it would fail to do so. It is a well-known and long-established conclusion of science and experience that promiscuity leads to a pathological condition very favorable to infecundity. Even if one could grant that promiscuity would promote this end of nature, it would do so only in a very imperfect way, to say the most.

But it should be noted that the welfare of mankind at large demands not a promiscuous procreation, but the generation of such offspring as will prove useful members of society. For this purpose and for the proper rearing of children, the family is indispensable.[49] Hence marriage by its very nature is calculated to promote the welfare of humanity.

31. The foregoing statements make us acquainted with the four purposes which constitute the objective ends of marriage, in contradistinction to the motives or subjective accidental ends which very frequently actuate the contracting parties.

32. Procreation of children is properly designated as the principal part of the primary end of marriage. This conclusion is drawn from nature's scheme brought into play by means of the difference in the sexes, the natural issue of whose union is the child. But the nature of the born offspring, its helplessness, its exalted destiny (heir of heaven) are so intimately interwoven with its procreation, that the child's education, which is the secondary part of the primary end, cannot be separated from its generation. Hence the two, *viz.,* the procreation and the education of the offspring, must unitedly be regarded as the primary end of marriage.

33. From this primary end naturally flows, as being

[48] *The Science of Ethics,* vol. II, pp. 394 ff., New York, 1917.
[49] St. Thomas, *Suppl. IIIae, p.,* q. LXV, a. III, c.

implicitly contained therein, the principal part of the secondary end, namely, the mutual help and support of the contracting parties. In other words it consists "in the mutual supplying of those things in which the sexes naturally supplement each other, both in the physical and psychical side of their respective natures."[50]

34. The principal and the secondary part of the primary end as well as the principal part of the secondary end of marriage would have been obtained, even if the state of innocence had not been discontinued.[51] This is proved from the circumstances relating to the creation of man.[52] After the fall of man the subordinate part of the secondary end of marriage became a relative necessity. This doctrine finds its succinct exposition in the teaching of St. Paul.[53]

35. From these various ends of marriage, when viewed cumulatively in all their relations, as a natural consequence flow the characteristics of the conjugal bond, namely, its unity and indissolubility. The numerous extensive treatises of the theologians defend absolutely the teaching of the Church on this point. A few concise statements will sufficiently serve our present purpose.

36. The unity of marriage forbids the simultaneous possession of more than one wife or of more than one husband. This prohibition is founded partly on the Christian religion, partly on nature, whether we consider the simultaneous possession of more than one wife (polygyny), or of more than one husband (polyandry).

That polyandry is directly opposed to divine and natural law as well as to all social order is so obvious

[50] CRONIN, *op. cit.*, vol. II, p. 391.
[51] GASPARRI, *op. cit.*, n. 208.
[52] *Gen.* I, 28; II, 18.
[53] *I Cor.* VII.

that it needs no proof. It is opposed to the divine law; hence it has never been permitted. It crosses the purposes of natural law, because it places an obstacle in the way of the realization of the primary end of marriage, and whatever thwarts the design of nature must needs militate against the social order. The first proposition is self-evident. The Old Covenant fails to record a single instance of legitimatized polyandry. That the polyandric marriage frustrates the scheme of nature is an incontrovertible fact, in itself sufficient to prove the second proposition. The plurality of husbands comes in conflict with the principal part of the primary end of marriage, namely, the propagation of the human race, because it is a positive hindrance, and places an unwarrantable limitation on the birth of children. Furthermore, it formally encourages a union which presupposes a waste antagonizing the scheme of nature, and in which the means, namely, the pleasure, is obtained, while the end, namely, procreation of children, is not realized. Nor can the subordinate part of the primary end of marriage, namely, the rearing of children according to the requirements of natural law, properly thrive in so degrading a union. It advocates the most unnatural inequality, because the man possesses less than the woman. In such a family there is no real head, and a child of such a union does not know his father. These and many other circumstances relieve the husband of his individual natural obligation.[54]

37. While it is generally admitted that monogyny, the possession of one wife, is the ideal marriage union, it must be said that polygyny, unlike polyandry, is not at variance with all the principles of natural law. It cannot be intrinsically evil, for on such supposition

[54] ST. THOMAS, *Suppl. IIIae. p.*, q. LXV, a. III, c.

God could not have permitted it. A polygynous union does not interfere with the principal primary end of marriage, and even the subordinate primary end, namely, the education of children, may be attained by it. But, because this latter end can be reached only as far as the mere essentials are concerned, it is safe to conclude that the polygynous union is not altogether in consonance with the primary end of marriage, and that it is absolutely opposed to the secondary end of marriage.

38. This statement concerning the principal primary end needs no explanation. In defense of the assertion made as regards the secondary end of marriage, the following arguments could be advanced. The success to be achieved in the attainment of the subordinate primary end of marriage depends to a great extent on the realization of its secondary end. But the conditions which obtain in a polygynous union are far from favoring the secondary end of marriage; consequently its subordinate primary end is attained only in a very imperfect way. There can be no harmony, happiness or mutual support in a union in which so pronounced an inequality reigns as that existing between the husband and his wives. The peace of each wife is disturbed by the well-founded fear of being displaced at any moment. Love, if it exists at all on the part of the wife, becomes a source of wounds to her sensibilities, while the affection of the husband is reduced almost to a mere animal passion. Add to all this the jealousy, the inevitable bane deteriorating such unions, and it is easy to see how the stability of such a family is undermined, and an atmosphere created, which, besides being unconducive to the proper rearing of the child, is obnoxious to the welfare of human society. Finally, a polygynous union militates absolutely against the subordinate secondary end of marriage, whose object is a remedy for concupiscence.

39. From the foregoing reasoning it is clear that polyandry can in no way be reconciled with natural law, and that polygyny is permissible, provided it is not explicitly forbidden by any law, and is practiced for an honest end with the express or tacit consent of the first legitimate wife.[55] This is the reason why the Creator in no obscure way expressed His preference of the ideal union of one man with one woman. Though this original design of the Maker in certain instances was permitted to undergo a change on account of the hardness of the hearts of men,[56] it has been restored in the New Law to its pristine ideality. Hence, polygyny can no longer be tolerated in the face of positive divine law.

40. This evangelical divine law affects all who live in the Christian era, irrespective of whether they are baptized or not, though it binds Christians in particular. Christ espoused Himself to only one Spouse, namely, the Church. To symbolize this mystical union, He prescribed monogyny and monandry. He raised matrimony to the dignity of a sacrament whose characteristics, namely, unity and indissolubility, have not only a special binding force but also a sacred significance.

The unity of marriage has already been discussed sufficiently. The following pages will present a brief summary of the most important proofs advanced in favor of the indissolubility of the marriage bond.

41. This characteristic of the marriage tie is in a certain sense founded on the requirements of natural law. Since indissolubility is not an indispensable requisite for the attainment of the primary end of

[55] PERRONE, *De Matrimonio Christiano,* vol. II, p. 35; Leodii, 1861,
[56] *Matt.* XIX, 8.

marriage, an absolute indissolubility cannot be attributed to a mere matrimonial contract on the ground of the primary precepts of natural law.[57] If the contrary of this opinion were true, the Church would be convicted of an unpardonable interference with the immutable laws of nature, for, by virtue of the Pauline privilege, she at times dissolves the matrimonial bond contracted in infidelity. Notwithstanding this fact, it may be maintained that both the secondary precepts of natural law and the perfect attainment of the primary end of marriage, plead gravely in behalf of the indissolubility of the marriage tie as a relative necessity.

42. The end intended by nature is not only the birth of the child but also its physical and moral training, to be imparted by both father and mother, two factors which must combine with the view of making the education complete. Therefore their combined co-operation is required during the whole period of tutelage, which lasts until the age when the child can safely be declared self-relying.[58] But in the meantime other children are likely to be born of the same union, who will stand in need of the same parental solicitude for the same space of time.[59] Following this process to its final analysis, we conclude that, as a general rule, the parents will not have satisfied the primary requirements of marriage until they have reached their declining years, when, more than at any other time, they are in need of each other's help and companionship. In favor of the indissolubility of the marriage tie as founded on natural law, St. Thomas adduces other arguments from analogy to nature.[60]

[57] PERRONE, *op. cit.*, vol. III, p. 106.

[58] ST. THOMAS, *Suppl. IIIae*, p., q. LXVIII, a. II, ad. 1.

[59] MEYER, *Institutiens Iuris Naturalis*, n. 408; Friburgi Brisgoviae, 1885.

[60] *S. Contra Gentiles*, III, 122.

43. No one would deny that the secondary end of marriage, namely, the good of the contracting parties, is best promoted in a union which is indissoluble. The natural duty to support the wife devolves on the husband for the various services she renders him. In this claim she is upheld by commutative justice.[61] Furthermore, the nature of the marital love, of the friendship and daily relationship, is such that it presupposes a lasting union, whose severance by divorce brings in its wake many sad consequences not only to the contracting parties and the unfortunate offspring, but to human society as well.[62] These reasons prove sufficiently that the indissolubility of the marriage tie is not only in perfect harmony with the ends of marriage, but also a relative necessity of the secondary end as well as for the perfect attainment of the primary end.

44. This relative indissolubility, founded on natural law, becomes absolute in case of a consummated Christian marriage. It is the sacramental character of the contract which communicates this stability to a Christian union,[63] because there is nothing on this earth that can mirror with a more perfect resemblance the absolutely inseparable union existing between Christ and His Spouse. This indissolubility must be sustained even against those who maintain that the matrimonial bond may be severed in case of adultery.[64] The teaching of the Church on this point has been ably defended by many theologians.[65]

45. The Church, being the divinely commissioned guardian of the Christian matrimonial contract, has

[61] CRONIN, *op. cit.*, vol. II, p. 439.

[62] MEYER, *op. cit.*, vol. II, n. 101.

[63] COD. IUR. CAN., Can. 1013, §2.

[64] CONC. TRID., Sessio XXIV, *De sacr. matr.*, Can. VIII.

[65] PERRONE, *op. cit.*, vol. III, pp. 137 ff.; PALMIERI, *De Matrimonio*, pp. 175 ff., Romae, 1880; CARRIÈRE, *De Matrimonio*, vol. I, pp. 25 ff., Parisiis, 1837; HEISS, *De Matrimonio*, pp. 9 ff., Monachii, 1861; DE SMET, *op. cit.*, nn. 179 ff.

canonized the principle that in case of doubt, the presumption is in favor of the validity of marriage. It must, therefore, always be considered valid until the contrary is proved.[66] This principle, however, is not to be emphasized to the detriment of the canonized axiom that in doubtful matters it is the privilege of the faith to be favored by the law.[67]

Therefore, whatever may be the nature of such existing doubt, matrimony must always be considered valid until its invalidity is proved beyond question. This principle binds in the external as well as in the internal forum, and it has a particular force when it is to be applied to a marriage contract invested with the dignity of a sacrament.

46. The Congregation of the Holy Office laid great stress on this principle in its instruction sent to the Vicar Apostolic of Central Oceania on December 18, 1872.[68] The missionaries, as appears from the way marriages were contracted in those parts, adopted the principle that in case of doubt the marriage is to be pronounced invalid. The Holy Office not only discountenanced such practice, but ordered that it be discontinued and be replaced by the long-adopted principle which holds that in case of doubt the rendered decision must always favor the validity of the marriage in question. The Sacred Congregations have always abided by this principle, and had it incorporated in the new Code, because it holds good for all contracts and because their experience has taught them that the course advocated by it is the safest to follow.[69]

47. This principle loses its force in a particular case, namely, when the nullity of a doubtful marriage

[66] COD. IUR. CAN., Can. 1014.
[67] *Op. cit.,* Can. 1127.
[68] New COLLECTANEA, vol. II, n. 1392.
[69] COD. IUR. CAN., Can. 1014.

would benefit the faith. Benedict XIV qualifies this conclusion as the constant rule to be followed,[70] and the new legislation adopts it in the same sense.[71] This principle was applied by the Sacred Congregation of the Holy Office in settling the doubt proposed by a Canadian Bishop. The decision declares that an infidel who practices polygyny and whose present marriage is doubtful, need not, on becoming a convert, retain his first wife, though she is regarded as the only legitimate one while he remains in infidelity; he may marry one of his other wives, provided she embraces the true faith.[72]

48. The more common opinion extends this principle even to marriages contracted through doubtful fear. In case the doubt is *dubium dubio facti* (when there is doubt as to whether the marriage has actually been contracted through fear) then, in our opinion, the 1014th canon is to be applied, and the marriage is to be considered valid. Should one be confronted with a case in which fear really existed but it is doubtful whether it was sufficiently grave to invalidate the marriage, then, according to some authors, the intimated party should not be deprived of the chance of being benefited by the doubt.[73] The more probable opinion, however, would even then pronounce in favor of the validity of marriage. The decision would be the same if a marriage was properly contracted (the dispensation from the impediment of disparity of worship having been obtained) between a baptized and an unbaptized person, but subsequently a doubt would arise as to its validity on account of fear to which the baptized

[70] BENEDICTUS XIV, *Bull. Rom. Cont.*, vol. III, p. I, Epist. *"Probe te,"* §27.

[71] COD. IUR. CAN., Can. 1127.

[72] *Inst. S. C. S. Officii* (Ad Ep. S. Alberti) 9 dec. 1874, n. 13; *Collect.*, n. 1427.

[73] SCHMALZGRÜBER, *op. cit.*, p. I, tit. I, n. 401.

party was subjected. All the foregoing statements are based on the new law whose tenor is that marriage should be regarded valid until the contrary is proved, regardless of whether it was contracted by two baptized persons, or by a baptized and an unbaptized individual, or by two infidels. The only possible exception in the application of this general principle would be the last case mentioned, when, namely, two infidels become united in marriage one of whom suffered from doubtful fear. As long as both remain in infidelity their marriage must be regarded as valid. But should one of them become a convert, especially if it were the party who was subject to fear, then the question of their marriage should be settled in a way favorable to faith. If the converted party should wish to marry a Catholic, he may be permitted to do so. This conclusion is drawn from the fact that in such a case the declaration of nullity as regards his former marriage (which he contracted in infidelity, but whose validity is questioned on account of the impediment of fear) would favor the faith. In such doubtful matters the Holy See should always be consulted.

V. Different Kinds of Marriage.

(Canon 1015.)

49. Matrimony between two baptized persons is called ratified (*ratum*) before its consummation. It is called ratified and consummated (*ratum et consummatum*) subsequently to a conjugal act by which the contracting parties become one flesh, and whose nature is such that it is sufficient in itself to promote the end for which marriage was instituted. Once a marriage has been contracted, unless the contrary is proved, its consummation is always presumed subsequently to the conjugal act. Marriage contracted by unbaptized per-

[74] GASPARRI, *op. cit.*, n. 812.

sons is called *legitimate*. An invalid marriage is called *putative,* if contracted in good faith by at least one of the contracting parties. It remains putative until both parties become certain of its invalidity.[75]

50. A marriage is valid and licit if neither a diriment nor impedient impediment stands in it sway. This kind of marriage is sometimes called true marriage. If it is contracted by baptized persons it is called ratified (*ratum*) before its consummation; ratified and consummated (*ratum et consummatum*) after it has been consummated. The term *ratum* is to be extended also to a marriage contracted with a dispensation from the impediment of disparity of worship,[76] and also to that entered into by infidels who subsequently become converts, for in this latter case, their marriage automatically becomes a sacrament; consequently, after its consummation, it is absolutely indissoluble.

51. The marriage of baptized persons is called ratified, not only because it is considered as such in the eyes of both God and the Church, but also on account of the special stability imparted to it by virtue of the sacramental grace. The Council of Trent uses the same term (*ratum*—ratified) in connection with marriages which were contracted illicitly but validly, as for instance, clandestine marriages (without consent of parents).[77]

52. The term *legitimate,* even before the time of Benedict XIV, was reserved, though not exclusively, for marriages contracted by infidels.[78] Needless to say that it may be applied also to the marriages of the faithful; but to be more correct, we must use it in its accepted traditional meaning, which is retained even

[75] Cod. Iur. Can., Can. 1015.
[76] De Smet, *op. cit.*, n. 91.
[77] *De Reformatione Matr.*, ses. XXIV, cap. I.
[78] Benedict XIV, *De Synodo,* VIII, XII, n. 5.

by the new legislation. Therefore, a marriage contracted by two infidels is legitimate (valid), provided no diriment impediment of divine, natural, or positive law, or of civil law, interferes with its validity. Such a marriage is called legitimate before its consummation; legitimate and consummated after the conjugal act whose nature is described below.

53. It will suffice to state here that consummation is always presumed unless the contrary is proved. Ratified marriages and legitimate marriages are considered consummated, if the conjugal act, whether voluntary or involuntary, was in itself sufficient for generation, irrespective of whether conception results from it or not; in other words, *si vir membro virili vas mulieris penetravit, et (rupto hymene, si adsit), semen in vaginam deposuit.* This conclusion is drawn from the *Causa Parisien.* The Sacred Congregation of the Council gave the following reply to a proposed doubt: "VI. *Matrimonium censendum esse tantum ratum et non consummatum, quoties hymen, qui vaginam claudit, sit intactus; quia ex integritate hymenis, virginitas inviolata deducitur.*" [79]

Formerly there was a controversy whether a marriage could be consummated by means of artificial fecundation, namely, by an onanistic or unnatural act which results in the effusion of *semen virile,* which *semen* would subsequently be transmitted *in vaginam mulieris* by means of a syringe. Some authors espoused the affirmative side and thus serious ground was afforded for controversy. The Sacred Congregation of the Holy Office having been consulted whether a recourse to artificial fecundation could be had, responded on March 24, 1897: "*Non licet.*" The answer, as is evident, brands such an act as illicit but it fails

[79] *Acta Sanctae Sedis,* vol. XXVII, pp. 331-339.

to settle the question whether artificial fecundation could be instrumental in consummating a marriage. The new law, if we are not mistaken, settles the question when it says that only a *coniugalis actus quo coniuges fiunt una caro* can consummate marriage. Therefore the union of the two bodies by which is implied the *effusio seminis virilis* must result from the conjugal act itself, which is not the case when the *semen virile* causes fecundation by means of an artificial contrivance.

54. The putative marriage is an invalid contract in which the pseudo-married parties are publicly reputed as husband and wife, and at least one of them believes they are lawfully wedded. As long as the good faith of at least one of the persons concerned perseveres, the putative marriage, according to a long established canonical rule, has all the effects of lawful wedlock, one of which is the legitimacy of the offspring.[80]

55. There are other kinds of marriage besides those already enumerated here. These are presumptive, clandestine, public, attempted, and morganatic marriages, and, finally, marriage of conscience. A few words about each of these will suffice.

56. Presumptive marriage is not a marriage in the strict sense. It is a union whose existence the law presumes with an incontrovertible presumption (*praesumptione iuris et de iure*), on account of a circumstance implying marital consent on the part of the man and the woman. Such a marriage used to arise, for instance, from free carnal intercourse between two betrothed persons, and also between two persons who through defect of age were not qualified to marry. Free carnal intercourse between them, after they reached the age of puberty, used to be interpreted as

[80] C. 13, X, *qui filii sint legitimi*, IV, 17.

ratifying and renewing the consent formally invalid on account of the impediment of age. The Tridentine decree and the decree *"Ne temere"* have abrogated this form of marriage.

57. Clandestine marriage, in the accepted sense of that term, is one contracted without the prescribed form of the Church. This form was the Tridentine form in the past. At the present time it is the form prescribed by the law of the new Code. It is called clandestine because it is entered into in secret, namely, without the presence of the parish priest and two witnesses.

58. Public marriage is one contracted publicly in conformity with the valid form of the Church. It presupposes the publication of the banns, or a dispensation from them for a legitimate reason.

59. Attempted marriage is a form of invalid marriage. It is called attempted, because, though both contracting parties are aware of the diriment impediment prohibiting their marriage, or of the lack of proper form, they go through the ceremony with a pretense of contracting marriage.

60. Morganatic marriage is a union contracted between a man of royal birth and a woman not of his station of life, with the understanding that the wife and the future children will be satisfied with only a stipulated portion of the paternal inheritance. This inheritance involves the rank of the husband, his titles, dignity and offices, and his other ancestral possessions. Since the objective matter constituting this contract limits itself to mere civil effects, the Church not only accepts such a marriage but lends her aid to its solemnization. Such marriages originated in Austria and Germany, and are confined almost exclusively to those countries.

61. Marriage of conscience is a union contracted by means of the proper form, namely, in presence of the Ordinary or the parish priest and two witnesses. It is called marriage of conscience or secret, because secrecy is to be observed on the part of all those who witness it. The cause of this secrecy is the presumption that an exposure of the marriage would bring with it very grave injury and inconvenience to the contracting parties. It is precisely for this reason, and in order to keep the marriage from the public that the customary ante-nuptial proclamations are dispensed with.[81] The new legislation makes a special provision in favor of such a marriage and declares that only a very grave and urgent reason can justify it.[82] The observance of its secrecy is imposed on the Ordinary and his successors as well as on the assisting priest and the two witnesses. Not even one of the contracting parties may divulge the secret without the consent of the other.[83] The obligation of secrecy ceases on the part of the Ordinary when a scandal or a grave injury desecrating the sanctity of the sacrament of matrimony is feared from its observance. He is free to make the marriage public by way of punishment imposed on the parties for the neglect of their duties. The new legislation states precisely the nature of this neglect. It consists in their failure to baptize their offspring, or to apprise the Ordinary of the child's true name, when they had him baptized under an assumed name. Apprising the Ordinary in this way is a duty with which they are expected to comply within thirty days after the baptism has taken place. A similar penalty may be imposed on them if they omit

[81] Const. BENED. XIV, *"Satis Vobis,"* nov. 27, 1741, §5; *Bull. Rom. Cont.*, vol. I.

[82] *"Nonisi ex gravissima et urgentissima causa . . . permitti potest ut matrimonium conscientiae ineatur."* (COD. IUR. CAN., Can. 1104.)

[83] COD. IUR. CAN., Can. 1106.

the Christian education of the child born of such union.[84]

62. Exceptional circumstances which may justify the contracting of such a marriage may arise in the case of an army officer who is barred from marriage except on the supposition that his future wife commands a dowry whose minimum is stipulated by the civil law. The same may be said of persons who for reasons of conscience are united in marriage but liable to civil penalty if their marriage be made public. A royal person who after the death of his first wife wishes to marry again for reasons of conscience, may also be permitted to have recourse to such marriage, provided a sufficiently grave reason makes it imperative to keep the second marriage secret.[85]

63. A marriage thus contracted and the names of the children born of such union should not be inscribed in the usual matrimonial and baptismal registers. A special record of them should be kept in the secret archives of the Diocesan Curia.[86] The law of the new Code insists that the Bishops should make provision for such a separate chest, whose exclusive purpose should be the preserving and keeping under lock and key of documents of this character.

VI. The Jurisdiction of the Church over Marriage.

(Canon 1016.)

64. All baptized persons belong to the jurisdiction of the Church. This principle finds its confirmation in the New Codex, in which the following canon is formulated: The marriage of baptized persons is regulated not only by divine but also by canon law, the

[84] Cod. Iur. Can., Can. 1106.
[85] De Smet., *op. cit.*, n. 94.
[86] Cod. Iur. Can., Can. 379; see this work, n. 526 ff.

competence of the civil authority to the mere civil effects of such marriage being granted. This canon is the natural sequel of the teaching of the Church upholding the sacramental character of all marriage contracts, whether the contracting parties profess Catholicity or not, provided they are validly baptized. A sacred thing must be regulated by a society which is especially constituted and authorized for that purpose.

65. Though all canonists admit this extensive jurisdiction of the Church, some (even of great renown) [87] have combated the opinion that the Church has actually made use of this right and always intends to bind with canonical impediments even those baptized outside the true fold. This canon settles the question once and for all. Thus has triumphed the more common opinion of the canonists of all ages, in which the modern are unanimous; [88] it was the only opinion consistent with the teaching of the Church. Hence no law, no custom can introduce an indiscriminate exemption of heretics, schismatics, apostates or the excommunicated from canonical impediments.[89] The numerous decisions of the Sacred Congregations plainly indicate that this has always been the practice of the Church. Therefore, unless an express exemption is given in favor of those who were not baptized in the Catholic Church, they are to be considered as bound by the canonical impediments. Their ignorance excuses them from sin; it may also endow their marriage with a putative validity, but it fails to render it valid in case of a diriment ecclesiastical impediment.

66. Canon 1016 expressly admits the competence of the civil forum to the mere civil effects of marriage even when it is contracted by Christians. The civil

[87] SCHMALZGRÜBER, *op. cit.*, p. I, tit. I, nn. 378 ff.
[88] COD. IUR. CAN., Can. 87.
[89] WERNZ, *op. cit.*, n. 66.

authority has the right to regulate these effects by legislation conducive to the welfare of the contracting parties and the community at large. It may enforce this regulation even by the infliction of punishment, but it cannot assume the right of denying capriciously those civil effects, which naturally flow from the marriage contract, and to which the parties concerned have a just claim.

67. Christians who validly and licitly contract marriage according to divine and canon law, should not, on the ground that they violated some civil law, be deprived of the natural beneficial civil effects, for instance, the acknowledgment of the legitimacy of their union and of the child born in such a wedlock. If the state refuses to attribute such civil effects to a marriage contracted validly and licitly according to the law of the Church, unless certain conditions are fulfilled beforehand, such prohibition is not to be placed on equal footing with an impediment. If the condition prescribed by civil law can be complied with without sin, the welfare of the future child demands a submission to it. But if, on the other hand, the spiritual welfare of the parties demands that they should get married, a condition specified by the civil law and violating the freedom of conscience may be ignored.[90]

68. To deny to a marriage the natural civil effects which are inseparable from the essence of the contract, would be equivalent to inflicting very grave punishment. But, since the civil authority has no competence over the validity of the Christian marriage contracts, it transgresses the legitimate limits of its jurisdiction when it imposes a penalty which results in depriving Christians of the natural civil effects of their valid marriage.

[90] FEIJE, *De impedimentis et dispensationibus matrimonialibus*, nn. 71, 72; Lovanii, 1874.

69. The civil authority is within its rights in prescribing the civil registration of marriages validly contracted before the Church. Failure to comply with this regulation within the specified time can be a just cause for even a severe penalty. This penalty, however, may not be so severe as to deprive the marriage contract of its validity for the time intervening between its actual celebration and its registration,[91] though to such an unreported and unregistered marriage may justly be denied *some* civil effects. Gasparri goes so far as to advance the opinion of an extremist, maintaining that a Christian who fails to have his valid marriage recorded in the civil register will *justly* be looked upon by the state as not being married, and consequently *may be deprived of all the civil effects of the marriage.*[92]

[91] WERNZ, *op. cit.*, n. 83.
[92] GASPARRI, *op. cit.*, n. 280.

CHAPTER II.

Espousals.

(Canons 1017 and 1018.)

I. Nature of the Espousals and Requirements for their Validity.

70. The new law modifies fundamentally the old discipline concerning espousals. The following is the translation of the canon which treats of this subject. The espousals, or the promise of marriage, whether unilateral or bilateral, are invalid in both forums, unless they were contracted in writing, signed by the parties and also by the parish priest or the Bishop of the place or by at least two witnesses. In case either party or both the parties know not how to write or are physically unable to write, for the validity it is required that this fact be noted in the document and that an additional witness be selected who with the parish priest or with the Ordinary of the place or with the two witnesses of whom mention has been made, must sign the document. But the promise of marriage, thought it may be valid and no just cause may excuse one from its fulfillment, does not confer the right to a juridical action to compel the celebration of marriage; the right to such action is admitted only for the purpose of recovering damages, if any are due.[1]

71. This canon contains the latest development in the espousals, and in substance retains the form

[1] Cod. Iur. Can., Can. 1017.

hitherto prescribed by the decree *"Ne temere"* for a valid betrothment. A radical change has been introduced in the scope of the matrimonial promise. The decree *"Ne temere"* made no provision for a unilateral matrimonial promise; the new legislation places both the unilateral and the bilateral promise in the same category, prescribing the same requirements for both.

72. The parish priest is an authorized witness of the engagement. He takes the place of two witnesses in all engagements made within the precincts of his parish, but outside its limits he constitutes only one witness. The same is to be said of a Bishop with regard to his diocese.

73. Concerning the signing of the document containing the engagement, the words, *vel nequeat* have been added to the texts of the decree *"Ne temere."* They have been placed after the words, *scribere nesciat.* Thus the present text makes a provision for any inability to sign one's name, whether it results from illiteracy, or from an accidental cause. In order that the document may be valid this inability must be distinctly stated, and an additional witness should testify to it by means of his signature.

74. It is a disputed question whether an engagement is valid, if made by persons who are laboring under impediments from which they cannot be freed without a dispensation. The more common opinion does not admit the validity of such engagements since it is presupposed that the parties make an illicit promise. Therefore, engagements contracted by a Catholic and a non-Catholic without the dispensation from the impediment of mixed religion are generally considered invalid.[2] Since the importance of the espousals has diminished considerably, it is of little

[2] S. Cong. de Prop. Fide, new *Collect.*, n. 1696.

consequence to note that the reasonable, serious objections of parents may invalidate them.

75. An engagement may be validly entered into even by proxy or procurator, provided there is a sufficient cause to justify a recourse to so extraordinary a measure.[3] This custom, having been in vogue for many centuries, retains its force until it is expressly abrogated.

II. Obligation Arising from the Espousals.

76. In the past the betrothal carried with it a grave obligation to marry. This was imposed by commutative justice on both contracting parties, if the contract was bilateral; and on one party, if it was unilateral. The marriage was to be contracted in due time, as specified by the contract, unless a legitimate cause excused its postponement. The obligation to enter into marriage could be forced even with censures and other ecclesiastical punishments,[4] especially if such promise had been made under oath.[5]

77. Even a juridical action could be instituted in the past before the ecclesiastical tribunal, if one of the contracting parties declined to abide by the promise made.[6] Of all these stringent measures only one has been retained, namely, the right to institute juridical proceedings to recover damages justly due.[7] In this respect the Church has practically canonized the civil law, which permits the violation of the promise thus given.

78. The new discipline abrogates the right which in

[3] Ferreres, *Los Esponsales y el Matrimonio,* n. 203; Madrid, 1909.
[4] Gasparri, *op. cit.,* nn. 62 ff.
[5] C. X, *De Sponsalibus et matrimoniis,* IV, 1.
[6] Dens, *Tractatus de Sponsalibus et Matrimonio,* n. 7, p. 18.
[7] Cod. Iur. Can., Can. 1017, §3.

the past was generally attributed to the parties making an engagement, namely, *ius ad rem* (not *in re*) or the right to their respective bodies in matrimony. This abrogation favors the opinion of those who maintained that a sin committed by one of the contracting parties with a third person, does not contain an additional guilt (against justice) of such magnitude that a special mention must be made of it in the tribunal of penance. The absence of legal obligation on the part of the betrothed to give their respective bodies to each other by means of matrimony, deprives the espousals of the force of an impedient impediment, if the parties wish to contract marriage with some one else. The espousals no longer possess the force of a diriment impediment of public honesty; hence one contracting party may freely enter into marriage with any blood-relative of the other. Even if an illicit intercourse has taken place between two espoused parties the impediment of affinity will no longer prevent them from marrying any of the blood-relatives of the other party. In the new legislation the impediment of affinity arises solely from a valid marriage, whether ratified or consummated,[8] and the impediment of public propriety from an invalid marriage, whether consummated or not, and from public or notorious concubinage.[9] A more comprehensive treatment of these two impediments will be submitted later.

79. Formerly the obligation to marry the person with whom the engagement was made, was urged *sub gravi* on the ground of natural law.[10] Such an obligation is no longer imposed. The new legislation accepts the discipline of those civil codes which enforce the reparation of the damages suffered by the innocent

[8] COD. IUR. CAN., Can. 97.
[9] *Op. cit.*, Can. 1078.
[10] GASPARRI, *op. cit.*, n. 62.

party, but do not legally compel the fulfilling of the promise of marriage.[11]

From this it follows that a subsequent engagement is not invalidated on account of a former unbroken betrothal. The new legislation does not attribute a superadded force to an engagement made firmer and more solemn by virtue of an oath taken. The person rescinding such an engagement without cause would sin against religion, but not against justice. The engagement dissolved through a just cause frees one even from the sin against religion, for ordinarily an oath is considered only as an accessory to espousals.[12] The same is to be said in case a betrothal confirmed by oath is broken by mutual consent.

80. Thus the whole ecclesiastical discipline concerning the espousals has been considerably simplified. The few principles here considered should be used as a guide in all other questions concerning the mutual consent and the violation of the given promise. The present canonical discipline disposes easily of the complicated cases of the past, even of those whose solution was rendered more difficult on account of some supervening causes which, had they been foreknown, would have deterred the grieved party from entering into an engagement. Nor should a difficulty arise in the solution of the case in which one of the parties wishes to embrace a more perfect state, for no one would question the permissibility of breaking such contracts in the given or a similar instance, which presupposes the presence of a just cause.

81. We are not to infer that the pledge given in an engagement entails no responsibility whatsoever, and

[11] A sample of such civil codes is the Italian Code in which we read: "La promessa scambievole di futuro matrimonio non produce obligazione legale di contrarlo, nè di eseguire ciò che si fosse convenuto pel caso di non adempimento della medesima."

[12] GASPARRI, *op. cit.*, n. 76.

may be broken without any further consequences, at the whim and fancy of either contracting party. It is true that to the party injured is denied the right to a juridical process instituted before an ecclesiastical court in order to compel the offender to make good his promise. But it must be borne in mind that the same court upholds the right of the injured party to recover damages. This duty of reparation devolves on the party who rescinds the engagement without just cause. The presence of a just cause frees one from the obligation of satisfying the other party for the damages sustained. Freedom from such obligation is limited to those damages which are the direct resultants of the promise. Any other injury directly caused through some other action must be repaired, though the legal obligation to marry is absent. Thus, for instance, damages resulting from an illicit intercourse extorted by force or a promise of marriage and subsequent to a valid engagement, must be repaired by the guilty party, even if he had a cause justifying the dissolution of the engagement. In such hypothesis the offender should be urged with pressing importunity to protect the honor of the injured party by marrying her. If all efforts made by ecclesiastical authority in this direction should fail, the innocent party should be advised to have recourse to the civil law in order to recover damages.[13] It must be noted that the offender is bound in conscience to make some reparation. It is left to the discretion and prudent judgment of the confessor to determine in the internal forum the extent of the guilt and the consequent obligation. The culpability of the guilty party in such a case would be greater or less according as there was or was not a justifying cause for the breaking of the engagement.

[13] GASPARRI, *op. cit.*, n. 113.

82. The following canon (1018) admonishes the pastors to instruct their flock prudently in the sacrament of matrimony and in its impediments. The purpose of this canon is not to point out a new obligation imposed on the pastors by the Codex of Pius X. The encyclicals of Gregory XVI,[14] Pius IX,[15] Leo XIII,[16] and the instructions of the Holy Office [17] make use of strong language in order to bring the pastors to the realization of the same duty. The word *prudenter* cannot be sufficiently emphasized in this connection. The instruction of the pastor should be accommodated to the circumstances, disposition and intellectual attainments of his hearers. His prudence will dictate what subjects should be touched extensively and what should be treated briefly; his discretion will aid him to decide what should be left unexplained. While he is expected to present a succinct, yet fairly thorough exposition of the new canonical discipline on matrimony, the instruction on certain subject ought to be reserved for individual explanation when the parties bring to his notice their intention to marry.

[14] *"Summo iugiter,"* 27 maii 1832; litt. ap. *"Quas vestro,"* 30 apr. 1841.
[15] Ep. *"Verbis exprimere,"* 15 aug. 1859.
[16] *"Arcanum,"* 10 febr. 1880.
[17] Instr. (pro Vic. Ap. ad Gallas), 20 iun., 1866, ad 25; instr. (ad Archiep. Corcyren.), 3 ian. 1871, n. 7; instr. (ad Ep. S. Alberti), 9 dec. 1874, n. 1.

CHAPTER III.

TRANSACTIONS PRECEDING THE CELEBRATION OF MARRIAGE.

I. Examination of the Parties.

(Canon 1019—Canon 1021.)

83. Before a marriage is celebrated it must be manifest that no obstacle is in the way of the valid and licit administration of the sacrament.[1] This presupposes an investigation involving a shorter or longer period of time. In danger of death, if no other proofs are available, it suffices, unless there are indications to the contrary, that the contracting parties give a sworn statement testifying to their baptism and freedom from impediment.[2] Such a statement made *in periculo mortis* serves instead of the preliminaries to marriage, as, for example, proclamation of banns, examination of witnesses, etc. The purpose of this special provision is to facilitate the contracting of marriage under circumstances which do not permit the enforcement of the ecclesiastical discipline prescribed for non-urgent cases. *Periculum mortis* here must not be confounded with *articulus mortis.* A soldier about to wage war, or a person about to undergo a major operation is *in periculo mortis,* but not *in articulo mortis,* and this canon is applicable to their case. For *articulus mortis,* which is equivalent to *urgens pericu-*

[1] COD. IUR. CAN., Can. 1019, §1.
[2] *Op. cit.,* Can. 1019, §2.

lum mortis, a special provision is made in canon 1043.[3]

84. The "contrary indications" to which this canon refers are circumstances calculated to show that the parties are either unbaptized or labor under an impediment. These indications must always have some probability in their favor. Thus, for instance, should both parties be well known in the locality in which the marriage is to take place, the fact of their blood-relationship or of their affinity would in all probability come to the knowledge of the pastor. Should the indications show that one of the parties is not baptized, after a short instruction baptism should be administered if the party so desires, and the pastor could proceed with the marriage. If, however, the infidel party declines to be baptized, or an impediment is detected from which the pastor has no power to dispense, he is not permitted to proceed any further until the necessary dispensation has been obtained.

85. The pastor to whom the law concedes the right to assist at the marriage, must investigate diligently at an opportune time before marriage whether there is an obstacle to its celebration. The nature of the investigation to be performed is clearly described in the new discipline. He should cautiously inquire from both the man and the woman, together and separately, whether they are laboring under an impediment and whether they, especially the woman, consent to the marriage freely. He should, furthermore, ascertain whether they are sufficiently instructed in Christian Doctrine. This latter precaution may be omitted only when their fitness in this regard is apparent. It devolves on the Ordinary to prescribe uniform rules by which the pastors should be guided in the course of this investigation.[4]

[3] See this work, n. 151 ff.

[4] COD. IUR. CAN., Can. 1020.

86. According to the decree *"Ne temere"* the *parochus* who is authorized to assist at marriages is the pastor of the place where the marriage is to be contracted. The same holds good also as regards the making of these inquiries. The law obliges the pastor who is to witness the marriage to investigate diligently as to whether there is any impediment between the parties, interfering with the validity or licitness of the prospective contract.[5] Formerly this duty devolved on the pastor who was the *parochus proprius* of the parties by virtue of domicile or quasi-domicile.

87. The former discipline required also that each of the contracting parties should produce two witnesses (unless the same two were willing to testify in favor of both) whose duty it was to prove that the contracting parties were free to marry.[6] The Codex states expressly that this discipline is still to be retained, but it is prescribed only for cases when there is a doubt in the mind of the pastor as to the absence of all impediments. A recourse to this mode of procedure is the most practical way to settle such a doubt. Such witnesses should be known to the one who is authorized to take their deposition, and they should preferably be the father, mother, sister, brother, or other relatives by blood or by marriage, of the parties in question.[7]

88. The "opportune time" to which this canon refers is any time preceding the publication of the banns. The *tempus opportunum* ends at the moment the banns are first announced.

[5] C. 3, X, *de clandestina desponsatione,* IV, 3; Benedictus XIV, cons. *"Firmandis,"* 6 nov. 1744, §9; S. C. C., *Romana et aliarum,* 1 febr. 1908 ad XI; Rituale Rom., tit. VII, c. I, *de sacramento matrimonii,* n. 1, 6.

[6] Instr. S. C. Inq. ad Ep. orient., 29 aug. 1890, n. 1; Clement X, const. *"Cum alias,"* 21 aug. 1670; Gasparri, *op. cit.,* n. 126.

[7] Gasparri, *op. cit.,* n. 129.

89. The obligation to make this prescribed investigation is a grave one, as is manifest from the words of the Lateran Council and of Benedict XIV.[8] Gasparri thinks that it is incumbent on the pastor to make it even if he should have a moral certainty as to the absence of all impediments.[9] While, on the one hand, such a moral certainty on the part of the pastor is generally a practical impossibility, it is hard to see, on the other hand, why the pastor should be obliged to enter into such inquiries if he *knows* beforehand that his investigation will not disclose anything militating against the contemplated marriage.

90. The pastor should not, without sufficient reason, delegate another to perform this task in his name. His inquiry should first be directed towards the public impediments, namely, ligamen, consanguinity, affinity, spiritual relationship, public honesty, etc. Then he ought to question separately and prudently, with great caution, both the prospective husband and the wife as to whether they consent freely to the marriage, and whether they are laboring under an occult impediment like that of vow, crime, etc. The parties are obliged *sub gravi* to reveal all impediments, even if these should incriminate them or redound to their dishonor.[10] In case it is difficult or inadvisable to interview the bride separately, as it happens in some localities, the presence of an elderly woman, who is obliged to secrecy, may be tolerated. She should be a friend or a relative of the bride, but not her mother.

91. Needless to say that the man and the woman about to be married must both present themselves per-

[8] WERNZ, *op. cit.*, n. 130; BANGEN, *op. cit.*, II, §1.

[9] *Op. cit.*, n. 142.

[10] BENEDICT XIV, const. *"Nimiam licentiam,"* 23 maii, 1743, §10; GASPARRI, *op. cit.*, n. 140; SCAVINI, *op. cit.*, III, n. 1038; WERNZ, *op. cit.*, n. 130.

sonally before the pastor. A local custom by virtue of which the prospective husband and the mother of the prospective wife betake themselves to the pastor for the purpose of submitting to the necessary inquiries, cannot be tolerated.[11]

92. As regards instruction in Christian Doctrine it ought to be borne in mind that no person should be permitted to contract marriage unless he is sufficiently familiar with the rudiments of faith. He ought to be able to recite the "Our Father," "Hail Mary," "Apostles' Creed," "Commandments of God and of the Church," "Acts of faith, hope, charity and contrition." He should, furthermore, be familiar with all those religious truths which are necessary *necessitate medii.*[12] Ignorance of truths necessary *necessitate praecepti* does not bar one from marriage. In these matters the authors generally advise the pastor to show some indulgence and leniency towards persons whose mind is very unreceptive and unretentive. Such individuals should not be prevented from marrying as long as they have a fairly correct understanding of the leading truths of the Catholic Church.[13] This principle may be safely followed in practice notwithstanding the stress the Codex of Pius X lays on the fact that the contracting parties must be sufficiently instructed. The possession of this necessary knowledge is not to be presumed; it must be tested.[14] The pastor is dispensed from the obligation of questioning the parties in Christian Doctrine only when the

[11] Gasparri, *op. cit.*, n. 143.

[12] Wernz, *op. cit.*, n. 131.

[13] De Becker, *op. cit.*, p. 258; Benedict XIV, *De synodo*, lib. VIII, c. XIV, n. 3sq; De Smet, *op. cit.*, n. 331; Gasparri, *op. cit.*, n. 484.

[14] C. 14, 17, 29, X, *de spons. et matr.* IV, 1; c. 3, X, *de clandest. desponsatione*, IV, 3; Benedict XIV, ep. encyc. *"Etsi minime,"* 7 febr. 1742; S. C. S. Off. (Kentucky), 9 maii 1821; S. Poenit., 5 sept. 1899; Rituale Romanum, tit. VII, c. 1, *de sacr. matr.*, n. 1, 10.

character of the persons makes such an inquiry entirely unnecessary.[15]

93. On account of the delicacy of the matter which forms the subject of this inquiry the Codex advises the Ordinaries to compose a uniform formula which would serve as a guide for all the pastors of their respective dioceses.[16] This ought to be committed to print, and it should contain in carefully chosen language the questions the pastor ought to ask on such occasions.

94. Unless the baptism was administered within the territorial limits of a pastor he must demand a baptismal certificate from both parties or only from the Catholic party if the marriage is to be contracted with a dispensation from the impediment of disparity of worship. Catholics who failed to receive the sacrament of Confirmation should receive it before they are permitted to enter into marriage. Nothing but a grave inconvenience can excuse them at that time from complying with this law.[17]

95. As regards the securing of the baptismal certificate the new law makes no innovation. In the case of a mixed marriage, one must determine whether the impediment is simple mixed religion, or disparity of worship. In the first instance the pastor should demand the baptismal certificate of the Catholic party as well as that of the baptized non-Catholic party. In the second instance he should require a baptismal certificate from the Catholic party only.[18] The baptismal certificate of the non-Catholic party must be demanded in every case, unless the pastor has personal access to the register recording his baptism. If

[15] Cod. Iur. Can., Can. 1020, §2.
[16] S. Poenit., 5 sept. 1899.
[17] Cod. Iur. Can., Can. 1021.
[18] S. C. de Sacramentis, instr. 6 mart. 1911, n. 1.

it is impossible to secure the baptismal certificate because the books were either lost or destroyed by fire, the testimony of a witness who is above all suspicion (*si nemini fiat praeiudicium*) will suffice. If the party was baptized as an adult, his sworn statement testifying to his reception of the sacrament of Baptism will also be sufficient.[19] If the doubt cannot be solved in any other way, the principle of presumption should be applied.[20]

96. It is important that the contracting parties should have benefited by the sacrament of Confirmation before they are permitted to administer to themselves the sacrament of Matrimony. Insistence on this demand is in perfect accord with the discipline of the former legislation.[21] The obligation to receive this sacrament rests with the parties; the determination whether the *incommodum* is sufficiently grave or not, rests with the pastor. If it is urgent that the parties should be married; if they are poor and reside at a long distance from the seat of the diocese and the Bishop will not administer the sacrament of Confirmation in their locality for some time to come; if the Bishop is far from his diocese and they cannot wait until his return; if the unconfirmed party is prevented by sickness from undertaking a journey to the episcopal city in order to present himself before the Bishop for confirmation; if some urgent circumstance hinders the unconfirmed party from leaving his home just at that time; these and many other reasons would certainly constitute a *grave incommodum* for the parties. If in the estimation of the pastor the inconvenience to the parties is grave, he may proceed to marry them,

[19] Cod. Iur. Can., Can. 779.

[20] See this work, n. 238.

[21] *Conc. Ep. Sicil.* (1880), and *Conc. prov. Vienn.* (1858) in *Collect. Lac.*, t. VI, col. 823, and t. V, col. 174.

but must see to it that they receive the sacrament of Confirmation at the earliest opportunity. Should the *incommodum* not seem grave and the parties decline to comply with this law, the pastor cannot admit them to the sacrament of Matrimony unless he first consults the Ordinary.

II. Proclamation of Banns.

(Canon 1022—Canon 1025.)

97. The announcement of the banns must be made publicly [22] by the proper pastor of the contracting parties.[23] If a party, after having reached the age of puberty, has resided elsewhere for six months the pastor should make this fact known to the Ordinary. To ascertain the free state of such an individual the Bishop may prescribe that proclamation of the banns be made at that place, or, should it be deemed preferable, may institute a juridical proceeding.[24] If there should be some suspicion as regards the presence of an impediment, the pastor should consult the Ordinary, even if such party's stay outside the parish limits was of a shorter duration than six months. Under such circumstances the Bishop should not permit the marriage to take place until this suspicion is removed by means of the provision suggested above.[25]

98. Though the pastor may have omitted nothing in the conscientious examination to which the contracting parties are to be subjected, such examination cannot preclude the possibility of the presence of an impedient or diriment impediment which the persons either knowingly withheld, or which, being unknown to

[22] Cod. Iur. Can., Can. 1022.
[23] *Op. cit.*, Can. 1023, §1.
[24] *Op. cit.*, Can. 1023, §2.
[25] *Op. cit.*, Can. 1023, §3.

them, did not come to light. It was this possibility that induced De Soliaco, Bishop of Paris, to issue a decree in 1198, prescribing three public announcements of all future marriages.[26] This local law was afterwards adopted by some provident Bishops as a matter of safeguard, and subsequently extended to the universal Church by the Fourth Lateran Council prescribing one public proclamation of every marriage.[27] It remained for the Council of Trent to cast this law in its final shape by amplifying it and expressing it more clearly.[28]

99. Both the old and the new legislation insist that the proclamation of the banns must be made by the proper pastor of the contracting parties.[29] He is obliged *sub gravi* to comply with this law even if he should have moral certainty as to the absence of all impediments.[30] By the expression *parochus proprius* the law means the pastor one acquires by means of a domicile or quasi-domicile.[31] The *parochus proprius* of the *vagi* is that pastor in whose parish they tarry *hic et nunc.*[32] The same is to be said of those who acquired only a diocesan domicile or quasi-domicile.[33] If both parties belong to the same parish without having acquired a domicile or quasi-domicile in another, the proclamation is to be restricted to this particular parish. If they belong to two distinct parishes, the

[26] BENEDICT XIV, const. *"Paucis abhinc,"* 19 mart. 1758; WERNZ, *op. cit.*, n. 135; GASPARRI, *op. cit.*, n. 149.

[27] *Conc. Lat.* in cap. III, *De clandest. desponsatione.*

[28] *Conc. Trid.*, sess. XXIV, cap. I, *De reform. matrimonii.*

[29] BENEDICT XIV, ep. encycl. *"Satis Vobis,"* 17 nov. 1741; ep. encycl. *"Paucis abhinc,"* 19 mart. 1758; S. C. S. Off., instr. (ad Ep. Orient.), 22 aug. 1890, n. 2; RITUALE ROM., tit., VII, cap. I, *de sacramento matrim.*, n. 7, 8.

[30] GASPARRI, *op. cit.*, n. 142; WERNZ, *op. cit.*, n. 136; DE SMET, *op cit.*, n. 36.

[31] COD. IUR. CAN., Can. 94, §1; S. C. de Sacramentis, *Romana et aliarum*, 13 mart. 1910, ad V, c.

[32] COD. IUR. CAN., Can. 94, §2.

[33] *Op. cit.*, Can. 94, §3.

other condition remaining the same, the proclamation is to be made in both. If either or both contracting parties have several domiciles or quasi-domiciles, according to the letter of the law, proclamation should be made in all, for, in that case all those pastors are considered their *parochi proprii.* The banns of *vagi* should be announced in the parish in which they reside at the time. If the party gave up his domicile or quasi-domicile, and established a residence in the parish in which he wishes to contract marriage, then the second and the third paragraph of this canon find their application.[34] Since the Codex fails to say that by means of one month's residence one acquires *parochum proprium,* the natural inference should be that though such a pastor, by virtue of a right expressly conceded to him, may marry people having such residence, he is not supposed to announce their banns.

100. The male child attains the age of puberty as soon as he has completed his sixteenth year and the female child after the completion of her fourteenth year.[35] If after the attainment of the age of puberty either one or both contracting parties resided outside the parish for at least six months, the pastor who is to assist at the marriage must apprise the Ordinary of that fact. The Bishop, should he deem it necessary, may order the proclamation of the banns to be made at that place. Or, if instead of such proclamation he should prefer a juridical process, he is free to institute one. In that case he should examine at least two witnesses who were acquainted with the party in question in the place in which he spent six months. The duty of such witnesses will be to furnish proofs whereby the freedom of the party to marry is established. If

[34] De Becker, *op. cit.,* p. 234; Gasparri, *op. cit.,* n. 163; Wernz, *op. cit.,* n. 139; De Smet, *op. cit.,* n. 36.

[35] Cod. Iur. Can., Can. 88, §2.

both the man and the woman were absent from their parish for that length of time, each of them should produce two witnesses, unless, in case they resided in the same locality, the same two witnesses are qualified to testify for both. The same is to be done for every six months that were spent in the territory of different parishes. The Bishop may have recourse to any other measure which in his estimation would serve the purpose of ascertaining the free state of the contracting parties.[36] Should a suspicion arise that the party contracted an impediment while residing in a place for even a shorter time than specified above, the Bishop should not permit the contemplated marriage until such a suspicion has been removed. This is to be accomplished by having recourse to the same process which is prescribed for those who resided outside their parish for six months. The Ordinary is empowered to dispense from the law promulgated in the two foregoing paragraphs if he has a well-founded probability that the parties did not contract an impediment during their absence from their parish.

101. The publications are to be made in the Church. Since this duty of making the publications devolves on the proper pastor, the natural inference is that they should not be made in a public chapel, unless it serves at the time the purpose of the parochial church and the parochial Mass is celebrated in it.[37] We must bear in mind that the main purpose of this law of publishing the banns in the parish church is not to emphasize the place of publication so much as the presence of a large gathering of people whom the Church wishes to apprise officially of the marriage about to be contracted. It was for this reason that St. Alphonsus attributed

[36] BENEDICT XIV, ep. "*Paucis abhinc,*" 19 mart. 1758; S. C. S. Off., instr., 21 aug. 1670; instr. (ad Ep. Orient.), 22 aug. 1890, n. 2.
[37] WERNZ, *op. cit.*, n. 139; S. C. C., 1 iul. 1724.

to this law so extensive an interpretation.[38] It seems probable, he says, that without mortal sin, and if there is a reason, even without any sin whatsoever, one may announce the banns of marriage even outside the church when a large concourse of people convenes for a sacred purpose, like a procession, a sermon, etc. Therefore it is legitimate to conclude that this law may be modified in certain instances at the discretion of the Bishop. A decree of the Sacred Congregation of the Council, dated July 1, 1724, gives an express permission to announce the banns even in a church in which the parishioners convene only on extraordinary occasions for the celebration of the divine mysteries.

102. Another important factor relative to banns is the time regulating their proclamation. On three consecutive Sundays or holydays of obligation, one announcement is to be made. An interruption is not only to be tolerated but commended, should the three days follow one immediately after another. Such a precaution would provide more time for the detection of an impediment, if there should be any.[39]

103. Formerly the canonists adhered to the opinion that no announcement of banns is permissible on suppressed feasts except with the consent of the Ordinary.[40] It would seem that the spirit pervading the new legislation on this point would permit the pastor to proclaim the banns of marriage even without consulting the Ordinary, provided there is a concourse of people present at the Mass celebrated on a suppressed feast.

104. The proclamation of banns must take place

[38] *Theologia Moralis*, lib. VI, n. 992.

[39] Gasparri, *op. cit.*, n. 165; Wernz, *op. cit.*, n. 138; De Becker, *op. cit.*, p. 233.

[40] Gasparri, *op. cit.*, n. 166; Wernz, *op. cit.*, n. 138; De Smet, *op. cit.*, n. 38; Feije, *op. cit.*, n. 247; *Synodus Dioecesana Albanensis*, pars II, art., X, n. 9, *De matrimonio*.

during Mass or during some other divine service, provided in the latter instance there is present a large gathering.[41] The words *"aut inter alia divina officia"* are to be interpreted in a broad sense. Under such services one may include Vespers, Benediction of the Blessed Sacrament, an announced sermon, a special novena or procession.

III. Dispensation from the Proclamation of Banns.

(Canon 1026—Canon 1034.)

105. Neither apparent uselessness nor moral certainty as to the absence of an impediment, nor publication made by civil authority can release the pastor from the obligation of proclaiming the banns of marriage for this law is not based on the presumption of fact but on universal danger. He may lay it aside in mixed marriages[42] (in which case the proclamation is forbidden), in cases of urgent necessity when the marriage cannto be delayed until a dispensation is obtained from the Ordinary,[43] and in marriages of princes by virtue of universal custom.[44] There are other instances in which the parties may be dispensed from having their banns announced. The Council of Trent reserves to the Bishop and to his delegates the right to decide whether the case under consideration warrants a dispensation or not.[45] To dispense from all publications *sine causa* would be exposing oneself to the danger of mortal sin.[46] This statement is not to be applied to a

[41] S. C. C., 25 oct. 1580; RITUALE ROMANUM, tit. VII, c. I, *de sacramento matrimonii*, n. 7, 12, 13.

[42] COD. IUR. CAN., Can. 1026; see this work, n. 108.

[43] *Op. cit.*, Can. 1019 and 1043; see this work, n. 83 ff. and n. 151 ff.

[44] SCAVINI, III, n. 897; GASPARRI, *op. cit.*, n. 154; DE SMET, *op. cit.*, n. 42; WERNZ, *op. cit.*, n. 136 note 17; BASSIBEY, *De la Clandest.*, n. 204.

[45] Sessio XXIV, c. I.

[46] GASPARRI, *op. cit.*, n. 184; BENEDICT XIV, const. *"Nimian licentiam,"* §13, 18 maii 1743.

hypothetical case when the Bishop has a moral certainty that the parties do not labor under an impediment.[47] If there is a well-founded suspicion of the presence of an impediment the Bishop should not dispense from all three publications. In the absence of such a suspicion, according to the common opinion of the canonists, he should never deny a dispensation, if its granting would be the occasion of signal spiritual or temporal good and its refusal the source of notable spiritual or temporal evil.[48] The gravity of the cause is the determinant of the number of publications from which the Bishop may dispense. D'Annibale puts it in very concise language: "*Caeterum Ordinarius non permittitur dispensare pro libito, sed ab una ex iusta causa, a duabus ex gravi, ab omnibus ex urgentissima causa.*" [49]

106. The Ordinary would have a sufficient cause for dispensing from one or more publications of the banns in the following instances: If on account of disparity of age the sacrament would be exposed to ridicule and the contracting parties to public derision; if the proclamation would prove an occasion of scandal or infamy for the parties who are wrongly reputed as united in marriage; if there is a question of a marriage of conscience; if one or both contracting parties must needs embark on a long journey and, without grave spiritual or material detriment, their marriage cannot be postponed; *in periculo mortis,* as already explained; [50] if it is feared that by delaying the mar-

[47] St. Alphonsus, *op. cit.*, lib. VI, n. 1006; Scavini, *op. cit.*, III, n. 905; Giovine, *op. cit.*, §356.

[48] Sanchez, *op. cit.*, III, IX; Schmalzgrüber, *op. cit.*, IV, III, n. 23 sq.; Giovine, *op. cit.*, §358; St. Alphonsus, *op. cit.*, VI, n. 1005; Yoder, *op. cit.*, c. I, art. I, §3; Gasparri, *op. cit.*, n. 186; Wernz, *op. cit.*, n. 142.

[49] *Op. cit.*, vol. III, n. 453, note 7; Benedict XIV, const. "*Nimiam licentiam,*" 18 maii, 1743, §5, 10, 11.

[50] See this work, n. 83 ff. and n. 151 ff.

riage one of the parties will change his mind and matrimony is the only means whereby the reputation of the other party can be safeguarded; if there is sufficient ground to fear that the marriage will be prevented by some evil machinations.[51] The pastor who asks for a dispensation from the banns should facilitate the task of the Bishop by rendering him morally certain that the parties are free to marry.

107. The Ordinary, instead of the foregoing form of proclaiming the banns, may use another. He may post publicly, for eight consecutive days, the names of the contracting parties at the door of the parochial church or of any other church, taking care that this period will include two holydays of obligation.[52] The prerogative contained in this canon is not altogether new. Some very large parishes enjoyed the same privilege for many years before the present legislation extended it to the universal Church. The Bishop alone has the right to benefit his diocese by prescribing for it this law. The names of the contracting parties must be placed conspicuously at the door of the church. As a matter of advisability the pastor who intends to make use of this privilege habitually, should reserve a determined place at the door for this purpose, to which he should call the attention of the congregation. Two of the eight days during which the names are to remain at the door must be holydays of obligation, as, for instance, two Sundays, or a Sunday and a holyday of obligation. It would seem that even a suppressed holyday of obligation should suffice for this purpose.

108. Marriages to be contracted with a dispensation from the impediment of disparity of worship or of mixed religion should not be announced unless the

[51] GASPARRI, *op. cit.*, n. 186; WERNZ, *op. cit.*, n. 142; DE SMET, *op. cit.*, n. 43.

[52] COD. IUR. CAN., Can. 1025.

judgment of the Ordinary, scandal having been removed, directs otherwise. Should the proclamation be made, the apostolic dispensation must first be obtained and no mention is to be made of the religion of the non-Catholic party.[53] If the Ordinary thinks the proclamation of banns in mixed marriages expedient, this canon must be followed to the very letter. The banns of such marriages must be published either *viva voce,* as was customary in the former discipline, or by placing the names of the contracting parties at the door of the church, if the parish enjoys that privilege.

109. Any impediments of which the faithful have knowledge must be revealed to the pastor or the Ordinary of the place before the celebration of marriage.[54]

The impediments must be manifested whether diriment or impedient, public or occult. The ordinary secrecy imposed by natural law, even if confirmed by oath, does not free one from this grave obligation.[55] *Secretum commissum, aut grave damnum, aut periculum damni gravis tum privati ipsius revelantis, tum propinquorum, tum societatis* justifies one in keeping silent.[56] Knowledge acquired under the seal of confession or *occasione confessionis* is not subject to manifestation.[57]

110. The duty to reveal matrimonial impediments is founded on natural and divine law, and the purpose of this ecclesiastical law is merely to emphasize, explain and enforce it. At the base of this obligation are charity towards one's neighbor and consideration for the general welfare of society. An occult impediment

[53] COD. IUR. CAN., Can. 1026; S. C. S. Off., litt. (Ad Vic. Ap. Mysurien.), 26 nov. 1862; litt. 4 iul. 1874.

[54] COD. IUR. CAN., Can. 1027.

[55] GASPARRI, *op. cit.*, n. 177; WERNZ, *op. cit.*, n. 143; DE SMET, *op. cit.*, n. 44; FEIJE, *op. cit.*, n. 269.

[56] C. 7, X, *de cog. spirit.* IV, 11; c. 27, X, *de spons.* IV, 1; c. 6, *qui matrimonium accusare possunt, vel contra illud testificari,* IV, 8.

[57] SCHMALZGRÜBER, *h. t.*, n. 51 sq.; GASPARRI, *op. cit.*, n. 174.

for which dispensation has been obtained *pro foro conscientiae* need not be revealed,[58] unless there is danger of scandal, in which case a dispensation should be received also *pro foro externo* before the marriage is contracted.

111. The proper Ordinary of the place at his own discretion is authorized to dispense for legitimate reason even from those publications which would have to be made in another diocese. If there are several proper Ordinaries the right to dispense is ceded to the one in whose diocese the marriage is actually to be contracted. If the marriage is celebrated outside the proper diocese, any proper Ordinary has the power to dispense.[59]

The words of this canon *"loci Ordinarius proprius"* refer to the Ordinary in whose diocese the contracting parties have acquired a domicile or a quasi-domicile.[60] If both of them have their domicile or quasi-domicile in the diocese within whose territory they intend to contract marriage, their Bishop has the power to dispense from publications which would have to be made in another diocese,[61] if, for instance, the parties in question spent at least six months in the latter after their attainment of the age of puberty.[62] If the contracting parties acquired a domicile or a quasi-domicile in several dioceses and in one of them they intend to contract marriage, then only that Ordinary has the right to dispense from the proclamation of banns in whose diocese the marriage is actually solemnized. Should the marriage be contracted in a diocese in which they do not possess a domicile or quasi-domicile,

[58] WERNZ, *op. cit.*, n. 144; GASPARRI, *op. cit.*, n. 178.

[59] COD. IUR. CAN., Can. 1028.

[60] *Op. cit.*, Can. 94.

[61] BENEDICT XIV, ep. encycl. *"Satis Vobis,"* 17 nov. 1741, §5; S. C. S. Off. (Quebec), 14 iun. 1703; S. C. de Prop. Fide, instr. (ad Archiep. Vic. Ap. Indiar, Orient.), 8 sept. 1869, n. 50.

[62] Consult COD. IUR. CAN., Can. 1023, §§2 and 3.

then any of the foregoing different proper Ordinaries, whom the parties acquired by virtue of their several domiciles or quasi-domiciles, may grant the dispensation. In the case of *vagi* only the *Ordinarius loci,* in whose diocese the marriage is contracted, has the power to grant such a dispensation.

112. The Codex states unequivocally that an individual can acquire a proper pastor or Ordinary in no other way than by means of a domicile or quasi-domicile. A person who merely to satisfy the letter of the law takes up his abode for a month in a strange parish in order to be qualified thereby to contract marriage in it licitly,[63] does not by that very fact necessarily lose his domicile or quasi-domicile nor can he be forced to acquire a new one. Perhaps it is for this reason that the Codex disqualifies the pastor or the Ordinary in whose parish or diocese such a residence has been established, from thereby becoming the *parochus* or the *Ordinarius proprius partium.*[64] The natural inference is that the Ordinary cannot dispense the parties (who established only one month's residence in some parish of his diocese) from proclamation of banns to be made in the diocese in which they formerly resided.

113. If another pastor made the investigation or announced the banns, the result must immediately be communicated by means of an authentic document to the pastor who is to assist at the marriage.[65] The pastors who are not to assist at the marriage but are connected with it either because they were called upon to make the investigation or to announce the banns, must send testimonial letters to the pastor who is to solemnize it. In this document they should apprise him of the result of their inquiry. They should not fail

[63] Cod. Iur. Can., Can. 1097, §1, n. 3,
[64] *Op. cit.,* Can. 95.
[65] *Op. cit.,* Can. 1029.

to state clearly whether their investigation revealed the presence or the absence of an impediment or a suspicion thereof. The Christian name and the surname of the contracting parties, the name of their parents and of their domicile should be distinctly stated in the document imparting the foregoing information. In addition to this, the foregoing document must also state the name of the church and the day on which the proclamation of the banns was made for the last time. If a dispensation was given from any publication this fact should also be noted. The date and the name of the place should never be omitted and the document should bear the signature of the pastor. If the marriage is to be celebrated in another diocese it should be countersigned by the Ordinary and brought to the notice of the Bishop in whose diocese the marriage is to be solemnized. The last two provisions may be disregarded if custom has established a contrary practice.

114. The pastor should not assist at the marriage unless, besides having made the investigation and announced the banns, he has secured all the necessary documents, and three days have elapsed since the last publication or a reasonable cause excuses from such delay. If the marriage is not solemnized within six months, the proclamation of the banns must be repeated, unless the Ordinary decides otherwise.[66]

The first part of the foregoing canon retains the former discipline,[67] but the prescription of a three days' delay is an innovation. In the past marriages did not have to be deferred for any prescribed time, but it was generally agreed that a delay of twenty-four hours sufficed after the last publication of the banns. The pastor is the authorized judge in deciding whether this

[66] Cod. Iur. Can., Can. 1030.

[67] Wernz, *op. cit.*, n. 147; Gasparri, *op. cit.*, n. 191.

law is to be observed in particular instances. He has the right to dispense himself from retarding the marriage in the presence of a reasonable cause. The term "*rationabilis,*" together with the fact that the decision is left to the judgment of the pastor, intimates that even a slight cause would be sufficient.

The other new regulation introduced by this canon is the repetition of the proclamation of banns in case the marriage was not contracted within six months. These six months begin to run with the fourth day following the publication of the banns for the last time, for the parties had no right to be married before that. To the Ordinary of the place is reserved the right to dispense from the renewal of the proclamation of banns if in his judgment there is a sufficient reason to put aside this law.[68]

115. Some questions might arise as to the proclamation of banns when there is a doubt as to the presence of an impediment. To provide for such contingencies the Codex of Pius X legislates specifically by prescribing the following course: In order to remove the doubt the pastor should give the matter a more thorough investigation by examining two witnesses and, if necessary, the contracting parties themselves, provided there is no question of an impediment whose revelation would bring infamy to the latter. The proclamations should be started or finished according as the doubt arose before they were commenced or subsequently, but before their completion. The pastor should not assist at the marriage without consulting the Ordinary if in his judgment the doubt is not removed. Should the presence of an impediment be ascertained, its nature will determine the course the pastor is to pursue in the announcement of the banns.

[68] S. C. S. Off., instr. (ad Ep. Orient.), 22 aug. 1890, n. 6; RITUALE ROM., tit. VII, c. I, *de sacramento matrimonii*, n. 11.

Should the detected impediment be occult the pastor is to start or, if already started, complete the proclamation of the banns and lay the matter before the Bishop of the place or before the Sacred Penitentiaria, suppressing the names. If the impediment is public and not discovered before the proclamation of the banns began, the pastor should not proceed any further until the impediment is removed, though he may have certainty that a dispensation was obtained from it but only for the internal forum. Should the impediment be detected after the first or the second publication the pastor is to complete the publication of the banns, and refer the matter to the Ordinary.[69] Finally, if neither a certain nor a doubtful impediment is discovered, the pastor, having finished the publications, should permit the parties to enter into marriage.[70]

116. The doubt of which this canon speaks must be a positive, not a negative doubt, *dubium facti,* not *dubium iuris,* for in the latter instance the laws would not urge.[71] In the matter of matrimonial impediments *dubium dubio iuris* is a doubt in which it is questioned whether a certain circumstance constitutes an obstacle disqualifying a person from contracting marriage validly or licitly. In the case of *dubium dubio facti* it is certain that this circumstance does constitute an impediment, but a doubt arises as to its presence in the case under consideration. Only in this latter instance is the pastor bound in conscience to settle the doubt. Should this doubt continue even after the proclamation of the banns, the pastor before permitting the parties to enter into marriage must inform the local Bishop of this fact.[72]

[69] BENEDICT XIV, ep. encycl. *"Nimiam licentiam,"* 18 maii, 1743, §10.

[70] COD. IUR. CAN., Can. 1031; see this work, n. 87.

[71] *Op. cit.*, Can. 15.

[72] S. C. S. Off., instr. 21 aug. 1670; 24 febr. 1847; instr. (ad Ep. S. Alberti), 9 dec. 1874; instr. (ad Ep. Orient.), 22 aug. 1890.

117. The witnesses of which this canon speaks need not have other qualifications than reliability and trustworthiness, they may be Catholics or non-Catholics, even infidels, men or women. Any impediment that can be proved in the external forum is regarded as public, otherwise it is occult.[73] If the pastor is aware of the fact that a dispensation has been obtained *pro foro interno* from a public impediment, it is legitimate to presume that such an impediment has already been lifted, and he may act on it also *pro foro externo, salvo scandalo.* It is necessary to have recourse to the Ordinary in all cases of doubt, even if one might run the risk of sinning by excess, for the pastor may admit the parties to marriage only when he has ascertained the absence of all impediments or at least has received a dispensation *ad cautelam* from those that are doubtful.[74]

118. Except in case of necessity the pastor should not assist at the marriage of the *vagi* of whom mention is made in canon 91, unless the matter is first laid before the Bishop or a priest delegated by him.[75]

The legislation embodied in this canon is the same as that enforced by the Council of Trent.[76] In large dioceses it is advisable on the part of the Bishop to authorize certain priests, preferably deans, located in different parts of the diocese, to whom the pastors can have recourse whenever they have occasion to witness the marriages of *vagi.*[77] If a *vagus* wishes to marry one who has a domicile or a quasi-domicile the proper

[73] Cod. Iur. Can., Can. 1037; see this work, n. 167 and 168.

[74] Benedict XIV, ep. encycl. *"Satis Vobis,"* 17 nov. 1741; Rituale Rom. tit. VII, c. I, *de sacramento matr.* n. 8; c. 2, *Ritus celebrandi matr.*, n. 1.

[75] Cod. Iur. Can., Can. 1032.

[76] *De reform. matr.*, sessio XXIV, c. VII.

[77] S. C. C., decr. *"Ne temere,"* 2 aug. 1907, art. V, §4; Rituale Rom., tit. VII, c. I, *de sacramento matr.*, n. 6.

course would dictate that the pastor of the latter should assist at the marriage. Thus, for instance, if the bride is a *vaga* and the bridegroom a *vagus,* any pastor with the permission of his Ordinary may assist at the marriage, but if the bride should have a domicile or a quasi-domicile, and the bridegroom is a *vagus,* the pastor of the former may witness the marriage without consulting the Ordinary. The Tridentine decree did not mean to affect individuals who are *momentanee vagi,* who, namely, have abandoned their former domicile or quasi-domicile but have failed as yet to acquire a new one.[78] The present law being the same, the majority of recent canonists distinguish between *momentanee vagi* and *habitualiter vagi.* Wouters,[79] Leitner [80] and a few of less note include both these classes under this law. If a delay would prove an occasion of scandal, of serious financial loss, or of a well-grounded hope that the parties will attempt marriage by a minister or a civil magistrate, or will live in concubinage, then the pastor, facing a case of necessity, may solemnize the marriage of *vagi* even without having previous recourse to the Ordinary, but he must first endeavor to the best of his ability to ascertain their free state.

119. The pastor should not neglect to direct an instruction to the parties, accommodated to their condition in life, in which he will point out the sanctity of the sacrament of matrimony, the mutual obligations of the consorts, and the duty of parents toward their offspring. He should urge them fervently to approach the tribunal of penance with sincerity, and the table of

[78] Wernz, *op. cit.*, n. 178; Gasparri, *op. cit.*, n. 146; De Smet, *op. cit.*, n. 75; Sanchez, *op. cit.*, III, XXV, n. 2; St. Alphonsus, *op. cit.*, VI, n. 1089; Ferreres, *Los. Esponsales y el Matrimonio*, n. 254, 271, 499.

[79] *Commentarius in decretum "Ne temere,"* p. 54. Amstelodami, 1910.

[80] *Die Verlobungs- und Eheschliessungsform nach dem Dekrete "Ne temere,"* p. 42. Regensburg, 1910.

the Lord with piety.[81] This instruction should not be omitted unless the case is extremely urgent. If it is not possible to impart it outside the tribunal of penance, it ought to be given during confession. The pastor should dwell on the holiness, dignity and importance of the sacrament, and on the piety with which it should be received. He must inculcate and explain the obligations of husband and wife, their mutual love, fidelity, trust, the protection of the wife by the husband and her submission to him, the honesty of the conjugal act, and the sinfulness of all actions tending to race-suicide. He must emphasize, furthermore, the duty of the parent toward the child, the latter's right to baptism as soon as possible, to Christian education from his tender years and to parental solicitude as regards his material wants.[82]

120. Confession is not to be regarded as a *conditio sine qua non,* not even if one or both of the contracting parties should be in the state of mortal sin. The pastor should do his utmost to deter such a party from so grave a sin, and should endeavor to prevail on him by pointing out the manifold necessary sacramental graces of which he deliberately deprives himself. If he fails in this attempt he should induce the person in question to make at least an act of perfect contrition. The state of mortal sin results in a sacrilegious reception of the sacrament, but it does not interfere with its validity.

If, however, the party is a public sinner, or is bound by a public censure, unless he first confesses his sins and reconciles himself with the Church, the pastor without grave cause is not permitted to witness his

[81] Cod. Iur. Can., Can. 1033.

[82] *Conc. Trident.*, sessio XIV, *de reform. matrim.*, c. I; S. C. S. Off. (Kentucky), 9 maii, 1821; (Vic. Ap. Sandwic.), 11 dec. 1850, ad 21; *Moguntina*, 28 aug. 1852; Rituale Rom., tit. VII, c. I, *de sacr. matrim.*, n. 17; Gasparri, *op. cit.*, n. 196.

marriage. If possible the Ordinary should be consulted about the grave cause in the case under consideration.[83] Should a public sinner confess his sins to another priest, the pastor should demand a testimonial to that effect.

121. The pastor should exhort the children who are still minors, not to enter into marriage without the knowledge of their parents, or against their will when they have a reasonable objection. Should the children disregard his counsel he is not to assist at their marriage unless he first consults the Ordinary of the place.[84]

The children to whom this canon refers are those who have not as yet completed their twenty-first year.[85] For the validity of the marriage it is required that the boy should have completed his sixteenth and the girl her fourteenth year.[86] Formerly the reasonable dissent of the parents was generally regarded as an impedient impediment.

122. The right to marriage has always been considered one of those rights which the minor was not supposed to exercise without the consent of his parents. Among the Hebrews and the Greeks it was generally the parents who selected a suitable consort for their children, regardless of whether the child was a minor or a major.[87] A similar practice prevailed among the Romans and in their law the consent of the parents was essential. Only in certain exceptional instances was the marriage considered valid without it.[88] The Germanic law prescribed the consent of the parents as

[83] COD. IUR. CAN., Can. 1066.
[84] *Op. cit.,* Can. 1034.
[85] *Op. cit.,* Can. 88.
[86] *Op. cit.,* Can. 1067.
[87] BENEDICT XIV, const. *"Postremo mense,"* febr. 28, 1747; S. AMBR., c. 13, C. XXXII, q. 2.
[88] L. 9, 10, 19D, *de ritu nupt.,* XXII, 2; L. 18, 25 C. *de nuptiis,* V, 4.

a necessary requisite for the marriage of a minor.[89] It cannot be proved that the Roman law was transplanted into the Church in all its rigor, namely, as invalidating marriages contracted without the consent of the parents. Though from an examination of the early laws this contention cannot be vindicated conclusively, yet no doubt can be entertained on the question since the twelfth century, owing to the apodictic proofs in which the Decretals abound.[90] By way of explanation it may be added that if, on the one hand, the Church laid such emphasis on the consent of the parents to protect their rights, on the other hand, it did not fail to safeguard the rights of the offspring by forbidding the parents to force their child to a marriage against his will.

123. The want of parental consent no longer constitutes an impediment, though the licitness or the illicitness of the assistance of the pastor is conditioned on it. To harken to the parents in a matter of such importance is a precept imposed on the children by virtue of natural law. The pastor may assist at the marriage without consulting the Ordinary if, in his estimation, the objection of the parents raised against the contemplated marriage is unreasonable.[91] The right to object is reserved to the parents alone and it is not to be extended to the tutor in the event of the parents' demise. If one parent assents and the other dissents the pastor is free to act. Among such reasonable causes could be enumerated disgrace, dissension or grave damage to the family from such a union.

[89] SCHULTE, *Handbuch des katholischen Eherechts,* §31. Giesen, 1855; MOY, *Das Eherecht der Christen in der morgenländischen und abendländischen Kirche,* p. 316 ff. Regensburg, 1833.

[90] C. 2, C. XXVII, q. 2; BENEDICT XIV, *De synodo,* vol. I, Lib. IX, c. XI, n. 3. PETR. LOMBARDI, *Sent.,* lib. IV, dist. XXVIII.

[91] C. 11, C. XXXVI, q. 2; c. 23, X, *de sponsalibus et matrim.,* IV, 1; BENEDICT XIV, ep. encycl., "*Nimiam licentiam,*" 18 maii 1743, §10.

CHAPTER IV.

Matrimonial Impediments.

I. General Notions about Matrimonial Impediments.

124. Though for about eleven centuries the word "*impedimentum*" was unknown in the vocabulary of the canonical discipline of the Church,[1] the canons of the Councils held as early as the sixth century give an unmistakable expression to the idea conveyed by it.[2] Gratian[3] and Peter Lombard employ various terms to express the notion connoted by the word "impediment," but the word itself never occurred to them. It is rightly associated with the name of Bernardus Papiensis (1139) for, to all appearances, it was he who used it for the first time,[4] in the list in which he enumerated the fourteen causes which "impede" matrimony.[5] Alexander III about half a century later borrowed this term as a vehicle of expression[6] in connec-

[1] Villien, *L'empêchement de mariage. Sa notion juridique d'après l'histoire.* In the *Canoniste Contemporain*, 1903, p. 421.

[2] *Synodus Agathensis* (506), can. LXI; Mansi, *op. cit.*, vol. VIII, col. 335. *Conc. Aurelianense* (511), can. XIII; Mansi, vol. VIII, col. 353. *Synodus Epaonensis* (517), can. XXX; Mansi, vol. VIII, col. 562. *Conc. Vermeriense* (753, 756), can. I; Mansi, vol. XII, col. 566.

[3] C. 6, 8, C. XXX, q. 5.

[4] Wernz, *op. cit.*, n. 217; Villien, *loc. cit.*, p. 422; Esmein, *op. cit.*, vol. I, p. 205.

[5] "Sunt autem quae, matrimonium impediunt, XIV: Votum, ordo, habitus, dispar cultus, error personae, conditio, ligatio, enormitas delicti, impossibilitas coeundi, coactio, publicae honestatis iustitia, tempus feriarum et interdictum Ecclesiae" (*Summa* Bernard. Pap.; IV, 1, §6, p. 221. Ratisbon, 1861; cf. *Summa de matrimonio*, p. 228; ib., Wernz, n. 217, foot-note, 22).

[6] C. 4, X, *qui clerici vel voventes matrimonium contrahere possunt*, IV, 6.

tion with the impedient impediment arising from a simple vow. The word was subsequently accepted by the majority of theologians [7] and received official recognition by the Council of Trent.[8]

125. The references already cited testify to the pronounced lack of uniformity disclosed by the authentic sources containing an account of the pre-medieval canonical discipline as to the number and force of matrimonial impediments. The fact that the early theologians placed indiscriminately in one and the same list the impedient and the diriment impediments without taking heed to point out the particular force of each, contributed not a little to the then prevailing perplexity whose most regrettable feature lay in the fact that some impediments were regarded as diriment in certain localities and as impedient in others. Thus, for example, the impediment of Holy Orders was not looked upon as a diriment impediment for the universal Church until the First Lateran Council expressly ruled so.

The Council of Trent failed to remove this disagreement existing among the theologians, for even the more modern authors differ when engaged in the determination of the number of matrimonial impediments.[9]

126. The rule of Innocent III as regards lawfulness to marry [10] has been practically incorporated into the Codex of Pius X. All persons may marry except those who are forbidden by law.[11] Such has always been the discipline of the Church as defended against Marcion-

[7] C. 1, *de cognatione spirituali,* IV, 3, in VI°; C. un. *de voto et voti redemptione,* tit. VI, in *Extravag. Joan.* XXII.

[8] Sessio XXIV, *De sacramento matrimonii,* can. III; and *De reformatione matrimonii,* cap. III.

[9] De Smet, *op. cit.*, n. 235; Wernz, *loc cit.*, Notae Historicae, II.

[10] C. 23, X, *de sponsalibus et matrimoniis,* IV, 1.

[11] Cod. Iur. Can., Can. 1035.

ism and Manichaeism.[12] The law which stands in the way of marriage may be either divine or human. The former may be either natural or positive. The latter may be either ecclesiastical or civil according as it proceeds from a competent ecclesiastical or civil authority.[13]

127. The impediments of divine law, whether natural or positive, affect all persons regardless of creed. The impediments of civil law bind the infidels, while those of ecclesiastical law affect only such persons as are brought under the immediate jurisdiction of the Church by means of baptism. Therefore, the lawfulness or validity of marriage contracted between two unbaptized persons depends on the divine and the civil law. The lawfulness or validity of marriage entered into by two baptized persons must be judged according to the positive divine and ecclesiastical law. The competence of the civil law in this last instance cannot go beyond the civil effects of such marriage.

128. A marriage forbidden by law may be illicit or invalid. The invalidating clause must be obvious, it may not be presumed.[14] Owing to the principle laid down in the foregoing paragraph a marriage between two infidels, though only illicit by virtue of the divine law, may be invalid by the force of the civil law. In the same way a marriage may be invalid owing to ecclesiastical law, though by virtue of divine law it may be only illicit if contracted between two baptized persons, or between a baptized and an unbaptized person.

[12] C. 2, X, *de coniugio leprosorum,* IV, 8; C. 1, *de coniugio servorum,* IV, 9; *Professio fidei* (in Conc. Lugdunen. II) *a Michaelo Palaeologo Gregorio X oblata* a. 1274.

[13] WERNZ, *op. cit.*, n. 215; GASPARRI, *op. cit.*, n. 245.

[14] *De regulis iuris,* Reg. LXIV, in VI°; SANCHEZ, lib. VII, Disp. II, and disp. LII, n. 5; BENEDICTUS XIV, *De Synodo,* lib. XII, Cap. I, n. 3.

129. Every marriage is licit and valid unless its lawfulness or validity is prevented by an impediment of divine or human origin. No absolute uniformity prevails as to the definition of a matrimonial impediment. The majority of authors maintain that it is a circumstance established by law rendering the matrimonial contract either illicit or invalid.[15] A matrimonial impediment, therefore, is the presence of a specified cause which under certain conditions or circumstances, by virtue of divine or human law, affects the lawfulness or the validity of a marriage contract. This definition contains all the factors connected with an impediment. It must be borne in mind that the sacrament of matrimony is affected by an impediment only indirectly. Directly it aims at the contract whose validity or invalidity determines the reception or non-reception of the sacrament between two baptized persons. The new discipline has abolished some impediments, while others it has modified. The impedient impediments are four:

1. Simple vows (*votum simplex*); [16]
2. Legal relationship (*cognatio legalis*) in conformity with the civil law of the country; [17]
3. Mixed religion (*mixta religio*); [18]
4. Unworthiness (*indignitas*).[19]

130. The diriment impediments are thirteen:

1. Want of required age (*aetas*); [20]

[15] GASPARRI, *op. cit.*, n. 247; WERNZ, *op. cit.*, n. 215; D'ANNIBALE, *op. cit.*, vol. III, n. 428; DE SMET, *op. cit.*, n. 234; HEINER, *Grundriss des katholischen Eherechts*, p. 54. Munster i. W. 1905.

The Codex of Pius X treats of the impediments of marriage in the following canons:

[16] Can. 1058.
[17] Can. 1059.
[18] Can. 1060-Can. 1064.
[19] Can. 1065 and 1066.
[20] Can. 1067.

2. Impotency (*impotentia*); [21]
3. Undissolved marriage bond (*ligamen*); [22]
4. Disparity of worship (*disparitas cultus*); [23]
5. Holy Orders (*ordo*); [24]
6. Religious profession (*professio religiosa*); [25]
7. Abduction (*raptus*); [26]
8. Crime (*crimen*); [27]
9. Consanguinity (*consanguinitas*); [28]
10. Affinity (*affinitas*); [29]
11. Public decency (*publica honestas*); [30]
12. Spiritual relationship (*cognatio spiritualis*); [31]
13. Legal relationship (*cognatio legalis*); in conformity with the civil law of the country.[32]

II. Different Kinds of Impediments.

(Canon 1036—Canon 1037.)

131. There are different kinds of impediments of which the new Code of Canon Law makes mention.

I. An impedient and a diriment impediment. The impedient impediment implies a grave prohibition to contract marriage. If, however, notwithstanding such prohibition the marriage should be contracted its validity is sustained by the Church.[33] A diriment impediment in addition to the grave prohibition contains also an invalidating force [34] in case a marriage should be attempted notwithstanding the presence of such an obstacle.[35] Since the individuality of the matrimonial contract presupposes the competence of both parties, the contract would be respectively illicit or invalid

[21] Can. 1068.
[22] Can. 1069.
[23] Can. 1070 and 1071.
[24] Can. 1072.
[25] Can. 1073.
[26] Can. 1074.
[27] Can. 1075.
[28] Can. 1076.
[29] Can. 1077.
[30] Can. 1078.
[31] Can. 1079.
[32] Can. 1080.

[33] Cod. Iur. Can., Can. 1036, §1.
[34] *Op. cit.*, Can. 1036, §2.
[35] C. un. *de voto et voti redemptione*, tit. VI, *in Extravag. Joan.* XXII.

according as one of the persons should be bound by an impedient or diriment impediment.[36] This last principle, formerly controverted but at present embodied in the new legislation, finds its practical application in marriages contracted with a dispensation from the impediment of disparity of worship. Thus, for instance, some states of North America, whose statutes prohibit miscegenation, establish a civil diriment impediment of marriage between a white person and a negro or an Indian or a Mongolian.[37] If a Catholic of the white race should attempt to marry an infidel belonging to any of the above mentioned races in a place where the latter has his domicile and where miscegenation is a grave statutory offence nullifying marriage, the Church would not uphold the validity of such contract by the mere fact that it was entered into according to the due form and with the necessary dispensation. The same is true in case a Catholic of the colored race should wish to marry an infidel of the white race under the same circumstances. An ecclesiastical dispensation from the impediment of disparity of worship gives permission to the Catholic to contract marriage with a competent infidel, but it does not mean to remove the civil impediment under which the latter may be laboring. The invalidity of the aforesaid marriage would not result from the impediment of disparity of worship, which according to the present discipline does not arise between a baptized non-Catholic and an infidel. It would be occasioned by the civil diriment impediment intending to prevent the amalgamation of races.

132. II. An impediment may be public or occult.[38]

[36] Cod. Iur. Can., Can. 1036, §3.

[37] Keezer, *The Law of Marriage and Divorce*, §26, p. 18. Boston, 1906.

[38] Cod. Iur. Can., Can. 1037.

It is regarded public when it can be proved in the external forum; otherwise it is considered occult.[39] With the adoption of this canon many of the insurmountable difficulties arising in the past will be eliminated. In the former discipline the impediments of consanguinity, of affinity arising from matrimonial carnal intercourse, of spiritual and legal relationship, of Holy Orders and of disparity of worship were considered public *ex natura sua.* The others were either public *simpliciter,* or occult *simpliciter,* or *omnino occult.* Gieran thinks that impediments public by their very nature will not be regarded as occult by the present legislation even if they could not be proved by the external forum.[40] Our opinion is just the contrary. It is precisely with that end in view that the canon employs the word "*censetur*" in preference to the word "*est.*" To decide whether an impediment is public or occult, namely, whether it can or cannot be proved in the external forum, one must possess *probationem plenam, probatio semi-plena* does not suffice. To exemplify this canon: If after a diligent inquiry it is concluded that the impediment of consanguinity existing between two parties cannot be proved in the external forum, then it must be treated as an occult impediment, for instance, if only one of the contracting parties knows of the blood-relationship. Therefore in this case as well as in any other where an occult impediment is involved the dispensation is to be asked from the internal forum, the external forum being mostly for public impediments. On the other hand, if the impediment of crime *utroque coniuge vel alterutro machinante* can be proved in the external forum, then it must be regarded as public. Thus, for example, per-

[39] S. C. C., *Mohiloven.* seu *Tiraspolen.,* 9 iul., 10 sept. 1881.

[40] *The new Canon Law in its practical aspects.* In the *American Ecclesiastical Review,* 1918, p. 149.

sons guilty of such a crime take up an abode in a distant country where their crime is unknown, but it is known in the place in which they resided formerly.

The other kinds of impediments of which the new legislation makes no explicit mention but implicitly approves the old division, are the following:

133. III. According as the impediment originates from divine law (positive or natural) or from human law (ecclesiastical or civil) it is called an impediment of natural or of divine positive law; of ecclesiastical or of civil law. The determination to which of the above-named categories of law any particular impediment belongs, must be left to that part of this work in which such impediment is treated individually.

134. IV. Impediments may be absolute or relative. The former may render the marriage either illicit or null as regards any person whatsoever, for instance, the impediment of simple vow, or of Holy Orders. The latter prohibits marriage with certain determined persons, for example, the impediment of consanguinity, affinity, spiritual relationship, crime, and disparity of worship.

135. V. Impediments may be certain or doubtful. The difference between the two is apparent. The doubt may arise either from fact or from law, or from both combined. The impediment is doubtful *dubio facti,* when it is beyond doubt that a certain fact gives rise to an impediment, but it is not certain that this fact actually exists in the case under consideration. An impediment is doubtful *dubio iuris* when the fact is self-evident, but it is questioned whether it constitutes an impediment. When both these kinds of doubts are present in one and the same case then the impediment is *dubium dubio iuris simul et facti.* Example for the first: It is certain that the impediment of consanguinity exists between those related in the third degree. It is doubtful, however, whether Joseph and Agnes are thus related. In all such instances the Ordinaries may dispense, provided the nature of the doubt is such that if the thing doubted should prove to be a fact the Holy See would dispense from the existing impediment. Example for the second: It is certain that Charles adopted Cecilia, but it is doubtful whether the adoption was such as to constitute an impediment. In all such cases the impediment may be ignored.[41] The same is to be said as regards the third kind of doubt.

136. VI. An impediment may be perpetual or temporary. The duration of the first is indefinite, that of the second, temporary. Consanguinity would be an example of the former; the impediment of age of the latter.

137. VII. An impediment may be dispensable or non-dispensable, according as a dispensation can or cannot be obtained from it.

138. VIII. An impediment may be antecedent or subsequent (supervenient). The first exists prior to the matrimonial contract, for instance, the impediment of consanguinity; the latter takes rise posterior to a valid marriage, for example, affinity.

139. IX. Impediments may be occult or public by their very nature. The first are constituted principally to promote private well-being. Therefore, if a juridical process should be started against the validity of a marriage owing to the presence of an impediment of the private right, the actors in such a case would, as a rule, be the contracting parties themselves. Such an impediment is, for instance, occult impotency. The impediments of public right are introduced for the welfare of the community; consequently, the right to expose the nullity of a marriage contracted with such

[41] Cod. Iur. Can., Can. 40.

an impediment is not reserved to the parties in question. It belongs *ex officio* to the judge or *promotor matrimonii,* and it may be used by any person whom the ecclesiastical law qualifies as legitimate actor.

All persons may contract marriage unless forbidden by law.[42] The right to marriage is founded on natural law.[43] Human authority may not forbid marriage absolutely, though it may relatively in certain instances and as regards certain persons who become disqualified by natural or ecclesiastical law, or by a just human law, or by virtue of an obligation freely assumed. The attitude of the Church on this point is best evidenced by the condemnation which it hurled against the erroneous doctrines of the Marcionites, Manichaeans and Eucratites as regards marriage.

Under the present order of things no individual is obliged to contract marriage except accidentally, namely, when the public good or his honor demands it. The direct commands *"crescite et multiplicamini et replete terram"* [44] was intended directly only for our first parents. Their descendants were to comply with it only collectively, namely, mankind as such, not individuals as such. Therefore celibacy is permissible as long as there are enough individuals complying with the foregoing precept. If celibacy were against natural law St. Paul would not have encouraged the unmarried of his audience to remain unmarried, saying "it is good for them if they so continue." [45]

III. Right to Legislate in Marriage.

(Canon 1038—Canon 1041.)

140. Only to the supreme ecclesiastical authority

[42] Cod. Iur. Can., Can. 1035.
[43] St. Thomas, *suppl. IIIae p.,* q. XLI, a. I.
[44] *Gen.* I, 28.
[45] I *Cor.* VII, 8.

belongs the right to declare peremptorily under what circumstances the divine law impedes marriage. The same ecclesiastical authority, by virtue of privative jurisdiction is empowered also to introduce diriment or impedient impediments by means of universal or particular law.[46]

This canon has already been explained.[47] By the words "supreme ecclesiastical authority" is meant the Roman Pontiff or the college of Bishops convened at an ecumenical council. The Church by virtue of divine right may decide what diriment or impedient impediments flow from the divine law as a natural consequence.[48] Such declaration binds both baptized persons and infidels. Because this canon mentions only divine law, one is not to infer that the Church renounces its claim to the right of making a similar declaration also with regard to natural law. The most general conclusion the wording of this canon would warrant is that the Church refrains from claiming that she has the *exclusive* right to declare under what circumstances the natural law prohibits or invalidates marriage. Her exclusive right to such a declaration cannot be questioned when only baptized persons are concerned, and should she make such a pronouncement it would bind the unbaptized also. The canon means to intimate that since the unbaptized are under the jurisdiction of the civil power, the civil law may go even so far as to interpret for them what impediments oblige by virtue of natural law.

141. The supreme ecclesiastical authority has also the exclusive right to establish impediments whereby marriages contracted by baptized persons are rendered

[46] COD. IUR. CAN., Can. 1038.
[47] See this work, n. 64 ff.
[48] S. C. S. Off., instr. (ad Ep. Geneven.), 3 sept. 1772; instr. (ad Praef. Mission. Martinicae, etc.), 6 iul. 1817.

illicit or invalid.[49] The word *"privative"* means to exclude two things, namely, the civil power and the power of the local Bishops (the latter by reservation). In former discipline the Ordinaries were within their rights when they established impediments of marriage for their own diocese. Not only their direct precept but even their indirect sanction, such as a law originating from custom presupposes, sufficed formerly to introduce an impediment. The new law suppresses this once admitted right of the Bishops and reserves to the supreme ecclesiastical authority all right to legislate for baptized persons in matters concerning matrimonial impediments.

142. In certain peculiar cases the local Ordinaries may forbid marriage for a time, but only for a just cause and while such a cause is present, to individuals actually residing in their diocese and to their subjects living outside its limits. Only the Apostolic See can add an invalidating clause to such an episcopal prohibition.[50]

The Ordinaries have not been deprived of all their power as regards matrimonial impediments. They still retain the right to establish a temporary impedient impediment, in the sense of barring from marriage, for a time, certain individuals in particular instances. Such a penalty may be meted out only for a just cause and the prohibition must be removed as soon as the cause ceases.[51] Should the parties contract marriage before the cessation of the cause and the removal of the episcopal prohibition their act would be illicit but valid. If for a grave reason the Bishop should deem it

[49] *Con. Trid.*, sess. XXIV, *de sacram. matrim.*, can. 3, 4, 9; BENEDICT XIV, *"Singulari,"* 9 febr. 1749, §2, 16, 17; PIUS VI, const. *"Auctorem fidei,"* 28 aug. 1794, prop. 59, 60, Synodi Pistorien. damn.; LEO XIII, ep. encyc. *"Arcanum,"* 10 febr. 1880.

[50] COD. IUR. CAN., Can. 1039.

[51] S. C. C., *Florentina*, 17 febr. 1629, ad 1, 2.

advisable to forbid the marriage absolutely, a *clausula irritans* should be asked from the Holy See.[52]

143. Only the Roman Pontiff may abrogate the impedient and diriment impediments of ecclesiastical law; nor may any one dispense from them unless such a power has been ceded to him either by common law or by reason of a special indult granted by the Holy See.[53]

The Roman Pontiff, being the supreme legislator and the fountain-head of all power enjoyed by those who are in possession of ecclesiastical jurisdiction, can reserve to himself all legislative, judicial and coercive power as regards matrimonial impediments. Such reservation was actually effected by the new law as a safeguard for the welfare of the Church and of society. The foregoing canon furnishes an ideal case for the application of the *prima regula iuris: "Omnis res per quascumque causas nascitur, per easdem dissolvitur."* The right of the Holy See to such a reservation was always admitted by the leading canonists, nor was it ever questioned that the same supreme authority alone may authorize another to dispense in its name from a matrimonial impediment.[54]

144. The canon referring to custom emphasizes still more this absolute control which the Holy See has over marriage impediments. Custom introducing a new impediment or one contrary to those already existing is reprobated.[55] Formerly Canon Law accepted various impediments originating in custom, but it was always maintained that no custom or human law can abrogate an impediment of divine law. In the future

[52] S. C. C., Russiae (Archiep. Chiovien.), 18 sept., 2 dec. 1628; 24 mart., 20 apr. 1629.

[53] Cod. Iur. Can., Can. 1040.

[54] Wernz, *op. cit.*, n. 63; Gasparri, *op. cit.*, n. 303; De Smet, *op. cit.*, n. 215; Benedict XIV, ep. encycl., *"Magnae Nobis,"* 29 iun. 1748; Pius VI, const., *"Auctorem fidei,"* 28 aug. 1749; prop. 59, 60; S. C. de Prop. Fide, (S. P. pro Sin.-Tunkin. Occident.), 4 iul. 1831.

[55] Cod. Iur. Can., Can. 1041.

it will be well nigh impossible for custom to establish a universal impediment, not only on account of the reprobation expressed above, but mostly on account of the difficulty which will be experienced in getting the consent of the supreme ecclesiastical legislator. It cannot be presumed that in our times a universal custom, before attaining the force of law, would fail to come to the notice of the Holy See, which would either approve it expressly or reprobate it.

145. The new legislation discriminates between impediments of minor grades and those of major grades. Under the former are classified the following:

1. Collateral consanguinity in the third degree.
2. Collateral affinity in the second degree.
3. Public propriety in the second degree.
4. Spiritual relationship.
5. Crime arising from adultery combined with a promise to marry, or with an attempt to contract even a civil marriage.[56]

All the other impediments belong to the class of the major grade.[57] An extensive and individual treatment of these impediments will be presented later. The foregoing differentiation finds its practical application in the dispensations to which the attention of the reader is called in the pages that follow.

IV. Dispensation from Matrimonial Impediments.

(Canon 1043—Canon 1057.)

146. Dispensation is a relaxation of the law in some particular instances. Only the author of the law, or his successor, or his superior, or an individual author-

[56] *Ordo servandus in S. Congregationibus, Tribunalibus, Officiis Romanae Curiae*, 29 sept. 1908, Pars II, *Normae peculiares*, cap. VII, art. III, n. 19.

[57] Cod. Iur. Can., Can. 1042.

ized by either has the right to grant a dispensation.[58] Ordinaries below the Roman Pontiff may not dispense from the general law of the Church, not even in a peculiar case, unless such power was given to them explicitly or implicitly, or unless recourse to the Holy See is difficult and grave harm is feared on account of delay. It is understood that, should these conditions be present, the Bishop will lift only those impediments from which the Holy See ordinarily dispenses.[59] Thus, for instance, he will not remove an impediment arising from any degree of lineal or from the first degree of collateral consanguinity, and only in extreme cases will he dispense from lineal affinity in the first degree (provided the marriage from which it arises has not been consummated), nor from crime *alterutro vel utroque coniuge machinante, praesertim si casus sit publicus.*

147. The Bishops and other Ordinaries of places may dispense from the diocesan laws; but only in particular instances and for a just cause from the laws of a Plenary or a Provincial Council. Should the Roman Pontiff deem it necessary to legislate for a certain territory, such particular law in that locality would be endowed with the force of a general law, in the sense that the Ordinaries of such places could not dispense from it in the absence of the conditions stated above as required for the dispensation from a general law.[60] Without an express authorization pastors have no power to relax either a general or a particular law.[61] Every relaxation of an ecclesiastical law must be occasioned by a just and reasonable cause commensurate with the gravity of the law from which a dispensation is to be granted, otherwise a dispensation given by an

[58] *Op. cit.*, Can. 80.
[59] *Op. cit.*, Can. 81.
[60] *Op. cit.*, Can. 82.
[61] *Op. cit.*, Can. 83.

inferior is illicit and invalid. Should there be a doubt as to the sufficiency of the cause, the asking of the dispensation would be licit, and its granting both licit and valid.[62] The wording of the rescript bestowing the faculty to grant the dispensation must be interpreted strictly.[63]

148. Since dispensations are generally given by means of rescripts which serve simultaneously as a proof, should the occasion require it, it is necessary that the reader should familiarize himself with the new law on this point. *Excommunicati vitandi*[64] or *personaliter interdicti,*[65] or *suspensi,*[66] as well as persons whom a declaratory or a condemnatory sentence excommunicates or interdicts or suspends cannot validly receive a dispensation from the Holy See, unless this fact is mentioned in the petition and in the rescript.[67] If the favor need not be bestowed through a third person (an executor), the effect follows as soon as the rescript is given; otherwise it is deferred until the authorized party executes it.[68] Only those conditions are regarded as essential for the validity of a rescript which are introduced by the conditional conjunctions "if," "unless," and others belonging to the same category.[69] Rescripts are granted under the implicit condition "*Si preces veritate nitantur.*" Should the causes stated in the petition be unfounded or imaginary the rescript is invalid, unless it is given "*motu proprio,*" or contains a dispensation from a minor impediment. In the case of a "*motu proprio*" rescript the granted favor is sustained,

[62] *Op. cit.*, Can. 84.
[63] *Op. cit.*, Can. 85.
[64] *Op. cit.*, Can. 2265, §2.
[65] *Op. cit.*, Can. 2275, n. 3.
[66] *Op. cit.*, Can. 2283.
[67] *Op. cit.*, Can. 36.
[68] *Op. cit.*, Can. 38.
[69] *Op. cit.*, Can. 39.

though a part of the truth was concealed by the petitioner, as long as the final or the only cause on which the petition was based was not false.[70] In the case of a dispensation from a minor impediment the rescript would be valid even if the whole truth should be concealed and an imaginary or even false reason substituted as the *causa motiva.*[71]

149. A favor denied by one Sacred Congregation or Office of the Roman Curia cannot be granted validly by another Congregation or Office or by the Ordinary of the place (should he have the power), except with the assent of that Sacred Congregation or Office by which it was declined in the first instance; the right of the Sacred Penitentiaria remaining intact.[72] No individual should ask another Ordinary for a favor denied by his own, without mentioning the fact of refusal; nor should the latter grant such a favor without having first informed himself of the reason by which the former was influenced when he refused the petition. In the same way a favor refused by the Vicar General and asked from the Bishop without mention of that fact is invalid, nor may a favor denied by the Bishop be asked from the Vicar General without the consent of the Ordinary, even if the fact of the Bishop's refusal should be exposed in the petition.[73]

150. Provided the Ordinary is unmistakably certain as to the identity of the person to whom a favor is granted, and as to the nature of the favor, the rescript is not invalidated by an error that may have been committed as regards the description of the nature of the concession, or as regards the name of the grantor or of the grantee or of the place of the latter's residence.[74]

[70] *Op. cit.*, Can. 45.
[71] *Op. cit.*, Can. 1054.
[72] *Op. cit.*, Can. 43.
[73] *Op. cit.*, Can. 44.
[74] *Op. cit.*, Can. 47.

Should the Apostolic See grant a rescript not necessitating an executor the recipient need not present it to the Bishop unless expressly ordered by the rescript to do so, or the nature of the concession obviously demands it, as, for example, when the favor regards a public matter, or the verification of certain conditions by the Bishop is required.[75] The executor must observe the essential conditions as well as the substantial form laid down in the rescript.[76] He may substitute another person for himself unless such privilege is expressly denied to him,[77] or, unless he has been chosen *industria personae* (by virtue of some personal merit).

V. The Power of the Bishops and Priests over Matrimonial Impediments.

151. The Ordinaries of places may dispense their own subjects in every place as well as all persons residing within the limits of their territory, not only from the form to be observed in the celebration of marriage, but also from every impediment of ecclesiastical law, excepting those arising from the order of the holy priesthood and from lineal affinity, if, in the latter case, the marriage was consummated. This faculty may be used whether the impediments are public, occult or multiple, provided scandal is removed and the customary conditions complied with, should the case demand a dispensation from the impediment of disparity of worship or of mixed religion. The conditions under which this extraordinary faculty may be used are clearly specified, namely: If urgent danger of death necessitates the adjustment of matters of conscience, and, should the case permit, the legitimation of offspring.[78]

[75] *Op. cit.,* Can. 51.
[76] *Op. cit.,* Can. 55.
[77] *Op. cit.,* Can. 56.
[78] Cod. Iur. Can., Can. 1043.

This is the most extensive faculty ever given to the Bishops by virtue of ordinary power in case of urgent danger of death. On February 20, 1888, the Congregation of the Holy Office issued a decree whereby the Bishops were authorized to dispense from all public matrimonial impediments established by ecclesiastical law in order to provide for the relief of conscience in behalf of those individuals who contracted a civil marriage, or "*vivunt in concubinatu.*"[79] The foregoing faculty was not ordinary but only delegated, with the privilege of subdelegation. The decree states distinctly that only *aegroti* and *in gravissimo mortis periculo constituti* may be benefited by this faculty. By virtue of the decree "*Ne temere,*" art. VII, for similar reasons plus the legitimation of offspring *imminente mortis periculo* any priest could convalidate a civil marriage provided neither the Ordinary, nor the parish priest of the place, nor a priest delegated by either was accessible. Finally on August 15, 1909, the Sacred Congregation of the Sacraments declared that a priest who according to the foregoing article of the decree "*Ne temere*" assists at a marriage is empowered to dispense from all the impediments mentioned in the decree on the Holy Office issued for the Bishops in 1888.

The present decree is the final development of the foregoing. Its extensiveness is due to the fact that it eliminates many restrictions found in the former decrees. They all show the unbounded mercy and solicitude the Church entertains for those sinners who are on the verge of eternity.

152. The first condition is the urgent danger of death. The law fails to specify the particular cause from which such a danger must result in order that the faculty may become operative. Therefore any

[79] New *Collectanea,* n. 1685.

cause whatsoever will suffice, provided it may be qualified as *urgens mortis periculum.* A soldier in the first trenches, a person on board a submerging ship, an individual living in a high story of a building that is all ablaze from below affording little possibility of escape, and one living in a house which owing to a severe earthquake is falling to pieces and whose exit is barred, are as much in urgent danger of death in the sense of this canon as one who is critically ill owing to grave sickness, or as the result of an unsuccessful major operation.

153. Such danger may threaten either the party who labors under an impediment, or the one who is free from it. The Holy Office decided that this faculty may be used even if only the healthy party is directly bound by the impediment and the other, exposed to an urgent danger of death, wishes to adjust his matters of conscience.[80] It is presumed in this case that both parties in question are Catholics.

154. But what is to be done under the same circumstances if they are both laboring under an impediment, for instance, *si monialis aegrotans in concubinatu viveret cum diacono bene valente?* The Holy Office decided that *ad consulendum conscientiae* the Ordinary could even in that case dispense from all ecclesiastical impediments, excepting the two mentioned above. It is very questionable, however, whether the opinion of Gieran [81] can be upheld, namely, that this faculty may be used even in order "to soothe the conscience of the party who is not in danger of death." If both parties are Catholics it is hardly imaginable that the conscience of the dying person can remain "unsoothed" after the convalidation of marriage and the legitimation of off-

[80] S. C. S. Off., 1 iul. 1891, in the new *Collectanea,* n. 1758.

[81] *The New Canon Law in its practical aspects,* p. 151; Philadelphia, 1918.

spring. In such a case his contention might hold. But suppose the dying party is a non-Catholic? In that case, if he should decline to become a convert, the Ordinary could go no further unless he possessed the faculty of granting a *sanatio in radice.* One should not lose sight of the fact that the purpose of this extraordinary faculty is to benefit the dying person (whose salvation the Church wants to secure) directly, the healthy person only indirectly.

155. The second condition in the absence of which the ordinary may not avail himself of this faculty is the very condition which occasioned its granting, namely, the necessity of adjusting matters of conscience, and, should the case permit it, of legitimating the offspring. It would be a mistake to imagine that the two reasons must always be combined in one and the same case, for the first can easily be imagined without the second but not *vice versa.* The necessity of settling matters of conscience affords in itself a sufficient ground for the Bishop to act and to avail himself of the faculty bestowed by this canon. A civil marriage, a concubinage not legitimatized even by the civil law, the wish to repair a wrong done to a woman or to fulfil the promise of marriage under which she was seduced, the intention to restore the good name of the accomplice or the desire to avoid grave scandal or a proximate occasion of sin are some of the reasons one could enumerate as necessitating an adjustment of matters of conscience and in themselves sufficient to justify the Ordinary in resorting to this faculty.

In some instances the validation of marriage may be desired for the sake of the children born out of wedlock. Though such might actually be the primary intention, the secondary, namely, the settling of matters of conscience, is implicitly included in it. It would seem that the word "and" here is not to be regarded as disjunctive but copulative, as connecting two things existing in the same case, namely, the adjustment of matters of conscience and the legitimation of offspring. The faculty may be used in a case where the first condition occurs without the second, but it is hard to see how the second condition could be verified without offering some relief to the conscience of the party who is in urgent danger of death.

156. Should the validation of marriage take place, the natural illegitimate offspring become *ipso facto* legitimatized; not so, however, the children born of an adulterous or of a sacrilegious union.[82] Even if such a union should be validated, in the former instance after the death of one of the consorts and in the latter by means of a dispensation, the children already born of a sacrilegious or adulterous union would still remain illegitimate. Take the case where a *monialis aegrotans in matrimonio civili viveret cum diacono bene valente.* The Ordinary by virtue of this faculty could grant the necessary dispensation and the marriage could be validated, but it would not benefit the children already born of that union. Such children can be legitimatized only by a special mandate of the Roman Pontiff.[83]

157. The faculty contained in this canon is granted to the Ordinaries of places. Besides the Roman Pontiff, under the name *Ordinary* in this connection are to be included: All residential Bishops, *Abbas* or *Praelatus nullius,* and their Vicar General, Administrator, Vicar and Prefect Apostolic.[84] They may exercise this faculty in behalf of their subjects wherever they may be, or in favor of all persons who *hic et nunc*

[82] Cod. Iur. Can., Can. 1051.

[83] Gasparri, *op. cit.*, n. 1123; Wouters, *op. cit.*, p. 68; S. C. S. Off., 8 iul. 1903, in the new *Collectanea,* n. 2171; S. Poenit., 1 iul. 1859.

[84] Cod. Iur. Can., Can. 198.

actually reside in their diocese. Thus the canon invests the Bishop with a personal jurisdiction over his own subjects and brings under it also persons tarrying within the limits of his diocese but not possessing either a domicile or a quasi-domicile therein. Therefore he may resort to this faculty even when *peregrini* or *vagi* are involved. In order to settle matters of conscience of a person who is in urgent danger of death outside his domicile or quasi-domicile, either his own Bishop or the Ordinary of the place may avail himself of this faculty.

158. The first dispensation which this canon empowers the Ordinary to grant, regards the non-observance of some customary formalities prescribed for marriage. (*Forma in matrimonii celebratione servanda.*) By this form is meant the presence of the Ordinary or of the parish priest and two witnesses. In other words, he can dispense from the presence of the two witnesses. Owing to conditions prevailing in some localities of China a petition requesting a similar privilege was sent to Rome by the Ordinaries of that country, and on July 28, 1908, the Holy See acceded to their wishes.[85]

As far as the impediments are concerned all those that were introduced by the Church law fall within the scope of this faculty, be they diriment or impedient, public or occult or multiple. The exempted impediments arise from the Order of the Priesthood and from lineal affinity, provided in the latter instance the marriage has been consummated. Should such marriage not be consummated the Ordinary under such circumstances could dispense even from the impediment of lineal affinity. Since the law fails to discriminate as regards the degree, it is legitimate to infer that the

[85] KUBELBECK, *The Sacred Penitentiaria*, p. 62; at the Catholic University of America, Washington, D. C., 1918.

expression *"ex affinitate in linea recta"* comprehends any degree of the direct line, if the marriage occasioning the affinity has not been consummated. Thus, for instance, the Bishop could grant a dispensation by virtue of which one could marry one's daughter-in-law or mother-in-law, or step-daughter or step-mother. He could also dispense from the impediment arising from the Order of Diaconate or Subdiaconate.

159. Even if all the above explained conditions should be verified in a particular case, the Bishop before actually applying the necessary dispensation must take heed to remove the scandal. His prudence will suggest the various means whereby such a purpose can be accomplished. If the parties show their repentance in the presence of witnesses, or if they are willing to do public penance, or if they give a sincere promise that as soon as the danger of death is removed they will leave the present place where their scandalous relations are known, and will go to a region where they are unknown, these and other precautionary measures, dependent on circumstances, would suffice to satisfy the obligation the words *"remoto scandalo"* impose. If the Bishop should find the removal of total scandal a practical impossibility, its partial removal linked with the parties' promise, or desire, or at least willingness to do more will give him enough ground to grant the dispensation. He can proceed even if the scandal is irreparable, but not if the parties out of mere obstinacy refuse to remove it when the difficulties to be confronted are inconsiderable. This treatment is to be accorded to them not as if the validity of the dispensation were conditioned on the words *"remoto scandalo,"* but on account of their frame of mind. The least the Church exacts under such circumstances is compunction of heart for the wrong done and the scandal created, which compunction cannot be conceived unless accompanied with readiness to embrace a little humiliation or inconvenience connected with the reparation of the given scandal.

160. Should the case require a dispensation from the impediment of disparity of worship or of mixed religion, the customary *cautiones* must be subscribed to, before the Ordinary proceeds any further in his task of adjusting the persons' matters of conscience. A thorough treatment of these cautiones is found in another part of this work.[86] The importance of exacting and of giving these guarantees can be inferred from the fact that as recently as July 21, 1912, the Holy Office declared null and void all marriages in which a dispensation from the impediment of disparity of worship was obtained without the exaction or after the refusal of such precautionary conditions.[87] We are inclined to think that, under such circumstances, the spirit of the Church would permit the Ordinary to make this faculty operative, at least *quoad validitatem*, even in case the *cautiones* are refused by the infidel party, as long as the Catholic party constituted in urgent danger of death is willing to do all in his power to comply with them should he recover. This inference is legitimate from the fact that according to the new legislation a rescript is not invalidated (though its use may be illicit) unless preceded by the conditional conjunction "if," "unless," "except," "provided" or any other belonging to the same class.[88] What course should the Ordinary take if he meets with an absolute refusal even on the part of the Catholic? It is hard to see how such an individual could be considered well disposed to have his marriage validated and his matters of con-

[86] See this work under n. 191 ff.

[87] *Acta Ap. Sedis*, vol. IV, p. 443.

[88] COD. IUR. CAN., Can. 39.

science adjusted, and these are the main reasons for the granting of the faculty expressed in this canon.

161. Under the circumstances described above, but exclusively in a case where no recourse can be had even to the Ordinary of the place, the same extensive faculty to dispense is enjoyed by the pastor, and by any priest who assists at marriage according to the norm of canon 1098, n. 2, and even by a confessor, the latter being restricted to the internal forum and in the act of sacramental confession.[89]

In order that the three classes of priests enumerated in this canon may validly apply the above-explained faculty it is necessary that the circumstances should be the same as stated before, namely, an urgent danger of death, the need to settle matters of conscience, and, should the case permit, the legitimation of offspring.

The case must be such that neither the proper Bishop (by virtue of domicile or quasi-domicile, or one month's residence) of either party in question, nor even the Ordinary of the place in which they tarry *hic et nunc* can be approached. This does not imply an absolute impossibility. It rather refers to the delay which such a recourse would inevitably necessitate, and which would expose the party concerned to the danger of dying before the affairs of his conscience could be settled. The priests mentioned in the foregoing canon need not resort to such extraordinary measures as the telephone or a telegram even if communication with the Bishop could thereby be established.[90]

162. The pastor has this faculty by virtue of his office, which fact carries with it the right to delegate the same faculty to others. Besides the pastor this faculty is enjoyed by *any* priest who, in danger of

[89] *Op. cit.*, Can. 1044.

[90] Litt. encycl. Secr. Stat., 10 dec. 1891; in the new *Collectanea*, n. 1775.

death, should assist at marriage when neither the Ordinary, nor the pastor, nor a priest delegated by either can be reached. The qualifying adjective "*alius*" permits any priest to resort to this faculty, the other conditions being verified, even if he should be suspended, or excommunicated, or deprived of all jurisdiction.[91]

Under the same circumstances a confessor is invested with the same power as the Ordinary, but he may exercise it only in the tribunal of penance.[92] The difference between the power granted to the first two and to the third is apparent. The pastor and the *sacerdos qui matrimonio ad norman can. 1098, n. 2, assistit* may make use of this faculty either outside the tribunal of penance, or in it; the confessor, as a *conditio sine qua non,* is limited to the sacramental confession. Should he dispense in *foro interno* from an occult impediment which subsequently becomes public, another dispensation must be obtained for the same *pro foro externo.*[93]

163. Should the pastor or the other priest mentioned in this canon (not the confessor) grant dispensation for the external forum, he is immediately to bring this fact to the knowledge of the Ordinary of the place, and the dispensation should be recorded in the Matrimonial Register.[94]

By the Ordinary of the place is understood the head of the diocese within whose territory such a dispensation is given. Dispensations granted *pro foro externo* are public acts and as such should be recorded in the

[91] DE SMET, *op. cit.*, n. 68; VERMEERSCH, *"Ne temere,"* n. 74; WOUTERS, *op. cit.*, n. 68; see this work, n. 508.

[92] S. C. S. Off., litt. encycl., 1 mart. 1889; 23 apr. 1890 ad 2-4; S. C. de Sacr., *Parmen. et aliarum,* 14 maii 1909.

[93] BENEDICT XIV, *De Synodo Dioecesana,* lib. IX, c. II, n. I.

[94] COD. IUR. CAN., Can. 1045.

Matrimonial Register.[95] Dispensation given by the confessor *pro foro interno* is a secret act, needing no recording, for it cannot be revealed without breaking the sacramental seal. It is for this reason that the new law does not oblige a confessor to notify the Ordinary of the place of a dispensation he has granted in the tribunal of Penance.

164. The Ordinaries of places may dispense from all impediments mentioned in canon 1043, heeding the clause placed at its end, whenever an impediment is detected after all the preparations have been made for the nuptials, and the marriage, without the probable danger of grave evil, cannot be deferred until a dispensation from the Holy See can be obtained. This faculty holds good even for the validation of a contracted marriage, should there be the same danger in delay, with no time to have recourse to the Holy See. Under the same circumstances the same faculty is enjoyed by all mentioned in canon 1044, but only in occult cases in which even the Ordinary of the place cannot be reached, or can be reached only with danger of violation of the sacramental secret.[96]

This canon legislates for an emergency styled in the past *"casus perplexus."* Sanchez was the first advocate of the opinion that in cases in which the circumstances specified in this canon are verified the Bishops have an ordinary power to dispense provided the impediment is occult.[97] This opinion was subsequently embraced by St. Alphonsus, and after a time was adopted by all leading canonists.[98] Though all kinds of reasons were contrived for its vindication and

[95] S. C. de Prop. Fide, instr. (ad Archiep. Hiberniae), 25 iul. 1791.

[96] Cod. Iur. Can., Can. 1045.

[97] *Op. cit., loc. cit.*, lib. VII, disp. 40, n. 5.

[98] Rosset, *op cit., loc. cit.*, n. 2389 ff; Gasparri, *op. cit.*, n. 409; Leitner, *op. cit.*, p. 504 ff.; Scherer, *loc. cit.*, p. 640; Wernz, *op. cit.*, n. 619; De Smet, *op. cit.*, n. 238; Feije, *op. cit.*, n. 635.

though some maintain that even the Holy Office sanctioned it indirectly,[99] it remained doubtful until the present legislation not only confirmed it by express approbation but augmented its scope by extending it to all impediments, whether occult, public, or multiple, diriment or impedient, provided they are of ecclesiastical origin, excepting only two, already referred to above. It must be borne in mind that this canon does not authorize a dispensation from the form of marriage.

The words "*cum iam omnia parata sunt ad nuptias*" do not necessarily convey the idea that before the Ordinary may resort to this faculty the parties must have already crossed the threshold of the church for the purpose of contracting marriage. It suffices that the invitations have been issued and all arrangements have been made, even if the impediment should be discovered a few days before the wedding, as long as the time allotted is not sufficint to permit recourse either to the Holy See or to one possessing delegated power.

165. If the above-stated conditions exist in a particular case, the *probabile gravis mali periculum* follows almost inevitably. Therefore the Ordinary will have reason to dispense in most of such instances, for the probable danger of grave evil will be present in almost every case, should the marriage not be celebrated on the day appointed. The Bishop may dispense even if the parties should purposely postpone the revelation of the impediment to the very last minute, and should thus be found in *mala fide*. He may furthermore exercise the same faculty even in marriages already contracted (invalidly), should a similar danger be present in delay, and should time not permit recourse either to the Holy See or to its delegate.[100]

[99] Wernz, *op. cit.*, n. 619 note 83.
[100] S. C. S. Off., 6 iul. 1898, in the new *Collectanea*, n. 2007.

Some conditions which the canonists laid down in the past in order that the Bishop may exercise the same faculty for validation of marriages invalidly contracted, are eliminated by the new legislation. Should the impediment have been discovered after the marriage was entered into, or should a delay caused by recourse to the Holy See be likely to occasion scandal, or incontinence, when there is no possibility of separation *a toro et mensa* without great inconvenience to the parties, no one would deny that such circumstances would not only justify but even make imperative the granting of a dispensation.[101]

166. Should the circumstances be such as described above, it being immaterial whether marriages to be contracted or already contracted are involved, and should recourse to the Ordinary be impossible on account of the danger in delay or on account of the danger of violating the secret, then, the pastor, or any priest (in the absence of the Ordinary, or of the pastor, or of a delegate of either) or even a confessor may grant the necessary dispensation, provided the case is occult. The difference between the faculties enjoyed by the Bishop and those by the three classes of priests mentioned above is apparent. The former may dispense from all impediments of ecclesiastical law (excepting the two already so often emphasized) regardless of the nature of the case, even if it be public; the latter may dispense from the same impediments, but only in occult cases. An occult case is not equivalent to an occult impediment, nor must the canon be interpreted in the sense that unless the impediment is occult, it is withdrawn from the jurisdiction of these three classes of priests. Be the impediment public or occult, as long as it is a secret case, the priests in question may dispense from

[101] WERNZ, *op. cit.*, n. 618; FEIJE, *op. cit.*, n. 633.

it. It was necessary that the Codex should make use of the expression *"pro casibus occultis"* for in the new legislation the publicity or occultness of an impediment is not determined by the fact whether it is known or unknown to others, but by the fact whether it can or cannot be proved in the external forum.[102] Let us take a hypothetical case in which the invalidity of a marriage is due to an impediment arising from collateral consanguinity in the second degree. Formerly this by its nature was a public impediment; consequently a public case in the old legislation, but not so in the new. Should only the contracting parties know of the existence of the impediment, the new law would consider the case an occult one and any one of the priests belonging to the three classes mentioned would be authorized to grant the necessary dispensation, since this canon gives them the right to dispense from all impediments of ecclesiastical origin except those arising from the Order of Holy Priesthood and, should the marriage have been consummated, from lineal affinity.

167. When a case is to be regarded as public or as occult is a question whose solution is yet pending. In the past the Sacred Penitentiaria made the publicness or the occultness of an impediment dependent on the size of the village or the city, and on the number and disposition of the individuals who were aware of its presence.[103] Though the question was never solved with mathematical precision, it was a generally accepted theory that if in a village only six and in a city only eight persons were aware of the impediment, it could still be considered occult. It would, perhaps, not be out of place to apply to public and occult cases the same principles which formerly decided the publicness or the occultness of an impediment.

[102] COD. IUR. CAN., Can. 1037.
[103] GASPARRI, *op. cit.*, n. 252.

168. Unless the rescript of the Sacred Penitentiaria orders otherwise, a dispensation granted in the internal non-sacramental forum from an occult impediment is to be carefully recorded in the register kept in the secret archives of the Curia in accordance with the instructions contained in canon 379, nor would the case demand another dispensation should such an impediment become public subsequently, unless the dispensation had been given only for the internal sacramental forum.[104]

The Church law distinguishes three kinds of *fora* (forums). The external forum is an ecclesiastical court in which public matters concerning the rights or the temporal and spiritual transactions of Christians are adjudicated. The evidence of this court is limited to things that come to light either by testimony or by public proofs. The internal forum is divided into sacramental and non-sacramental. The former is confined to sins as confessed by the penitent, the latter handles all affairs pertaining to the spiritual welfare of the individual and the society. The evidence of the external forum consists of the exonerating or self-accusing declaration of the individual and of those who testify for or against his cause. The internal forum decides on the testimony of the individual alone.[105]

With this explanation in our possession the foregoing canon should create no difficulty. The Church in order to save the contracting parties from disgrace, or to obviate scandal, takes all these precautions in case of occult impediments. For this reason it insists on recording the marriage in which a dispensation was obtained from the non-sacramental forum, in a register used especially for that purpose, and kept under lock

[104] COD. IUR. CAN., Can. 1047.
[105] REIFFENSTUEL. *op. cit.* III, 5, n. 348; BENEDICTUS XIV, *De Synodo Dioecesana*, lib. XIII, c. XXII, n. 8; D'ANNIBALE, *op. cit.*, vol. I, n. 25.

and key in the diocesan archives.[106] A secret communicated in the non-sacramental forum obliges, though its divulgation would not involve *violationem sigilli sacramentalis.* If such a secret should become public it ceases to bind. Consequently, the secret being divulged, the dispensation granted privily on account of it will of itself become public. Should the dispensation be given in the sacramental forum the secret would continue to oblige notwithstanding the fact that it became public. For this reason, to justify the contracting parties in the eyes of the public and to prevent scandal, a dispensation for the external forum must be procured when the knowledge of an impediment dispensed from in the internal sacramental forum alone becomes the property of others.

169. Should in a particular case a petition for a dispensation be dispatched to the Holy See, the Ordinaries, even if they should possess the faculties required by the case, must refrain from making use of them, except in accordance with the norm laid down in canon, 204, §2.[107]

Sometimes it may happen that the parish priest or the party laboring under an impediment forwards a petition to the Holy See for a dispensation. In such instances the Ordinary, though he might have power to dispense from the impediment in question, should abstain from making use of it, unless there is danger in delaying until a response comes from the Holy See. A dispensation granted under such circumstances must immediately be brought to the knowledge of the Holy see.[108] This canon does not mean to suspend the faculty of the Bishop in a case in which the Holy See has been petitioned to dispense. A dispensation granted by him

[106] COD. IUR. CAN., Can. 379.
[107] *Op. cit.,* Can. 1048.
[108] *Op. cit.,* Can. 204, §2.

would be valid though the grave and urgent cause described above be absent. He would, however, be guilty of presumption, and would act illicitly, for *non decet ut rei ad superiorem delatae se immisceat inferior.* If he is obliged to notify the Holy See should he dispense in grave and urgent necessity, *a fortiori* must he do so should the dispensation be given *sine gravi urgentique causa.*

170. Unless the rescript ordains otherwise all persons having a general indult to dispense from a certain impediment may dispense from the same in prospective marriages or in those already contracted, even if the impediment be multiple.[109] This canon embodies a modification in what was formerly called *facultas cumulandi.* By virtue of the present discipline if a missionary possesses the general indult to dispense from the impediment of collateral consanguinity up to the second degree of the equal line inclusively, he may dispense also in cases in which the same impediment is multiplex, when, for instance, the same parties are related in the second and also in the third degree of consanguinity.[110]

171. Persons having a general indult to dispense from several impediments of different species, either diriment or impedient, are authorized to lift such impediments even if they should be public, or occur in one and the same case.[111] For instance, if a person in possession of a general indult may dispense from the impediments of affinity, of disparity of worship, and of crime, by virtue of the same indult he may dispense from the same three impediments even if they should occur in one and the same case. Formerly this was not

[109] *Op. cit.*, Can. 1049, §1.
[110] S. C. S. Off., 19 iun. 1875; (Mission. Trichinopol.), 2 apr. 1892; S. Poenit., 20 apr. 1883.
[111] Cod. Iur. Can., Can. 1049, §2.

possible unless one received the so-called faculties for cumulating.

172. If together with one or several public impediments which one can remove by virtue of a general indult, one finds that in the same case there is another impediment from which he has no power to dispense, the Holy See must lift all of them. If, however, the impediment or impediments from which one can dispense were discovered only after the Holy See has already been petitioned for a dispensation, then one is free to use his faculties.[112] The tenor of this canon shows that it legislates for public impediments. Should there be three public impediments in a case and should the Ordinary have power to dispense only from two, all three must be removed by the Holy See. If, however, the two impediments from which the Ordinary can dispense were not discovered until after the Holy See has already been petitioned for the removal of the third, the Ordinary is free to remove them.[113]

173. The offspring, except adulterine and sacrilegious, born or conceived by the parties in question is legitimated when a dispensation is granted from a diriment impediment. Such effect follows whether the dispensation is given by virtue of ordinary power, or by virtue of power delegated by means of a general indult, not by rescript given for particular cases.[114]

Those children are in need of legitimation who descend from parents whose marriage was neither valid nor putative. Illegitimate children may be either spurious or natural according as the parents, at the time the child was conceived or born, or at any time during the period of gestation, were or were not labor-

[112] COD. IUR. CAN., Can. 1050.
[113] S. C. de Prop. Fide, litt. (ad Deleg. Ap. Syriae), 10 maii, 1887.
[114] COD. IUR. CAN., Can. 1051; S. C. S. Off., 12 dec. 1748 ad 1; 8 iul. 1903, litt., 11 dec. 1906.

ing under a diriment impediment. There are four classes of spurious children, namely, adulterine (born of adulterous union), sacrilegious (born of a union in which one or both parties were bound by solemn religious vows, or the father was a cleric in major Orders), incestuous (born of a union in which the parties labored under the impediment of consanguinity or affinity), and nefarious (the child of a father and his daughter, or of any direct descendant and ascendant). It is certain that the foregoing canon legislates for the natural children. The question might arise to what extent does it affect the spurious children? It expressly exempts the two classes, namely, the adulterine and the sacrilegious offspring. What are we to say about incestuous children and nefarious children? It would seem that an incestuous offspring, if its parents are related within those degrees of consanguinity or affinity from which the Church dispenses, is meant to be benefited by this new law. Not so, however, as regards nefarious children for their parents can entertain no hope of a dispensation. The foregoing canon therefore implies that a dispensation given by virtue of ordinary power, or by virtue of power delegated by means of a general indult effects an automatic legitimation of the offspring if one excludes those above mentioned. Should the faculty to dispense be obtained by means of a rescript for a particular case, no such effect would follow unless a clause inserted in the same rescript would make a special provision for it.

174. A dispensation given from an impediment of consanguinity or affinity in a determined degree retains its force even if a mistake crept into the petition or concession as regards the degree, provided the degree really existing is inferior. The same is to be said when another impediment of the same species but of an equal or inferior degree was omitted.[115]

The first part of this canon is founded on the principle that a dispensation granted from a higher degree includes the lower degree,[116] but not *vice versa.* Let us suppose a case with an impediment of consanguinity in the third degree. Should either the petition or the concession, or both, speak of the second degree, the rescript would not be invalidated thereby. Nor would it be vitiated should a dispensation be asked from the second degree of simple consanguinity, whereas in reality one would have to deal with an impediment of multiple consanguinity in the same degree or in the second and the third degree.

175. When the Holy See grants a dispensation from a ratified non-consummated marriage, or gives permission to contract a new marriage on the ground of the presumed death of the other consort, it intends to remove simultaneously the impediment of crime arising from adultery combined with a promise of, or with an attempt at marriage, but not so when the same impediment originates from the causes mentioned in canon 1075 under numbers 2 and 3.[117]

There are four various causes which may give rise to the impediment of crime. This canon legislates for the first two, namely, when it arises from adultery combined with a promise of marriage, or from adultery combined with an attempt at marriage. Should A. marry B., and should he contract such an impediment with C., he would not require a dispensation to marry her in case his first marriage is dissolved as *ratum non consummatum.* Again, should A. receive permission to

[115] COD. IUR. CAN., Can. 1052.

[116] *Reg.* 35 and 53, *De regulis iuris,* in VI°; S. PIUS V, const. "*Sanctissimus.*" 20 aug. 1506, §1.

[117] COD. IUR. CAN., Can. 1053; see this work, n. 308 ff. and 311 ff.

remarry *ob praesumptam coniugis mortem,* he could contract marriage with B. notwithstanding the impediment of crime that might exist between them for either of the two causes mentioned above. The discipline embodied in this canon was handed down by the Congregation of the Sacraments on June 3, 1912, and is now extended to the universal Church.

176. Dispensation from a minor impediment is always valid. It is not vitiated either on account of suppression of truth (*subreptio*), or of assertion of falsehood (*obreptio*),[118] even if the only final cause alleged be false.[119] The meaning of this canon can be made clearer by means of an example. Let us suppose that the only cause advanced in the *supplica* for dispensation is *aetas superadulta.* Though the petition should be faulty on account of obreption, and though the parties should be in bad faith (having knowingly stated a false cause), the rescript would be valid nevertheless if the impediment which it removes belongs to a minor grade.[120]

177. Dispensations from public impediments committed to the care of the Ordinary of the petitioners, should be executed by the Bishop who gave the testimonial letters or transmitted the petition to the Holy See. This duty is incumbent on him even if the petitioners, by the time the dispensation is to be executed, abandoned the domicile or quasi-domicile they had in his diocese and, with no intention of returning, established themselves in another diocese. In such case he must bring the dispensation to the knowledge of the Ordinary in whose diocese the parties in question in-

[118] COD. IUR. CAN., Can. 42.

[119] *Op. cit.*, Can. 1054; *Ordo servandus in S. Congr., Trib., Officiis, Rom. Curiae,* 29 sept. 1908, Pars II, *Normae peculiares,* cap. VII, art. III, n. 21.

[120] *Acta Ap. Sedis,* vol. 1, p. 90.

tend to contract marriage.[121] This canon legislates for dispensation granted by the Holy See *in forma commissoria.* Such dispensations do not take effect until they are actually executed by the person to whom such a task was entrusted. Should a Bishop send a petition for a dispensation to the Holy See, his task is not completed until the granted favor is actually conferred by means of execution. Should he be commissioned as executor, he retains his jurisdiction over the parties for this one case even if they moved into another diocese. If he should be constrained to execute the rescript in another diocese, the Ordinary of that place should be notified of the nature of this dispensation. It is to be noted that such an executor, whether he be a Bishop or a priest, is implicitly vested with the power to absolve from any ecclesiastical penalties or censures whose removal is absolutely necessary in order that the persons may be benefited by the dispensation.[122] Should the person in question be an *excommunicatus vitandus,* or *personaliter interdictus,* or one whom a declaratory or a condemnatory sentence excommunicates or interdicts, the executor could not apply the dispensation validly unless a special clause inserted in the rescript expressly authorized him to absolve from such severe penalties. Persons thus branded cannot be the recipients of a favor unless the rescript takes cognizance of their censure.[123]

178. Without an express permission given by the Holy See the Ordinaries of places or their officials are forbidden to exact any fees for dispensations granted to those who are not poor except the slight amount required to defray the expenses of the chancery. All

[121] Cod. Iur. Can., Can. 1055.
[122] *Op. cit.,* Can. 66, §3; S. Poenit., 2 iul. 1891; Cod. Iur. Can., Can. 200, §1.
[123] *Op. cit.,* Can. 36; Can. 2265, §2; Can. 2275, n. 3.

contrary customs are reprobated, and the Bishops are bound to restitution should they receive any other fees.[124]

The history of ecclesiastical taxes is rather lengthy and it records several regrettable abuses committed by individuals. These abuses the Church tried to remedy by various repressive measures. The earliest document containing a tax list dates from the time of Benedict XII. Already the Council of Constance had found it necessary to mete out punishment against those who trafficked with spiritual things. Pius II decreed that scribes accepting more than the law allowed should be removed from their office, and Innocent VII, besides confirming the foregoing punishment, threatened them with excommunication reserved to the Holy See. In spite of such drastic measures the abuses continued, and the subsequent pontiffs, especially Alexander VI, Julius II, and Leo X, were constrained to have recourse to repeated legislation intended to check this mercenary tendency regarding things spiritual. The Council of Trent decreed that under certain circumstances the dispensation should be given *gratis.*[125] Innocent XI on October 1, 1678, regulated the fees and permitted moderate charges for matrimonial dispensations, which alms were to be used for pious purposes. The Sacred Congregation of the Council under Leo XIII, modified the *Taxa Innocentiana* on June 10, 1896, and allowed the provincial councils to regulate the taxes according to the customs prevailing in the different localities. The tax-list adopted by such councils required the approbation of the Holy See before it could become operative. This decree of the Sacred Congregation is embodied in the new Codex.[126]

[124] Cod. Iur. Can., Can. 1056.
[125] Sess. XXIV, cap. V. *De reformatione matrimonii.*
[126] Cod. Iur. Can., Can. 1507.

179. Taxes are not to be confounded with *componenda.* They both represent money received in exchange for granted favors, but while the purpose of the taxes is to defray the expenses of the chancery, the *componenda* are used for pious works, and assume thereby a penal character, for they may be looked upon as alms calculated to make partial reparation for the transgression of the law of the Church.

The words of this canon "*modica praestatio*" refer to the postage and other actual expense the chancery incurs in connection with a particular dispensation. From the poor even this amount may not be exacted. Should the Ordinaries wish to retain the privilege of demanding some *componenda* as was customary under the former discipline, they must obtain a special permission from the Holy See. The new law abrogates all previous customs to the contrary, and restitution must be made by all who disregard it by collecting a compensation beyond what the present canon authorizes.

180. Persons dispensing by virtue of power delegated by the Holy See must expressly mention the pontifical indult when they make use of the given faculty.[127] Failure to comply with this provision in the former discipline, as a rule, invalidated the dispensation.[128] Under the same circumstances according to the new legislation the dispensation would be illicit but valid. The purpose of this canon is to protect the rights of the superior.

It has already been stated that a rescript is generally given with the tacit understanding that the causes expressed in the petition are based on truth. The question might arise: When must such causes conform to

[127] *Op. cit.*, Can. 1057.

[128] BENEDICT. XIV, ep. "*Ad tuas,*" 8 aug. 1748; S. C. S. Off. (S. Ludovici), 15 iun. 1875; 12 apr. 1899; S. C. de Prop. Fide, litt. (ad Vic. Ap. Myssur.), 3 iun. 1853; instr. (ad Vic. Ap. Indiar. Orient.), 8 sept. 1869, n. 53.

the truth? The new law distinguishes whether one deals with a rescript which needs an executor, or with one that does not stand in need of being executed.[129] In the former supposition it will be necessary that the cause expressed in the petition and on the ground of which the favor in question was granted be true at the time the rescript is executed. In that hypothesis the rescript will be valid even if the advanced cause was false at the time the petition was dispatched. In the latter case the causes must be true at the time the favor was granted, otherwise the rescript is null and void, unless it is actuated *"Motu proprio"* [130] or the favor it bestows is a dispensation from an impediment of minor grade.[131]

[129] COD. IUR. CAN., Can. 41.
[130] See this work, n. 148.
[131] See this work, n. 176.

CHAPTER V.

Impedient Impediments.
(Canon 1058—Canon 1066.)

1. Impediment of Simple Vows.

181. Marriage is prohibited to those who take the simple vow of virginity, of perfect chastity or of celibacy; likewise to those who vow to receive Holy Orders, or to embrace the religious state. A simple vow does not invalidate marriage, unless the Holy See endowed it with such a force.[1]

Vow of virginity is a deliberate promise made to God by virtue of which one imposes on oneself a voluntary obligation to preserve one's body intact from acts which violate its integrity, or which are instrumental to *primum opus carnale consummatum.* Persons bound by such a vow would contract marriage validly but illicitly. The reason for the first lies in the fact that the Church has never bestowed an irritant clause on the vow of virginity. The marriage would be illicit because such a step would expose the person to the danger of violating the vow, *cum altero coniuge postulante debitum reddere tenetur.* It would, furthermore, imply the intention to consummate marriage, which is equivalent to a formal violation of the vow.

In certain instances a marriage with such a vow would be not only valid but also licit, namely, (1) if both parties mutually vowed chastity; (2) if the one bound by the vow of chastity is determined to refrain from asking the *debitum,* and God reveals to him that

[1] Cod. Iur. Can., Can. 1058.

the other party has the same determination; (3) if the former has a firm resolution not to consummate marriage but to enter religion within a reasonable time. In this last case he would sin gravely if he neglected to inform the other party of such future intention. Only before the first *opus carnale* is consummated does the vow of virginity deprive one of the right to ask the *debitum,* though it does not free one from rendering it.

182. The vow of perfect chastity implies abstinence from every carnal gratification whether external or internal. The principles explained above in connection with the vow of virginity are to be applied also to the vow of perfect chastity.[2]

The vow of celibacy is violated only by actual marriage but not by a sin of the flesh. After one has contracted marriage its use is perfectly licit.

Some persons do not possess a clear idea of the difference existing among the three foregoing vows. In such case the intention with which one meant to bind himself, or the obligation one meant to assume, should be the determinants as to whether one took the vow of celibacy, or of virginity, or of chastity.

183. A person who contracts marriage places himself in the moral impossibility of fulfilling the vow whereby he obliged himself to receive Holy Orders. But under the circumstances he is not bound either to enter religion or to abstain from asking the marriage debt. Only in few and extraordinary instances does the obligation to receive Holy Orders revive. Such would be the case if the wife should lose her right to *debitum* on account of having taken a vow of chastity.[3]

If a person made a simple vow to embrace the religious state, the marriage he would contract would be

[2] Gasparri, *op. cit.*, n. 438; Wernz, *op. cit.*, n. 566; Feije, *op. cit.*, n. 559; De Smet, *op. cit.*, n. 247; De Becker, *op. cit.*, p. 246.

[3] Gasparri, *op. cit.*, n. 440.

valid but gravely illicit and he would have to abstain from its use. He may not ask for the marriage debt, nor is he permitted to render it, but should avail himself, if possible, of the earliest opportunity to fulfill his vow within a reasonable time without having consummated the marriage. Should he consummate it without having been dispensed from his vow, he would sin gravely but the subsequent use of marriage would be licit.

To form an idea how the foregoing five vows may affect the *debitum coniugale* the reader is referred to the moralists.[4]

184. The Holy See has reserved to itself the right to dispense from private vows, whether they regard perfect and perpetual chastity, or the embracing of a religious order of solemn vows, provided both were made absolutely and after the completion of the eighteenth year.[5] Vows that are not reserved may be commuted or dispensed from for a just cause (if such a dispensation does not violate the right of another) by the Ordinary of the place or by the Superior for clerics who are exempted, or by a special delegate of the Holy See.[6]

The vows here considered are simple vows which constitute only a prohibitive impediment to marriage,[7] unless the Holy See ordains otherwise in particular instances, as it ruled for the scholastics of the Society of Jesus, whose simple vows taken after a novitiate of two years it endowed with the force of nullifying marriage.[8]

[4] SANCHEZ, *op. cit.*, lib. IX, disp. 33 ff.; ROSSET, *op. cit.*, n. 1230 ff.

[5] COD. IUR. CAN., Can. 1309.

[6] *Op. cit.*, Can. 1313.

[7] *Op. cit.*, Can. 1073; c. 3, 4, 6, X, *qui clerici vel voventes matrimonium contrahere possunt*, IV, 6; c. un., *de voto et voti redemptione*, III, 15, in VI°; S. C. C., *Canarien.*, 26 mart., 9 apr. 1718.

[8] GREGORIUS XIII, const. *"Ascendente Domino,"* 25 maii 1584. §22.

II. Impediment of Adoption.
(Canon 1059.)

185. All marriages regarded illicit by the civil law of a country on account of legal relationship arising from adoption, will be considered as such also in the eyes of the Canon Law.[9]

The reader is referred to another part of this work in which the origin, history and other features of this impediment are treated more extensively.[10] It will sufficiently serve our present purpose to note here that practically all civilized nations adopted this impediment which has its origin in the Roman law. The lack of uniformity in the legal modes of adoption, and in the force attributed to it by the civil legislation of the various countries, occasioned frequent frictions between the Church and the civil law. To avoid these frictions the Church modified her discipline in this respect and hence resulted the hitherto unknown impedient impediment of adoption. Many of the difficulties and controversies are now happily ended. By conforming itself to the civil law the Church leaves it to the decision of the various countries whether in a particular locality the relationship arising from adoption should constitute a diriment or impedient impediment of marriage.

For marriages, therefore, to be contracted in various countries, the Church will not only adopt the civil law as the measure of the force of the impediment of adoption, but will guide itself also by the scope of the impediment as well as by the particular mode of adoption prevailing in the respective countries.

186. The adoption may be perfect or imperfect. By perfect adoption the person who is *sui iuris* (*arrogatio*) or *alieni iuris* is incorporated into the family of

[9] Cod. Iur. Can., Can. 1059.

[10] See this work, n. 288 ff., treating on the diriment impediment of adoption.

the adopter with all the duties, rights and privileges of a legitimate child. The imperfect adoption, unlike the former, permits the offspring to remain in his parental home, and under the authority of his natural parents, nor does it require of the adopter to transfer any part of his property to the child, though the latter may assert his claim to it should the adopter die intestate. The law of some countries admits only perfect adoption, that of others permits both perfect and imperfect. According as the civil law conditions the illicitness of a marriage only on perfect adoption or on both kinds of adoption, the ecclesiastical law will also condition it only on perfect adoption or on both perfect and imperfect adoption.

The scope of the ecclesiastical impediment of adoption is likewise determined by the scope of the civil impediment of adoption. In other words, persons whom the civil law disqualifies from licit marriage on account of the presence of a prohibitive impediment of adoption, will be declared incompetent also on the ground of the ecclesiastical law.

III. Impediment of Mixed Religion.

(Canon 1060—Canon 1064.)

1. Nature of the Impediment.

187. The Church most strictly forbids all marriages between two baptized persons one of whom is a Catholic and the other a member of a heretical or of a schismatic sect. Even the divine law prohibits such a wedlock, should there be danger of perversion for the Catholic consort and offspring.[11]

This canon defines the nature of a mixed marriage. In order that the impediment of mixed religion may

[11] Cod. Iur. Can., Can. 1060.

arise between two persons, one must be a Catholic and the other *sectae hereticae seu schismaticae adscripta.* The word *"adscripta"* means an express affiliation with such a sect. Therefore this impediment would not arise between a practical Catholic and one who fell away from the Catholic communion without having become a professed adherent of a heretical or a schismatic sect. In order that a person may be regarded a heretic or a schismatic, it is not absolutely necessary that he be incorporated into the sect by virtue of baptism. It is sufficient that, after receiving Catholic baptism, he allies himself with such sects by frequenting their services or outwardly professing their doctrines. A Catholic child, even if he should be brought up by heretics from his very infancy, is not considered a heretic, unless they enrolled his name on the official register of such a sect, or unless he worshiped in it even without such enrollment.

188. Mixed marriages are forbidden by natural, divine, and positive ecclesiastical law. The latter's prohibition is based on the former's. Natural divine law forbids such marriages on account of the serious danger of perversion to which are exposed the Catholic consort and the offspring.[12] Even if this danger should cease in some particular instances, and thus the prohibition arising from the divine law be lifted, the ecclesiastical law would not be relaxed and without a dispensation the marriage would be illicit.[13]

In the early years of the Church St. Paul [14] and St.

[12] C. 15, 16, C. XXVIII, q. 1; BENEDICT. XIV, ep. encycl. *"Magnae Nobis."* 29 iunii, 1748; ep. *"Singulari,"* 9 febr. 1749, §11; LEO XIII, ep. encycl. *"Arcanum,"* 10 febr. 1880; ep. encycl. *"Constanti Hungarorum,"* 2 sept. 1893; Secret. Status, instr. 27 mart. 1830; instr. 22 maii, 1841; instr. 15 nov. 1858.

[13] WERNZ, *op. cit.*, n. 578; GASPARRI, *op. cit.*, n. 446; DE SMET, *op. cit.*, n. 252.

[14] I. *Cor.* V, 11; *Titus,* III, 10.

John [15] found it necessary to raise their voice in admonishing their coreligionists against communicating with heretics in things sacred. The same warning found expression in the early Councils which forbade the Christians all intermarriages with persons prefessing a different belief.[16] This prohibition was very rigorous in the early ages, but by virtue of sheer necessity it was somewhat relaxed after the pseudoreformation period. At the present time, in order to avoid a still greater evil, the Church tolerates mixed marriages provided certain conditions are fulfilled.

2. *Dispensation from the Impediment.*

189. The Church does not dispense from the impediment of mixed religion, unless:

1. Just and grave causes urge such a dispensation.
2. The non-Catholic consort furnishes *cautiones* whereby he obliges himself to remove all danger of perversion from the Catholic consort, and both consorts bind themselves to baptize and educate all their offspring in the Catholic faith.
3. There is a moral certainty that the *cautiones* will be fulfilled. These guarantees, as a rule, should be given in writing.[17]

A mixed marriage, though all formalities required for its validity may be complied with, must be always regarded as illicit unless a dispensation is obtained. A contrary custom, even of the longest duration, would be always considered as *corruptela*, and hence could never make such a marriage licit.[18] When a dis-

[15] II. ep. I, 10 and 11.
[16] Cap. XVI, *Conc. Illiberit.* (300-306); cap. X, XXI, *Conc. Laodicen.* (343-381).
[17] Cod. Iur. Can., Can. 1061.
[18] Benedict. XIV, *De Synodo Dioecesana*, lib. IX, cap. III, n. 2.

pensation is granted from this impediment the Church dispenses also from the law prohibiting communication *in divinis* with heretics and schismatics.

The following pages will be devoted to the explanation of the foregoing conditions.

190. I. Benedict XIV [19] deemed it necessary to accentuate the fact that though all the other conditions may be verified in a particular instance the Church does not dispense *sine gravi aliqua, ac plerumque publica causa.* The Sacred Congregation of Propaganda gave expression to the same doctrine when it admonished the delegates of the Holy See that only *iustae gravesque causae* should influence them to grant a dispensation.[20] That the Church does not intend to relax its discipline on this point is apparent from the fact that the new legislation following in the footsteps of the old, requires the same *iustae ac graves causae* as a condition in whose absence a dispensation from this impediment will not be granted.

It is easier to determine whether a cause is sufficiently grave when one deals with a specific rather than with an abstract instance. Some of the causes justifying the granting of such a dispensation would be: (1) The welfare of a Christian republic; (2) the predominence of heretics or schismatics in a certain country; (3) a written promise made by a heretic to embrace the Catholic faith after marriage; [21] (4) a well-founded hope that a favorably disposed non-Catholic family would return to the unity of the true faith; (5) the fact that such marriage is the only means whereby children born of a former union can be educated in the Catholic faith, or whereby (6) scandal,

[19] *Op. cit., loc. cit.*, n. 5.

[20] Litt. encycl. S. C. de Prop. Fide, 11 mart. 1868; in the new *Collectanea*, n. 1324.

[21] Zitelli, *op. cit.*, p. 60.

concubinage, diffamation or attempt at marriage can be avoided.[22] Causes of private nature, like superadult age, lack of dowry, poverty of the widow, *angustia loci,* and others enumerated in the instruction given by the Sacred Congregation of Propaganda [23] do not suffice singly, but when several concur in one and the same case the circumstances may justify the granting of a dispensation.

The importance of a sufficiently grave cause is apparent from the fact that without it even the Roman Pontiff would dispense illicitly, though validly, while the Bishop under the same circumstances would not remove the impediment for the apostolic indult which he enjoys requires the *cautiones* as a *conditio sine qua non.*

191. II. The second condition without which the dispensation should not be granted regards certain guarantees to be exacted from the two contracting parties. Formerly only the non-Catholic consort was expected to give the *cautiones;* the new law demands a promise also from the Catholic party. The former, according to the tenor of the past discipline, had to promise that he will not interfere with the religious freedom of the latter. The new law requires that he should go even further, and that by a positive act he should remove whatever is calculated to jeopardize the faith of the Catholic consort (circumstances exposing her to the danger of perversion). Besides, both consorts must promise that their children will be baptized and educated exclusively in the Catholic faith. Formerly the Catholic party was not required to make this promise expressly for it was tacitly presumed that such was his intention. Now the Church,

[22] BANGEN, *op. cit.*, vol. IV, p. 20.

[23] Instr. S. C. de Prop. Fide, 9 maii 1877; in the new *Collectanea,* n. 1470.

more emphatically than ever before, will call to his mind this duty, thus making the non-compliance with it so much more sinful.

192. III. These promises are founded on natural and divine law;[24] therefore, not only should they be exacted but a moral certainty should be had as to their fulfillment. The Holy Office in an instruction given to the Primate of Hungary on July 7, 1890, insists that unless the foregoing conditions are subscribed to a dispensation should never be granted. The same instruction, like the canon of the new law, emphasizes the moral certainty which the pastor should have as regards the future fulfillment of the accepted conditions.[25] Should the indication show that their fulfillment is impossible under the contemplated circumstances, or should the insincerity of one or both contracting parties be apparent, the persons in question could not be considered worthy applicants for a dispensation.

In case of urgent danger of death, to adjust matters of conscience and, should the case permit, to legitimate the offspring, a dispensation from this impediment may be granted by the Bishop or by the priests when recourse to the Bishop is difficult, even if the non-Catholic party should refuse to give the customary guarantees, provided the Catholic party is favorably disposed.[26]

In order that the importance of the embraced obligations may be more deeply impressed on the contracting parties and that the proof of their voluntary assumption be available for the external forum, if need

[24] Instr. Secr. Status, 15 nov. 1858.

[25] Benedict. XIV, ep. encycl. "*Magnae Nobis,*" 29 iun. 1748; Gregorious XVI, ep. encycl., "*Summo iugiter,*" 27 maii 1732; Leo XIII, ep. encycl. "*Quod multum,*" 26 aug. 1886; Pius X, litt. ap. "*Provida,*" 18 ian. 1906, n. II.

[26] Cod. Iur. Can., Can. 1043 and 1044; see this work, n. 160.

be, the present discipline prescribes that, as a general rule, the guarantees should be given in writing.[27]

3. Injunctions Relative to Mixed Marriages.

193. The Catholic consort is bound by the obligation of endeavoring by prudent means to procure the conversion of the non-Catholic party.[28] The legislation contained in this canon formerly constituted one of the promises to which the Catholic party was expected to subscribe expressly, and on which the granting of the dispensation was conditioned.[29] This obligation does not lose its force by the fact that it is no longer included in, but separated from the conditions explained above. While the Catholic party's readiness to that effect need not be signified in the petition for dispensation, the law of charity, receiving a special sanction and an added force by virtue of the foregoing ecclesiastical canon, nevertheless continues to oblige him. The former discipline employed the words *"pro viribus"* to express the effort which the Catholic party was expected to make toward converting the non-Catholic consort. The new legislation supplants those terms with the word *"prudenter."* By this change the supreme legislator means to emphasize the circumspection and the discretion which must be exercised in order that the Catholic party may succeed in bringing the dissenting consort to the unity of the faith. A faithful performance of all conjugal duties is without doubt the first and one of the most effective means contributing toward the attainment of that end.

194. Though the Church should grant a dispensa-

[27] Pius VI, rescript. ad Card. Archiep. Mechlinen., 3 iul. 1782; S. C. S. Off. (ad. Ep. Aurelianen.), 6 iun. 1879; S. C. de Prop. Fide, litt. (ad Ep. Ottavien.), 17 apr. 1879.

[28] Cod. Iur. Can., Can. 1062.

[29] S. C. S. Off., instr. (ad Archiep. Quebecen.), 16 sept. 1834, ad 5; instr. (ad Archiep. Corcyren.), 3 ian. 1871, n. 3; S. C. de Prop. Fide, instr. (ad Vic. Ap. Sveciae), 6 sept. 1785; litt. encycl. 11 mart. 1868.

tion from the impediment of mixed religion the contracting parties are nevertheless forbidden to present themselves either personally or by proxy, whether before or after the marriage, before a non-Catholic minister in order to give or to renew their consent while he officiates in his religious capacity.[30] The laws of some countries impose an obligation to give or renew one's consent before a representative of the state as a *conditio sine qua non* to the gaining of the civil effects of marriage. Should the magistrate of such places be a non-Catholic minister, employed for a purely civil function, the parties would not violate this ecclesiastical law by making use of his services.[31] They would not be permitted, however, either to give or to renew their consent before him should his office as civil functionary and as minister of a sect be inseparable, and should he officiate in both capacities simultaneously, namely, by one and the same act.

If the parish priest is certain that the contracting parties will disregard this law, or that they have already transgressed it, he should abstain from witnessing their marriage, unless a very grave cause urges otherwise, and then he must first consult the Ordinary and remove the scandal.[32] Such a very grave cause would exist in every case where the fear is present that a civil marriage will be attempted or that the already attempted invalid marriage will be consummated. It is to be noted that in case the marriage is attempted before the minister of a sect the parties incur an excommunication *latae sententiae* reserved to the Bishop.[33] Absolution from this censure must precede the celebration of such a marriage.

[30] Cod. Iur. Can., Can. 1063, §1.

[31] Instr. S. C. S. Off., 12 dec. 1888, n. 7; in the new *Collectanea*, n. 1696.

[32] Cod. Iur. Can., Can. 1063, §2.

[33] *Op. cit.*, Can. 2319, §1, n. 1.

195. Besides the foregoing injunctions directed to the contracting parties the new legislation inculcates also the duties of the Ordinaries and other pastors of souls when it admonishes them that they (1) should dissuade the faithful to the best of their ability from mixed marriages; (2) should exert every effort not to permit them to be contracted against the law of God and of the Church if they are unable to prevent them altogether; (3) should watch vigilantly over the faithful fulfillment of the *cautiones* which were given in marriages contracted in their own territory or outside it; (4) should be guided in their assistance at such marriages by the instructions contained in canon 1102.[34]

The duties of the Bishop and pastors as outlined in the first three points of the foregoing canon need no explanation. It is sufficient to note that the pastor will not consent to witness a mixed marriage until all his efforts to dissuade the Catholic party from such a step prove abortive. If the latter remains immovable and there is a serious danger that marriage will be contracted outside the Church, provided the parties express a willingness to comply at least with the minimum requirements of the law, the pastor should rather assist at their marriage than allow them to resort to an action which is contrary to the law of God and of the Church, besides being invalid.

196. Even if the dispensation should be granted, the banns of such marriage are not to be proclaimed in the Church, as has already been explained in connection with canon 1026.[35] Should the Ordinary deem it expedient to make such proclamation, no mention should be made of the religious sect with which the non-Catholic party is affiliated. For the validity of

[34] *Op. cit.*, Can. 1064.
[35] See this work, n. 108.

the assistance at such marriages it is required that no extrinsic force or fear should be brought to bear on the pastor in order thus to constrain him to ask and receive the consent of the contracting parties.[36]

According to an instruction Pius IX ordained on November 15, 1858, that such marriages should not take place within the church (*extra ecclesiam*), and that all religious rites whatsoever must be barred.[37] As regards religious rites the new law conforms to the foregoing decree. Since we treat here *de odiosis* the word "*ecclesia*" must be interpreted strictly, in which case it should not be applied to the sacristy or to a private chapel. Such is the meaning of a decision of the Holy Office handed down on January 17, 1877.[38]

If from the observance of this law grave evils are feared, the Ordinary may permit one or the other of the usual ceremonies but the celebration of the Mass must always be excluded.[39] The exclusion of the Mass contains an indirect prohibition against the the imparting of the solemn nuptial blessing with the usual prayers found in the Romal Missal, for such a blessing may not be bestowed outside the Mass.[40]

197. From all this legislation it is manifest that under ordinary circumstances the Church wants the parish priest to render more than a passive assistance to such marriages, since he must ask and receive their consent. By passive assistance is meant the mere presence of the pastor and the witnesses in order to testify to the consent given by the contracting parties. The only official act of the pastor would be the recording of the marriage in the matrimonial register. Should the obviation of serious evils necessitate it, the

[36] Cod. Iur. Can., Can. 1095, §1, n. 3.
[37] Gasparri, *op. cit.* n. 456: De Becker, *op. cit.*, p. 264.
[38] Gasparri, *op. cit.*, n. 463.
[39] Cod. Iur. Can., Can. 1102, §2.
[40] Cod. Iur. Can., Can. 1101.

Bishop may, by way of exception, permit even the active assistance of the pastor which could extend to all the marriage ceremonies contained in the ritual, including the blessing of the ring and all the prayers, barring always the celebration of the nuptial Mass and the solemn blessing usually imparted in it.

198. The guarantees must be exacted even after the marriage is already contracted validly but unlawfully. Until they are given and at least the Catholic education of the children is secured, the Catholic party cannot be admitted to the sacraments.[41] Should the non-Catholic party decline to give the *cautiones,* the well-disposed Catholic party, provided she made the required promises, may be admitted to the frequentation of the sacraments, *scandale remoto.*[42]

It is incumbent on the pastor to validate the marriage as soon as possible should it be invalid either on account of the lack of form or of the presence of some diriment impediment and separation is not practicable, as is generally the case. The exacting of the customary *cautiones* ought to be the first step under such circumstances. Absolution from the censure of excommunication *latae sententiae* should follow next if the marriage was attempted not before a civil magistrate but before a heretical minister. This absolution should be given *in foro externo.* Only in case the attempted marriage is secret and there is no danger of its becoming publicly known, may the absolution be given *in foro interno.* Should the non-Catholic party refuse the giving of *cautiones,* as long as the Catholic party is favorably disposed and the former is willing to renew his consent, the dispensation may still be ob-

[41] S. C. S. Off., 2 mar. 1842; S. C. S. Off., 3 ian. 1871; in the new *Collectanea,* n. 1362, §7.

[42] GASPARRI, *op. cit.,* n. 468; DE SMET, *op. cit.,* n. 257; WERNZ, *op. cit.,* n. 588.

tained for the purpose of validating the marriage, especially if there be some children who stand in need of being legitimated. If the non-Catholic party declines both the giving of *cautiones* and the renewal of consent, recourse should be had to *sanatio in radice*.[43]

VI. Impediment of Unworthiness.

199. The new law bases the state of indignity or unworthiness on the following causes: (1) Public rejection of the Catholic faith (without joining a heretical sect); (2) Profession of membership in societies condemned by the Church; and (3) Public crime or censure coupled with unwillingness to show any sign of repentance. The impediment of unworthiness is thus contracted between a practical Catholic and one who is stigmatized on account of any of the foregoing three reasons. Formerly other causes beside those enumerated could contribute to the origin of this impediment. It is called impediment of unworthiness because one party approaches the sacrament of matrimony unworthily, and exposes himself to the danger of being guilty of sacrilege.

It is generally taught that a worthy party contracting marriage with an unworthy party does not sin gravely, notwithtsanding the fact that he is cognizant of the state of unworthiness under which the other is laboring and that he not only assists to administer the sacrament to him but also asks it from him. Even those theologians who accuse the *pars digna* of venial sin because he becomes a tool offering *parti indignae* an occasion to receive the sacrament unworthily excuse him from all culpability, should he be in possession of some reason justifying his act.[44] Furthermore, neither

[43] GASPARRI, *op. cit.*, n. 468; DE SMET, *op. cit.*, n. 257; WERNZ, *op. cit.*, n. 588.

[44] D'ANNIBALE, vol. III, n. 329; BENEDICT. XIV, *De synodo Dioecesana*, lib. IX, cap. III, n. 5.

the pastor nor the witnesses are obliged *ex officio* to prevent the sacrilege of another, but only *ex caritate,* and they may even permit it indirectly, if the avoidance of greater evil, as is generally the case, demands this.[45]

200. The faithful should be discouraged from contracting marriages with persons who publicly renounced the Catholic faith, even if they did not join a non-Catholic sect, or who profess membership in societies condemned by the Church. The pastor should not assist at such marriages without consulting the Ordinary, who, after having weighed all the circumstances in the case, may permit his assistance. Only grave cause may influence the Bishop to such leniency, and it cannot be shown until, in his prudent judgment, the Catholic education of all the future offspring has been safeguarded and the danger of perversion of the other consort has been removed.[46]

The question will naturally arise: Which are those societies whose condemnation by the Church makes a member liable to be the cause of the impediment of unworthiness? Since we treat here *de odiosis,* the terms: *"societatibus ab Ecclesia damnatis adscripti sunt"* must be interpreted strictly.[47] We would therefore conclude that the canon has in mind only the members of those societies which are expressly and *nominatim* condemned. Such societies are the Masons or the Carbonari, censured by the well-known constitution *"Apostolicae Sedis"* of Pius IX, and the Odd Fellows, the Sons of Temperance and the Knights of Pythias condemned by the Congregation of the Holy Office on August 20, 1894, in a Decree addressed to the Hierarchy of the United States. According to a decla-

[45] GASPARRI, *op. cit.*, n. 475.

[46] COD. IUR. CAN., Can. 1065.

[47] S. C. S. Off. (Portus Aloisii), 1 aug. 1855; (Marysville), 21 aug. 1861; (Leodien.), 30 ian. 1867; 25 maii 1897; consult the new *Collectanea* under numbers 1300, 1495 and 1969.

ration dated August 2, 1907, by the Apostolic delegation at Washington this condemnation is to be extended to the female secret societies which are to be regarded as branches, if affiliated with male societies already nominally condemned.[48]

Any reason justifying the granting of a dispensation from the impediment of mixed religion would suffice for the Ordinary to permit the pastor to witness marriages whose illicitness would be due to the presence of the impediment of unworthiness. Before such permission is given all precautions must be taken in order to safeguard the Catholic education of the children and to remove from the Catholic consort the danger of perversion.[49] The good judgment of the Bishop will determine whether the assistance of the pastor should be passive or active. Should he decide in favor of the latter, he should not be so indulgent as to permit also the celebration of the nuptial Mass "*nisi gravia adjuncta aliter exigant.*" [50]

201. So much as regards condemned societies. A few words must now be said on another aspect of this impediment, namely, when it arises from the third cause. The new law reads as follows: if a public sinner or one laboring under a public censure declines to make use of the sacrament of penance or to be reconciled with the Church, the pastor should not witness his marriage unless there is a grave and urgent reason, about which, if possible, he should consult the Ordinary.[51]

St. Alphonsus says [52] that a person is considered a public sinner when his crime is notorious either by

[48] FANNING, in the *Catholic Encyclopedia*, art., *Secret Societies*, n. VII.

[49] S. C. S. Off. (Marysville), 21 aug. 1861; (S. Bonifacii), 23 apr. 1873; 25 maii 1897; 11 ian. 1899.

[50] S. C. S. Off., 21 febr. 1883; in the new *Collectanea*, n. 1591.

[51] COD. IUR. CAN., Can. 1066.

[52] *Theologia Moralis*, vol. VI, n. 44, ib., GASPARRI, *op cit.*, n. 477.

law, he having been convicted of it by judicial process, or by fact, when it is committed in a public place, or by fame, when the indications are such that many have already come to the knowledge of it, though to some of those present it may be unknown. The *Rituale Romanum*[53] classifies in the category of publicly unworthy all those who are *excommunicati, interdicti, manifesteque infames; ut meretrices, concubinarii, foeneratores, magi, sortilegi, blasphemi et alii eius generis publici peccatores.*

202. Should a pastor be asked to assist at the marriage of a public sinner who refuses to confess his sins, if at all possible, he should lay the case before the Bishop.[54] This obligation would be incumbent on him for a double reason when, by virtue of a particular law, all marriages must be preceded by a sacramental confession. The Sacred Congregation of Propaganda on April 17, 1820, decreed that Catholics who are public sinners and who refuse to confess their sins should not be admitted to marriage *"nisi parochus ex causis vere gravibus excusari possit."*[55] This decision is founded on the opinion of the authors that the assistance of a priest at such marriages is sinful unless he is exonerated on the ground of grave reason.

203. Similar should be the mode of procedure in marriages of those against whom a public censure was fulminated. The Sacred Penitentiaria having been consulted about such a case answered that the pastor is to exert every effort to induce such a person to be reconciled with the Church. Should his efforts prove unavailing, recourse must be had to the Bishop,[56] who

[53] *De SS. Eucharistiae Sacramento*, §8.

[54] S. C. S. Off. (Portus Aloisii), 1 aug. 1855; (Hong-Kong), 14 mart. 1860.

[55] Gasparri, *op. cit.*, n. 478.

[56] S. C. S. Off. (Bombay), 21 febr. 1883; S. C. de Prop. Fide (C. G. Quebec.), 17 apr. 1820; S. Poenit., 10 dec. 1860, ad 18.

(*si gravia damna imminere videantur*) may permit even his active assistance, always excluding the celebration of the Mass.[57] Should an unrepentant *excommunicatus vitandus* ask for a similar favor the Ordinary may not grant it without *causa gravissima*.[58]

[57] St. Alphonsus, *Theologia Moralis*, vol. VI, n. 54; ib., Gasparri, *op. cit.*, n. 483.
[58] Feije, *op. cit.*, n. 277.

CHAPTER VI.

The Diriment Impediments.

I. The Impediment of Age.

(Canon 1067.)

204. The impediment of age is an obstacle by virtue of which a man and a woman, not having reached either the use of reason or the age prescribed by ecclesiastical law are barred from contracting a valid marriage. This impediment, as is manifest from the foregoing definition, can arise either from natural law (want of use of reason), or from ecclesiastical law (want of certain required age). The marriages of unbaptized persons, provided they are contracted after the parties reached the use of reason, must be considered valid unless invalidated by a civil impediment of age. The marriages of baptized persons are invalid if the parties concerned lack the age prescribed by ecclesiastical law.

205. In the former discipline the Church accommodated itself to the Roman law[1] which regarded as *puberes* and marriageable the female children after the completion of their twelfth year and the male children after the completion of their fourteenth year.[2] While the age of puberty required for the validity of

[1] L. 3 C. *Quando tutores.*

[2] C. 12, 13, X, *de desponsatione impuberum,* IV, 2; c. 2, X, *de frigidis et maleficiatis, et impotentia coeundi,* IV, 15; c. un. *de desponsatione impuberum,* IV, 2, in VI°; Benedict. XIV, Const., *"Omnium solicitudinum,"* 12 sept. 1744, §14, dub. V, §40.

other contracts has remained unchanged,[3] it has undergone some modification in relation to matrimonial contracts. Formerly precocity could supply the defect of age. In other words, parties legally in the state of impuberty, but actually in possession of physiological or natural puberty (implying the potency to procreate) could contract a valid marriage even before they reached the age required by ecclesiastical law. This gave rise to many doubts which the present discipline happily eliminates by not permitting a valid marriage unless the male child has completed his sixteenth year and the female child her fourteenth year.[4] After that age, in the eyes of the Church, the marriage is valid or may be contracted validly though neither of the parties may possess the actual physiological faculty to generate, for this condition is not required by natural law. But, the Codex adds, it is the duty of the shepherds of souls to dissuade from marriage all young people who have not reached the age at which marriage is usually contracted according to the prevailing local customs.[5]

From the foregoing statements it is obvious that the power of the Roman Pontiff over this impediment extends only to the period at which the parties reached the use of reason. Should a dispensation be granted, the consorts are not permitted to cohabit *usque dum ambo potentes evaserint,* or reached the nubile age.[6] The Holy See may not dispense below the age of reason, for it would be equivalent to crossing the purpose of natural law.

206. The civil laws of the various countries are not uniform in their demand of age required for a valid marriage. Such laws are absolutely obligatory on the

[3] Cod. Iur. Can., Can. 88, §2.
[4] *Op. cit.,* Can. 1067, §1.
[5] *Op. cit.,* Can. 1067, §2.
[6] S. C. S. Off., 2 maii 1866; Gasparri, *op. cit.,* n. 508.

unbaptized, for the baptized the compliance with them is not *ad validitatem,* for such persons are governed by the foregoing legislation of the Church. *E. g.,* the civil law of Belgium requires the age of eighteen years on the part of the man and of fifteen on the part of the woman, but extends to them the privilege of dispensation before that age should the highest civil authority deem it advisable.[7] Therefore, without a civil dispensation a man of seventeen and a woman of fourteen years could not contract a valid marriage in the eyes of the state, but they could do so in the eyes of the Church provided both were baptized. Should the woman in this case be an infidel and the man a Catholic, their marriage would be null and void even in the eyes of the Church, unless besides the dispensation from the ecclesiastical impediment of disparity of worship (for the man) a civil dispensation from the impediment of age (for the woman) is also obtained. If the civil law does not specify any particular age, then the marriage between a baptized and an unbaptized person would be valid provided the former is in possession of the legal age (prescribed by the Church) and the latter of the age of reason (the dispensation from the impediment of disparity of worship being presupposed should the former be baptized in the Catholic Church).

II. The Impediment of Impotency.

(Canon 1068.)

207. Impotency, in the wide sense, is an inability to procreate offspring and to propagate the species. One must be on his guard not to confuse *impotentia coeundi* with *impotentia generandi.* The former is a natural or accidental defect in the genital organs of one or both

[7] *Code Napoléon,* art., 144 and 145; ib., De Smet, *op. cit.,* n. 275, Scholion.

contracting parties preventing *copulam de se aptam ad generationem prolis.* Such *copula* presupposes *completam perforationem vaginae mulieris per erectum membrum viri cum effusione veri seminis virilis in vaginam.*[8] *Impotentia generandi,* or in other words, sterility, implies the inability to procreate, but presupposes the ability for coition in the way described above. *Impotentia generandi* is neither a diriment nor an impedient impediment of matrimony.[9] Therefore, the infecundity of the sperm (on the part of man), and ovariotomy, oöphorectomy or fallectomy calculated to prevent conception by having recourse to the Porro operation causing an unnatural sterility in the woman, imply only *impotentiam generandi* but not *coeundi.*[10]

208. *Impotentia coeundi* in so far as it is a diriment impediment to marriage may be defined: Perpetual and antecedent, absolute or relative inaptitude, on the part of the man and the woman, for a conjugal act *de se* required for the procreation of offspring. Impotency may be:

1. Antecedent or subsequent according as its existence preceded or followed the matrimonial contract.

2. Perpetual or temporal. It is called perpetual when it is irremediable, or, if curable, not so without a miracle or means illicit or dangerous to life. It is temporal when its cure is effected of itself in the course of time, or when it can be remedied by means that are honest, licit and void of danger.

3. Absolute or relative, according as the *incapacitas coeundi* extends to all persons of the opposite sex, or only to some.

[8] Gasparri, *op. cit.,* n. 510; De Smet, *op. cit.,* n. 276; Wernz, *op. cit.,* n. 342; De Becker, *op. cit.,* p. 156.

[9] Cod. Iur. Can., Can. 1068, §2; c. 18, C. XXXII, q. 5; c. 27, C. XXXII, q. 7.

[10] Dr. O'Malley, in the *American Ecclesiastical Review,* vol. XLIV, p. 684 ff.

4. Natural or accidental. The former has its origin in some intrinsic organic defect of the body, the latter in some extrinsic cause, generally in some functional defect of a pathological nature, as in the case of anaphrodisia, aphrodisia and vaginism.

209. With these preliminaries in his possession the reader should experience no difficulty in interpreting the first paragraph of canon 1068, which runs as follows: Antecedent and perpetual impotency, whether on the part of the man or of the woman, whether known to the other party or not, whether absolute or relative, invalidates marriage by virtue of natural law. This canon settles the much-mooted question concerning the source from which the diriment force of this impediment originates. The majority of theologians always maintained that natural law, apart from ecclesiastical law, endows impotency with the force of nullifying marriage. This conclusion must force itself on every one who analyzes the nature of the matrimonial contract, which, as all admit, consists in the mutual tradition of the exclusive and perpetual right which each of the contracting parties bestows on the other for the purpose of procreating children. But impotency frustrates this end absolutely and at the very outset, for it bars the possibility of even the first requisite, namely, an act apt in itself to promote the primary end to which this contract tends by its very nature. Furthermore, a person laboring under antecedent and perpetual impotency is not in a position to transfer such a right to another *quia debitum carnale solvere non potest.*

210. Impotency does not invalidate marriage unless it is antecedent. The subsequent impotency can effect only the use of marriage or the right one acquires by it, but not the marriage itself, which remains valid even though under such circumstances its use might become illicit.

Temporary impotency even if it should be antecedent does not invalidate marriage because it admits a remedy. For marriage already contracted it matters very little whether the impotency is absolute or relative (provided it is antecedent) for in either hypothesis such marriage would be rendered invalid. The party laboring under relative impotency may be admitted to another marriage, not so, however, in the case of absolute impotency.

The canon states distinctly that the marriage entered into with an antecedent perpetual impotency is invalid regardless of whether the fact of impotency was known or unknown to the other party. If it was known, some authors bind the parties to a cohabitation as brother and sister; others again permit a new marriage obliging the man to a support of the impotent consort.[11] This latter opinion receives an indirect sanction by the new law, though it fails to take into account the question of support. Such obligation would, however, arise *ex caritate* should the party who is free from impediment have the marriage annulled and subsequently contract another. The imposition of such an obligation supposes that the marriage was contracted with a full knowledge of the existence of antecedent impotency.

211. Both the man and the woman are impotent when they lack the genital organs proper to their respective sex. The latter's impotency may be caused also by the *arctitudo vaginae* and *vaginism.*[12] Towards the impotency of the former, besides the cause already stated, may contribute the want of semen, also the ab-

[11] Gasparri, *op. cit.*, n. 526; Schmalzgrüber, IV, XV, n. 42.
[12] Vaginismus est in hyperesthesia vulvae omnem coitum impediente.

sence of both testicles (as is the case with eunuchs),[13] aphrodisia,[14] and anaphrodisia.[15] Before a definite declaration is made as regards the objective invalidity of the marriage on the ground of any of these reasons, it must be carefully ascertained whether the impotency to which they give rise was antecedent and by its nature perpetual or incurable.

212. The aptitude or inaptitude to normal marital intercourse is therefore the touchstone of the presence or absence of the impediment of impotency. This gives us occasion to say a few words about hermaphrodites, or persons who are in possession of more or less perfectly developed genital organs of both sexes. Though the organ of one sex, as a rule, shows a more perfect or complete development than that of the other, *possunt in utroque sexu copulam perfectam habere.*[16] De Smet quotes Brouardel as the authority for the opinion that no example has as yet been found of a person who both externally and internally would possess the attributes of both sexes.[17]

The co-possession of organs of the other sex does not in itself disqualify a hermaphrodite from marriage. The question is easy of solution when he is impotent according to the undeveloped or defective sex, for then he can make use of marriage only by means of the developed sexual organ, and he must even make a deposition to the effect that he intends to renounce absolutely the use of the other. Should he be equally *potens* in both sexes, which is a practical im-

[13] Sixtus V, const. *"Cum frequenter,"* 27 iun. 1587.

[14] Caliditas viri si ille nequeat expectare vas mulieris, quin totum semen defluat extra vas. S. C. C., in *Neapolitana Matrim.*, 5 iul. 1862.

[15] Si vir membrum virile adeo flaccidum habeat, ut capax erectionis saltem sufficientis non sit. S. C. C., in causa nullitatis matrimonii, 24 ian. 1871.

[16] Gasparri, *op. cit.*, n. 536.

[17] *Op. cit.*, n. 280.

possibility, he is free to choose the organ which he intends to use in marriage.[18] He may be barred from marriage only when there is a moral certainty as to his absolute inaptitude to carnal intercourse. In case of doubtful impotency, though his marriage should be discountenanced as much as possible, it could not be absolutely forbidden. The new law distinctly states that when the impediment of impotency is doubtful, whether by law or by fact, the possibility of marriage is not to be absolutely excluded.[19] This settles a controversy regarding women who have undergone a surgical operation resulting in the removal of ovaries, of matrix, or causing infecundity by some other way. All these in the new law, which agrees with the practice established during the former discipline, will have their way open to marriage.[20]

It must be borne in mind that a marriage null and void on the ground of impotency cannot be rendered valid solely by means of artificial fecundation.[21]

213. The impediment of impotency is not recognized by the civil law of every country, though on the ground of error a declaration of nullity can be obtained even from those courts which do not admit the existence of this impediment.[22] The civil law of Austria, Italy, Spain and the United States of North America practically accepts the canonical impediment of impotency.[23]

[18] WERNZ, *op. cit.*, n. 353; S. C. C., in *Ferrentina Matrim.*, 24 mart. 1888; 18 aug. 1888.

[19] COD. IUR. CAN., Can. 1068, §2.

[20] S. C. S. Off. (Quebec), 23 iul. 1890; (Westmonasterien), 3 iul. 1895; S. C. C. (Bosnonien), 30 ian., 27 febr., 30 apr., 25 iun. 1836; 26 febr., 23 apr., 1842.

[21] GASPARRI, *op. cit.*, n. 533; see this work, n. 53.

[22] *Cod. Civil. Germ.*, §1333; Lex Hung. de matrim. civ., §54; SCHULTE, *op. cit.*, p. 514.

[23] WERNZ, *op. cit.*, n. 354; KEEZER, *Treatise on the Law of Marriage and Divorce*, n. 12, 160, 164.

III. The Impediment of Ligamen.
(Canon 1069.)

214. *Ligamen* is the bond of a previous and existing marriage. The Creator by uniting one man to one woman, and Christ by restoring marriage to its pristine ideality showed unmistakable preference for the monogyny and monandry. It is generally agreed that natural law proscribes both polygamy and polyandry, the former relatively, the latter absolutely. Without doubt, positive divine law, contained in the New Testament, forbids both absolutely.[24]

215. A person bound by the bond of a former marriage cannot validly contract a new marriage, though his present one is non-consummated, *salvo privilegio fidei.*[25] The presence of the impediment of *ligamen* indicates the objective validity of previous wedlock. It does not matter whether the latter is only a mere natural contract (when both parties are infidels), or a sacrament (when both parties are Catholics). Should another marriage be attempted while the bond of the previous one continues and should the parties be guilty of adultery, they would contract a diriment impediment of crime, necessitating a dispensation before they could validly marry each other, even if the former marriage should be dissolved by the death of the consort. Regardless of the cause invalidating or dissolving a previous marriage, no new marriage may be contracted until the nullity or the dissolution of the former is established legitimately and beyond all doubt.[26]

In case of doubt no new marriage should be attempted until a definite decision is reached, otherwise

[24] See this work, n. 36 ff.; GASPARRI, *op. cit.*, n. 631.
[25] COD. IUR. CAN., Can. 1069, §1.
[26] COD. IUR. CAN., Can. 1069, §2.

the objective value of a subsequent marriage would depend entirely on the fact whether the parties were free or not. If the new marriage is contracted in good faith it will enjoy all the advantages of a putative marriage [27] even if subsequent investigation should reveal the presence of the impediment of *ligamen,* in which case the parties would have to separate immediately after such discovery.

The declaration of nullity must always proceed from a higher ecclesiastical tribunal, namely, the Holy See or the Bishop. This law should never be disregarded when the marriage has all the appearances of a valid contract. When the marriage is invalid on the face of it, so that the fact is manifest to all, recourse to a juridical process may be dispensed with. Canon 1990 legislates that in such cases the Ordinary, after having cited the parties, may declare the marriage null and void with the intervention of the *defensor vinculi.*

216. The impediment of *ligamen* ceases by the death of the former consort,[28] in case of non-consummated marriages by solemn religious profession,[29] or by an authoritative dispensation of the Roman Pontiff, and in legitimate marriages among the unbaptized by Pauline privilege.[30] An extensive treatment of these individual causes is presented in another part of this work.[31]

217. On May 14, 1868,[32] the Sacred Congregation of the Holy Office laid down special rules to be followed in cases in which the ascertainment of the death of the former consort is connected with some difficulties. The

[27] C. 8, X, *qui filii sint legitimi,* IV, 17.
[28] Cod. Iur. Can., Can. 1118.
[29] *Op. cit.,* Can. 1119.
[30] *Op. cit.,* Can. 1120.
[31] See this work, n. 547 ff.
[32] In the new *Collectanea,* n. 1321.

following is a brief summary of the instruction. The first step should be directed toward demanding an authentic death-certificate. This should be based on the reliable records of the death-register of the parish, or of the hospital, or of military authorities. If such a document cannot be obtained from the ecclesiastical authority recourse should be had to the civil authority of the place where the consort died. In the absence of such a document at least two witnesses, worthy of belief, should be placed under oath testifying to their former acquaintance with the dead consort as well as to the cause of his death and the place where it occurred. If only one eye-witness can be adduced, provided he is above all suspicion, his deposition may suffice, but of itself it does not constitute a *probationem plenam.* If no eye-witnesses can be procured, secondary or hearsay witnesses may be summoned whose knowledge of the death of the consort is founded on the testimony of eye-witnesses. In the absence of any witnesses whatsoever the case should be solved by calling to aid the principle of presumption. In doing so inquiry should be made into the moral character, religious attitude, occupation, age and health of the presumably defunct person, and into the circumstances preceding, accompanying and following his absence. Light should be thrown also on his relations with the surviving consort. As partial testimony the letters he wrote and the newspapers giving an account of his death may also be requisitioned. The sworn statement of the living consort does not of itself constitute a sufficient evidence of the death of the other consort, and in the absence of other proofs corroborating such testimony the Holy See must be consulted in every case individually.[33]

[33] S. C. S. Off., 3 maii, 1893; *Nouv. Rev. Théol.*, vol. XXVI, p. 153; ib., De Becker, *op. cit.*, p. 141.

A moral certainty is required as to the severance of the former matrimonial bond before another marriage may be contracted. The new law enacts severe punishments against the bigamists. It binds them with irregularity *ipso facto* incurred [34] and brands them as *infames* even if they should attempt only a civil marriage while the bond of the former continues. Should they continue *in illicito contubernio,* notwithstanding the admonition of the Bishop, according to the gravity of their guilt they may be placed under excommunication or even under personal interdict.[35]

Because the impediment of *ligamen* arises from natural law it cannot be lifted by means of a dispensation. To maintain that Pontiffs did dispense from it is to repeat an old calumny which has no foundation in history.[36]

IV. Impediment of Disparity of Worship.

(Canon 1070—Canon 1072.)

1. History and Nature of the Impediment.

218. An adumbration of this impediment may be found in the Old Covenant, in which God's chosen people were forbidden to intermarry with the seven Gentile nations who inhabited the Promised Land before it was given as an inheritance to the Israelites.[37] The main reason for this divine prohibition was founded in the same cause that inspired the matrimonial legislation of the Catholic Church, namely, the danger of perversion. This danger and that of spiritual apathy find fertile soil in a home where oneness of faith does not contribute to happiness and peaceful

[34] COD. IUR. CAN., Can. 984, n. 4.

[35] *Op. cit.*, Can. 2356.

[36] ROSKOVÁNY, *De matrim. mixt.*, t. IV, p. 84; WERNZ, *op. cit.*, n. 365; GASPARRI, *op. cit.*, n. 631.

[37] *Deut.* XXXIV, 16; I. *Esdras* X, 10, 11, 18, 19.

cohabitation. The difference of religion is often the contributory cause of much dissension whose avoidance very frequently is bought by the Catholic party at the cost of abandoning all religious practices and of neglecting to safeguard properly the spiritual interests of the future offspring. St. Paul compares a marriage between a Christian and an infidel to a fellowship which light makes with darkness.[38] St. Cyprian[39] and Tertullian[40] are perhaps the first ecclesiastical writers who with St. Paul discountenanced such marriages, and said to the early Christians: "Bear not the yoke with unbelievers."[41]

219. Despite the promptness with which the early Christians complied with all disciplinary measures of the Church, the Council of Elvira (300-306) found it necessary to incorporate a positive law among its enactments, forbidding Christian girls to contract marriages with infidels, Jews, heretics or priests of the pagan rites.[42] The rigor of this law was enhanced by the Constantinian legislation (339) which threatened with capital punishment all Christians attempting to marry a Jew.[43] The law of Theodosius (388) branded as adulterous the marriages contracted between a Christian and a Jew. Estius, interpreting this law, remarks that this stigma was attached to these unions not on account of their nullity, but by reason of the gravity of the sin of which the Christian who thus degraded his character was guilty.[44] It was in Spain that this impediment first obtained the force of invalidating a marriage. Such force may have been attributed to it in some localities of other countries also, but,

[38] II *Cor.* VI, 14.
[39] MIGNE, *P. L.*, vol. IV, col. 767.
[40] MIGNE, *P. L.*, vol. I, cols. 1290 and 1291.
[41] II *Cor.*, VI, 14.
[42] MANSI, *Conc. cit.*, cap. XV, XVI.
[43] WERNZ, *op. cit.*, n. 504.
[44] *Bul. Rom. Con.*, BENEDICT XIV, vol. III, *"Singulari Nobis,"* §7.

more commonly, it was considered only an impedient impediment.[45] Its incorporation into the Gratian collection did not of itself endow it with the force of a universal law of the Church. The practically unanimous opinion of canonists holds that the diriment impediment of disparity of worship was introduced by virtue of an accepted custom prevailing in the Eastern and the Western Church in the period intervening between the ninth and the twelfth century.[46] This custom implicitly accepted by the Church in the past has been canonized officially by the present ecclesiastical legislation, invested with the force of written law and declared binding on all persons baptized in the Catholic Church, or converted to the Catholic Church from heresy or schism, when they contract marriage with an infidel.

220. This short historical survey proves sufficiently that its diriment force did not originate from natural or divine law. By virtue of these laws it is only an impedient impediment, otherwise the Church could neither dispense from it nor modify it to the extent evidenced in the most recent matrimonial legislation. With these facts in our possession we can see the difference between a perfect and an imperfect disparity of worship. The former has its origin partly in the ecclesiastical and partly in the natural divine law, and according to the old discipline it used to arise between a baptized and an unbaptized person. This was in the past the diriment impediment of disparity of worship in the strict sense. The imperfect impediment of disparity of worship is founded on divine and natural law. It is only an impedient impediment, more properly designated by the name impediment of mixed

[45] BENEDICT XIV, *loc. cit.*, §9.

[46] BENEDICT XIV, *loc. cit.*, §10; GASPARRI, *op. cit.*, n. 607; ESMEIN, *Le mariage en droit canonique*, tit. cit., vol. I, pp. 216 ff.; WERNZ, *op. cit.*, n. 504.

religion. It arises between two baptized persons of whom one is Catholic and the other a heretic or a schismatic. The impediment of mixed religion renders the marriage illicit; that of disparity of worship both illicit and invalid. The impedient impediment of mixed religion has undergone no change in the new matrimonial legislation. The diriment impediment of the disparity of worship has been considerably modified. Both the old and the new discipline base this impediment not on the profession of faith, but on the indelible character impressed by the sacrament of baptism. The new legislation lays stress on the Catholic baptism in contradistinction to any other, administered by other religious denominations.[47] According to the old discipline a marriage contracted between an unbaptized and a baptized person was invalid irrespective of the sect in which the baptism was received. But, since the new discipline distinguishes between Catholic and non-Catholic baptism, it is manifest that by means of this impediment the Church does not mean to legislate for marriages contracted by two persons of whom neither was baptized in the Catholic Church. Hence, the impediment of disparity of worship is restricted to marriages entered into by persons of whom one is baptized in the Catholic Church or has been received into the Church from heresy or schism and the other is unbaptized. This sweeping change forces the conclusion that after the Feast of Pentecost, 1918, the Church will consider valid all those marriages that shall be contracted between an unbaptized person and a baptized non-Catholic, the latter in this one case being exempted from contracting the impediment of disparity of worship on account of

[47] Nullum est matrimonium contractum a persona non baptizata cum persona baptizata in Ecclesia catholica vel ad eandem ex haeresi aut schismate conversa. (CODEX IUR. CAN., Can. 1070, §1.)

the reception of non-Catholic baptism. Such marriages will be valid provided no impediment of natural or divine law or of ecclesiastical law stands in the way of their validity. Thus, the impediment of disparity of worship will no longer invalidate a union contracted by an unbaptized person with a person baptized outside the Catholic Church. The form which must be observed for the validity of such marriages is discussed in another part of this work.

221. By the impediment of disparity of worship the Catholic party is affected directly and the unbaptized party indirectly. Thus, the Catholic party is declared incompetent to contract marriage with an infidel. Since, however, the nature of the marriage contract requires that both parties be qualified, such marriages would be invalid even if the Catholic party were not bound by a particular form of marriage. By virtue of the individuality of this contract the incompetence of one party is communicated to the other.

A double prohibition stands in the way of a marriage between a Catholic and an unbaptized person. On the one hand, there is the divine and natural law as an impedient impediment, and, on the other hand, the ecclesiastical law as a diriment impediment. In some instances the first prohibtion may cease, namely, when the danger of perversion is absent. But, even in such cases, the ecclesiastical prohibition retains its force, and such marriages are neither licit nor valid without a dispensation given by the Roman Pontiff or his delegate.

2. *Catholic Baptism.*

222. Since it is the Catholic baptism from which the impediment of disparity of worship draws its origin in the new legislation, it will be well at this point of our investigation to acquaint ourselves with the full meaning and scope which the words Catholic baptism imply.

For the general guidance of the reader one could premise that the foregoing words are to be interpreted in the sense in which the decree "*Ne temere*" employs them, namely, baptism administered in the Roman Catholic Church.

223. 1. They do not include the baptism administered by the Uniat Greek Churches. Such baptism makes one a member of the Catholic Church, but not subject to this legislation. The Codex of Pius X, as a general rule, does not legislate for the Churches of the Oriental Rites, unless an express mention is made of them, or the tenor of the canon is such that its very nature presupposes its observance on the part of the Orientals.[48] Thus the new legislation expressly conforms in this respect to the traditional custom of the Church whose first exponent was Innocent III in his Constitution "*Licet Graecos*" given in the Fourth Lateran Council.[49] Therefore members of the Oriental Church, as long as they adhere to that Rite, do not have to submit to the requirements prescribed by the decree "*Ne temere*" unless the other party to the contract, being a Roman Catholic, is bound by it. But if a member of the Uniat Greek Church affiliates himself officially with the Latin Rite, then he falls under the scope of the decree, and by this very act becomes

[48] Cod. Iur. Can., Can. 1.

[49] An assembly of renowned theologians convened in 1631, headed by Cardinal Pamphili, thus interprets the tenor of this Constitution: Nelle Constituzioni Apostoliche non s'intendano compresi gli orientali se non nei tre seguenti casi: 1. Nei punti di fede e dottrina cattolica; 2. dove la materia stessa dimostra la comprensione, in quanto non è una legge soltanto ecclesiastica ma una dichiarazione della legge divina e naturale. 3. Quando, benchè si tratti di ordinazioni disciplinari, gli orientali vi sono espressamente nominati. Ex litt. encycl. S. C. de Prop. Fide, nov. 8, 1882; *Collectanea*, n. 113; New *Collectanea*, n. 1578; Papp-Szilágyi, *Enchiridion iuris Ecclesiae orientalis Catholicae*, §55, p. 68, Magno-Varadini, 1880; Wernz, *op. cit.*, n. 104; Ferreres, *op. cit.*, n. 510; *Acta Ap. Sedis*, vol. I, p. 408.

liable to all matrimonial impediments enforced by the canonical discipline of the Western Church, including those impediments which are ignored by the Rite which he leaves. He could therefore contract the impediment of disparity of worship which according to the new legislation is based on the reception of baptism in the Roman (not Greek) Catholic Church.

224. 2. The words Catholic Baptism include those adults who in the reception of baptism were actuated by the motive of becoming Catholics.

3. They include those heretics and schismatics who return to the true fold, though they may subsequently relapse into their former heresy or schism. If the baptism of such converts is doubtful, they are to be re-baptized conditionally. If it is valid, then the mere profession of faith and absolution from heresy will suffice to give them the same standing in the eyes of the ecclesiastical law as if they had actually received Catholic Baptism.

4. In the case of infants, baptism depends (a) on the intention of its minister; (b) on the intention of the child's parents. Both the minister and the parents may be of the same faith or of different faiths. In the first instance they may both be either Catholic or non-Catholic. In the second supposition the agent administering baptism may be Catholic and the parents of the child non-Catholics, or *vice versa.* In the following pages we shall consider these hypotheses by connecting them with cases in which baptism is given in urgent necessity. Outside such necessity no doubt is entertained as to the nature of baptism, since it is generally conferred by the minister of that religious denomination into which the parents intend to incorporate their offspring. The child of non-Catholic parents receives Catholic baptism, if it is administered by the priest. The child of Catholic parents receives a non-

Catholic baptism, if it is baptized by a clergyman outside the Catholic Church.

In placing the following considerations before the reader we do not intend to determine conditions necessary for the validity of baptism. Our purpose is to ascertain those conditions only which must affect the child in order that it may become subject to the new law regulating the impediment of disparity of worship.

225. A. If the parents of the child and the person who baptized it are of the same faith (Catholic or Protestant), it is presumed that the latter wished the child to become a member of that religious body to which its parents belongs. In such a case a Catholic, regardless of his intention, could administer only Catholic baptism to a child both of whose parents are Catholics. In case one of the parents is non-Catholic, even if the baptizing Catholic should expressly exclude a Catholic baptism, and should intend to baptize the child for the sect of the non-Catholic parent, the baptism would still remain Catholic. The same is to be said if a non-Catholic in case of urgent necessity baptizes a child whose parents are of mixed religion. To defend this opinion the following reasons are advanced. The baptism in such cases is either valid or invalid. Its proper administration on the part of the baptizing agent presupposes an act in conformity with the intention of the Church or of Christ. But neither the Church nor Christ intends that the child whose parents, whether both or only one, are Catholics, should be affiliated with a non-Catholic sect. Such affiliation would, furthermore, be against the will of the parents. If both parents are Catholics, the reason is self-evident. If one of them is a non-Catholic, then it is presumed that the parents have virtually interpreted and expressed on this point the intention of all their future children, when they gave the *cautiones,* submitting to all the conditions which the Church prescribes before a dispensation from the impediment of mixed religion or disparity of worship can be obtained.

If neither the person baptizing nor the parents of the child are Catholic, there is still a possibility as to the administration of a Catholic baptism. While ordinarily it is presumed that the child is incorporated into the sect of its parents, this presumption must give way to fact, if the minister of such baptism, though he be a non-Catholic, explicitly states that his intention is to administer a Catholic Baptism.

226. B. If the parents are non-Catholic and the person administering baptism is a Catholic, then two possibilities may arise, namely, the Catholic agent either expresses his intention as to the administration of Catholic baptism or fails to do so. If his intention is expressed, then the baptism thus administered is Catholic. This would be true even if the parents objected to such an act. We presuppose here a case of urgent necessity when the Catholic is bound in conscience to administer baptism. He is released from this obligation if the parents themselves wish to baptize the child or authorize a non-Catholic present to do so.

If the Catholic fails to give expression to his intention and the parents subsequently to such a baptism inscribe the child's name in the baptismal record of their sect, according to Lehmkuhl,[50] such baptism is not to be considered Catholic. The question could arise, does the mere entering of a child's name in a non-Catholic register settle the nature of this baptism? It is hard to see how an accidental circumstance, posterior to baptism, brought into play by the act of an external agent unrelated to this baptism, could in any way affect the objectivity of the sacrament. The bap-

[50] *Theologia Moralis*, n. 893, Friburgi Brisgoviae, 1910.

tism, therefore, must be considered from its very beginning either Catholic or non-Catholic. In our opinion the registration cannot change its nature. We are inclined to pronounce in favor of its Catholicity.

227. C. If both parents are Catholic and the person who in case of urgent necessity administers baptism is a non-Catholic, the baptism must be considered Catholic. The same is to be said though one of the parents be non-Catholic. The reason for the latter statement is contained in the *cautiones* with which the present marriage is supposed to have been contracted. If the mixed marriage is invalid, the child illegitimate, and the non-Catholic agent administering baptism wishes to incorporate the child into a non-Catholic sect, a serious doubt might then arise as to the true nature of such baptism. Even in such a case the child ought to get the benefit of the doubt, especially if the marriage is putative, in which case the child would be considered legitimate. Cases like these will have to be solved by the Holy See.

If the baptism is not administered in case of urgent necessity, and the parents, whether they are both Catholic or only one of them, intentionally make use of the services of a non-Catholic clergyman, then two possibilities may arise. Such parents may be either in good faith or in bad faith. In the former instance such a baptism is to be considered Catholic. In the latter case it is to be regarded as non-Catholic. If the parents in case of urgent necessity, permit their child to be baptized by a non-Catholic clergyman, they must instruct him that the child is to be a member of the Catholic Church, or rather, if nobody else is present, they should baptize it themselves. If they fell away from the Church, and leave the matter to the non-Catholic clergyman, it is presumed that he is at liberty to incorporate the child into his own sect.

228. D. Some theologians maintain that we are not to regard as Catholics those infants who, not yet seven years old, were validly baptized in the schismatic Church, even if subsequently educated in the Catholic faith by their converted parents. The advocates of this opinion [51] do not admit that such a child, not yet enjoying the use of reason, becomes a convert by the very fact of the conversion of its parents. We decline to subscribe to their opinion. It is admitted by all that parents are the interpreters of the child's intention before it reaches the use of reason. They are expected to safeguard not only their own spiritual welfare, but also that of their child. Therefore, what they have considered their duty expressly, namely, to embrace the Catholic faith, their offspring is to consider its duty interpretatively. Thus it would seem that the conversion of the parents of itself postulates the simultaneous conversion of their child who is validly baptized but below the age of reason. This opinion is more in harmony with both the spirit of the Church and the wish of the parents, granted the condition mentioned above. The other opinion which advocates that the child must be permitted to decide this question after it reaches the use of reason, cannot be sustained. The Church insists on the Catholic education of such a child. If analogy has any force, we could adduce the civil law which, by the naturalization of the father, *eo ipso* admits to citizenship his child who is a minor.

In the foregoing paragraphs the child's legitimate superiors play the same rôle as the parents themselves in the absence of the latter.

229. If the child has completed its seventh year it is considered adult *in ordine ad baptismum.* Consequently, the parents or its legitimate superiors cease

[51] WOUTERS, *Commentarius in Decretum "Ne temere,"* p. 85, Amstelodami, 1910.

to be its interpreters in these matters. The child at that age is expected to express its own wish for the reception of baptism.[52]

Until very recently there was no particular reason for a more specific determination of the true nature of a Catholic baptism as differentiated from a non-Catholic baptism. Therefore the authors gave a very inadequate treatment of this question and the Church itself did not consider it necessary to lay down rules that would embrace all contingencies in connection with the administration of baptism. Since the introduction of the new Church-law this question carries with it far-reaching consequences. The foregoing statements are a tentative explanation of the author, *salvo meliori iudicio*. Several doubts will have to be solved in the near future by positive legislation of the Church. The definition of the true nature of Catholic baptism will determine who are bound by the new form of marriage and who are liable to contract the impediment of disparity of worship.

230. To summarize the rules enunciated above, we can state that the validly baptized children of Catholic parents will certainly be subject to the new legislation on the two points just mentioned, unless the circumstances under which the baptism was administered plainly indicate that the parents did not intend to bring the children up in the Catholic Church, for instance, if they deliberately and in bad faith requested a non-Catholic clergyman to administer the baptism. Children of non-Catholic parents, if baptized by a Catholic, will be regarded as having received a Catholic baptism. Therefore, if they are subsequently educated in the Catholic faith, the ecclesiastical law will not discriminate between them and the children of Catholic parents. This is evident from the unusual concession

[52] COD. IUR. CAN., Can. 745, §2, n. 2.

which the new law makes in their behalf, provided certain conditions are verified. Such baptized children, when they marry a non-Catholic, are exempted from the Catholic form of marriage, provided, from their very infancy, they have been brought up in heresy or schism or infidelity or without any religious training whatsoever.[53] Such persons are not bound by the Catholic form of marriage because a special ecclesiastical law exempts them. Since no such special exemption is granted to them as regards the impediment of disparity of worship one must conclude that they would contract the impediment should they attempt marriage with an infidel.

With this explanation in mind we may state that the impediment of disparity of worship will always arise between an unbaptized person and

1. The offspring of Catholic parents, baptized as an infant in the Catholic Church.

2. One who, as an adult, received Catholic baptism, but consequently relapsed into his former heresy, or lost all faith.

3. A person born of non-Catholic parents and in his infancy (whether in urgent necessity or outside such necessity) was baptized in the faith.

4. A person baptized validly outside the Catholic Church and admitted into its membership by profession of faith and absolution from heresy.

5. The child of Catholic parents who after its Catholic baptism has fallen away from the Faith, either in infancy or in adult age.

231. A few years after the promulgation of the decree *"Ne temere"* an inquiry was made whether the new marriage law was to be applied to a marriage between an infidel and the child of non-Catholic parents, who, after his reception of Catholic baptism, had been

[53] COD. IUR. CAN., Can. 1099, §2.

brought up a Protestant, or without any religion whatsoever. The Holy Office on March 31, 1911, replied that the Holy See has reserved to itself the exclusive right of settling such questions.[54] Therefore, a recourse was to be had to Rome in all such cases individually. The present general law promulgated in the Codex of Pius X implicitly abrogates this decision of the Holy Office when it expressly exempts from the new form of marriage all persons who, being born of non-Catholic parents, from their very infancy, after their reception of Catholic baptism, are brought up in heresy, or schism, or infidelity, or without any religious training.

Thus the present legislation, as is seen from the foregoing exposition of its tenor, modifies to some extent the rule interpreting the scope of the Benedictine declaration as approved by the Holy Office on April 6, 1859.[55] In this decree under the name heretics are included:

1. Those who, though baptized in the Catholic Church, have been brought up in heresy before their seventh year, and still continue to profess its doctrine.

2. Those who were educated by heretics rather than in heresy, having received little or no instruction in that doctrine, and having seldom or never worshipped in it.

3. Those who as children fell into the hands of heretics, and were incorporated into a heretical sect.

4. Apostates who fell away from the Catholic Church, and allied themselves with a heretical sect.

3. *Doubtful Baptism.*

232. The impediment of disparity of worship hav-

[54] S. C. S. Officii, 31 mart., 1911. *Acta Apost. Sedis*, vol. III, p. 163; *American Ecclesiastical Review*, vol. XLV, p. 84.

[55] Feije, *op. cit.*, n. 319; Gasparri, *op. cit.*, n. 977; Lehmkuhl, *op. cit.*, n. 905, note 1.

ing been modified, some of the principles formerly held must also undergo a change. Though the impediment will no longer prevent the validity of marriages entered into by one baptized outside the Catholic Church and an unbaptized person, a part of the old discipline on this point will be applicable in cases where parties thus married will wish to become converts. It goes without saying that their marriage will be the first thing claiming the attention of the Church. Its objective validity must be decided by the form which such persons are bound to employ as a *conditio sine qua non.* Since they are bound by all the other ecclesiastical impediments as well as by those of the natural and the divine law, extreme care must be exercised in the inquiry into the objective validity of such marriages.

233. Baptism will no longer constitute the same difficulty as was experienced in the past in marriages when neither of the parties was baptized in the Catholic Church. If two Catholics wish to contract marriage and a doubt arises as to the validity of the baptism of one of them, then the party whose baptism is questioned should be baptized conditionally before the marriage ceremony is performed. If, however, the marriage is contracted without this doubt being first removed, such a union is considered valid. The administration of conditional baptism may be postponed for a good reason till after the marriage ceremony, but it should not be neglected. Such a conditional baptism should be administered secretly and without prejudice to the validity of the marriage in question as long as this doubt perseveres. If the subsequent investigation should disclose that the supposed Catholic party whose baptism was doubted was never baptized, then, we maintain, the impediment of disparity of worship would assert its force by invalidating such a marriage.

Gasparri [56] holds that it would be valid from the very beginning, even if the doubt should subsequently be settled in favor of the non-reception or the invalid administration of the sacrament of baptism. This opinion, which can hardly be admitted, is combated by several leading canonists. An incontrovertible presumption (*praesumptio iuris et de iure*) favoring the validity of baptism is at the bottom of such opinion, when there is a question as to the validity of the marriage contracted by two parties one of whom is baptized and the other is doubtfully baptized. Since this kind of presumption admits no proof to the contrary, the conclusion is logical, but the premises are by no means certain. The decrees of the Sacred Congregation when followed to their final analysis fail to support this opinion of Gasparri which is accepted by Leitner [57] and Marsella.[58] Wernz [59] shows how the following *Causa Tarvisina* cannot be adduced in its vindication.

The question was asked whether Laura Delfini (she married a Catholic and subsequently a doubt arose as to her baptism) is to be baptized conditionally? On May 4, 1737, the Sacred Congregation of the Council answered: "affirmatively, and without prejudice to the marriage." Giraldi [60] adds: It is to be specially noted that whenever baptism is to be reiterated in case of adults, it should be done secretly, whether they are married or single, and without prejudice to the marriage in the former case, if it was properly contracted. It is this reply of the Sacred Congregation of the Council which gives rise to such conflicting opinions. The opinion of Gasparri, Leitner, and Mansella has

[56] *Op. cit.*, n. 598.
[57] *Lehrb. des kath. Ehcrechts*, p. 279; Paderborn, 1902.
[58] *De Impedimentis Matr. dirimentibus*, p. 79, n. 1; Romae, 1881.
[59] *Op. cit.*, n. 507.
[60] *Exp. Iur. Pont.*, p. I, sect. 615.

already been given. Scherer [61] maintains that the decision of the Sacred Congregation of the Holy Office handed down on November 17, 1836; [62] on February 5, 1851; [63] and on September 9, 1868,[64] are based on a principle which directly contradicts the opinion expressed by the three authors just named. It is manifest that Scherer claims too much for these decisions; nor do they reflect his opinion expressly, though it must be admitted that they favor it.

234. Gasparri's opinion intimates that in case there is a doubt as to the valid administration of baptism (especially if it is *dubium dubio iuris*) the Church accepts its validity by a presumption that cannot be controverted (*presumptione iuris et de iure*). No one will deny that in an impediment of ecclesiastical origin the Church has a free hand, and therefore she may so legislate in favor of baptism regardless of the sect by which it was administered, as long as its nullity is not certain. The Church could surely be guided by such principle, especially when doubt arises as to the validity of the baptism of one whose parents were Catholics,

[61] *Handbuch des Kirchenrechts*, p. 374, n. 12; Graz, 1886.

[62] It was asked whether the Calvinists and Lutherans whose baptism is doubtful are to be regarded as infidels so that the impediment of disparity of worship arises between them and the Catholics. Reply: Each individual case must be examined when such heretics belong to sects whose rituals do not insist on the essential matter and form to be used in the administration of baptism. If their rituals prescribe the proper matter and form, then the baptism is to be regarded as valid. If a doubt should arise in the first case, the baptism is to be considered valid in relation to the validity of marriage. But if it is discovered that the baptism is null . . . the marriage is likewise null. (S. C. S. Off., *Collectanea*, n. 649.)

[63] The inhabitants of Holland converted to Catholicism are generally to be considered validly married on the ground of their baptism. If it is discovered that in a particular case the baptism is invalid, recourse must be had to the Holy See. (Feije, *De Imped. et Disp. Matrimonialibus*, n. 467; Lovanii, 1874.)

[64] The Vicar Apostolic of Japan asked: Are the doubtfully baptized Japanese to be regarded as validly baptized if they wish to contract marriage? Answer: A doubtful baptism is to be considered as valid in relation to the validity of marriage. (S. C. S. Off., *Collectanea*, n. 657.)

who always professed the Catholic faith, and married a Catholic after having made use of the prescribed form. But, *de facto,* it is questionable whether the Church actually means to take such an attitude. Furthermore, even if it should regard such a doubtful baptism as if it were absolutely valid in relation to marriage, the objective validity of the baptism, and consequently the objective validity of the marriage contracted under such circumstances, would not depend on this particular subjective attitude of the Church. Therefore, unless the Church intends to dispense implicitly every time this impediment may arise subsequently to marriage (after the doubt concerning the validity of baptism is solved) such unions objectively taken must be considered and treated as contracted, *at the very beginning,* by persons of whom one was baptized and the other unbaptized. It is precisely the implicit disposition Gasparri gratuitously attributes to the Church, which cannot be demonstrated nor presumed, because the decision rather favors the contrary opinion. If we interpret the decree issued by the Sacred Congregation of the Council in the above-quoted *Causa Tarvisina* (namely, Laura Delfini should be baptized conditionally, without prejudice to the validity of the marriage) in the light of this reasoning, the marriage in question does not necessarily have to be regarded as valid from the very beginning. Wernz [65] thinks that this clause has no more force than others, couched in different language, but rendered in similar cases, for instance, "From reasons thus far adduced the nullity of marriage is not apparent." (*Ex hactenus deductis non constare de nullitate matrimonii*). Such clause does not necessarily affirm the objective validity of the marriage. It leaves the consorts *in statu quo* until the doubt is settled. After the doubt is once re-

[65] *Op. cit.*, n. 507, n. 28.

moved the presumption must give way to certainty. Therefore, if the invalidity of the baptism is proved, the impediment of disparity of worship reveals itself and invalidates the marriage from its very beginning. If it is discovered that the baptism (whose validity was questioned) was valid, then, this impediment being absent, the marriage from the very beginning was objectively valid.

235. The decision of the Holy Office, rendered on July 20, 1840, if followed to its logical analysis, corroborates the view here proposed.[66] Gasparri remarks[67] that if in this case the heretical party (Anglican) is not baptized, then the first marriage was legitimate, because neither one of them would have been under the jurisdiction of the Church at the time their marriage was contracted. Thus he plainly admits that on account of the subjective doubt the objective validity of the marriage is not subject to change. Nor is the indelible character of Baptism conferred or removed by such a doubt.[68] Therefore, the Holy Office in its ruling, it may be supposed, was influenced by the presumption that the Anabaptist woman was never baptized, and that the Anglican was baptized. But, had it been subsequently discovered that the latter was unbaptized, the second marriage would have been null on account of the impediment of *ligamen.* This circumstance leads one to conclude that the first marriage could not have been declared valid objectively but sub-

[66] An Anglican wishes to become a Catholic. He was formerly married to an Anabaptist woman who maintains that she was never baptized. A serious doubt, however, may arise also as to the validity of the man's baptism on the ground that it was administered by an Anglican minister. The husband left his first wife and married a Lutheran woman. The question was asked: Which of the two women is his legitimate wife? Reply: As long as it is evident that the first wife was not baptized, the first marriage is invalid. The second, provided no other impediment is in the way, is valid. (FEIJE, *op. cit.*, n. 464.)

[67] *Op. cit.*, n. 603.

[68] WERNZ, *op. cit.*, n. 508, note 33.

jectively and by a mere presumption. It is in the light of this principle one is to view the decision of the Holy Office concerning the Calvinists and Lutherans whose baptism is doubtful. They are to be considered validly married to Catholics, but only on condition that this doubt perseveres. If it is evident that the baptism is null, the marriage is null.[69]

236. In the foregoing decisions the majority of modern canonists [70] see the implicit application of the principle that the validity of such marriages is to be presumed with a presumption which can be controverted (*praesumptione iuris tantum*). Such decisions do not mean to attribute an objective validity or invalidity to a doubtful union. They bestow on it only a presumptive validity or invalidity, as the case may demand. This presumption must cede to fact when the objective validity or invalidity of the baptism is established, and it is detected that the presumption has no foundation in fact. Therefore, if the subsequent investigation proves that the presumed impediment of disparity of worship has foundation in fact, the marriage is invalid. If the contrary is proved, then the marriage is valid, provided no impediment of natural or divine or ecclesiastical law militates against its validity. This opinion has been canonized and incorporated into the new Codex.[71] It states distinctly that if at the time of the marriage one of the parties was generally considered baptized, or his baptism was doubtful, his union with a Catholic must be considered valid,

[69] "Si autem certe cognoscatur nullum baptisma . . . nullum est matrimonium." (17 nov. 1830; FEIJE, *op. cit.*, n. 464.)

[70] DE BECKER, *De Sponsalibus et Matrimonio*, p. 218; Bruxelles, 1896. WERNZ, *op. cit.*, n. 507; DE SMET, *De Sponsalibus et Matrimonio*, n. 290; Brugis, 1909; and others.

[71] Si pars tempore contracti matrimonii tanquam baptizata communiter habebatur aut eius baptismus erat dubius, standum est pro valore matrimonii, donec certo probetur alteram partem baptizatam esse, alteram vero non baptizatam. (COD. IUR. CAN., Can. 1070, §2.)

until it is proved beyond doubt that one party is baptized and the other unbaptized. The words: *"Donec certo probetur alteram partem baptizatam esse, alteram vero non baptizatam"* clearly indicate that a decision issued in all such inquiries does not pretend to pronounce upon the objective validity of the marriage under consideration, but only upon its presumptive (subjective) validity.

237. The validity of baptism may be questioned on two grounds, namely, a doubt may arise as to the fact of its actual administration (*dubium dubio facti*), or its administration being certain, there may be a doubt whether the proper matter and form were used (*dubium dubio iuris*). It is generally admitted that either of these doubts is sufficient to invest the baptism with a presumptive validity in relation to marriage,[72] and the same kind of validity would be communicated to the marriage contracted in such doubts. The Holy Office expressly confirmed this opinion by a decision rendered on July 7, 1880.[73] The principle involved in this decision has been somewhat modified in its application to several more recent cases. Thus on July 10, 1896, the Holy Office declared that if two heretics or schismatics wish to be married, as long as the administration of their baptism is certain, though its validity may not be self-evident, they are to be considered as validly baptized.[74] While this decree seems to lay a particular stress on the fact of administration, its tenor must not be so construed as to lead one to maintain that if such fact of administration is questioned (*dubium dubio facti*) the Sacred Congregation does not mean to bestow on the baptism that presumptive valid-

[72] WERNZ, *op. cit.*, n. 507; DE BECKER, *op. cit.*, p. 223; GASPARRI, *op. cit.*, n. 603.

[73] GASPARRI, *loc. cit.*

[74] S. C. de Prop. Fide, *Collectanea*, n. 1940.

ity which is the first and least requisite *in ordine ad validitatem matrimonii.*

238. The principle that doubtful baptism is regarded as valid in relation to marriage is applicable both to prospective and to contracted marriages.[75] This principle affects the validity of baptism directly; that of the marriage indirectly. Since the objective validity or invalidity of the marriage depends on the objective validity or invalidity of the baptism, it is imperative that in each particular case a thorough investigation should be made into the baptism of the non-Catholic party. If the doubt cannot be removed even after a conscientious inquiry, then the decisions sent to Bishop Gross, of Savannah, by the Congregation of Propaganda will be of notable assistance.[76] Their scope is so comprehensive that it comprises practically all the contingent circumstances that can render a baptism doubtful. Their perusal will disclose the conditions under which one may be justified in forming a presumption in favor of baptism. The document being the most significant ever issued on this perplexing question, we deem it advisable to reproduce it here in substance.

Bishop Gross asked: I. Whether, when there is a doubt as to the administration or non-administration of baptism, we may pronounce judgment on the principle of presumption, when such baptism affects the validity or nullity of the contracted marriages?

II. Whether, when the fact of administration of baptism is unknown, one may apply the principle of presumption in relation to the validity of a contracted marriage, in the following cases:

[75] S. C. S. Off., 9 sept., 1868; see *Collectanea*, n. 657.

[76] *Collectanea*, n. 662; *Acta Sanctae Sedis*, XXV, pp. 261-263; *Conc. Plen. Balt.* III, ap. ad num. 122, p. 246; *Am. Eccl. Review*, vol. VIII, pp. 140-142.

1. If the non-Catholic party or parties are the offspring of parents who belong to a sect which rejects baptism, then the baptism is not to be presumed.

2. A similar pronouncement is to be made in the case of those whose parents professed a religion which does not admit infant-baptism, namely, in which baptism is not administered except to adults, for instance, those reaching the age of thirty years, as is the case with the baptists.

3. The same is to be said of those whose parents while living failed to ally themselves with any particular sect; pretending to worship a supreme being by their honest and upright conduct rather than by the teachings of any determined religion.

4. If the parents were zealous members of a sect which believes in the necessity of baptism, or in which it is generally administered, then the baptism of their children should be presumed. But what is to be said of children whose parents were indifferent or negligent members of such a sect, or professed a religion which does not reject baptism absolutely but disbelieves in its necessity and generally fails to administer it? Is the baptism to be presumed in both instances or in either of them?

5. If only one parent professes and practices the teachings of a sect in which baptism is generally administered, and this parent has the unquestioned ascendancy over the child's education, then the baptism is to be presumed.

The same is to be said when, after a sufficient inquiry, it is doubtful whether such a parent exercised the chief control over the child's education. But what pronouncement should be made when it is discovered that neither the sect nor the disposition of mind of the parent having the principal control over the child's education favors baptism, while the disposition of the less influential parent and his sect are favorably inclined towards baptism?

6. Cases in which no presumption favors baptism should be decided on the principle: Fact is not to be presumed, but must be proved.

The Congregation of Propaganda on August 1, 1883, replied:

To the I. Affirmatively, investigation of each case having first been made.

To the II. Affirmatively concerning the first, the second and the third article, the first part of the fourth article, and the first part of the fifth article; in the latter article after the words "chief control over the child's education" are to be added the words: "and the other parent is not known to be positively opposed to baptism, then baptism must be presumed." In other cases noted in the second part of the fifth article recourse must be had to the Holy See with a complete statement of all the circumstances calculated to shed light on the case under consideration. The foregoing decisions provide the answer to the sixth inquiry.

239. The guiding principles approved in this decree enjoyed a very extensive application in the old discipline. In the new legislation there applicability is limited to marriages contracted between a Catholic and a non-Catholic about whose baptism there is a doubt. In such a case a dispensation from the impedient impediment of mixed religion will suffice, though it is desirable that all such petitions should be accompanied (*ad cautelam*) with a request also for the dispensation from the impediment of disparity of worship. The Sacred Congregation in our days is more disposed than in the past to respond to such appeals. Though there may be a doubt as to the validity of the baptism of the non-Catholic party, as soon as the dispensation from the impediment of mixed religion is granted, the marriage is licit. The priest is not permitted to baptize such a person conditionally with the view of obviating the possibility of the marriage's nullity. Such baptism may be conferred only on the condition that the non-Catholic party is willing to make a profession of faith and join the true fold.[77]

240. If a doubt should arise as to the validity of the baptism of the Catholic party, its conditional administration should not be neglected, irrespective of whether the doubt arose before or after the marriage. A clear distinction should be made here between baptism which is necessary to salvation *necessitate medii,* and baptism which is necessary for the validity of the marriage in question. The first must be objectively valid; but a doubtful baptism will suffice in relation to marriage. Therefore, it is not absolutely wrong, under certain circumstances, to unite in marriage two Catholics without having previously administered conditional baptism to the one whose baptism is not altogether certain. The Church permits even the sacrament of Holy Orders to be administered to candidates who cannot prove by means either of a letter or of a witness that they were baptized; in that case the baptism is presumed, provided they are the offspring of Catholic parents.[78] When, however, there is a prudent doubt, it ought to be removed by a conditional administration of the sacrament which is the gate to all other sacraments.[79]

241. The opinion of Lehmkuhl[80] that whenever the Church dispenses from the impediment of mixed religion it means to dispense simultaneously (*ad cautelam*) also from the impediment of disparity of worship,

[77] S. C. Inq., 13 apr., 1878; ib., WERNZ, *op. cit.*, n. 507, n. 29.
[78] S. C. de Prop. Fide, litt. (ad Vic. Ap. Cocinc. Occid.), 30 sept., 1848; *Collectanea*, n. 652.
[79] *Am. Eccl. Review*, vol. XII, pp. 241, 406, 407.
[80] *Theol. Moralis*, vol. II, p. 566; Friburgi Brisgoviae, 1910.

has long been discredited by modern canonists.[81] Therefore a dispensation from the latter is never to be presumed unless the rescript alludes to it explicitly. This opinion is based on a decision of the Sacred Congregation rendered on April 29, 1842,[82] and is corroborated by the new legislation.[83] Therefore, if a marriage is contracted with a dispensation from the impediment of mixed religion (without *ad cautelam* from the impediment of disparity of worship) and it is subsequently ascertained that the non-Catholic party whose baptism was doubtful is unbaptized, the marriage is null. The declaration of nullity may be made by the Ordinary,[84] provided a judicial process is established; a course necessitated by the fact that unions of this kind possess the true form of marriage. In all doubtful cases recourse should be had to the Holy See.[85] The impediment of disparity of worship ceases to bind when Catholics live under circumstances which make it morally impossible for them either to ask for a dispensation or to marry one of their own faith. Thus, for instance, the conditions prescribed by the ecclesiastical law are impossible of observance by those living in some parts of China.[86] A similar case should be imagined, if some Christians should strand on an island where they could intermarry only with infidels. Under such circumstances, when they are obliged to choose between marrying an infidel and remaining single, provided they do not expose their faith to very serious danger, and are in good conscience, this im-

[81] WERNZ, *op. cit.*, n. 508, n. 33; DE BECKER, *op. cit.*, p. 224; DE SMET, *op. cit.*, n. 290.

[82] DE SMET, *loc. cit.*

[83] COD. IUR. CAN., Can. 1070, §2.

[84] Cum interventu, tamen defensoris vinculi matrimonialis. S. C. S. Off., 5 iun., 1889. (*Collectanea*, n. 1706.)

[85] DE BECKER, *op. cit.*, p. 224; DE SMET, *op. cit.*, n. 290.

[86] S. C. S. Off., ep. (ad Vic. Ap. Mandciuriae), 4 iun., 1851; see *Collectanea*, n. 1275.

pediment would not be considered as invalidating their unions.[87] Such environments, can very rarely exist in our times, though they may easily be imagined in places like Alaska. The missionaries of those regions should submit an exposition of facts to the consideration of the Holy See, and abide by its decision.[88] It is only a theoretical question whether the Church means to dispense in advance in such infrequent instances, whether it only tolerates such marriages, or, owing to peculiar circumstances, it intends to suspend a law whose observance is manifestly impossible. All three hypotheses contribute to the same final result.[89]

4. *Dispensation from the Impediment.*

242. It has already been stated that the diriment force of this impediment does not arise either from natural or from divine positive law, but was introduced by custom.[90] Consequently it is in the power of the Holy See to permit that a Catholic for grave reasons may contract marriage with an infidel. A dispensation in all such instances implies also the declaration that the danger of perversion, which is the cause of the existence of this impediment, is either absent or remote. The Church does not dispense from this impediment unless:

I. The marriage in question is contracted in a place in which there are more infidels than Catholics.[91]

II. Just and grave causes urge such a dispensation.

[87] DE BECKER, *op. cit.*, p. 217; DE SMET, *op. cit.*, n. 289.

[88] DE BECKER, *op. cit.*, p. 218.

[89] GASPARRI, *op. cit.*, n. 623; WERNZ, *op. cit.*, n. 510, note 37; DE BECKER, *op. cit.*, p. 217; DE SMET, *loc. cit.;* see also Decree of the Holy Office, on June 4, 1851; *Collectanea*, n. 1275, and St. Alphonsus, *op. cit.*, lib. III, n. 763.

[90] BENEDICT XIV, *"Singulari Nobis," Bull. Rom. Con.*, vol. III.

[91] This condition is not embodied in the new Code. It is a local law, and its application to countries where infidels predominate will no doubt continue.

III. The non-Catholic consort furnishes *cautiones* whereby he obliges himself to remove all danger of perversion from the Catholic consort, and both consorts bind themselves to educate all their offspring in the Catholic faith.

IV. There is moral certainty that the *cautiones* will be fulfilled.

These *cautiones,* as a rule, should be given in writing.[92] It is to be noted that when a dispensation is granted from this impediment the Church dispenses also from the law forbidding communication *in divinis* with infidels. Sometimes certain restrictions are placed in the rescript, as, for example, (1) the Catholic woman is not permitted to marry a Jew; (2) the parties shall not, either before or after the marriage, present themselves before a non-Catholic minister for the purpose of having him witness their consent in his religious capacity.[93]

The following pages will be devoted to the explanation of the conditions just mentioned.

243. I. The first condition, as Gasparri remarks,[94] is not appended to dispensations granted to Christian countries, but only to those granted to missionary places. We may add that the new Codex makes no mention at all of this first condition. Formerly in missionary regions this condition was verified only when in the village where the Catholic party resided, the infidels outnumbered the Christians. This requirement was somewhat modified by a special indult granted by the Congregation of Propaganda on January 14, 1806, to the missionaries of China and the East Indies.[95] This decree states that the first condition re-

[92] COD. IUR. CAN., Can. 1061.
[93] *Op. cit.,* Can. 1063, §1.
[94] *Op. cit.,* n. 611.
[95] *Collectanea,* n. 1270.

quired for the granting of the dispensation is fulfilled though in a certain village or town (*pago*) the Catholics predominate, as long as they are in the minority in the district (*toparchia*) to which this particular town belongs. Gasparri remarks [96] that unless this extensive interpretation is distinctly stated in the faculties, the faculty to dispense is restricted to cases which occur in towns where the Catholics are in the minority. It is hard to see why such a conclusion should be drawn from the wording of the decree. It distinctly states that in the future the words of the clause ("in places where there are more infidels than Catholics") are generally to be applied to separate districts.[97] It would seem that the words "*generatim in posterum*" indicate a rule whereby, in the future, faculties to dispense will be given with the understanding that the first condition for granting the dispensation will be verified when the above-quoted words find their true application in their amplified sense, namely, when they refer to the *toparchia* (district) in which the person has a domicile or quasi-domicile. Therefore, no such territorial restriction as Gasparri indicates should be put on these words, unless the faculty to dispense distinctly contains such a restriction.

244. II. Natural, divine, as well as ecclesiastical law prohibit the granting of such dispensation without the verification of the conditions specified in the second point, for otherwise the granting of the dispensation would amount to offering contumely to the Creator. Even if in certain instances natural law would not militate against such a union, the apostolical impedient and the ecclesiastical diriment law would

[96] *Op. cit., loc. cit.*

[97] "Conditio illa, in locis ubi sunt plures infideles quam fideles, generatim, in posterum intelligenda sit, non de singulis pagis vel vicis, sed de singulis toparchiis." (*Collectanea*, n. 1270.)

still retain their full force. In case the circumstances were such that the natural law would forbid the marriage, the Holy See, even in the absence of a just cause, could dispense validly, though illicitly. Under the same circumstances neither licit nor valid dispensation could be granted by one who has only a delegated power.

Benedict XIV [98] deemed it necessary to accentuate the fact that though all the other conditions may be verified in a particular instance the Church does not dispense *sine gravi aliqua, ac plerumque publica causa.* The Sacred Congregation of Propaganda gave expression to the same doctrine when it admonished the delegates of the Holy See that only *iustae gravesque causae* should influence them to grant a dispensation.[99] That the Church does not intend to relax its discipline on this point is apparent from the fact that the new legislation following in the footsteps of the old, requires the same *iustae ac graves causae* as a condition in whose absence a dispensation from this impediment will not be granted.

245. It is easier to determine whether a cause is sufficiently grave when one deals with a specific rather than with an abstract instance. Some of the causes justifying the granting of such a dispensation would be: (1) The welfare of a Christian republic; (2) the predominance of infidels in a certain country; (3) the fact that such marriage is the only means whereby children born of a former union can be educated in the Catholic faith, or whereby (4) scandal, concubinage, diffamation or attempt at marriage can be avoided.[100] Causes of private nature, like superadult age, lack of

[98] *De Synodo Dioecesana,* lib. IX, cap. III, n. 5.

[99] Litt. encycl. S. C. de Prop. Fide, 11 mart. 1868; in the new *Collectanea,* n. 1324.

[100] Bangen, *op. cit.,* vol. IV, p. 20.

dowry, poverty of the widow, *angustia loci,* and others enumerated in the instruction given by the Sacred Congregation of Propaganda [101] do not suffice singly, but when several concur in one and the same case the circumstances may justify the granting of a dispensation.

The importance of a sufficiently grave cause is apparent from the fact that without it even the Roman Pontiff would dispense illicitly, though validly, while the Bishop under the same circumstances would not remove the impediment even if he should grant a dispensation by virtue of the power which an apostolic indult would give him.

246. III. The third condition without which the dispensation should not be granted regards certain guarantees to be exacted from the two contracting parties. Formerly only the non-Catholic consort was expected to give the *cautiones,* the new law demands a promise also from the Catholic party. The former, according to the tenor of the past discipline, had to promise that he will not interfere with the religious freedom of the latter. The new law requires that he should go even further, and that by a positive act he should remove whatever is calculated to jeopardize the faith of the Catholic consort (circumstances exposing her to the danger of perversion). Besides, both consorts must promise that their children will be baptized and educated exclusively in the Catholic faith. Formerly the Catholic party was not required to make this promise expressly, for it was tacitly presumed that such was his intention. Now the Church, more emphatically than ever before, will call to his mind this duty, thus making the non-compliance with it so much more sinful.

[101] Instr. S. C. de Prop. Fide, 9 maii, 1877; in the new *Collectanea,* n. 1470.

247. IV. These promises are founded on natural and divine law,[102] therefore, not only should they be exacted but a moral certainty should be had as to their fulfillment. The Holy Office in an instruction given to the Primate of Hungary on July 7, 1890, insists that unless the foregoing conditions are subscribed to, a dispensation should never be granted. The same instruction, like the canon of the new law, emphasizes the moral certainty which the pastor should have as regards the future fulfillment of the accepted conditions.[103] Should the indications show that their fulfillment is impossible under the contemplated circumstances, or, should the insincerity of one or both contracting parties be apparent, the persons in questions could not be considered worthy applicants for a dispensation.

In order that the importance of the embraced obligations may be more deeply impressed on the contracting parties and that the proof of their voluntary assumption be available for the external forum, if need be, the present discipline prescribes that, as a general rule, the guarantees should be given in writing.[104]

248. The Sacred Congregation distinguishes between dispensation of disparity of worship given to prospective marriages and those granted to contracted marriages. According to an instruction given by the Congregation of Propaganda on February 15, 1780, this dispensation should very rarely be granted to Catholic women wishing to contract marriages with infidels, because experience teaches that in their case the danger of perversion seldom ceases.[105] The danger

[102] Instr. Secr. Status, 15 nov., 1858. *"Magnae Nobis."*

[103] BENEDICT XIV, ep. encycl., 29 iun., 1748; GREGORIUS XVI, ep. encycl., *"Summo iugiter,"* 27 maii, 1732; LEO XIII, ep. encycl. *"Quod multum,"* 26 aug., 1886; PIUS X, litt. ap. *"Provida,"* 18 ian., 1906, n. II.

[104] PIUS VI, rescript. ad Card. Archiep. Mechlinen., 3 iul., 1782; S. C. S. Off. (ad Ep. Aurelianen.), 6 iun., 1879; S. C. de Prop. Fide, litt. (ad Ep. Ottavien.), 17 apr., 1879.

[105] *Collectanea,* n. 1266.

being less in case a Catholic man wishes to marry an infidel, a dispensation may be granted more readily.[106]

249. After the marriage has been contracted, though invalidly, and the Catholic party wishes to have it validated, if the danger of perversion is removed, the request to dispense should not be denied. Such a dispensation in favor of a well-disposed person is more readily granted than in the case of mixed marriages, when the validity of the marriage does not depend on the dispensation.[107] If he danger remains, it is preferable to leave the Catholic party in good faith as to the validity of the marriage rather than grant a dispensation.[108] If the Catholic party, being aware of the nullity of the marriage, asks for a dispensation, such favor cannot be granted unless the danger of perversion is first removed. If this cannot be done, she should be advised to have recourse to a civil divorce rather than jeopardize her spiritual welfare.[109]

This remedy is practicable, but only among civilized nations. The Congregation of Propaganda in one of its above-quoted decrees[110] has provided for similar emergencies arising in uncivilized countries. If a married woman through no fault of her own, by force of circumstances, is so situated that her faith is seriously endangered, and she is constrained by violence to continue in such circumstances, she should be reminded of her miserable plight, and, if possible, freed from the spiritual danger surrounding her. If her actions clearly indicate that she is doing all in her power to liberate herself from the degrading environments, then she may be strengthened and comforted even by a

[106] S. C. S. Off., 29 apr., 1891; see *Collectanea*, n. 1279.
[107] De Smet, *op. cit.*, n. 291.
[108] S. C. de Prop. Fide, 13 sept., 1760; *Collectanea*, n. 1261.
[109] Gasparri, *op. cit.*, n. 615.
[110] See above, foot-note 108.

prudent administration of the sacraments, but a dispensation should never be given to her.[111]

250. The reprint of the answer given by the Congregation of Propaganda on May 3, 1828, and the request which occasioned it, will perhaps help to give a clearer notion of the discipline of the Church in these matters. The Vicar Apostolic of Tonkin asked whether this dispensation may be granted to one (1) who, having formerly lived with an infidel *cum contumelia Creatoris,* now wishes to be dispensed from the impediment of disparity of worship. It is hoped that the danger of perversion is absent, and a faint hope is entertained even for the conversion of the infidel party; (2) who hopes to be able to live *sine contumelia Creatoris* as far as the infidel consort and the little children already born or to be born are concerned, though the adult children will not be converted; (3) whose infidel consort consents to everything except the Catholic education of the first born, or the first male child already born or to be born. May the dispensation, in this third case, be granted, in a most urgent necessity, as, for instance, when the proximate danger of death demands it? To the first and the second inquiry the reply was affirmative. The third also was affirmative with the proviso that the Catholic party is at the point of death. But even then it is necessary to exact a promise that in case of recovery she will endeavor to convert the infidel party and to bring up all the children in the Catholic faith.[112]

[111] "Che se non si fosse ella volontariemente costituita in tale stato, ma per violenza e per forza tirata e ritenuta, allora dovrebbe procurarsi, che l'uno e l'altro pericolo della perversione e della fornicazione da prossimo si facesse rimoto, e l'esperienza presa da' suoi sforzi e dissensi continui, per conforto, con prudenza accordarle i Sagramenti, veduta la sua disposizione, ma non accordare la dispensa giammai. (*Collectanea,* n. 1261.)

[112] S. C. de Prop. Fide, litt. (ad Vic. Ap. Tunk. Orient.), 3 maii, 1828; see *Collectanea,* n. 1273.

251. Clement XIII in his instruction to the Vicar Apostolic of Oriental Su-tchuen insists that these faculties must be used only within the territory of the grantee. The dispensation can be given only to true Catholics whose consorts refuse to be baptized, and only in case a grave inconvenience would result in consequence of a separation. They must always be given *gratis,* and with an injunction on the Catholic party to educate all the children in the true faith and to strive to bring about the conversion of the infidel. Both parties must be instructed about the necessity of renewing their consent, which, in order to avoid persecutions or scandal, may be done without witnesses, and, if possible, the infidel party should be informed of the nullity of the present marriage.[113]

252. A grave cause can more easily be found in contracted marriages than in prospective marriages. It is of more frequent occurrence in missionary places than in Christian countries. Consequently the dispensation, as a rule, is more readily given in the first two instances than in the latter two.[114] It is left to the good judgment of the dispenser to determine whether the existing cause is of sufficient gravity to justify the granting of the dispensation.

253. The decisions of the Sacred Congregations of Propaganda and of the Holy Office will furnish considerable help towards forming an idea of such justifying causes. If a Catholic and an infidel have contracted marriage, and have lived *sine contumelia Creatoris,* their spiritual welfare is considered a sufficient cause for the granting of a dispensation, especially if they have children and a separation from the infidel party is connected with grave difficulties.[115]

[113] S. C. S. Off., 12 ian., 1769; see *Collectanea,* n. 1263.
[114] Gasparri, *op. cit.,* n. 619; Cod. Iur. Can., Can. 1061, n. 1.
[115] S. C. S. Off., 15 sept., 1736; *Collectanea,* n. 1258.

Gasparri, from the decisions of the Sacred Congregation of Propaganda, draws the inference that the faculty received by an indult to dispense from the impediment of disparity of worship cannot be sub-delegated, unless so extraordinary a privilege is expressly communicated by the Holy See.[116] This statement has to be somewhat modified. In the new legislation it is distinctly stated that one who has an ordinary power of jurisdiction may sub-delegate a faculty which the Holy See has granted him by a special delegation, unless such a power is expressly withdrawn in the rescript.[117]

Dispensation from this impediment, though all the conditions are willingly subscribed to, should not be granted with readiness, because experience teaches that many unforseen dangers arise threatening the spiritual welfare of the Catholic party.[118] It is for this reason that the Church prefers marriages which Catholics contract among themselves even with a dispensed impediment of affinity or consanguinity, to those in which she would be called upon to give a dispensation from the impediment of which we treat.[119] Each individual case must be examined carefully, so as to avoid exposing the dispensation to the danger of nullity on account of the absence of a sufficiently grave cause.[120]

254. The spiritual danger threatening the Catholic party in such marriages is emphasized by the insistence with which the Church urges that the promises be made by the infidel party. These promises must be exacted even *in articulo mortis.*[121] In the old legislation, *in*

[116] *Op. cit.*, n. 620.
[117] Cod. Iur. Can., Can. 199.
[118] Litt. Ap. Gregorii PP., XVI, 30 apr., 1841; *Collectanea*, n. 1428.
[119] S. C. S. Off., 12 ian., 1769; *Collectanea*, n. 1263.
[120] S. C. S. Off., 15 febr., 1780; *Collectanea*, n. 1266.
[121] S. C. S. Off., 18 mart., 1891; *Collectanea*, n. 2188; *Acta S. Sedis*, vol. XXIX, p. 638.

articulo mortis, all the Bishops could dispense (in favor of contracted marriages) from this impediment (*sive per se, sive per alios*) when recourse to the Holy See was impossible.[122] They enjoyed this special indult on condition that the required promises were made.[123] De Becker [124] interprets this decision in the sense that, without regard to the circumstances brought about by the threatening death, all the promises must be urged on both parties. A dispensation, in his estimation, may, however, be granted *in articulo mortis,* though the infidel party refuses to consent to the conditions, provided the danger of perversion for the Catholic party is removed and the latter gives all the assurances to abide by the *cautiones.* This lenient interpretation is quite comformable to the spirit of the Church, as evidenced in the various decrees of the Sacred Congregation,[125] and in the new Code.

255. In accordance with the tenor of the most recent legislation the Ordinaries have very extensive faculties *urgente mortis periculo.* These faculties are personal; therefore, they may be exercised in behalf of their subjects, without regard to territory, and in behalf of all those who actually tarry in their diocese. They may dispense from the form of marriage and from all ecclesiastical impediments (excepting the impediment arising from the Holy Priesthood and from affinity in the direct line provided the marriage was consummated) whether occult or public, even if they be multiple. This faculty is granted for the spiritual welfare of the parties concerned, and, if need be, for the legitimation of offspring. If this privilege is used to dispense from the impediment of disparity of wor-

[122] Litt. encycl. S. C. S. Off., 20 febr., 1888; *Collectanea,* n. 1685.
[123] S. C. S. Off., 18 mart., 1891; *Collectanea,* n. 2188.
[124] *Op. cit.,* p. 228.
[125] Decrees of *Collectanea,* nn. 1263; 1264; 1271; 1273.

ship, its use should be preceded by the giving of the *cautiones*.[126] Under the same circumstances, in case an immediate recourse cannot be had to the Ordinary, a parish priest, or, when the case is very urgent, any priest who happens to be present,[127] enjoys the same extensive power. For the internal forum (in the act of sacramental confession) the confessor may make use of the same extensive faculty.[128] The priest who has exercised so extraordinary a power in the external forum must without delay make it known to the Bishop, and must note it in the marriage register.[129]

The wording of the Canon 1043 allows one to infer that under the circumstances therein related a Bishop or a priest may not only dispense from the impediment of disparity of worship, but may also lend his passive presence to the marriage, notwithstanding the fact that the *cautiones* are not given. This extreme leniency of the Church should be extended only as the last resort, namely, when all efforts made towards prevailing on the parties to give the *cautiones* prove abortive.

256. A decision of the Holy Office rendered on September 16, 1824, in doubtful matrimonial cases submitted by the Bishop of Quebec, discloses the special effect possessed by a dispensation from the impediment of disparity of worship. The instruction specifies that: The Church in dispensing a Catholic from the impediment of disparity of worship with the view of permitting his marriage to an infidel, intends to remove those impediments also from which the infidel is exempted.[130] This automatic dispensation from co-existing impediments was restricted to relative impedi-

[126] Cod. Iur. Can., Can. 1043.
[127] *Op. cit.*, Can. 1098, n. 2.
[128] *Op. cit.*, Can. 1044.
[129] *Op. cit.*, Can. 1046.
[130] *Acta S. Sedis*, vol. XXV, p. 584; Gasparri, *op. cit.*, n. 672; Wernz, *op. cit.*, n. 510; De Becker, *op. cit.*, p. 228; De Smet, *op. cit.*, n. 291.

ments and to those only from which the Church dispenses. Thus the exemption was not extended to the impediments of vow, Holy Orders, affinity or consanguinity in the direct line, nor to consanguinity in the first degree of the collateral line. Since in the new Code an emphasis is laid on the fact that both parties must be competent, and since no such special effect is attributed to a dispensation from this impediment, it would seem that the above instruction has been deprived of its significance.

257. As we have already stated, this dispensation is not given unless all the requisite promises have been made previously by both the Catholic and the infidel party who are about to enter into marriage. But it must be borne in mind that the mere promises do not suffice in themselves. The Holy See insists that the Ordinaries and the pastors of the flock have a moral certainty as to their actual fulfillment [131] and that they watch vigilantly that the promises be not disregarded.[132]

Sometimes the infidel party feigns a willingness to subscribe to these conditions in order to obtain the necessary dispensation. But it might be discovered subsequently that he was in bad faith, for, the dispensation having been obtained, he retracts what he previously promised. If it can be proved that at the time the promises were made he had no serious intentions of complying with them, then the dispensation would be invalid. If he meant to give the *cautiones* when the dispensation was applied for, but subsequently retracted, then canon 41 finds application. The removal of the impediment and the validity of marriage would require that, as a *conditio sine qua non,* his intention of keeping the *cautiones* should be expressed at the

[131] Cod. Iur. Can., Can. 1061, n. 3.
[132] *Op. cit.,* Can. 1064, n. 3.

time the dispensation is applied, when, namely, the marriage is solemnized.

5. *Injunctions Relative to Mixed Marriages.*

258. The Catholic consort is bound by the obligation of endeavoring by prudent means to procure the conversion of the non-Catholic party.[133] The legislation contained in this canon formerly constituted one of the promises to which the Catholic party was expected to subscribe expressly, and on which the granting of the dispensation was conditioned.[134] This obligation does not lose its force by the fact that it is no longer included in, but separated from the conditions explained above. While the Catholic party's readiness to that effect need not be signified in the petition for dispensation, the law of charity, receiving a special sanction and an added force by virtue of the foregoing ecclesiastical canon, nevertheless continues to oblige him. The former discipline employed the words "*pro viribus*" to express the effort which the Catholic party was expected to make toward converting the non-Catholic consort. The new legislation supplants those terms with the words "*prudenter.*" By this change the supreme legislator means to emphasize the circumspection and the discretion which must be exercised in order that the Catholic party may succeed in bringing the dissentient consort to the unity of the faith. A faithful performance of all conjugal duties is without doubt the first and one of the most effective means contributing toward the attainment of that end.

259. Though the Church should grant a dispensation from this impediment the contracting parties are

[133] *Op. cit.*, Can. 1062.

[134] S. C. S. Off., instr. (ad Archiep. Quebecen.), 16 sept., 1834; ad 5; instr. (ad Archiep. Corcyren.), 3 ian., 1871, n. 3; S. C. de Prop. Fide, instr. (ad. Vic. Ap. Sveciae), 6 sept., 1785; litt. encycl., 11 mart., 1868.

nevertheless forbidden to present themselves either personally or by proxy, whether before or after the marriage, before a non-Catholic minister in order to give or renew their consent while he officiates in his religious capacity.[135] The laws of some countries impose an obligation to give or renew one's consent before a representative of the state as a *conditio sine qua non* to the gaining of the civil effects of marriage. Should the magistrate of such places be a non-Catholic minister, employed for a purely civil function, the parties would not violate this ecclesiastical law by making use of his services.[136] They would not be permitted, however, either to give or renew their consent before him should his office as a civil functionary and as a minister of a sect be inseparable, and should he officiate in both capacities simultaneously, namely, by one and the same act.

260. If the parish priest is certain that the contracting parties will disregard this law, or that they have already transgressed it, he should abstain from witnessing their marriage, unless a very grave cause urges otherwise, and then he must first consult the Ordinary and remove the scandal.[137] Such a very grave cause would exist in every case where the fear is present that a civil marriage will be attempted or that the already attempted invalid marriage will be consummated. It is to be noted that in case the marriage is attempted before the minister of a sect the parties incur an excommunication *latae sententiae* reserved to the Bishop.[138] Absolution from this censure must precede the celebration of such a marriage.

261. Besides the foregoing injunctions directed to

[135] Cod. Iur. Can., Can. 1063, §1.

[136] Instr. S. C. S. Off., 12 dec., 1888, n. 7; in the new *Collectanea*, n. 1696.

[137] Cod. Iur. Can., Can. 1063, §2.

[138] *Op. cit.*, Can. 2319, §1, n. 1.

the contracting parties the Codex of Piux X inculcates also the duties of the Ordinaries and other pastors of souls when it admonishes them that they (1) should dissuade the faithful to the best of their ability from mixed marriages; (2) should exert every effort not to permit them to be contracted against the law of God and of the Church if they are unable to prevent them altogether; (3) should watch vigilantly over the faithful fulfillment of the *cautiones* which were given in marriages contracted in their own territory or outside it; (4) should be guided in their assistance at such marriages by the instructions contained in canon 1102.[139]

262. The duties of the Bishop and pastors as outlined in the first three points of the foregoing canon need no explanation. It is sufficient to note that the pastor will not consent to witness a mixed marriage until all his efforts to dissuade the Catholic party from such a step prove abortive. If the latter remains immovable and there is a serious danger that marriage will be contracted outside the Church, provided the parties express a willingness to comply at least with minimum requirements of the law, the pastor should rather assist at their marriage than allow them to resort to an action which is contrary to the law of God and of the Church, besides being invalid.

263. Even if the dispensation should be granted the banns of such marriages are not to be proclaimed in the Church, as has already been explained in connection with canon 1026.[140] Should the Ordinary deem it expedient to make such proclamation, no mention should be made of the religious sect with which the non-Catholic party is affiliated. For the validity of the assistance at such marriages it is required that no

[139] *Op. cit.*, Can. 1064.
[140] See this work, n. 108.

extrinsic force or fear should be brought to bear on the pastor in order thus to constrain him to ask and receive the consent of the contracting parties.[141]

264. According to an instruction Pius IX ordained on November 15, 1858, that such marriages should take place outside and not within the edifice of the church (*extra ecclesiam*), and that all religious rites whatsoever must be barred.[142] As regards the religious rites the new law conforms to the foregoing decree. Since we treat here *de odiosis* the word *"ecclesia"* must be interpreted strictly, in which case it should not be applied to the sacristy or to a private chapel. Such is the meaning of a decision of the Holy Office handed down on January 17, 1877.[143]

265. If from the observance of this law grave evils are feared, the Ordinary may permit one or the other of the usual ceremonies, but the celebration of the Mass must always be excluded.[144] The exclusion of the Mass contains an indirect prohibition against the imparting of the solemn nuptial blessing with the usual prayers found in the Roman Missal, for such a blessing may not be bestowed outside the Mass.[145]

266. Under ordinary circumstances the Church wants the parish priest to render more than a passive assistance to such marriages since he must ask and receive their consent. By passive assistance is meant the mere presence of the pastor and the witnesses in order to testify to the consent given by the contracting parties. The only official act of the pastor would be the recording of the marriage in the matrimonial register. Should the obviation of serious evils necessitate it the Bishop may, by way of exception, permit all the

[141] Cod. Iur. Can., Can. 1095, §1, n. 3.
[142] Gasparri, *op. cit.*, n. 456; De Becker, *op. cit.*, p. 264.
[143] Gasparri, *op. cit.*, n. 463.
[144] Cod. Iur. Can., Can. 1102, §2.
[145] *Op. cit.*, Can. 1101.

marriage ceremonies contained in the ritual including the blessing of the ring and all the prayers, barring always the celebration of the nuptial Mass and the blessing usually imparted in it.

267. It is incumbent on the pastor to validate the marriage as soon as possible should it be invalid either on account of the lack of form or of the presence of some diriment impediment and separation is not practicable as is generally the case. The exacting of the cutomary *cautiones* ought to be the first step under such circumstances. Then absolution from the censure of excommunication *latae sententiae* should follow next if the marriage was attempted not before a civil magistrate but before a heretical minister. This absolution should be given *in foro externo.* Only in case the attempted marriage is secret and there is no danger of its becoming publicly known, may the absolution be given *in foro interno.* Should the non-Catholic party refuse the giving of *cautiones* as long as the Catholic party is favorably disposed and the former is willing to renew his consent, the dispensation may still be obtained for the purpose of convalidating the marriage, especially if there be some children who stand in need of being legitimated. If the non-Catholic party declines both the giving of *cautiones* and the renewal of consent, recourse should be had to *sanatio in radice.*[146]

268. It may happen that the Catholic party entered into an agreement whereby she intends to permit the non-Catholic education of the future offspring in the way that is found in some countries where the boys follow the religion of their father and the girls that of their mother. Consequently, both her defection from the faith and her readiness to contract outside the Church are seriously feared. The case may be ren-

[146] GASPARRI, *op. cit.*, n. 468; DE SMET, *op. cit.*, n. 257; WERNZ, *op. cit.*, n. 588.

dered more difficult by the aggravating circumstance that she will neither retract her previous impious promise nor give the *cautiones.* In all such cases the assistance of the parish priest must be unfalteringly denied.[147] Such instances occasionally do occur in prospective marriages between a Catholic and a baptized non-Catholic. Because they are of more frequent occurrence in Germany, Bavaria and some parts of Austria and Hungary, a special concession was granted to those countries. Though the Ordinaries of those places cannot dispense from the impediment of mixed religion under the circumstances, they may permit the passive assistance of the priest to witness a marriage which the Catholic party is about to contract in mortal sin.[148] That such marriages are most reluctantly tolerated by the Church is manifest from their emphatic denunciation contained in the declaration of Benedict XIV, sent to Belgium and Holland.[149]

269. The question was asked whether this signal concession is to be restricted to the place for whose special benefit it was granted. The Holy Office, on June 21, 1912, replied: ***Standum est taxative praecedentibus S. Sedis ac praesertim s. m. Gregorii PP. XVI (Litt. app. diei 30 aprilis 1841 ad Episcopos Hungariae), ad rem concessionibus.***[150] Basing their opinion on this decision several theologians maintain that in similar cases the Bishop may permit such passive assistance of the parish priest even in places for which the above-mentioned decree was not intended. Bar-

[147] *Conc. Plen. Balt. II*, n. 338; PUTZER, *op. cit.*, p. 342.

[148] SABETTI-BARRETT, *op. cit.*, n. 903. q. 10; GASPARRI, *op. cit.*, n. 447; PUTZER, *op. cit.*, p. 342; Litt. Ap. Pii PP. VIII, 25 mart., 1830 (ad Archiep. Colonien. et ad Epp. Treviren. Paderbonen. et Monasterien.): *Collectanea.* n. 426; Litt. Ap. Gregorii PP. XIV, 30 apr., 1841, ad Episcopos Hungariae; *Collectanea,* n. 1428; Instruction to the Bavarian Bishops, on Sept. 12, 1834.

[149] Declaratio Bened. XIV, 4 nov., 1741; *Collectanea.* n. 1420.

[150] In the *American Ecclesiastical Review,* vol. XLVII, p. 331.

rett [151] adduces several good reasons in vindication of such opinion. The decree *Ne temere,* he argues, prescribes the presence of a priest as a *conditio sine qua non* of the validity of the marriage. It is easy to see how the extension of this concession would reduce not only the number of invalid marriages, but also the number of those unfortunate Catholics who, owing to the uncompromising attitude of the Church in this matter, betake themselves to a non-Catholic minister for marriage, so that they themselves and their children become lost to the faith. He quotes Lehmkuhl, Prümmer and Göpfert as advocates of the same extensive interpretation. While the manifold advantages of such interpretation must be conceded, one should not overlook the grave danger which such a concession, if universally applied, would inevitably bring in its wake.[152] Therefore, unless the Church should rule otherwise, all such instances, occurring in places to which this privilege has not been officially extended, must be referred to the Bishop. The latter should not consent to the passive assistance of a priest without having previously consulted the Holy See, if time permits. If, however, there is *periculum in mora* it would seem advisable to grant such permission, rather than suffer the contracting of an invalid marriage, and all the subsequent evils and sins resulting from it.[153]

6. *Ecclesiastical Penalty.*

270. Those who attempt to contract marriage before a non-Catholic minister incur an excommunication *latae sententiae* reserved to the Ordinary.[154] It does not matter whether both parties are Catholics or only

[151] SABETTI-BARRETT, *loc. cit.*, q. 11.

[152] MARTIN, S. J., *The New Decree on Mixed Marriages*, in the *American Ecclesiastical Review*, vol. XLVII, pp. 477 ff.

[153] GASPARRI, *op. cit.*, n. 447; FEIJE, *op. cit.*, n. 570; PUTZER, *op. cit.*, p. 343.

[154] COD. IUR. CAN., Can. 2319.

one of them, as is generally the rule. This censure is incurred by all who either before or after marriage have recourse to a non-Catholic clergyman with the intention of having him witness their consent in his religious capacity.[155] Those who contract marriage with the implicit or explicit understanding that one or all their children shall be educated outside the Catholic Church, or knowingly permit their children to be baptized by a non-Catholic clergyman, besides incurring a similar censure, are also suspected of heresy.[156] If the marriage entered into with such agreement is contracted before the priest, the Catholic incurs an excommunication. The text of this canon is to be interpreted strictly. Therefore, the Catholic who would attempt marriage before a non-Catholic clergyman incurs only one excommunication. He would not incur another censure because the marriage was attempted with an explicit or implicit understanding that one or all of the children should be brought up outside the Church. The word marriage is to be taken here in its strictly canonical sense, implying a valid contract. In the case given the marriage being invalid, the understanding with which it is attempted does not occasion another censure. If in such a marriage the consent was given before a priest and subsequently renewed in presence of a non-Catholic minister, the Catholic party incurs a double excommunication.[157] The priest applying to the Bishop for the necessary faculties should not fail to make known these facts. One absolution, after the faculties have been granted, will suffice to remove both censures. If a person, suspected of heresy on account of the agreement whose nature is explained above, fails to amend or remove the cause of suspicion within

[155] *Op. cit.*, Can. 1063, §1.
[156] *Op. cit.*, Can. 2319, §1, nn. 2-4.
[157] Cod. Iur. Can., Can. 2244.

six months from the time the censure was incurred, he is to be classed as a real heretic and is liable to all the penalties imposed on such.[158] Any one presuming to contract a mixed marriage, whether validly or invalidly, without the necessary dispensation of the Church, is excluded from all *legitimate ecclesiastical acts,* and from the sacramentals until a dispensation has been obtained from the Ordinary.[159] Such persons are not permitted to exercise the functions of administrator in ecclesiastical goods. They are barred from ecclesiastical trials and forbidden to act as judges, auditors, promoters of justice or of faith, *defensores vinculi,* notaries, chancellors or prosecutors. They cannot be accepted as sponsors at baptism or confirmation, nor may they vote in Ecclesiastical trials, or exercise the right of patronage (*ius patronatus*).[160]

7. *Civil Legislation.*

271. The impediment of disparity of worship and that of mixed religion in its strictly canonical form have been eliminated from the statutes of the Civil Codes. The Code of Napoleon ignores it entirely.[161] An imperial enactment issued on February 6, 1875, suppressed it in Germany.[162] In Hungary it met with a similar fate through a recent legislative measure. The civil laws of Austria do not admit the validity of marriage between one professing the Christian religion and an infidel. Thus the impediment is invested with a distorted form, becoming inherent in the profession of faith, and not in the baptismal character.[163] Such a

[158] *Op. cit.,* Can. 2315.
[159] *Op. cit.,* Can. 2319, §1, nn. 2-4.
[160] *Op. cit.,* Can. 2256, n. 2; HOLWECK, *Die kirchlichen Strafgesetze,* p. 150, §79, n. 3, Mainz, 1899.
[161] DE SMET, *op. cit.,* n. 292.
[162] AICHNER, *Comp. Iur. Ecc.,* §172, note 4, Brixinae, 1887.
[163] ORTOLAN, in the *Vacant & Mangenot Dictionnaire du Théol. Cath.,* art., *Disparité de Culte,* col. 1427.

civil enactment cannot fail to favor apostasy, for, provided one declares himself *confessionslos,* by this very fact a way is open to him to marry an infidel; while, on the other hand, a civil impediment of disparity of worship arises between a person once baptized but subsequently confessing infidelity, and a Catholic. This impediment is singularly characterized by Wernz[164] as the Austrian impediment of disparity of worship. The present Austrian legislation still upholds the impediment of Holy Orders, and of solemn religious profession, but it divests the impediment of disparity of worship of its canonical form. It legitimatizes two forms of marriage, namely, a canonical and a civil form. It opens the way to apostasy by enforcing the former only on those who profess the Catholic faith. The mere renunciation of faith is sufficient to make one competent to be married according to the civil form.[165]

V. Impediment of Holy Orders.
(Canon 1072.)

272. The impediment of Holy Orders is a circumstance bringing with it an inability disqualifying a cleric constituted in Sacred Orders from contracting a valid marriage,[166] or from continuing its licit use should the matrimonial bond have been contracted before his ordination in the Western Church. Among the major orders are to be enumerated: The Episcopate, the Priesthood, the Diaconate, and the Subdiaconate. Some rites of the Oriental Church class the subdiaconate among the minor orders.[167]

273. The impediment of Holy Orders was founded

[164] *Op. cit.*, n. 513.

[165] HIRSCHEL, in the *Archiv für katholisches Kirchenrecht*, vol. XXX, pp. 252 ff.; DE SMET, *op. cit.*, n. 292; GASPARRI, *op. cit.*, n. 624.

[166] COD. IUR. CAN., Can. 1072.

[167] *Conc. Prov. Alba Iul.* (1872), p. 88, 90, 142; *Synodus Sciarf.* (1888), p. 141, 201 ff.

on custom which, by specific legislation, became a universal law of the Church. This custom was probably based on the words of St. Paul: "He that is without a wife is solicitous for the things that belong to the Lord, how he may please God, but he that is with a wife is solicitous for the things of the world, how he may please his wife, and he is divided." [168] This scriptural quotation, to which others could be added,[169] furnishes an argument in favor of the state of celibacy which is better suited than that of matrimony to one whose life-task, by virtue of a free choice, is to consist of a special endeavor to promote his own and his fellowmen's spiritual welfare.

For a fuller history and development of this impediment the reader is referred to other sources.[170] It will suffice to note here that from the earliest ages both the Oriental and the Occidental Church forbade marriage to clerics who as celibate were promoted to the priesthood or even to the diaconate.[171]

274. The law of Emperor Justinian prohibiting marriage to clerics was subsequently adopted by the Oriental Church at the Synod of Trullo (692) whose sixth canon legislates that no priest or deacon or subdeacon after his promotion to Holy Orders may contract marriage.[172] The penalty of deposition was meted out against those who transgressed this law. This

[168] I *Cor.* VIII, 32 and 33.

[169] *Loc. cit.*, VII, 8.

[170] VACANDARD, in the *Dict. de Théologie*, s. v. *Célibat;* PHILLIPS, in the *Kirchenlexikon*, s. v. *Cölibat;* ZACCARIA, *Storia Polemica del Celibato Sacro* (Fuligno, 1785); PAVY, *Du Célibat Ecclésiastique* (Paris, 1852); CARRY, *Le Célibat Ecclésiastique* (Paris, 1901); ROSKOVÁNY, *Coelibatus et Breviarium* (Pesth, 1861-1890); LAURIN, *Der Cölibat der Geistlichen nach canonischen Rechte* (Wien, 1880); WERNZ, *Ius Decretalium*, vol. II, n. 295 ff., and vol. IV, n. 391 ff.; ESMEIN, *Le Marriage en Droit Canonique*, vol. I, p. 282 ff. (Paris, 1891); MILASCH, *Das Kirchenrecht der Morgenländischen Kirche* (Mostar, 1905).

[171] WERNZ, *op. cit.*, n. 391.

[172] GASPARRI, *op. cit.* n. 591; SANTI-LEITNER, *op. cit.*, lib. IV, tit. VI, n. 5; WERNZ, *op. cit.*, n. 391.

penalty was not only sanctioned but even enhanced when an excommunication *latae sententiae* was added to it by Benedict XIV in his constitution issued for the Italo-Greeks.[173] The same decree ordains that all marriages contracted after the reception of priesthood, of deaconship or of subdeaconship are null and void. Similar is the discipline of the Maronites, if one exempts the subdiaconate which they do not regard as a major order.[174] The same prohibition under the same penalty is emphasized by the Ruthenian Synod, but the law confines itself to the priesthood, disregarding the orders preceding it.[175] The Provincial Synod of the Roumanians by special legislation declares null and void all marriages contracted by clerics already in major Orders.[176] The Synod of Scharfa in 1888 legislating for the Syrians and the Synod of Alexandria in 1898 for the Copts approached the present discipline of the Occidental Church when they decreed that all candidates for higher Orders should be celibate.

275. This lack of uniformity in the Oriental Church is owing to the fact that the Holy See has failed to legislate specifically, universally and uniformly for all its rites, and in the absence of such legislation a controversy arose as regards the validity of marriages contracted by deacons and subdeacons. This question finds its practical application in case a schismatic cleric in major Orders, who marries after his promotion to subdeaconship, deaconship or priesthood, wishes to become a convert. In practice one should be guided by the instruction of Benedict XIV [177] which the Sacred

[173] *"Etsi Pastoralis,"* §VII, n. 27; 27 maii, 1742.

[174] *Synodus Maronitarum in Monte Libano* (1736), p. II, c. XI, §8, n. 9.

[175] *Synodus Zamoscensis,* tit. III, §8.

[176] *Synodus Provincialis pro Rumenis* (1883), art. XI, sect. I, cap II, §2.

[177] Const. *"Anno Vertente,"* §12, 19 iun., 1750; Const. *"Eo quamvis tempore,"* 4 maii, 1745.

Congregation of Propaganda repeatedly approved in its decisions.

276. If a cleric of the Oriental rite while in major Orders wishes to contract marriage, he should ask for a dispensation. This the Holy See does not always deny.[178] If the validity or the invalidity of a marriage already contracted is questioned the Holy See should be consulted in each individual case.

277. The law of the Western Church, forbidding marriage to clerics in major Orders does not present the same vagueness.[179] While up to the eleventh century there might have been a doubt as to its intrinsic force, this doubt gradually began to disappear after the Roman Synod (1049) held under Leo IX. It remained for the First Lateran Council (1123) to pronounce invalid marriages of high ecclesiastics who had received subdeaconship.[180] This law was subsequently more clearly defined by the Second and the Fourth Lateran Council, and was again accentuated by the Council of Trent.[181]

278. Benedict XIV decreed that neither celibacy nor the duty to recite the Breviary can be imposed on a cleric who was promoted to Holy Orders before he reached the age of puberty, unless after that age he either expressly or tacitly embraced the obligations attached to the Order he received.[182] He is not quite so indulgent toward the cleric who was constrained either by force or by grave fear to receive major Orders.[183] There was ground for controversy whether under such conditions the ordination was conferred validly or not.

[178] GASPARRI, *op. cit.*, n. 594.

[179] C. 1, 2, X, *qui clerici vel voventes matrimonium contrahere possunt*, IV, 6; c. 1, 4, X, *de clericis coniugatis*, III, 3; c. un. *de consanguinitate et affinitate*, IV, in *Clem.*

[180] THURSTON, in the *Catholic Encyclopedia*, art., *Celibacy*.

[181] Sess. XXIV, *De sacram. matrim.*, can. IX.

[182] Const. *"Eo quamvis tempore,"* 4 maii, 1745, §23 sq.

[183] *Loc. cit.*, §21; and *De Synodo Dioecesana*, lib. XII, cap. IV, n. 2.

The validity of the ordination being questioned, the arising obligation was also doubtful.

279. The new law ordains that a cleric promoted to Holy Orders under coercion, owing to grave fear, may be reduced to the state of the laity by the sentence of a competent judge, provided the coercion is proved and it is likewise manifest that he never acquiesced in his ordination, not even tacitly by exercising the rights the Order bestows and intending thereby to submit to the obligation. In possession of such evidence the cleric in question is freed from the obligation of celibacy and of the recitation of canonical hours.[184] Notwithstanding this definite legislation it would seem that if a cleric ordained under coercion should contract marriage while the sentence was pending, the validity of such a marriage should be upheld on the principle that *in dubio standum est pro valore matrimonii.*[185]

280. The coercion and the subsequent lack of acquiescence in the ordination must be proved by a juridical process clearly defined in the law.[186] In cases in which the obligations contracted by ordination are impugned, or in which the validity of the ordination is challenged, a *libellus* must be sent to the Sacred Congregation of the Sacraments, or to the Holy Office should the ordination be questioned on account of a substantial defect in the sacred rite. This preliminary step having been taken the Sacred Congregation will decide whether the cause is to be treated by a judicial process, or by way of a disciplinary measure. Should the decision favor the former course the Sacred Congregation will entrust the cause to the tribunal of the diocese to which the cleric belonged at the time of his ordination.

[184] Cod. Iur. Can., Can. 214.

[185] *Op. cit.*, Can. 1014; Suarez, *De virt. et de stat. relig.*, tract. VII, 1, 9, cap. XVII, n. 11; Ballerini, *Op. theol.*, t. IV, p. 181 sq.; Sanchez, *op. cit.*, lib. VII, disp. XXVII, n. 9.

[186] Cod. Iur. Can., Can. 1993.

Should the ordination be impugned on account of a substantial defect in the sacred rite, the case will be committed to the care of the diocese in which the ordination took place. Should the decision favor a recourse to the disciplinary measure the Sacred Congregation itself will settle the question after the competent tribunal of the Curia instituted the proper process in order to place itself in possession of all the necessary information. The validity of the ordination may be impugned either by the cleric himself or by the Ordinary to whose diocese he belongs or in whose diocese he was ordained. The absolution from the obligations attached to the clerical state must be asked by the ecclesiastic himself.[187] The *defensor* of the bond arising from Sacred Orders enjoys the same rights and has the same duties as the *defensor vinculi matrimonialis.*[188] Even if the action was instituted only against the obligations imposed by Sacred Orders and not against the validity of the ordination, the cleric *ad cautelam* is to be barred from the exercise of the Order.[189] Freedom from such obligations is not to be presumed until two judicial sentences agreeing in the same decision have been handed down by the competent ecclesiastical court.[190]

281. This impediment is of ecclesiastical origin; therefore it is in the power of the Church to dispense from it. Giovine [191] enumerates several cases in which such a dispensation was actually granted by Benedict IX, Pius VII, and other Pontiffs, in behalf of ecclesiastics below the Episcopate. The contrary opinion of St. Alphonsus, holding that the Church cannot lift the

[187] *Op. cit.,* Can. 1994.
[188] *Op. cit.,* Can. 1996.
[189] *Op. cit.,* Can. 1997.
[190] *Op. cit.,* Can. 1998.
[191] *Op. cit.,* §245; litt. encycl. S. C. S. Off., 20 febr., 1888; Cod. Iur. Can., Can. 1043.

impediment arising from the Order of the Holy Priesthood, must be rejected as untenable.[192] While strictly speaking the Church could dispense even in the case of a Bishop, history does not show that it has ever exercised such a right either in the Oriental or in the Occidental Church.[193]

282. The present law disqualifies a cleric constituted in major Orders from contracting a valid marriage, and imposes on him the obligation to observe chastity.[194] This inability to contract marriage validly does not cease even if the cleric as the consequence of a crime be penalized by a permanent irregularity, or suspension, or deposition, or even degradation. The impediment of Holy Orders retains its force even if such an ecclesiastic should be reduced to the state of a layman,[195] and subsequently should become a heretic or a schismatic or an apostate. Clerics attempting marriage, even if it be only a civil ceremony, incur an excommunication *latae sententiae* simply reserved to the Holy See. If after due admonition they continue in their obstinacy, they are to be degraded, and *ipso iure* all their offices become vacant.[196]

VI. The Impediment of Religious Profession.

(Canon 1073.)

283. No marriage can be contracted validly by a religious who embraced solemn vows or such simple vows as have the effect of nullifying marriage by virtue of a superadded force communicated to them through a special decree of the Holy See.[197] These solemn vows

[192] *Theol. Moralis, De Sacramento Ordinis,* lib. VI, n. 808.

[193] SANTI-LEITNER, *op. cit.,* lib. IV, tit. VI, n. 6; GASPARRI, *op. cit.,* n. 589.

[194] COD. IUR. CAN., Can. 132.

[195] *Op. cit.,* Can. 213, §2.

[196] *Op. cit.,* Can. 188, n. 5; Can. 2388.

[197] *Op cit.,* Can. 1073.

are chastity, poverty and obedience. It is only the first of the three that has a direct bearing on the question under consideration.

The vow of chastity finds its justification in the Sacred Scripture. The example and the counsel of the Founder of Christianity served as incentives for the Christians living even in the time of the Apostles, to bind themselves by a vow of chastity.[198] The words of St. Paul not only approved such a resolution but even extolled it.[199] It was therefore nothing surprising that as early as the third century history recorded two classes of individuals who publicly pledged themselves to observe a vow of chastity.[200] These were called *virgines velatae* and *virgines non velatae*.[201] Tertullian [202] mentions also a third class, namely, virgins who took a secret vow of virginity.

284. While the breaking of a vow entailed severe ecclesiastical penalties, it is a controverted point whether even before the First Lateran Council it possessed a universal force invalidating all marriages. There can be no doubt that by virtue of particular law enforced in certain localities the vow did produce such an effect even as early as the beginning of the seventh century.[203] A universal law drawn at the First Lateran Council (1123) declares all marriages contracted by men belonging to a religious order null and void,[204] and the Second Lateran Council (1139) makes a similar declaration as regards the religious communities of women.[205] After the distinction between the simple

[198] *Matt.* XVI, 24; XIX, 11 and 12.

[199] I. *Cor.* VII, 7, 8, 25 ff.

[200] VERMEERSCH, in the *Catholic Encyclopedia*, art., *Profession, Religious*.

[201] THOMASSINUS, p. I, lib. III, c. 42.

[202] *De veland. virginibus*, cap. XIV.

[203] Cap. XIV, *Conc. Paris.* (615); cap. II and III, *Conc. Rom.* (721); cap. VIII, *Conc. Trosl.* (909).

[204] Can. VIII, dist. XXVII.

[205] C. 40, C. XXVII, q. 1.

and the solemn vow came into existence, around the time of Gratian, the solemn vow was generally associated with the religious professed in an order. This gave rise to a doubt as regards the force of a simple vow. Solution was offered by the decree of Boniface VIII who endowed with a force nullifying marriage only those vows which were taken solemnly in the reception of Sacred Orders, or in the profession, whether express or tacit, made in a religious community, possessing the approbation of the Holy See.[206]

The foregoing decree of Pope Boniface was subsequently emphasized by the Council of Trent which anathemizes those who maintain that a cleric in Sacred Orders or one who has taken a solemn vow of chastity may contract marriage validly.[207]

285. The new law while legislating profusely for religious congregations introduced no fundamental change in this respect. The determination whether a vow is solemn or simple depends entirely upon its recognition as such by the Church.[208] In concrete cases the juridical recognition presupposes that the Church has permitted a certain religious institute to bind its members by solemn vows, and that all the conditions required for the validity of such vows have been verified.[209] Therefore the solemnity of a vow is determined by its effects rather than by the external rite which is the means of its administration.

286. The solemn vow may affect marriage in two ways, namely, by nullifying it, should it be attempted after the vow has been taken, or by dissolving it, should the vow be taken after a non-consummated marriage.[210]

[206] C. un. *de voto et voti redemptione,* III, 15, in VI°.
[207] Sess. XXIV, *De sacram. Matrim.,* can. IX.
[208] Cod. Iur. Can., Can. 1308, §2.
[209] Papi, *Religious Profession,* p. 9 (New York, 1918).
[210] Cod. Iur. Can., Can. 1119.

287. The simple vow is only an impedient impediment to marriage unless taken by the Scholastics of the Society of Jesus, in which case by virtue of special legislation it constitutes a diriment impediment.[211] Some maintain that a simple vow of chastity taken by a woman consenting to her husband's promotion to the Priesthood, has also the effect of dissolving marriage, regardless of whether she should contract it before or after the death of her former consort, if he was actually ordained.[212] The opinion permitting a valid marriage after the consort's death is, however, more probable. Since all agree that such a marriage would be illicit a dispensation should be obtained from the Holy See from the taken vow. Should the marriage be contracted without such a dispensation, unless the Holy See declares otherwise, its validity must be upheld.[213]

288. It must be borne in mind that only the solemn religious vows possess the effect explained above, namely, when taken and administered in conformity with the new law. The conditions of validity are clearly specified:[214] (1) The candidate must have the required age, namely, the age of twenty-one years for a perpetual profession, be it solemn or simple;[215] (2) Admission to the profession must be given by the lawful superior according to the constitution; (3) The profession must be preceded by a valid novitiate;[216] (4) It should not be the result of coercion, fear or fraud; (5) It must be explicit and administered by the

[211] GREGORIUS XIII, const. *"Ascendente Domino,"* 25 maii, 1584, §22.

[212] SANTI-LEITNER, tit. VI, *De voto,* n. 8; SANCHEZ, VII, disp. 40; BENEDICT. XIV, *De Synodo Dioecesana,* lib. XIII, cap. XII, n. 16; see also DE BECKER, *op. cit.,* p. 152; SCHMALZGRÜBER, ad tit. *qui clerici vel voventes,* n. 67; DE SMET, *op. cit.,* n. 284, note; c. 10, X, *de conversione coniugum,* III, 32.

[213] WERNZ, *op. cit.,* n. 380; GASPARRI, *op. cit.,* n. 576.

[214] COD. IUR. CAN., Can. 572.

[215] *Op. cit.,* Can. 573.

[216] See canons 542 and 555 of the new Code.

legitimate Superior or his delegate; (6) It must be preceded by a temporary and simple profession.[217]

The impediment of religious profession is of ecclesiastical origin, for the efficacy of the vows, whether simple or solemn, is dependent entirely on the legislation of the Church. This doctrine is contained in the above-quoted decree of Boniface VIII, and practically all leading canonists admit that the Holy See may dispense from a solemn vow; *a fortiori* from a simple vow.[218] Such dispensation has actually been granted on several occasions. The best known instance is perhaps the indult of Pius VII, who at the beginning of the nineteenth century *"sanavit in radice multarum monialium et monachorum sacrilega matrimonia."* [219]

289. In urgent danger of death the Bishops and the priests, as already explained, have the power to dispense even from a solemn vow, provided it is detached from the Priesthood.[220] Outside such danger only the Roman Pontiff may dispense, unless the Ordinary enjoys a special indult. A very grave cause involving individual or public welfare is usually required for such a dispensation.[221]

290. The *Clementinae* record an excommunication fulminated against those men and women of religious communities who attempt marriage notwithstanding the fact that they are solemnly professed.[222] Pius IX reserved this excommunication *latae sententiae* to the Ordinaries,[223] and the Codex of Pius X qualifies it as *excommunicatio simpliciter reservata Sedi Apos-*

[217] *Op. cit.*, Can. 574.

[218] St. Alphonsus, *op. cit.*, vol. III, n. 256; Giovine, *op. cit.*, §241; n. 2; St. Thomas, 4, *Sent.*, dist. XXXVIII, q. 1, ad 3; Wernz, *op. cit.*, n. 381; De Becker, *op. cit.*, p. 152.

[219] Gasparri, *op. cit.*, n. 567.

[220] Cod. Iur. Can., Can. 1043; see this work, n. 151 ff.

[221] Gasparri, *op. cit.*, n. 508; Wernz, *op. cit.*, n. 381.

[222] C. un. *de consanguinitate et affinitate*, IV, in *Clem.*

[223] Const. *"Apostolicae Sedis,"* 12 oct., 1869, §III, n. 1.

tolicae.[224] To the Bishop is reserved only the excommunication *latae sententiae* incurred in consequence of a marriage attempted by those who took perpetual simple vows in a religious community.[225] Besides this excommunication such religious bound by solemn or simple vows, whether perpetual or temporary, incur irregularity, which is communicated to the other party attempting to contract marriage with them.[226]

VII. The Impediment of Abduction.

(Canon 1074.)

291. Abduction considered as a matrimonial impediment consists in a criminal act whereby one violently and with a matrimonial intent detains a woman in a place where she lives or to which she repairs of her own volition; or whereby with the same intent one violently carries her away from a safe place where she is free to a morally different place where she is subject to the direct or indirect control of the abductor until she consents to marry him. The authors generally distinguish between *raptus seductionis* and *raptus violentiae.* The former is abduction by seduction, popularly styled elopement. The latter implies violence employed by the captor in order to accomplish his end. Abduction by seduction does not give rise to a diriment impediment, for it presupposes that the woman signified her willingness both to the flight and to the marriage, regardless of the fact whether her consent was spontaneous or the result of flattery, allurement or cajolery. In this case should the woman be under age an injustice is offered to the non-consenting parents or guardians, but the Tridentine decree on which this law

[224] COD. IUR. CAN., Can. 2388.
[225] *Op. cit.,* Can. 2388, §2.
[226] *Op. cit.,* Can. 985.

is based does not take their will into consideration, its purpose is merely to safeguard the freedom of the woman in the choice of her consort. This freedom about which the Church is so solicitous is threatened only in the case of detention or abduction by violence; hence, either of those acts would induce the impediment.

292. The impediment of abduction would arise in any of the following cases: (1) When a woman is seized against her will and transferred into another place, not secure, without consenting to a marriage to which the abductor endeavors to coerce her, and for that reason detains her by force physical or moral (fear or fraud being equivalent to force); (2) When a woman yielding to fraud or enticement consents to repair to another place, but with another intention than matrimony, and in that place she is subsequently detained by the abductor who uses physical or moral coercion to force her into marrying him; (3) When a woman already espoused to the abductor, is carried away violently to a place unsafe for her, and objecting both to the abduction and to the marriage is detained there until she consents.

293. The perusal of a few historical facts will suffice to acquaint the reader with the development of this impediment. Some maintain that even the untutored tribes stigmatized abduction as something dishonorable, and for that reason inaugurated the custom of paying for the woman they wished to marry.[227] Though this statement may be impugned it is certain that the Jewish law did not favor marriages between the abductor and the abducted.[228] Rock maintains that the old Roman law (*Ius Vetus*) permitted the solemniza-

[227] Wernz, *op. cit.*, n. 278.

[228] *Deut.* XXII, 25 ff.; c. 8, 9, C. XXXVI, q. 2; Schegg, *Bibl. Archeolog.*, p. 643 ff.

tion of marriage between the *raptor* and the *rapta.*[229] Constantine the Great forbade such marriages and Justinian decreed a capital punishment against those who perpetrated the crime of *raptus.*[230] Owing, on the one hand, to the ample provisions made by the Roman law to punish the crime of abduction and, on the other hand, to its infrequency among the early Christians, the Church was not constrained in the first three centuries to legislate on this point.[231] In the fifth century the Council of Chalcedon (451) in canon 27 anathematized those who resorted to abduction in order to procure a wife, and degraded them if they were clerics. Leo VI contented himself with approving the former laws in all their rigor, while the old Spanish law inflicted a capital punishment on the abductor who also ravished the woman. In the ninth century abduction was associated with a kind of impedient impediment[232] perpetual by its nature.[233] The law of Innocent III[234] favored the wife-captors inasmuch as it permitted them to contract marriage with the *rapta* even while she was still in their power, provided she consented.[235] One commendable feature of this law was that the consent was not to be presumed, it had to be proved. The Innocentian law divested the impediment of abduction of its identity by making it practically indistinguishable from the impediment of *vis et metus.*

294. An important change in the history of this impediment was inaugurated by the Tridentine law. The Fathers convened at the Council of Trent, seeking a

[229] In the *Catholic Encyclopedia,* art., *Abduction.*

[230] L. 1, Cod. Theod. *de raptu virg.* IX, 24; L. un. Cod. *de raptu virg.,* IX, 13.

[231] St. Basil., *Epistol. canon. secund. ad Amphiloch.,* c. XXII and XXX.

[232] C. 4, 10, 11, C. XXXVI, q. 2.

[233] De Becker, *op. cit.,* p. 68.

[234] C. 7, X, *de raptoribus,* V. 17.

[235] Gasparri, *op. cit.,* n. 539.

remedy for the evils resulting from the frequency with which the crime of abduction was committed suggested that the impediment be made diriment. The result was the following decree as incorporated in the official acts: Between the *raptor* and the *rapta* no marriage can take place as long as the latter is under the control of the former. Should the abducted, after having been separated from the abductor and conducted to a safe and free place, consent to take the *raptor* for her husband, he may marry her; nevertheless, the *raptor* with all his counsellors, abettors and accomplices becomes by law excommunicated, declared forever infamous and incapable of acquiring any dignities, and, should they be clerics, they are to be deposed. The *raptor* is furthermore obliged, whether he marries the *rapta* or not, to invest her with a decent dowry whose amount is left to the decision of the judge.[236]

295. The foregoing discipline, in its substance, receives the official recognition of the Church by being promulgated in the Codex of Pius X. The canon embodying the new law reads: There can be no marriage between the man who is a *raptor* and a woman abducted with matrimonial intent, as long as she remains in the power of the abductor.[237] Should the *rapta* be separated from the *raptor* and conducted to a safe and free place the impediment ceases, provided she consents to have him for her husband.[238] As regards the nullity of marriage the violent detention of a woman is to be regarded equivalent to abduction, when, namely, a man violently detains a woman with matrimonial intent in a place where she tarries or to which she repairs of her own free will.[239]

[236] Sess. XXIV, *De reform. matrim.*, cap. VI.
[237] COD. IUR. CAN., Can. 1074, §1.
[238] *Op. cit., loc. cit.*, §2.
[239] *Op. cit., loc. cit.*, §3.

296. The following pages will be devoted to the elucidation of the foregoing law.

1. Abduction in the former discipline had to be combined with violence, namely, the woman had to be transferred reluctantly from a place in which she was free to another place controlled by the *raptor* either directly or indirectly. It was immaterial whether the abduction was accomplished by the principal or by his agent. The impediment did not arise unless the removal from a place *a quo* to a morally different place *ad quem* was realized in every case.[240] The impediment was induced even if the woman in question consented to the flight but not to the marriage,[241] but not so when she acquiesced in both.[242] Even moral force sufficed to give rise to this impediment, for threats, grave fear or fraud were equivalent to physical force. It was a controverted question whether the impediment arose in consequence of what used to be called an act of sequestration, namely, when the woman went to a certain place of her own volition and subsequently violence was used to coerce her to marriage. Much of the doubt that formerly existed disappears owing to the definiteness with which the new law legislates on this point. According to the present discipline the change of locality is only one of the causes giving rise to this impediment, the other cause is a violent detention with matrimonial intent regardless of the place where the woman is detained, even if it should be her own home.

2. Any woman, whatever her character, even one's own betrothed may be the occasion of the impediment of abduction, if the other conditions are verified. The impediment is not contracted should a woman abduct a man, but she would incur the same penalties as the

[240] S. C. C., *Herbipolen.*, 24 apr., 1858; 18 iun., 1859.
[241] S. C. C., *Olomucen.*, 14 mart., 1772.
[242] S. C. C., *Mediolanen.*, 24 aug., 1661.

abductor if she should participate in his crime as an abettor or a procurator. A public woman when abducted is presumed *volens explendae libidinis causa,* therefore, her unwillingness is to be proved.[243]

3. Removal from one place to another formerly constituted a *condito sine qua non* of the impediment of abduction. The present discipline has been considerably simplified by the fact that the law lays main stress not on the change of locality but rather on the fact of violent detention with matrimonial intent.

4. Matrimonial intent must enter into the abduction in order that an impediment may be contracted. Should the crime be perpetrated for another purpose as, for instance, robbery, gratification of lust, revenge, etc., the impediment would not arise. In doubt the matrimonial intent is always presumed. In the former discipline the initial motive (which was difficult to prove) of abduction had to be marriage. In the new discipline the initial motive, whatever its nature, is not a decisive factor, for the impediment is contracted by virtue of a mere act whereby a woman is detained by force provided the final motive is marriage. This wise change was suggested by the difficulty encountered in impugning the statement of an abductor who in his endeavor to liberate himself from the incurred penalty would make the assertion that his initial purpose in committing the crime was not marriage.

297. The impediment arises between the *raptor* and the *rapta.* The abettor or the procurator would incur the penalty but would not contract the impediment, unless after he abducted the woman for someone else he would detain her by force and coerce her to marry him instead of the principal agent.

Since the impediment is of ecclesiastical origin it does not bind infidels (provided neither *vis* nor *metus*

[243] GASPARRI, *op. cit.,* n. 547.

is present) unless the civil law conforms to the Church law. It does, however, regard all marriages in which at least one of the parties, the man or the woman, is baptized.

298. The Church very seldom dispenses from this impediment, not only because the presumption is in favor of coercion but also because by setting the woman free the marriage can be contracted without a dispensation.[244] With so deep a detestation does the Church regard this crime that even dispensations from other impediments she conditions on the clause: "Provided the woman was not abducted for that (namely, matrimonial) purpose."[245] Should the impediment of consanguinity exist between the *raptor* and the *rapta* a dispensation conditioned on such a clause would fail to remove it though subsequently to the abduction the woman was *in loco tuto constituta.* The faculties issued on February 20, 1888, conferring the power to dispense from public impediments in urgent danger of death, include the faculty to dispense from the impediment of abduction. The new law bestows on the Bishops and priests the same power by virtue of canon 1043.[246]

299. The penalty specified by the Tridentine law is somewhat modified by the new legislation. The new law omits all mention of dowry. One may therefore legitimately conclude that such an obligation will no longer be imposed on the abductor. Formerly an excommunication *latae sententiae nemini reservata* was fulminated against the perpetrator of such a crime. The new law reads: He who with matrimonial intent

[244] C. 10, C. XXXVI, q. 2; *Reg.* 27, *R. J.* in VI°; S. C. S. Off., instr. (ad Ep. Albaniae), 15 febr., 1901; S. C. de Prop. Fide (C. P. pro Sin-Cochin-chin.), 11 febr., 1804; 22 nov., 1860.

[245] PUTZER, *Commentarium in Facultates Apostolicas*, n. 126 (New York, 1893).

[246] See this work, n. 151 ff.

or with a motive to pander to his lust abducts a reluctant woman whether by force or fraud, or a woman who being a minor consents while her parents or guardians object and dissent, is by law excluded from all legitimate ecclesiastical acts, and should be punished also with other penalties proportionate to the gravity of his crime.[247]

300. All those who in accordance with canon 2209 co-operate in abduction with the principal are subject to the same penalties as the principal himself.[248] The priest and the witnesses before whom the *raptor* attempts to contract marriage while the *rapta* is still under his control do not incur these penalties, for they are not instrumental in his crime of abduction but only in his marriage. They would be liable to the same punishment only in case they abetted him by promising to witness his marriage should he succeed in his project.

To impugn the validity of a marriage contracted under such circumstances is the right of the abducted woman, but not of the *raptor*. She ought to avail herself of the earliest opportunity to bring to the knowledge of the proper ecclesiastical authority the cause that might be advanced for the nullity of her wedlock.

VIII. The Impediment of Crime.
(Canon 1075.)

301. The impediment of crime is a circumstance occasioning an inability which precludes the possibility of a valid marriage between a man and a woman when certain conditions specified by law have been verified in their mutual guilt of adultery or of homicide resulting in the death of the consort of either. The new law legislates [249] that no marriage can exist between those:

[247] COD. IUR. CAN., Can. 2353.
[248] *Op. cit.*, Can. 2231.
[249] COD. IUR. CAN., Can. 1075.

(1) Who, while bound by one and the same legitimate matrimonial bond committed adultery and mutually promised to marry or actually attempted a civil marriage; (2) Who while bound by one and the same legitimate matrimonial bond committed adultery and then either of them became guilty of the murder of his consort; (3) Who, by mutual physical or moral deeds, caused the death of a consort, even if they are free from the guilt of adultery.

302. The early Roman law prohibited marriage between an adulterer and an adulteress, which prohibition was endowed with an invalidating force by the law of Justinian.[250] The statement of Devoti [251] that the early Church canonized this Roman law is untenable, for the early canons fail to reveal the existence of a diriment impediment of crime.[252] The first intimation of such an impediment comes from the time of Pope St. Leo. The Council of Tribur (895) decreed: *"Nullus ducat in matrimonium, quam prius polluit per adulterium."* [253] This law was subsequently incorporated in the various collections including the Gratian.[254] Gratian records only two phases of this impediment, namely, when it arises from adultery linked with machination against the life of the husband of the adulteress,[255] or with a promise of marriage to be contracted after the death of her husband. Probably on the ground of the principle *"plus est ducere quam fidem dare,"* Clement III (1187-1191) [256] added the

[250] L. 21, §11, l. 40 ff. ad leg. Iuliam *de adulter.;* L. 13 ff. *de iis quae ut indign.,* Nov. 134, cap. 12.

[251] Lib. II, §140.

[252] Cap. IX, *Conc. Illiberit.* (300-306); C. 8, C. XXXII, q. 7; c. 2, C. XXXI, q. 1.

[253] C. 1, C. XXXI, q. 1.

[254] C. 4, C. XXXI, q. 1.

[255] C. 3, C. XXXI, q. 1.

[256] C. 4, X, *de eo qui duxit in matrimonium, quam polluit per adulterium,* IV, 7.

third cause from which this impediment drew its origin, namely, adultery coupled with an attempted marriage. Finally, his successor Celestine III (1191-1198) introduced the fourth phase of this impediment, namely, murder of a consort procured by mutual conspiracy even if adultery did not intervene.[257] Gregory IX (1227-1234) was the next Pontiff who had occasion to legislate on the impediment.[258] To a doubt submitted to him for solution he answered that the impediment of crime does not arise from the mere promise of marriage nor from the mere attempt at marriage, *nisi prius vel postea vivente coniuge adulterium intercessit.*[259] The Council of Trent refrained from legislating any further on this impediment, and the Code of Pius X simply approves the traditional discipline as handed down by the Decretals.

303. Though the new law is couched in clear terms, it is not sufficiently comprehensive to solve all doubts that in the past arose in connection with this impediment. The force of this statement will be better appreciated by submitting to individual consideration the various causes which are instrumental in giving rise to the impediment of crime.

304. I. The new law declares that no marriage can exist between those who, while one and the same legitimate matrimonial bond existed, committed adultery and promised to marry each other or attempted a civil marriage.[260] To become a partial contributory cause of this impediment the adultery must be:

1. Real and not merely putative, namely, one of the accomplices must be bound by a matrimonial bond ob-

[257] C. 1, X, *de conversione infidelium,* III, 33.

[258] C. 8, X, *de eo qui duxit in matrimonium, quam polluit per adulterium,* IV, 7.

[259] ESMEIN, *op. cit.,* t. I, p. 384 ff.; t. II, p. 65 ff.; WERNZ, *op cit.,* n. 518.

[260] COD. IUR. CAN., Can. 1075, §1.

jectively valid. It is immaterial whether such a marriage is consummated or not, nor would the guilt be lessened by the fact that in consequence of a civil divorce a separation a *toro et mensa* was obtained.

2. Consummated, namely, resulting from a perfect *copula in se* fitted for generation. An incomplete *copula,* or sodomy or onanism would not suffice, for in criminal cases the specified penalty is not incurred unless the crime is completed. The attempt at the crime is not penalized with the same rigor as the crime itself, unless the law so ordains. In case of doubt whether the *copula* was perfect or not, both forums presume the former.[261]

3. Formal on the part of the two accomplices, namely, both parties must be aware of the fact that one of them is married, for the law presupposes that both offend against one and the same matrimonial bond. Consequently, the impediment would not arise if each of the offenders would have a knowledge of only his own marriage without being aware of the marriage of his accomplice. An ignorance of such a fact, unless it is affected, would excuse one from contracting this impediment even if all the other conditions should be verified. There is a controversy whether vincible ignorance, called crass or supine, which is gravely culpable, would excuse under the circumstances. The majority of authors take the affirmative side of the question.[262]

305. Adultery, even if it should possess all the characteristics pointed out above, would fail to induce the impediment of crime unless accompanied by the promise of marriage. This promise is not a partial

[261] GASPARRI, *op. cit.,* n. 647.

[262] DE BECKER, *op. cit.,* p. 166; SCHMALZGRÜBER, *h. t.,* n. 11; GASPARRI, *op. cit.,* n. 647; SANCHEZ, *op. cit.,* VII, disp. LXXIX, n. 35; ST. ALPHONSUS, *op. cit.,* vol. VI, n. 1036; D'ANNIBALE, vol. III, n. 439.

contributory cause to the impediment of crime, unless it is:

1. True, differing from a desire or an intention by the fact that it is manifested externally. In case of doubt neither the internal nor the external forum presumes it to have been serious and true.

2. Manifested externally to the accomplice, who in turn employs such words or signs, or displays such conduct as can be interpreted as a positive acceptation of the proposal. One may not have recourse in this connection to the principal *"qui tacet consentire videtur."* Some canonists insist so strongly on the express acceptation that they require even a re-promise, though there is a controversy whether a re-promise is a *conditio sine qua non.* The express acceptation, in the opinion of some, implicitly contains a re-promise. Should such a re-promise not be included, or should it be excluded, the impediment would not arise or would be doubtful, to say the least.[263]

3. Absolute, for conditional promise does not suffice to give rise to the impediment unless the condition is such that its fulfillment is likely before the dissolution of the matrimonial bond. The impediment takes effect as soon as the past or present event on which the promise is conditioned is known to have actually taken place. It is contracted even by virtue of a promise conditioned on *de futuro necessario, impossibili aut turpi.* If the promise is *de futuro contingenti ac honesto,* the impediment arises provided the condition was verified before the dissolution of marriage; not so, should its fulfillment take place only after the matrimonial bond was dissolved. This opinion is to be held against Sanchez[264] and a few others.

4. Matrimonial, namely, its object should be mar-

[263] WERNZ, *op. cit.*, n. 524, note 35; GASPARRI, *op. cit.*, n. 648.
[264] Lib. VII, disp. LXXIX, n. 11.

riage to be contracted after the death of the consort.[265] Should its object be marriage after the civil divorce of the consort, the impediment would not arise.[266] It is immaterial whether this promise is antecedent, concomitant, or subsequent to adultery, as long as both occur during the same marriage. The impediment is not contracted if the adultery follows after the retraction of the previously given promise, and the promise is not renewed after the moral offense.

5. Finally, detrimental to an existing marriage. This presupposes the knowledge of the *ligamen* binding at least one of the parties. One might ask: Does an impediment arise between A. and B. when A. not knowing that B. was married promises her marriage and subsequently, after having learned of her marriage, knows her carnally? Should A. renew his promise after he was apprised of the marriage of his accomplice the impediment would unquestionably arise. In failure of such a renewal the impediment is doubtful. Some advocate that the renewal of such a promise is included implicitly in the commission of the crime of adultery, others again deny such a tacit inclusion. Owing to this controversy the impediment, at least on the ground of reflex principle, should not be urged.

306. Neither adultery nor the promise of marriage taken independently of each other would induce the impediment of crime. They must be correlated, or, in other words, both must take place during the same marriage. If A. unmarried, promised marriage to B. who is married, and during the same marriage they have known each other carnally, the impediment would arise. But if the promise of marriage was made during the life-time of B.'s first husband and the adultery

[265] SANCHEZ, lib. VII, disp. LXXIX, n. 2; SCHMALZGRÜBER, *h. t.*, n. 8 and 9; FEIJE, *op. cit.*, n. 649.

[266] GASPARRI, *op. cit.*, n. 648; WERNZ, *op. cit.*, n. 524.

followed after she was remarried, the impediment would not be contracted unless the promise was renewed, for both the promise and the adultery must be injurious to the matrimonial bond which bound B. by virtue of her second marriage.

307. On the ground of the principle *"plus est ducere quam fidem dare"* the impediment arises should an actual attempt at marriage be substituted for the mere promise, for such action is construed as offering even a more direct and manifest injury to the innocent consort. In this connection it must be borne in mind that any marriage, though it be only civil, will give rise to this impediment, provided it is correlated with adultery such as described above.[267] It is immaterial whether the adultery preceded or followed the attempt at marriage, as long as both took place during the existence of one and the same matrimonial bond of which the offenders were aware. If after the attempt at marriage the parties repented and the adultery followed without a new attempt at, or without a promise of marriage; or, if the attempt was made during the lifetime of the first consort the impediment would not arise in either case.[268]

308. II. The second phase of this impediment arises when during the existence of one and the same legitimate matrimonial bond the two offenders commit adultery and either of them is guilty of the murder of his own consort.[269]

A. Adultery mentioned in this canon would not become a partial contributory cause of this impediment unless it were real, consummated and formal in the sense already indicated above.[270]

[267] S. C. de Prop. Fide, 14 ian., 1844.

[268] GASPARRI, *op. cit.*, n. 649; DE SMET, *op. cit.*, n. 324; WERNZ, *op. cit.*, n. 526.

[269] COD. IUR. CAN., Can. 1075, §2.

[270] See this work, n. 304.

309. B. The murder of the consort:

1. Must be the outcome of the machination directed against the life of the innocent partner. It is immaterial whether the murder results from physical violence (by means of direct killing), or from moral violence (by means of indirect killing, the outcome of a mandate or of an advice).

2. Must be committed by one of those guilty of adultery, and it must be one's own consort, namely, real husband or wife. Furthermore, death as occasioned by the plotting itself must follow either immediately, or mediately, in the latter case the wound inflicted must have proved fatal.

3. Must have for its object the intention to contract marriage with the adulterous accomplice. Should it be actuated by a revenge, or by any other reason, the murder would fail to become a partial contributory cause to this impediment. It is sufficient that such a matrimonial motive should actuate only the party guilty of homicide.

310. There is a controversy to the effect whether it is necessary that this intention be manifested to the accomplice in adultery. Some take the affirmative [271] others again the negative side [272] of the question. The affirmative side can hardly be sustained in view of the sources which speak of the plotting of one party only.[273] Should the intention be manifested to the other party it would be equivalent to a conspiracy and we would be confronted with the third phase of this impediment when the death of the innocent consort results from the mutual machination of the two accomplices, in which case adultery is not a requisite. We

[271] GASPARRI, *op. cit.*, n. 650; D'ANNIBALE, vol. III, n. 441.

[272] WERNZ, *op. cit.*, n. 531; note 61; ROSSET, *De Sacramento Matrimonii*, n. 2048 ff.; LEITNER, *op. cit.*, tit. VII, n. 6, vol. IV, p. 215.

[273] C. 6, 7, X, *de eo qui duxit in matrimonium quam polluit per adulterium*, IV, 7.

must therefore conclude that the second phase of this impediment does not require that the intention (to enter into marriage) of the party guilty of murder be revealed to the accomplice in adultery. It is to be noted that, generally speaking, this intention is presumed, should all the conditions be verified. This presumption is not *praesumptio iuris et de iure;* consequently, it admits a contrary proof.[274] The adultery and the murder of one's consort must be so correlated that the former follows before death overtakes the consort against whom the plot was aimed. It is immaterial whether the adultery is committed before or after the machination, for example, before or after the administration of poison from which the death of the innocent consort resulted.

311. III. The third phase of this impediment arises from the murder of a consort, even when unaccompanied by the guilt of adultery, provided it was the outcome of mutual physical or moral acts of violence.[275]

In order that the murder of a consort may of itself give rise to this impediment it is required:

1. That the consort whose death is procured be bound by a valid matrimonial bond to one of the accomplices, and that this bond should exist at the time the homicide is perpetrated. Therefore in case of a putative marriage the impediment would not be contracted, for the murder would be qualified as a simple homicide and not a *coniugicidium.* The marriage need not be consummated, ratified marriage suffices.[276] It is immaterial whether the husband is guilty of uxoricide or whether the wife murders her husband.

2. The co-operation of the accomplice must be of such a nature that he may justly be reputed as the

[274] S. C. C., *Ulixbonen.,* 28 sept., 1726.
[275] COD. IUR. CAN., Can. 1075, n. 3.
[276] SANCHEZ, lib. VII, disp. LXXVIII, n. 20; WERNZ, *op. cit.,* n. 527.

co-criminal in the felonious act.[277] A mere approval given to the act after its commission would not involve the required criminality. It is immaterial whether the murder resulted from the physical or moral co-operation of the accomplice, as would be implied by physical acts of violence in the former case, or a mandate or advice in the latter. If, therefore, A. reveals to B. his intention relative to the murder of his wife, in order to marry her, and the deed is perpetrated after her approbation is given, it is presumed that B.'s approval was an incentive to the commission of the crime.[278]

3. That the death should be directly intended and that it should not result from an accident but from acts of violence either immediately or mediately through the inflicted wound. If, however, the wound is not deadly, and the death can be traced to the inexperience of the physician the impediment would not arise.[279]

4. Finally, that the murder be committed with the intention of entering into marriage with the accomplice, or with one of those who participated in the criminal act. It is precisely this hope of such a marriage the Church wishes to obviate by the introduction of this impediment. There is a controversy whether the accomplices must be actuated by this intention, or whether they must have mutually manifested it to each other. Since the murder of the consort must be committed with some hope of marrying the accomplice, it is reasonable to suppose that the principal should manifest his motive to his accomplice, whereupon the

[277] C. 1, X, *de conversione infidelium*, III, 33.

[278] GASPARRI, *op. cit.*, n. 644; D'ANNIBALE questions the tenableness of such an inference, vol. III, n. 440, note 25.

[279] SCHMALZGRÜBER, *h. t.*, n. 53; SANCHEZ, lib. VII, disp. LXXVII, n. 9; REIFFENSTÜL, IV, VII, 22, 25; GASPARRI, *op. cit.*, n. 644; D'ANNIBALE, vol. III, n. 440, note 24.

latter by lending his aid to the murder not only accepts it, but helps to make its realization possible. St. Alphonsus maintains[280] that familiarity or exchange of love-letters preceding the murder would constitute a sufficient intimation of the matrimonial intention. Other authors hold that in the external forum such intention is to be presumed in every case, especially if the accomplices, subsequently to the murder, should wish to contract marriage. Such a presumption could be *praesumptio iuris tantum,* to say the most, therefore it would admit a contrary proof. Nevertheless, should such a doubt remain unsolved the marriage once contracted must be sustained.[281]

312. The new law is silent as regards the multiplication of this impediment, therefore under the present discipline this impediment will not be subject to multiplication. Since marriages contracted under the old law are to be judged according to the old discipline, it must be borne in mind that formerly the impediment could become multiplex either by virtue of crime or by virtue of marriage. Should the various phases of this impediment occur during one and the same marriage, namely, should the same guilt of adultery be followed successively by the promise of marriage, then by an attempt at marriage, and finally by the murder of one's consort, the impediment would be threefold. Should, in addition to the foregoing, the murder be the outcome of the plotting of both accomplices, the impediment would probably become fourfold.[282] The impediment may become multiplex also by virtue of the injury offered to two marriages should both accomplices be married. Should A. (married) commit adultery, accompanied by a promise of marriage, with B.

[280] *Op. cit.,* vol. VI, n. 1033.
[281] S. C. C., *Bitunt.,* 15 ian., 2 iul., 1718.
[282] De Smet, *op. cit.,* n. 327.

(also married) the impediment of crime would be twofold. Should they also attempt marriage, the impediment would become fourfold. If A. should murder his wife and also B.'s husband the impediment would become sixfold.

313. From the foregoing facts it is evident that the impediment of crime is established by the Church law and its purpose is to safeguard the sanctity and the integrity of Christian marriage and thereby the welfare of the commonwealth. Therefore infidels, not being under the jurisdiction of the Church, do not contract this impediment unless the civil law of the country to which they are subject corresponds to the Church law. Two infidels, after their conversion, may contract marriage even without a dispensation though, while in infidelity, they were guilty of a crime which would have given rise to this impediment had either of them been baptized.

314. Some maintain that if the adultery took place before the conversion and the promise of marriage after it, the impediment would arise. This opinion is justly rejected by modern canonists, for it would be equivalent to saying that the promise of marriage independently of adultery is sufficient to induce such an impediment.[283] Should the crime be committed by a baptized and an unbaptized person, the impediment would arise owing to the fact that one of them is directly subject to the jurisdiction of the Church, and rendered thereby incapable of contracting marriage, which inability is communicated to the other party.[284] This statement is to be modified when one is confronted with the third phase of this impediment affecting directly only the party guilty of adultery *plus* the

[283] SANCHEZ, lib. VII, disp. LXXIX, n. 43; GASPARRI, *op. cit.*, n. 652; DE SMET, *op. cit.*, n. 328, Corollary II; WERNZ, *op. cit.*, n. 521.

[284] S. C. de Prop. Fide, 23 aug., 1852.

murder of the consort, the party guilty only of adultery being affected only indirectly. If it is the baptized party that is guilty of the two crimes, the impediment would be contracted. Should the baptized party be guilty only of adultery, and the unbaptized party of adultery combined with the murder of the consort, the impediment would not be incurred.

315. It is necessary to say a few words on the much-mooted question: How does ignorance affect the impediment of crime? It is well to bear in mind at the very outset that ignorance generally does not prevent one from contracting an impediment. But the impediment of crime serves the purpose of a penalty for and of a preventive against the crimes which constitute the three phases of the impediment as explained above. It would therefore be natural to infer that ignorance of the penalty would excuse one from contracting the impediment. To this opinion adhered Gasparri,[285] D'Annibale,[286] Ballerini and Gury,[287] and Slater.[288] The other opinion holds that the vindictive punishment is only a secondary cause of the existence of this impediment, the primary cause being the common decency militating against a marriage which can be traced to a grave moral offence (as adultery combined with the promise of marriage or with an attempt at marriage), or whose possibility was procured by the commission of a crime (as in the case of the murder of a consort). This opinion which is defended by the majority of canonists was always held as the more probable.[289] It might be

[285] *Op. cit.*, n. 658.

[286] *Summa Theolog. Moralis*, vol. III, n. 442.

[287] *Theolog. Moralis*, vol. II, n. 778.

[288] *A manual of Moral Theology*, vol. II, p. 317.

[289] KRIMER, IV, VII, n. 1011 ff.; DE ANGELIS, IV, VII, n. ult.; WERNZ, *op. cit.*, n. 522; SANTI-LEITNER, *loc. cit.*, n. 7 ff.; DE SMET, *op. cit.*, n. 328; DE BECKER, *op. cit.*, p. 165; BURTSELL, in the *Catholic Encyclopedia*, art., *Crime, impediment of;* FEIJE, *op. cit.*, n. 466; REIFFENSTÜL, *h. t.*, n. 26; add to these ZALLINGER, BOECKHN, WIESTNER, SCHMALZGRÜBER and others.

said in its favor that the decisions of the Sacred Penitentiaria and Dataria have never contradicted it, and that the old canons do not record a single example in which a person ignorant of the fact that such a penalty is annexed to these crimes was freed from incurring the impediment.

316. While the opinion holding that ignorance of the penalty does not excuse one from contracting the impediment had more weight the contrary opinion being also well-founded was regarded as possessing an extrinsic probability. Consequently, if in the past there was a question of dissolving a marriage whose nullity was claimed by reason of the presence of the impediment of crime, the authors advised for the sake of safety to have recourse to the Holy See, should the penalty attached to such a crime have been unknown to the parties in question. In such instances on the ground of reflex principle Gasparri would not urge the impediment, but counsels either a dispensation *ad cautelam* or a *sanatio in radice.*[290] This would hold good only as regards marriages contracted before the new law went into effect. The subsequent marriages must be judged according to the new Code which espouses the opinion of the majority of canonists when it legislates that ignorance does not excuse one from a nullifying or a disqualifying law unless the contrary is expressly stated.[291] The same is to be said with regard to the ignorance of an impediment.[292]

317. As regards dispensation from this impediment the new law legislates specifically when it declares that a dispensation from a ratified non-consummated marriage, and the permission to contract marriage *ob praesumptam coniugis mortem* always include also a

[290] *Op. cit.,* n. 658.
[291] COD. IUR. CAN., Can. 16, §1.
[292] *Op. cit.,* Can. 988.

dispensation from the first phase of this impediment, namely, when it arises from adultery combined with a promise of marriage or with an attempt at marriage.[293] It follows that from this phase of the impediment the Church dispenses without much difficulty.

318. A very grave reason is required for the dispensation when the impediment is contracted on account of the other two causes, namely, adultery combined with the murder of the consort, or murder of the consort as the outcome of the plotting of both accomplices. In these two cases, owing to the enormity of the crime, Wernz maintains that the Church never dispensed nor is it inclined to do so when the murder is public.[294] Should it be occult the Sacred Penitentiaria, though very rarely, in some instances does dispense, for the forum of conscience, namely, when the guilt of the parties in question is not likely to be divulged, and the cause is most urgent. If the death of the consort resulted from the administration of poison, an additional difficulty is placed in the way of obtaining a dispensation.[295] If the marriage is already contracted and the separation is not possible without occasioning grave scandal, and danger of incontinence threatens; or when the parties are so determined to marry that a public concubinage or an attempt at marriage is feared, then the dispensation is granted provided the murder is secret.

319. In case of urgent danger of death none of the four species of this impediment is reserved. Under circumstances already explained[296] Bishop and priests could dispense from it notwithstanding the fact that the murder of the consort was a public act.[297] Similar

[293] *Op. cit.*, Can. 1053.
[294] *Op. cit.*, n. 534.
[295] Gasparri, *op. cit.*, n. 654.
[296] See this work, n. 151 ff.
[297] Cod. Iur. Can., Can. 1043.

is the power of the Bishop over this impediment, whether the murder is public or secret, whenever the conditions formerly styled as *casus perplexus* are verified.[298] The priest in this case could dispense only if the murder is an occult act and recourse to the Bishop is difficult. It is to be noted that the new law classes the first phase of this impediment (namely, when it arises from adultery combined with a promise of marriage, or with an attempt at marriage) under impediments of minor grade.[299] Consequently an error either in the petition or in the rescript, and even *obreptio* or *subreptio* would not impair the validity of the dispensation.[300]

320. The new law does not impose specific penalties on those who contract the impediment of crime. The punishments must be gathered from the various penalties meted out on account of separate offences implied in the impediment. These offences are: Adultery, bigamy, attempt at marriage and homicide. Persons guilty of public adultery are barred from all ecclesiastical acts until they give unmistakable signs of repentance and amendment.[301] Bigamists, namely, persons who while bound by a matrimonial bond attempt another marriage, even if it be only civil, are *ipso facto* infamous. Should they persevere in an illicit familiarity, spurning the admonition of the Bishop, they are to be excommunicated or placed under personal interdict, according to the gravity of their offence.[302] The new law brands homicides as *irregulares ex delicto*.[303] Their crime brings with it exclusion from all legitimate ecclesiastical acts, from every office they

[298] *Op. cit.*, Can. 1045.
[299] *Op. cit.*, Can. 1042, §2, n. 5.
[300] *Op. cit.*, Can. 1054.
[301] *Op. cit.*, Can. 2357, §2.
[302] *Op. cit.*, Can. 2356.
[303] *Op. cit.*, Can. 985, n. 4.

may hold in the Church, and the burden to repair all damages.[304]

IX. Impediment of Consanguinity.
(Canon 1076.)

1. Preliminary Notions about Consanguinity.

321. Consanguinity or blood-relationship is a natural bond, a blood union, existing between persons who within degrees specified by Civil or Ecclesiastical Law descend from a common ancestor, or one directly from the other.

The degree (*gradus*) represents the distance between persons related in the same line. The descent from the common ancestor, who is the root or source (*stipes*) of consanguinity, may be traced either in direct line (*linea recta*) or in collateral or transverse line (*linea obliqua, seu transversa, seu collateralis*). Line in this connection represents a series of persons united with one another by a bond of consanguinity. According as the descent is direct or indirect we distinguish lineal and collateral consanguinity. Lineal consanguinity exists between persons of whom one descends directly from the other, for example, father and son; grandfather and grandchild. The direct line is descending (*descendentalis*), if the computation begins from the highest and goes down to the lowest degree of relationship. In the ascending (*ascendentalis*) direct line relationship is traced from the lowest to the highest degree. Collateral consanguinity springs from the same ancestor, not by direct but by indirect descent. In this case the common ancestor is the trunk (*stipes*) from which the different blood relations branch out, not one from the other, but side by side,

[304] *Op. cit.*, Can. 2354; see this work, n. 270.

for example, brother and sister; two cousins, two nephews. The collateral line is equal (*aequalis*) when the persons in question are equally distant from the common stock, for example, first cousins. It is unequal (*inaequalis*) when the distance is not the same, namely, when one is farther from, or nearer to, the common ancestor, than the other, for instance, uncle and niece.

322. Consanguinity may be: 1. Legitimate and illegitimate. The former presupposes the legitimacy, the latter the illegitimacy of the union from which the child was born. In either case the impediment of consanguinity has the same force.

2. Perfect and imperfect. Those persons are related by perfect consanguinity whose father and mother are the same. They are called brothers-german, or "whole" brothers or sisters. If they come from the same father but from different mothers, or from the same mother but from different fathers, then we have an example of imperfect consanguinity. In the former instance they are called half-brothers, or half-sisters, in the latter uterine brothers.

3. The blood relatives on the father's side are sometimes caled *agnates,* those on the mother's side *cognates.* This designation must not be confused with the idea of agnation and cognation as interpreted by the Roman Law.

4. Simple and multiplex. In the former the related persons trace their descent to the common ancestor by one line only; in the latter by two or more lines. The impediment of consanguinity is multiplied as often as the common ancestor is multiplied.[305] Thus the relationship is multiplex as often as the ascending lines of the parties in question meet within degrees specified by the law. These lines must continue until, having

[305] Cod. Iur. Can., Can. 1076, §2.

passed beyond the persons constituting the intermediate root, they converge in one and the same ancestor, common to both.

2. *History and Nature of the Impediment.*

323. A few reflections on the most important historical aspects of this impediment will suffice for our purpose. The Mosaic Law, for reasons inherent in the history, calling and character of the Israelites, prescribed only a few degrees within which marriage among blood-relatives was prohibited.[306] The prohibition of the Roman Law was extended to more remote degrees. It included all the blood-relatives legitimate and illegitimate, of the direct line ascending or descending.[307] It is also certain that in the collateral line it never permitted marriage between brother and sister. The extent and force of the prohibition regarding other degrees of the same line are a matter of controversy among the various authors. The law of Theodosius (384) extended this prohibition to first cousins inclusively,[308] but for the Eastern Church the prohibition was subsequently revoked by the edict of Arcadius (400).[309] Justinian approved the Arcadian enactment and promulgated it in the East and the West, extending the prohibition to first cousins and reserving for the emperor the right to dispense.[310] At this period the Germanic Law, following in the footsteps of the Roman Law, introduced its prohibition to the seventh degree of consanguinity.

Up to the sixth century the Church permitted itself

[306] *Lev.* XVIII, 6 ff.; XX, 11 ff.; *Deut.* XXXVII, 20, 22, 23.

[307] ESMEIN, *op. cit.*, pp. 336 ff.; L. 17, C. de nupt. v. 4; L. 53, 54, 37, 17, §2; D. de ritu nupt. XXIII, 2.

[308] ST. AUGUSTINE, *De Civitate Dei*, XV, XVI; ST. AMBROSE, *Ep.* LX, *ad Paternum: Ambrosii Op. Omnia*, tom IV, p. 369, Parisiis, 1836; WERNZ, *op. cit.*, n. 409.

[309] ESMEIN, *op cit.*, p. 339; L. 19, C. *de nupt.*, V, 4.

[310] L. 1, C. Th., *de incest. nupt.*, III, 10.

to be guided by the civil legislation. In the middle of that century it expressly prohibited marriage between second cousins.[311] The Oriental Church half a century after the Second Trullan Synod[312] (692) submitted to the same regulation. The lack of absolute uniformity in insisting on the universal observance of the law, in computing the different degrees of consanguinity, and in determining with certainty the last prohibiting degree, created not a little confusion, which lasted to the eighth century. Desirous to establish uniformity of discipline, the Church adopted the Germanic method of computation and, in accordance with the Germanic and Roman laws, the impediment was extended to the seventh degree. It is a controverted question whether at that time the impediment was regarded as diriment in all Christian localities. The majority of authors agree that it was considered as such in Italy and Rome, but that in some countries the last three degrees were regarded only as impedient and not as diriment impediments.[313] It was only after prolonged controversy and repeated ecclesiastical legislation that a more positive step toward unifying the discipline of the Church was undertaken. The Second Lateran Council (1139) canonized the then prevailing discipline,[314] extending it to the universal Church, and presumably prohibiting marriages to the seventh degree of consanguinity inclusively. Even subsequently some doubts were entertained as to the binding force of the last two degrees. Finally the Fourth Lateran Council (1215)[315] restricted the prohibition to the fourth degree of the collateral line owing to the grave inconveni-

[311] C. 30, *Con. Epaun;* C. 8, C. XXXV, q. 2 and 3.

[312] *Conc. Trul.*, c. LIV; ib. WERNZ, *op. cit.*, n. 409.

[313] WERNZ, *op. cit., loc. cit.*

[314] *Conc. Lat.* II, c. XVII, see MANSI, *Amplissima Col. Con.*, vol. 21, col. 530.

[315] PETR. LOMBARDI, in *Sent.*, lib. IV, dist. XXXIX and XL.

ence arising from its observance in the more remote degrees.[316]

324. Several Fathers of the Council of Trent proposed a reform favoring the restriction of the impediment to the third degree.[317] Their suggestion after the third reading was overruled and the former discipline retained.[318] This tendency, shown by several of the convened Fathers, may have influenced Paul III (1534-1549) in restricting the impediment to the second degree for American Indians,[319] and also for the natives of the Philippines.[320]

What the consensus of several Fathers convened at the Council of Trent considered expedient has been introduced by the promulgation of the most recent matrimonial discipline. The impediment of consanguinity in its present form is restricted to the third degree of the collateral line.[321] In the direct line, both descending and ascending, it prohibits and invalidates all marriages between persons related by consanguinity whether natural or legitimate.[322] The computation will begin with great-grandfather and great-grandmother, and the last in the direct line is the great-grandson and great-granddaughter. The last degree in the collateral line is second cousins, grand-nephew and grand-niece on either the father's or the mother's side.

Marriage may never be permitted if there is a doubt

[316] "Prohibitio quoque copulae coniugalis quartum consanguinitatis et affinitatis gradum de cetero non excedat; quoniam in ulterioribus gradibus non iam potest absque gravi dispendio huiusmodi prohibitio generaliter observari." MANSI, *op. cit.*, vol. XXII, col., 1038.

[317] THEINER, *Acta*, II, 342.

[318] *De Reform. Matr.*, sessio XXIV, can. III.

[319] ZITELLI, *Apparat. Iur. ecc.*, p. 439; Romae, 1888; MANSI, *op. cit.*, vol. 36, bis; *Conc. Prov. Limanum* I, col. 251.

[320] Litt. Ap. Leonis PP. XIII, 18 apr., 1897; new *Collect.*, n. 1965; WERNZ, *op. cit.*, n. 409; BURTSELL, in the *Cath. Encyclopedia*, art., "*Consanguinity.*"

[321] COD. IUR. CAN., Can. 1076, §2.

[322] *Op. cit.*, Can. 1076, §1.

whether the persons to be married are related in any degree of the direct line or in the first degree of the collateral line.[323] Though it is a controverted question whether marriage between brother and sister is against the law of nature, the Church has never granted a dispensation in such cases.[324] By prohibiting the marriage absolutely even in case of a prudent doubt whether the persons in question are related in that degree, the Church seems to favor the opinion of those who extend the prohibition of the natural law outside the direct line.

325. In the Uniat Greek Churches the discipline is not uniform. Their method of computation is that used by the Civil Law. The prohibition of some extends to the seventh,[325] of others to the eighth civil degree. According to the canonical computation the former would be second cousins touching third (third degree touching fourth), and the latter the fourth degree of the equal collateral line. Among the Syrians,[326] Copts,[327] Italo-Greeks and the Maronites the former legislation of the Catholic Church obtains, namely, the last prohibiting degree is the fourth, according to the canonical, or the eighth, according to the Oriental computation.

326. Since the new legislation contained in the Codex of Pius X does not affect the Oriental Churches, their discipline, until reformed, will remain unchanged. The Constitutions of Benedict XIV, namely *"Etsi pastoralis"* [328] and *"Singularis"* [329] (this latter ap-

[323] *Op. cit.*, Can. 1076, §3.

[324] BENEDICT XIV, *"Aestas Anni,"* oct. 11, 1757; see *Bull. Rom. Cont.*, vol. IV, p. 473, n. XIII.

[325] WERNZ, *op. cit.*, n. 409, note 51.

[326] *Synodus Sciarfensis Syrorum*, c. V, art. XIV, §7, p. 179. Romae, 1896.

[327] *Synodus Alexandrinus Coptorum*, c. VIII, de Sacr. Matr., p. 168. Romae, 1899.

[328] BENEDICT XIV, *Bull Rom. Cont.*, vol. I, p. 197.

[329] *Loc. cit.*, p. 100.

proves the letter of Innocent IV relating to the provincial Synod of the Maronites held in 1736) intended expressly for the Uniat Churches, enforce the same discipline as that in vogue in the Roman Catholic Church. Papp-Szilágyi [330] remark that owing to the prudent economy of the Holy See, the above-mentioned epistle of Innocent IV has never been enforced. They also state that the Constitution "*Etsi pastoralis*" was intended exclusively for the Italo-Greeks and not for all the Uniat Churches. From these two statements they draw the inference that marriages contracted within the eighth degree of consanguinity (fourth canonical degree, namely, third cousins) are not to be considered invalid, unless the marriage takes place in a province for which the Holy See has expressly legislated to that effect. In the Churches of the East all marriages between persons related in the direct line are forbidden, and in the collateral line to the seventh civil degree. The remotest degree is only an impedient impediment.[331] The national Greek Church prohibits marriage within the sixth degree, which corresponds to the present ecclesiastical discipline.

3. *Mode of Computation.*

327. Roman Law is in agreement with Civil Law in the method of computing the degrees of consanguinity arising from the direct line, but the two differ in reckoning the degrees of the collateral line. The following rules will prove a guide in the canonical method of computation:

(A). In the direct line there are as many degrees as there are generations, or as there are persons minus the common ancestor.[332] Thus, for example, a grand-

[330] *Enchiridion Iuris Ecclesiae Orientalis Catholicae*, P. 2, §109, Magno Varadini, 1862; ib. FEIJE, *op. cit.*, n. 365.

[331] BURTSELL, *loc. cit.*, art., "*Consanguinity*" (mode of calculation).

[332] COD. IUR. CAN., Can. 96, §1.

child is removed by two degrees from his grandfather.

(B). In the equal collateral line there are as many degrees as there are generations on one side of the line. Thus, for example, first cousins are related in the second degree of equal collateral line.

(C). In the unequal collateral line there are as many degrees as there are generations [333] on the longer side of the line. But for the sake of completeness and accuracy the number of generations in the shorter line must also be indicated. Thus, for instance, uncle and niece are related in the second degree touching the first.

According to the English mode of calculation all persons are counted, in both the lineal and the collateral blood-relationship, the common stock being omitted. Thus, for instance, the grandfather and the granddaughter are related in the third degree of lineal consanguinity. Uncle and niece are related in the third degree, first cousins in the fourth degree, second cousins in the sixth degree of collateral blood-relationship.

328. Consanguinity may be duplicated. The multiplication of blood-relationship is due to any of the following causes:

(A). The persons in question descend from ancestors who, being related to each other, married persons likewise related, for instance, two brothers marry two sisters and the child of one brother and sister wishes to marry the child of the other brother and sister.

(B). The persons in question descend from a common ancestor whose two children contracted marriage successively with one and the same person; thus, for example, they descend from the same grandfather whose two daughters married one and the same person, or whose two sons married one and the same person.

[333] *Op. cit.*, Can. 96, §2.

To elucidate these hypotheses it will be well to illustrate them by diagrams to which the authors generally resort.

I. DIAGRAM.

(Hypothesis A.)

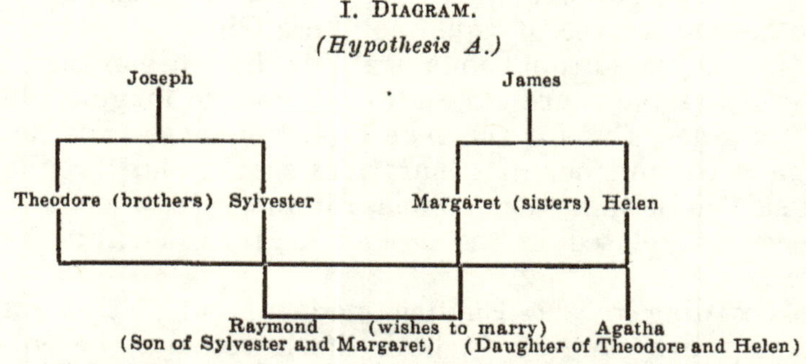

In this diagram Raymond and Agatha are twice related in the second degree of the equal collateral line. The former is traced to both Joseph and James through Sylvester and Margaret. Agatha is traced to the same ancestors through Helen and Theodore.

II. DIAGRAM.

(Hypothesis B.)

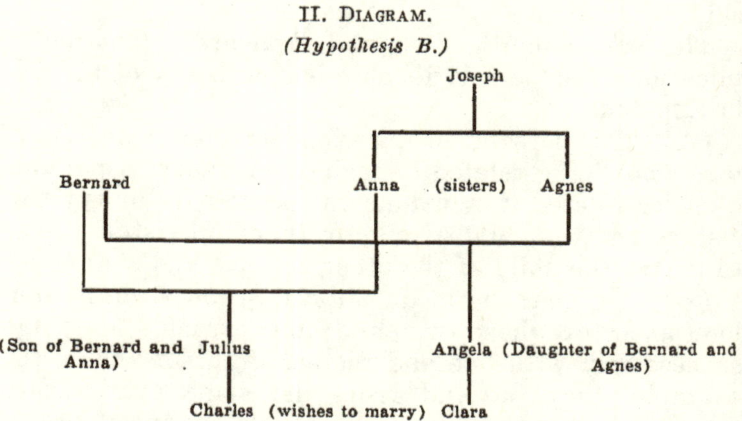

In this diagram Clara can be traced to the common ancestor (Joseph) through Angela and Agnes; Charles through Julius and Anna. Having Joseph for their common great-grandfather, they are related in the third degree of the equal collateral line. Having Bernard for common grandfather, they are related in the second degree of the same line.

To arrive at the degree of consanguinity in which the prospective consorts are related one may begin either with the common ancestor and descend to the persons in question, or with the prospective consorts and ascend to the common ancestor.

III. DIAGRAM.

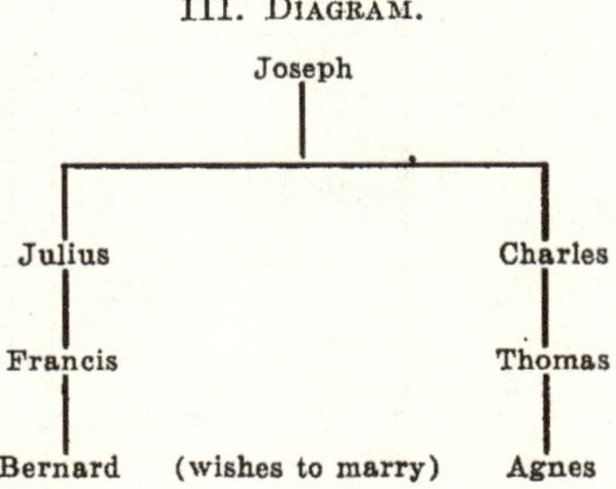

From this diagram it is obvious that the prospective consorts are related in the third degree of the equal collateral line.

Genealogical Tree.

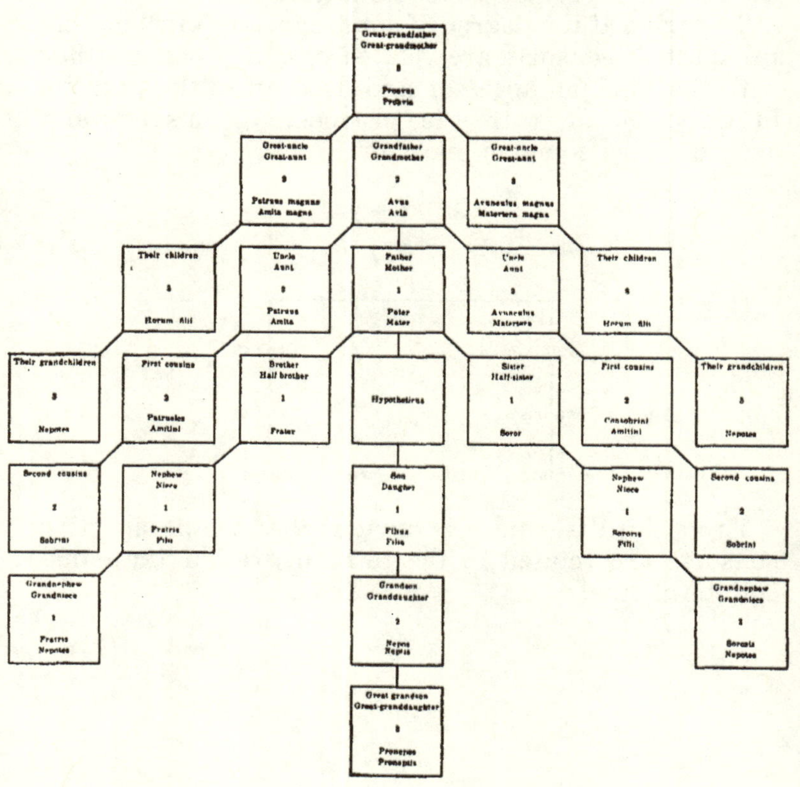

4. *Motives of This Impediment.*

329. There are three leading reasons which actuated the Church in approving and enforcing the impediment as it is accepted by the Mosaic and the Roman Law, namely: 1. To safeguard the observance of the prohibition arising from natural law; 2. To establish a barrier against early corruption which threatens young persons related and living under the same roof; 3. To promote a more extensive bond of union among men by means of intermarriages and to prevent the inbreeding of blood-relatives (a practice which very frequently occasions procreation of defective offspring, and transmission, in an intensified degree, of any physical, mental, or moral weaknesses under which the parents may be laboring). For a more comprehensive development of the aforesaid reasons the reader should consult the authors suggested below. A few remarks by way of explanation will sufficiently serve our present purpose.

I. The cause of consanguinity is identity of blood.[334] This identity becomes more pronounced the nearer a person approaches the common ancestor. It is generally admitted that marriage in the first degree of the direct line, between parent and child, is prohibited by natural law,[335] for the reason that the blood of parents and children is practically identical. To avert the deleterious effects of consanguineous marriages, the intermingling of foreign blood is necessary, which can be acquired only outside the family, for, as St. Thomas expresses it, blood-relatives are of the same substance.[336]

[334] St. Thomas, *Suppl.* IIIae, p., q. LIV, a. 3, c.

[335] Suarez, *De leg.*, lib. II, cap. XII, n. 3; Perrone, *op. cit.*, vol. II, p. 137; St. Ambrose, *ep.* XL, *ad Paternum;* St. Thomas, in *Sent.*, lib. IV, dist. XL, a. III, ad arg.; Sanchez, *De Matrimonio*, lib. VII, disp. LI; Wernz, *op. cit.*, n. 410; Gasparri, *op. cit.*, n. 675; De Smet, *op. cit.*, n. 299; De Becker, *op. cit.*, p. 181.

[336] *Suppl.* IIIae, p., q. LIV, a. IV, ad. 7.

330. Marriage between parent and child does not absolutely exclude the possibility of the realization of the primary end of nature. But this is attained very imperfectly, while the secondary end is not likely to be attained at all. Besides, such unions advocate the most unnatural condition, by reversing the essential natural position existing between parent and child.[337] By natural law the child owes to his parents deep reverence, obedience and subjection. Marriage makes them equal, or makes the mother even inferior to her son in case the two should be united in matrimony. Though, generally speaking, it is repugnant to a rational being to contemplate such unions, history is not without precedents showing that the Church had repeated occasions to insist on the observance of natural law in this respect. She had to deal with nations like the Persians who were addicted to practices contrary to the law of nature,[338] and who justly merited the vituperation of St. Chrysostom and St. Augustine, and even of the Pagan Aristotle and Pliny. The Church, wishing to bring such Gentiles under her spiritual domain, encountered the task of disabusing them of their unnatural notions, by gently inoculating them with Christian ideas, or, whenever such remedy proved insufficient, by enforcing stringently some of her legislative measures.[339]

It is a disputed question whether natural law forbids all marriages beyond the first degree of consanguinity in the direct line. The affirmative opinion is generaly advanced as the leading one.[340] In support of this view the authors draw attention in particular

[337] St. Thomas, loc. cit., q. LIV, a. III, c.

[338] De Becker, *op. cit.*, p. 179.

[339] Perrone, *op. cit.*, vol. II, p. 138.

[340] Schmalzgrüber, p. III, tit. XIV, n. 30 ff.; Wernz, *op. cit.*, n. 410; Gasparri, *op. cit.*, n. 674; De Becker, *op. cit.*, p. 181; De Smet, *op. cit.*, n. 299.

to the answer of Pope Nicolas I (858-867) occasioned by an inquiry on the part of the Bulgarians, there being no more authoritative declaration available relative to the matter in question.[341]

Though the Church fails to state expressly that her prohibition of marriages between persons related in any degree of lineal consanguinity is equivalent to a mere enforcement of natural law, we are inclined to believe that such is the case. It is true that this opinion may be controverted, but in practice no difficulty can be experienced, because the Church has legislated by positive law. The discipline of the Church, dissolving all marriages of lineal consanguinity and those contracted in the first degree of collateral consanguinity,[342] is certainly in favor of our opinion. Not a single instance can be adduced in which after the conversion of one or of both parties the Church has ratified such marriages. Nor has it ever dispensed in these degrees of consanguinity, not even in the case of the most urgent necessity.

331. While the primary laws of nature do not seem to prohibit marriage in the first degree of collateral blood-relationship (between brother and sister), the deordination of such a union strikingly militates against the secondary laws of nature. This departure from the natural order of things is sufficiently grave to permit the inference that though natural law may not put the same extreme ban on such marriages as it does on those of lineal consanguinity, it tolerates them

[341] "Nam quarundam nuptiis abstinere debemus, inter eas nempe personas quae parentum liberorumve locum inter se obtinent, nuptiae contrahi non possunt, veluti inter patrem et filiam, vel avum et neptem, matrem et filium, aviam et nepotem, et usque ad infinitum." (Opusc., *Responsa Nicolai I, ad consulta Bulgarorum*, cap. XXXIX, p. 23, Romae, 1860; ib., MANSELLA, *op. cit.*, p. I, c. III, a. I, n. 6, note; GASPARRI, *op. cit.*, n. 674, FEIJE, *op. cit.*, n. 364; SCHMALZGRÜBER, *op. cit.*, p. III, tit. XIV, n. 35; DE BECKER, *op. cit.*, p. 182; DE SMET, *op. cit.*, n. 298.

[342] *Synodus Limana* I, 15 aug., 1582, MANSI, *op. cit.* vol. 36 bis, col. 199; WERNZ, *op. cit.*, n. 410 note, 58; DE BECKER, *op cit.*, p. 181.

only on the supposition that they are absolutely necessary for the propagation of the human race, as a *conditio sine qua non.*[343] Advocates of this opinion maintain that natural law yielded to such necessity in the case of the sons and daughters of our first parents.[344]

On the ground of the immutability of natural law other authors maintain that marriages in the first degree of collateral consanguinity are forbidden by divine positive law which became obligatory on and operative with the grandchildren of Adam and their descendants. One should not presume, they argue, without an unavoidable necessity, that God dispensed from and suspended a law which, inhering in nature and man, and having a universal binding force, is immutable.[345] Other arguments as regards this question will be found in the following section which treats of the dispensation from this impediment.

The teaching of theologians, based on the practice of the Church, gives the latter the right to dissolve marriages contracted in infidelity within the prohibitory canonical degrees, provided both parties become converts, and there is a just cause. This dissolution cannot take place, if the persons in question have consummated the marriage subsequently to their conversion.[346] This point will be explained more fully later.

Though marriages contracted in the other degrees of collateral consanguinity do not interfere seriously with either the primary or the secondary laws of nature, they are not thereby altogether reconcilable with natural law by virtue of which they are considered illicit. The Church has not only approved this mild

[343] WERNZ, *op. cit.*, n. 411; DE SMET, *op. cit.*, n. 299, note 2.

[344] GASPARRI, *op. cit.*, n. 678.

[345] SANTI-LEITNER, *Praelectiones Iur. Can.*, vol. IV, tit. XIV, n. 13, Ratisbonae, 1905.

[346] FEIJE, *op. cit.*, n. 367; PERRONE, *op. cit.*, vol. II, p. 313; WERNZ, *op. cit.*, n. 699; D'ANNIBALE, *op. cit.*, vol. III, n. 470.

prohibition of the natural law, but enhanced its force. Thus an impediment which, by virtue of natural law, is only impedient in some degrees of collateral consanguinity, becomes diriment by special ecclesiastical legislation. That the Church was justified in annexing the penalty of nullity to an act which by natural law is only illicit will be evidenced from the discussion of the following two points.

332. II. The bond uniting blood-relatives is a different bond from the one which arises among persons related by marriage. In the first instance it springs from natural relation, it is an inherited tie. In the second it is acquired. Consequently the sentiments of love and confidence arising from the first relation differ substantially from those to which the acquired bond gives rise.

The sanctity of home and the pure love which ought to exist among consanguineous persons would be exposed to grave danger if such marriages were not discountenanced by the Church and also by public opinion. The natural bond by which such persons are united, instead of being instrumental in procuring an unlimited amount of good, would become the means of perverted intimacies, which would result in creating a poisonous atmosphere at the very base of society. It must be admitted that the occasion for evil is nearer among blood-relatives on account of their free companionship and intercommunion.[347] To counteract the influence of this threatening evil, as a matter of advisability the Church surrounds with safeguards and additional precautionary measures those who are exposed to it.

[347] "Finis matrimonii . . . deperiret, si quaelibet consanguinea posset in matrimonium duci, quia magnus concupiscentiae aditus praeberetur, nisi inter illas personas quas oportet in eodem domo conversari esset carnalis copula interdicta." ST. THOMAS, *Suppl.* IIIae, p., q. LIV, a. III, c.; and in IIa-IIae, q. CLIV, a. IX, c.

333. III. Marriage, the only legitimate means for the propagation of the human race, is the office of the community. The reasons thus far advanced may be regarded as requisites for the moral welfare of society. But the institution of marriage is to promote not only the moral but also the social and physical well-being of the community. The most effective means calculated to promote the social welfare of a community is the tangible bond, be it ever so remote, linking the different persons and originating in matrimony. The most ideal society is one in which all the persons are related, for then its units will endeavor to promote, and take a personal interest in one another's happiness and prosperity. To cultivate this feeling of friendship and brotherhood is one of the ends of matrimony,[348] thus to aid men to the realization of the Fatherhood of God.[349] By the prohibition of consanguineous marriages, this connecting link is extended to persons heretofore unrelated, and thus the fact that mankind is one huge family is visualized more tangibly.

Furthermore, both the Church and the State are authorized by God to guard the physical welfare of humanity. They exercise this authorization when they lay down certain laws tending to promote that end. The community implicitly admits such authority when it conforms to such rules regulating its actions. The legislation thus enforced may be either remedial (intending to remove an existing evil) or prescriptive (upholding for prudential reasons a hereditary law

[348] "Habita est enim ratio rectissima caritatis, ut homines . . . diversarum necessitudinum vinculo necterentur . . . atque ita se non in paucitate coarctatum, sed latius atque numerosius propinquitatibus crebris vinculum sociale diffunderet . . . ne habeat duas necessitudines una persona, cum duae possint eas habere, et numerus propinquitatis augeri." (ST. AUGUSTINE, *De Civitate Dei*, lib. XV, cap. XVI, Lipsiae, 1867; ST. THOMAS, IIa-IIae, q. CLXIV, a. IX, c.; again, *Suppl.* IIIae, p., q. LIV, a. III, c.; I *Peter* II, 17.

[349] *Acts*, VII, 26.

transmitted by foregoing generations). The prohibition expressed by such laws is founded on experience and observation. They provide against acts which in the past proved detrimental to the physical welfare of society.

The impediment of consanguinity belongs to the category of hereditary prescriptive laws. It is an established fact of experience that consanguineous marriages are injurious to the physical welfare of the child. The modern physiologists accept this fact established on, and corroborated by, statistical information, but they fail to agree as to the gravity of the harm inflicted on offspring of incestuous unions.

334. The nature and scope of this work will not permit us to enter into the discussion of the different theories suggested in explanation of exogamy and endogamy as practiced by some savage races. The reader is referred to the authors quoted below.[350] Westermarck mentions several writers who positively exclude the possibility that the harmful consequences resulting from endogamic marriages, as ascertained by facts of observation, could have been instrumental in influencing the untutored tribes to form laws prescribing exogamic unions.[351] Granting that no positive traces can be found favoring a contrary assumption, we cannot legitimately conclude that the available facts, namely, the obvious mental and physical deficiencies of offspring born of incestuous marriages, entirely escaped their attention. Unless there is positive

[350] SPENCER, *Principles of Sociology*, I, 614 ff.; London, 1885; FRAZER, *Totemism*, Edinburgh, 1887; MAINE, *Dissertations on Early Law and Customs*, London, 1883; MCLENNAN, *Studies in Ancient History*, London, 1886; *Exogamy and Endogamy*, in the *Fortnightly Review*, vol. XXI, London, 1887; MELODY, *Marriage and Near Kin*, in the *Catholic University Bulletin*, Jan., 1903, pp. 40-60, Washington, D. C.; CRONIN, *op. cit.*, vol. II, pp. 45 ff.

[351] WESTERMARCK, *Geschichte der menschlichen Ehe*, ch. XIV and XV, pp. 289-356, Yena, 1893.

evidence to the contrary one is not justified in placing gratuitous limitations on the knowledge of peoples who displayed so remarkable an ingenuity in exploring the secrets of nature, and so striking a familiarity with its serviceableness and adaptability to their daily wants.[352] While we do not contend that the uncivilized tribes were in possession of a "sagacious calculation" of these harmful effects,[353] we maintain that they were not altogether ignorant of them, and that their knowledge, combined with their natural repugnance to such unions, gave birth to the prohibitory laws against endogamic marriages.

335. We already had occasion to hint at the fact that there is a lack of unanimous belief as to the gravity of the physiological evils resulting from incestuous marriages. That these evils have frequently been exaggerated we readily agree with Arner.[354] Though, to all appearances, he is inclined to minimize these harmful consequences, he admits with frankness that "successive generations of offspring of incestuous connection . . . are very often degenerate." [355]

The intensification by double inheritance of the hereditary family characteristics is certainly an undoubted physiological fact. In the case of mental or physical weakness on the part of the parents, degeneracy is a serious menace to be feared, though it may fail to assert itself in every case individually, or even in the first generation. Statisticians interested in such investigations have almost unanimously come to the conclusion that such hereditary defects on the part of the parents are transmitted in an intensified degree to

[352] MAINE, *op. cit.*, p. 228.
[353] CRONIN, *op. cit.* vol. II, p. 453.
[354] *Consanguineous Marriages in the American Population.* A Doctorate Dissertation, Columbia University, 1908; THOMPSON, *Heredity*, pp. 386 ff., London, 1912.
[355] ARNER, *op. cit.*, p. 88.

the offspring.[356] This intensification is greatly increased in case the parents are living in an incestuous union. Such unions, if not childless, as is often the case, beget offspring subject to grave physical and mental weakness, for instance, epilepsy, deaf-muteness, and nervous diseases. The child of such a union acquires and transmits easily the defects of its parents, especially when the inbreeding of blood-relations is repeated.[357] The statistics of Fay bear out this fact. He ascertained that deafness, whether congenital or adventitious, is more likely to be transmitted in a consanguineous union than in a non-consanguineous union [358] and undoubtedly with increased intensity.

Viewing the foregoing facts cumulatively, no one should deny that the Church has sufficient ground for the stand she takes in these matters. Since under present conditions the blood-relationship beyond the third degree of consanguinity does not seem prejudicial to offspring, the Church has lifted her ban from the fourth degree.

5. *Dispensation from the Impediment.*

336. Those degrees of consanguinity which are based on natural law bind both baptized persons and infidels. Therefore marriages attempted between persons related within such degrees are *ipso facto* null and void and such consorts must separate in case one or both embrace the Catholic faith. The authors fail to agree as to the degrees prohibitory by natural law.

[356] HUTH, *The Marriage of Near-Kin considered with respect to law of nations, the results of experience, and the teachings of biology*, London, 1875; SURBLED, *La morale dans ses rapports avec la médicine, et l'hygiène*, Paris, 1896; LUKOCK, *The history of marriage, Jewish and Christian, in relation to divorce and certain forbidden degrees*, London, 1895; PETERSON, in the *Encyclopaedia Brittanica* (Eleventh edition), vol. XIV, art., *"Insanity,"* n. 6 (Consanguinity).

[357] BURTSELL, *loc. cit., "Consanguinity"* (Motives of Impediment).

[358] FAY, *Marriages of the Deaf in America*, pp. 132-133; Washington, 1898, Gibson Brothers.

There are three opinions. Some include all the degrees of the direct line and the first degree of the collateral line.[359] Others maintain that the prohibition of natural law does not extend beyond the first degree of lineal and collateral blood-relationship.[360] A third class of authors confines the prohibition of natural law to the first degree of lineal consanguinity.[361]

The solution of this doubt is of paramount importance when a marriage contracted in infidelity is to be ratified after the conversion of the parties. We presume here that the civil law to which the persons in question are subject does permit marriages within the above-enumerated controverted degrees. If it should prohibit such unions, then the civil impediment has already suspended the validity of their marriage and it cannot be revalidated, if they should be related within any of these controverted degrees, from which the Church never dispenses.

337. The advocates of the first opinion, the most comprehensive, draw the conclusion that persons who before their conversion contracted marriage in lineal consanguinity or in the first degree of collateral blood-relationship, cannot be permited to remain in a union invalidated on the ground of natural law. Such consorts, on their conversion, should be separated and permitted to remarry. In all the other degrees, provided the civil law does not interfere, the marriages

[359] WERNZ, *op. cit.*, n. 410 and n. 417; FEIJE, *op. cit.*, n. 366 and 367; LEHMKUHL, *Theologia Moralis*, vol. II, n. 990; Friburgi Brisgoviae, 1910; HEISS, *De Matrimonio*, pp. 139-142, Monachii, 1861; SANTI-LEITNER, *op. cit.*, *h. t.*, n. 13, p. 250; SCHMALZGRÜBER, *op. cit.*, p. III, tit. XIV, n. 35. The latter admits that marriage between the descendants and ascendants is invalid *in infinitum* on the ground of natural law, but, in his opinion, marriage in the first degree of collateral blood-relationship is not forbidden on the same ground. (*Op. cit.*, *loc. cit.*, n. 46.)

[360] SANCHEZ, *op. cit.*, lib. VII, dis. LI, n. 11 and disp. LII, n. 21.

[361] GASPARRI, *op. cit.*, n. 680; VERRICELLI, *De Apostolicis Missionibus*, q. XCVIII, dub. 14; GIOVINE, *De Disp. Matr.*, I, §209, n. 1.

of infidels are valid, for they are not bound by canonical impediments which, in the estimation of these authors, begin with the second degree of collateral consanguinity.

The advocates of the second opinion, less comprehensive, true to their principle, maintain that only those marriages should be dissolved which the infidels contract in the first degree of either lineal or collateral consanguinity.

The advocates of the third opinion, least comprehensive, base their decision on the fact that it is doubtful whether natural law actually forbids any marriages except those contracted in the first degree of lineal blood-relationship. Such being the case, they maintain that we must emphasize here the principle that in doubt one is to pronounce in favor of the validity of the marriage. Therefore they conclude that all unions may be ratified on the conversion of the infidel parties except those contracted within the first degree of lineal consanguinity. The others, *nisi favor fidei aliter exposcat,*[362] should not be dissolved.

338. There is no positive proof or categorical declaration at hand which would help one to decide with certainty that natural law forbids marriages in any other degree except the first of the direct line. Innocent III[363] distinctly declares that those who in infidelity contracted marriage (*praecisione facta a civili lege*) within the second degree of consanguinity, in the collateral line, should not be separated after their conversion. This instruction may be used as a negative argument. Since he does not extend the same privilege to those married within the first degree of collateral blood-relationship, it may be justly concluded that persons so married must be separated.

[362] Gasparri, *op. cit., loc. cit.,* ut supra.
[363] C. 8, X, *De divortiis,* IV, 19.

This separation would be the result of natural law prohibiting unions in that degree.

There is no explicit decree proving that such has actually been the discipline of the Church, though indirect proofs are not wanting. Thus, for instance, the Sacred Congregation of the Holy Office on two different occasions has given very extensive faculties to the Ordinaries (and even to the parish priests when recourse to the Ordinary is very difficult and there is *periculum in mora, urgente mortis periculo*).[364] The tenor of these decrees permits the Ordinary to dispense from any and all impediments of ecclesiastical origin excepting the impediment arising from the Holy Priesthood and from affinity in the direct line arising from *copula licita.* This same faculty is given under the same circumstances to all the Ordinaries and parish priests by the new legislation.[365] It is admitted that the aforesaid impediments are of ecclesiastical origin. Therefore, had the Church considered the second and other degrees of lineal and the first degree of collateral consanguinity of the same origin, these also should have been added as exceptional cases withdrawn from the conferred faculty. Since no explicit mention is made of them, and no one has ever presumed to include them in the faculty (for the delegate does not possess a more extensive faculty than the one by whom he is commissioned) the natural inference is that they are impediments of a higher order.

339. Furthermore, there is express legislation enacted by Provincial Synods and subsequently approved by the Church, ruling that all marriages contracted in infidelity within the first degree of collateral consanguinity, must be dissolved on the conversion of the

[364] Litt. encycl. S. C. S. Off., 20 febr., 1888; new *Collectanea,* n. 1685; 1 mart., 1889; new *Collectanea,* n. 1698.

[365] Cod. Iur. Can., Can. 1043; see this work, n. 151 ff.

parties.[366] No such declaration can be found as regards lineal consanguinity, since it is generally regarded as founded on natural law, while the former has constituted a bone of contention for many centuries.

As an additional proof, it may be added that the Council of Trent, legislating on the dispensation to be given from this impediment, insists that in the second degree the dispensation should not be granted except in very rare cases, and then only in behalf of influential princes and to serve a public cause.[367] This insistence plainly indicates that the legislative authority of the Church over this impediment begins with the second degree of collateral blood-relationship. The severity of this decree and the failure to make mention of the other controverted degrees, permit the tacit inference that a higher law has withdrawn from the Church the power to dispense from them. Whether this higher law is natural law or positive divine law (which permitted such marriages only in the case of the children of our first parents) has little bearing on the question.

The weight of the evidence thus far adduced, when viewed cumulatively, and corroborated by the fact that not a single instance can be advanced in which the Church dispensed from lineal consanguinity or from collateral blood-relationship in the first degree, ought to induce one to pronounce in favor of the first and most comprehensive opinion. Therefore, marriages contracted in infidelity within the controverted degrees as specified above, ought to be dissolved after the conversion of the parties and the persons thus parted ought to be permitted to remarry.

[366] *Synodus Limana,* I, 15 aug., 1582, MANSI, *op. cit.*, vol. 36 bis, col. 199.

[367] "In secundo gradu consanguinitatis nunquam dispensetur, nisi inter magnos principes, et ob publicam causam." (*De Ref. Matr.*, sessio XXIV, c. V.)

340. The canonical discipline as regards this impediment binds all baptized persons. At the present time the Church shows more leniency in these matters than in the past. It is certain that for just causes she may and does dispense from the impediment of consanguinity in the second and third degrees of the collateral line. The Council of Trent in the instruction quoted above enumerates two causes justifying the granting of a dispensation in the second degree of blood-relationship, namely, if it is asked by an influential prince and for public cause. The recent discipline interprets this decree in the sense that these two causes suffice whether they be taken connectedly or disjunctively, and even in the case of private persons.

341. The causes for which the Holy See usually dispenses from the equal second degree or from the mixed second touching the first, in the case of illustrious persons, or persons of noble descent, are the following: (1) Conservation of the noble family and its estate within the family; (2) Avoidance of grave scandal; (3) Infamy threatening a woman of noble birth either on account of carnal intercourse or suspected familiarity with a blood-relative; (4) Non-possession of dowry; (5) Bitter enmities that can be healed or avoided by marriage; (6) Marriage contracted in good faith, or even in bad faith provided the woman is already with child; (7) Superadult age of the woman.

It is to be noted that causes mentioned in points 3, 4, 5, 6, 7, if other, though less consequential reasons concur with them in the same case, are generally considered sufficient to justify the granting of a dispensation even in the case of poor applicants.[368] The reasons just given which are looked upon as more grave suffice for a dispensation from the second degree of the

[368] GASPARRI, *op. cit.*, n. 681.

equal line, or from the second and first, and third and first mixed. Any canonical reason will suffice for a dispensation from the equal third degree or second touching the third.

The impediment ceases to bind in case one of the contracting parties is related in the fourth degree to the prospective consort, even if it should be fourth mixed with the first.[369]

It is understood that the petition for dispensation involves only collateral blood-relationship removed further than the first equal line. A mention of the degree of consanguinity should never be omitted, and if the line should happen to be unequal and the consanguinity multiple, these facts must also be expressed. If the fact of the unequal line was concealed, provided the degree expressed in the petition is less remote (and the one concealed more remote) the dispensation is valid. Thus, for example, a petition is asked from the second degree. If in reality it should happen to be second mixed with the first, the dispensation is invalid. If it should be the second mixed with the third, the dispensation is valid. Such was the discipline under the old law. Though the new law fails to legislate specifically on these points, it would seem that the former discipline will remain in force.

342. The third degree of consanguinity has been placed in the category of minor impediments, therefore the dispensation granted from such a degree is also regarded as minor. Such being the case, obreption or subreption does not vitiate the dispensation. The mere exposition of the fact of consanguinity suffices, and the dispensation retains its validity even if it should happen to be asked and granted on fictitious

[369] SCHMALZGRÜBER, *op. cit.*, p. III, tit. XIV, a. 60; GASPARRI, *op. cit.*, n. 682.

grounds.[370] It is further to be noted that dispensation in any degree of consanguinity is valid though the petition or concession should contain an oversight about the degree, provided the actual degree is inferior to the one expressed. The same is to be said in case a coexisting impediment of the same kind in similar or inferior degree, should be withheld.[371]

6. *Ecclesiastical Penalty and the Exposure of the Impediment.*

343. Consanguineous persons attempting to contract marriage without a dispensation are guilty of incest. The Gratian collection enumerates several penalties to which such parties were liable unless excused by ignorance or fear. Thus, for example, they were declared *infames* by both civil and ecclesiastical law;[372] they were separated and, if they attempted marriage in bad faith, neither of them could remarry during the life-time of the other.[373] They were to be separated from the communion of the faithful,[374] and the children of such parents were not to succeed to paternal inheritance.[375] Schmalzgrüber mentions other penalties besides those already enumerated.[376] The Council of Trent imposes separation and intimates that such persons, if in bad faith, should give up all hope of ever being dispensed, especially if the marriage has been consummated.[377] The censure of excommunication fulminated by Clement V was repealed by Pius IX in his Constitution *"Apostolicae Sedis"*

[370] Cod. Iur. Can., Can. 1054, and Can. 42.
[371] Cod. Iur. Can., Can. 1052.
[372] C. 2, C. XXXV, q. 2.
[373] C. 4, C. XXXV, q. 2.
[374] C. 3, C. XXXV, q. 8.
[375] C. 1, C. XXXV, q. 7.
[376] *De Consanguinitate and Affinitate*, nn. 62-63.
[377] *De Reform. Matr.*, sessio XXIV, c. V.

issued on October 12, 1869, but that Constitution authorized the Bishops to inflict the same penalty, if they deemed it necessary in particular instances. A vestige of the impediment of incest, which in the opinion of the leading authors[378] was considered only an impedient impediment in the past, is still retained in the form of a clause placed as an adjunct to certain dispensations. The tenor of this clause is that a person who knowingly has attempted marriage with one related to him in a forbidden degree of consanguinity, cannot licitly contract marriage without the express permission of the Holy See, not even after the death of the consort in case his attempted marriage was subsequently revaliditated.[379]

The impediment of consanguinity is public whenever it can be proved in the external forum.[380] Therefore, not only the parties involved but also persons free from suspicion have the right to apprise the ecclesiastical authorities of the nullity of a marriage contracted without a dispensation from an impediment of blood-relationship. The old discipline laid down special legislation to be followed in all such juridical processes.[381] Since the old discipline still obtains in this respect, parents, relatives by blood or marriage, neighbors, acquaintances, whether Catholic or non-Catholic, all alike possess the right to expose the hidden fact of consanguinity.[382]

344. If the parish priest is informed as regards the blood-relationship of two prospective consorts, before he assists at their marriage he must inquire into the

[378] WERNZ, *op. cit.*, n. 412, note 85; SANCHEZ, *op. cit.*, lib. VII, disp. XV, n. 15; GASPARRI, *op. cit.*, n. 683.

[379] FEIJE, *op. cit.*, n. 369; WERNZ, *op. cit.*, n. 412, note 86; GASPARRI, *op. cit.*, *loc. cit.*

[380] COD. IUR. CAN., Can. 1037.

[381] C. 3, X, *qui matrimonium accusare possunt,* IV, 18.

[382] *Acta Apostolicae Sedis,* vol. V, pp. 201 ff.

grounds on which such information is based. Should the fact of consanguinity be revealed, a dispensation must be asked. If his investigation should result in a prudent doubt, leaving room for the presence of the impediment of consanguinity, he must abstain from assisting at the marriage without having first consulted the Ordinary.[383] The parish priest should not neglect to give heed to a trustworthy informant who undertakes the task of revealing an impediment existing between persons intending to contract marriage. The present canonical discipline,[384] as well as the past [385] insists that those who are in possession of such knowledge, should bring it to the notice of the Church.

345. The ecclesiastical judge or *defensor matrimonii* is bound *ex officio* to institute a juridical procedure as soon as he has sufficient data on hand testifying to the existence of consanguinity militating against the validity of a marriage. The mode of procedure which is to be pursued in all such cases is described extensively in the instruction given by the Sacred Congregation of Propaganda which in its substance is retained by the new Code. For the present it will suffice to know that no marriage may be declared invalid unless the evidence against its validity is absolutely convincing (*probatio plena requiritur; semi-plena non sufficit*). It is precisely in this feature that the two processes, namely, the one instituted for marriage to be contracted, and the other for matrimony already contracted, differ. In the first instance the marriage is suspended or prevented (without dispensation), though the evidence on hand does not ab-

[383] Cod. Iur. Can., Can. 1031.

[384] *Op. cit.*, Can. 1027.

[385] C. 10, X, *de cognatione spirituali*, IV, 11; c. 3, X, *de eo, qui cognovit*, IV, 13; c. 9, X, *de testibus et attest.*, II, 20; c. 3, X, *de matrim. contr. contra interd. Ecclesiae*, IV, 16; c. 27, X, *de sponsalibus et matrimoniis*, IV, 1; c. 3, X, *de clandestina desponsatione*, IV, 3; c. 13, X, *de desponsatione impuberum*, IV, 2.

solutely prove the existence of the impediment in question; such would be the testimony of a person worthy of belief,[386] or *publica fama.*[387] (*Probatio semi-plena de consanguinitate sufficit ut matrimonium contrahendum impediatur.*)

In order that the doubt as to the fact of the existing consanguinity may be solved, all sources calculated to shed light on the case under investigation should be diligently consulted. Reliable data will be furnished in this matter by the authentic records of marriages, baptisms and interments,[388] which evidence ought to be corroborated by the testimony of witnesses worthy of belief. The discipline of the Church in the past permits one to conclude that the testimony of two witnesses, especially if they should be relatives of the parties in question, will certainly constitute sufficient evidence (*probationem plenam*).[389]

7. *Civil Legislation.*

346. The Civil Law of the different nations generally conforms to the Canon Law in as much as it does not discriminate between consanguinity arising from the tie of legitimate procreation and that arising from natural procreation. A lack of uniformity prevails in the Civil Law as to the degrees within which consanguineous marriages are prohibited. In England the statute (32 Hen. VIII, c. 38) of Henry VIII, repealed by his son Edward VI, but revived by Elizabeth (I Eliz., c. 1), restricted the prohibition of such unions

[386] C. 4, 27, *de sponsalibus et matrimoniis,* IV, 1; S. C. C., 4 ian., 1884; ib., WERNZ, *op. cit.*, n. 423, note 92.

[387] C. 2, X, *de consang. et Affi.*, IV, 14; C. 3, X, *de matr. contracto contra interd. Ecc.*, IV, 16.

[388] Instr. S. C. de Prop. Fide, 1883, new *Collectanea,* n. 1587; 14 ian., 1884, in the *Acta S. Sedis,* vol. XVII, pp. 178 ff.

[389] C. 1-4, C. XXXV, q. 6; c. 1, 14, X, *de consang. et Affi.*, IV, 14.

within the "Levitical degrees." The prohibited marriages were those contracted between persons in the ascending and the descending line *in infinitum,* and in the collateral line to the third degree inclusively according to the computation of the Civil Law. The Act of 1835 decreed that: "All marriages which shall hereafter be celebrated between persons within the prohibited degrees of consanguinity or affinity shall be absolutely null and void to all intents and purposes whatsoever." Before this enactment such marriages had been regarded as only voidable.

The English law has been transplanted into Scotland practically in its native form, but it has been somewhat modified in the United States of North America. The States of New Hampshire, Ohio, Indiana, Kansas, Arkansas, Nevada, Washington, North Dakota, South Dakota, and Montana have for a long time prohibited consanguineous marriages between first cousins. The example of the foregoing States was subsequently followed by Louisiana, Oregon, Pennsylvania, Michigan, Nebraska, Utah and Wisconsin.

In France the code of Napoleon forbids marriages between (art. 161) all descendants and ascendants legitimate or natural in the direct line, and between (art. 162) brother and sister, legitimate or natural, and between (art. 163) uncle and niece or aunt and nephew.[390]

The Civil Law in Italy,[391] Hungary and Switzerland conforms to the Civil Law of France. The Civil Law of Spain distinguishes betwen consanguinity arising from a legitimate and that arising from a natural bond. In the former instance the impediment extends to the second degree of collateral blood-relationship, in

[390] De Smet, *op. cit.,* n. 301. Scholion, III.

[391] *Manuale de Udienza, Codice Civile,* tit. V, *Del matrimonio,* sec. II, art., 58 and 59, p. 18, Milano, 1911.

the latter it is restricted to the first degree of the same line. The civil authority according to art. 85 of the Spanish Code reserves to itself the right to dispense for just causes in the third and the fourth civil degree of legitimate consanguinity.[392]

In Germany all marriages are null and void between descendants and ascendants in the direct line, and between brother and sister of whole or half blood in the collateral line.

The German Civil Law on this point was incorporated into the Civil Code of the State of New York of the United States of North America.[393]

347. As is seen from the foregoing exposition of the civil legislation, the present discipline of the Church on this impediment approaches more closely the discipline of the Civil Laws owing to the elimination of the fourth degree. Needless to say that this relaxation favors only those who are under the jurisdiction of the Church, namely, who are baptized. If the Civil Law of a country should forbid marriages up to the fourth degree of consanguinity, a Catholic and an infidel, related in the fourth degree could not contract a valid marriage by the mere fact that they obtained a dispensation from the impediment of disparity of worship. The unbaptized party in the case would be bound by the civil diriment impediment of consanguinity, and unless a dispensation from the state is obtained, no valid contract can be made be-

[392] Wernz, *op. cit.*, n. 424.

[393] For a more comprehensive exposition of the civil legislation on this point the reader is referred to the following works: Eversley, *The Law and Domestic Relations*, London, 1906; Geary, *Marriage and Family Relations*, London, 1892; Murray (Scotland), *The Law Relating to the Property of Married Persons*, Glasgow, 1892; Bishop (America), *Marriage, Divorce and Separation*, Chicago, 1892; Neustadt, *Kritische Studien zum Familienrecht des bürgerlichen Gesetzbuches*, Berlin, 1907; André-Wagner, *Dict. de droit canon.*, Paris, 1901; art., *"Mariage," "Affinité"*; Desmond, *The Church and the Law*, Chicago, 1898.

tween the two. This inference is based on the new law.[394]

X. *Impediment of Affinity.*

(Canon 1077.)

1. *General Notions about Affinity.*

348. Affinity in the present canonical discipline is a bond of relationship arising from valid marriage (ratified, or ratified and consummated) [395] between the husband and the blood-relatives of the wife, and between the wife and the blood-relatives of the husband. The two consorts do not become related in the strict sense of the term, they are only the source of relationship.[396] Since the Church condemned the principle of Nestorius holding that affinity begets affinity, the blood-relatives of the husband do not become related to those of the wife, or *vice versa.* Affinity is always restricted to persons related to the consorts by consanguinity. No relationship is acquired on the part of one of the consorts with persons related to the other consort by marriage.

In order that affinity may arise, the contracted marriage must be valid. An extra-conjugal carnal intercourse or a putative marriage will no longer constitute a source of affinity. The two consorts are the source (*stipes*) from which affinity originates. The wife is the *stipes* of affinity arising between her husband and

[394] "Quanquam impedimentum ex una tantum parte se habet matrimonium tamen reddit aut illicitum aut invalidum." (Cod. Iur. Can., Can. 1036, §3.)

[395] Cod. Iur. Can., Can. 97, §1; c. 11, C. XXVII, q. 2; c. 3, C. XXV, q. 5; c. 1, C. XXV, q. 10; c. 5, X, *de consanguinitate et affinitate,* IV, 14; Benedictus XIV, ep. encycl. *"Inter omnigenas,"* 2 febr., 1744, §15: C. S. S. Off. (Yunnan), 20 sept., 1854; instr. (ad Ep. S. Alberti), 9 dec., 1874; instr. (ad Vic. Ap. Nankin.), 26 aug., 1891.

[396] Gasparri, *op. cit.,* n. 688; Schmalzgrüber, *op. cit.,* p. III, tit. XIV, n. 89; c. 20, C. XXXII, q. 7; c. 13, 22, C. XXXV, q. 2, et 3; c. XXXV, q. 5; c. 5, X, *de consanguinitate et affinitate,* IV, 14.

her blood-relatives. The husband is the *stipes* of affinity arising between his wife and his blood-relatives.[397] In affinity there are no generations. The terms "line" and "degree" refer to the consanguineous relatives of the respective consorts.

349. In order to compute the degrees of lineal or collateral affinity, one must apply the following principle: The degree and line of consanguinity determine the degree and line of affinity. A person related to one consort in a certain line and degree of consanguinity becomes related to the other consort in the same degree and line of affinity.[398]

A. 1. In the direct ascendental line the relatives (*affines*) are: I. degree: father-in-law (*socer*), mother-in-law (*socrus*); II. degree: wife's or husband's grandfather (*prosocer*), wife's or husband's grandmother (*prosocrus*); III. degree: wife's or husband's great-grandfather (*absocer*), wife's or husband's great-grandmother (*absocrus*).

A. 2. In the direct descendental line the *affines* are: I. degree: son-in-law (*gener*), daughter-in-law (*nurus*); II: degree: grand-daughter's husband (*progener*), grandson's wife (*pronurus*).

B. 1. In the case of second marriage the relatives in the direct ascendental line are: I. degree: step-father (*vitricus*), step-mother (*noverca*); II. degree: grandmother's husband (*provitricus*), grandfather's wife (*pronoverca*).

B. 2. In the descendental direct line the *affines* are: I. degree: stepson (*privignus,* son of a father or mother born of a former marriage), stepdaughter (*privigna,* daughter of a father or mother born of a former marriage).

[397] Cod. Iur. Can., Can. 97, §2.

[398] Cod. Iur. Can., Can. 97, §3; c. 3, C. XXXV, q. 5; S. C. S. Off., instr. (ad Archiep. Quebecen.), 16 sept., 1824, ad 2, 4.

C. In the collateral line the *affines* are: I. degree: brother-in-law (*levir*), sister-in-law (*glos*); brother's wife (*fratria*), sister's husband (*sororius*). The other relatives have no special name. They are designated by the various degrees of affinity.[399]

350. Affinity is multiplied as often as the consanguinity is multiplied.[400] A person related to one consort by a double tie of consanguinity becomes related to the other by a double tie of affinity. Thus, for instance, Charles contracted marriage with Agnes. If Agnes should happen to be twice related to Cecilia in two different degrees of consanguinity, then Charles also becomes twice related to Cecilia in the same degree of affinity. Affinity is multiplied also by a marriage contracted successively with a blood-relative of the deceased consort.[401] If Joseph should marry successively Agnes and Cecilia, related to Bertha in the first and the second degree of consanguinity respectively, he becomes twice related to Bertha.

2. *History and Nature of the Impediment.*

351. The impediment of affinity is a mere enforcement, in a modified form, of the prohibition of the Mosaic Law. *Leviticus* forbids marriages between relatives in the first and the second degree of the direct line, in the first degree of the collateral line, and in the first degree mixed with the second of the same line, between a man and the widow of his father's brother.[402] By prescribing that the surviving brother should marry the childless widow of his deceased brother, the law of the levirate removed from such cases the ban under which they were placed by the general law, by

[399] SANTI-LEITNER, *h. t.*, n. 34; GASPARRI, *op. cit.*, n. 691; GIOVINE, *op. cit.*, §303.

[400] COD. IUR. CAN., Can. 1077, §2, n. 1.

[401] *Op. cit.*, Can. 1077, §2, n. 2.

[402] *Levit.* XVIII, 8 ff.; XX, 20, 21.

virtue of its prohibition directed against affinity in the first degree of the collateral line.[403]

The cause of affinity in the Roman Law was a valid marriage (*iustae nuptiae*) even if unconsummated. The prohibition of marriage was confined to lineal affinity, namely, between stepfather or stepmother and stepdaughter or stepson (the two born of a previous marriage); and between father-in-law or mother-in-law and daughter-in-law or son-in-law.[404]

352. The Mosaic and the Roman Law are the two sources on which Canon Law has drawn as regards its legislation concerning affinity. For the first three centuries the Church contented itself with the mere enforcement of the Mosaic Law. Towards the end of the third and in the first quarter of the fourth century there are evidences proving that the Church has extended the impediment beyond the degrees specified in the Mosaic Law and began to legislate independently of any civil influence.[405] The Councils of Elvira (300-306)[406] and of Neo-Caesarea (314-325),[407] as well as the Synod of Rome,[408] establish this fact beyond doubt. The various Councils held in Gaul in the sixth and the seventh century either emphasized the already existing discipline or introduced new legislative measures modifying the impediment of affinity by extending it to further degrees. They threaten with severe penalties one who should attempt to marry "the widow of his brother, or the sister of his wife, or his stepdaughter, or his stepmother, or the widow of an uncle whether

[403] *Deut.* XXV, 5; *Matt.* XXII, 24; *Mark* XII, 19; *Luke* XX, 28.

[404] WERNZ, *op. cit.*, n. 429; DE SMET, *op. cit.*, n. 307; ESMEIN, *op. cit.*, vol. I, pp. 375 ff.; §7, *inst. de nuptiis*, I. 10; L. 14, §4, *D. de ritu nuptiarum*, XXIII, 2; L. 4, §§3 sq., *D. de gradibus*, XXXVIII, 10; L. 17, *C. de nuptiis*, V. 4.

[405] WERNZ, *op. cit.*, n. 429; ESMEIN, *op. cit.*, vol. I, p. 375.

[406] MANSI, *op. cit.*, vol. II, col. 15, c. 61.

[407] MANSI, *op. cit.*, vol. II, col. 540, c. 2.

[408] MANSI, *op. cit.*, vol. III, col. 1137 and 1138.

on the father's or on the mother's side." The canonical discipline adopted at these Councils was subsequently incorporated into the civil Codes of Burgundy, of the Visigoths in Spain, of the Longobards in Italy and of other nations.

The reason adduced in favor of the impediment of consanguinity may be applied to that of affinity, but it does not possess the same force. By virtue of the conjugal intercourse, which is the cause of affinity, a certain similarity is established between the two impediments owing to the natural bond which such an intercourse creates between one consort and the blood-relatives of the other.[409] The reverence, respect and love which this particular tie occasions, are ill disposed to encourage conjugal alliances among the persons thus related.[410] The legislation of nations not altogether untutored, as well as the Roman law,[411] intimates that the voice of nature makes itself heard by dissuading from such unions.

353. The impediment of affinity being closely allied with that of consanguinity, there was a tendency to limit both to the same degree. This was done by the Council of Rome (1059) [412] by virtue of whose legislation the two impediments reached the seventh, their furthest prohibitory degree. But the force of the prohibition attached to the last two degrees remained a controverted question. In some localities they were regarded as diriment, in others only as impedient impediments.[413]

The early discipline of the Church was rendered

[409] C. 15, C. XXXV, q. 2 and 3; ST. THOMAS, *Suppl.* IIIae, p., q. LV, a. VI, ad 1 and 2.

[410] WERNZ, *op. cit.*, n. 431; GASPARRI, *op. cit.*, n. 697.

[411] §6, *Inst. de nupt.*, I. 10; L. 16 sq., *D. soluto matrimonio*, XXIV. 3.

[412] MANSI, *op. cit.*, vol. XIX, col. 909.

[413] C, 1 8, X, *de consanguinitate et affinitate*, IV. 14; SANCHEZ, *de imped. aff.*, lib., VII, disp. LXVII, n. 3; PETRI LOMBARDI, lib. IV, in *Sent.*, dist. XLI.

very complicated on this point and it unnecessarily affected many persons by the fact that the accepted custom distinguished four different kinds of affinity. The period in which the impediment arising from illicit affinity (from extra-matrimonial carnal intercourse) was introduced into the canonical discipline, is a disputed question. Whether its first trace is found in the pseudo-Isidorian decretals, or whether it was anterior to their date,[414] has little bearing on the present question. Suffice it to say that about the ninth century the first kind of affinity arose through either matrimonial or extra-conjugal carnal intercourse.[415] The other kinds of affinity were introduced after that date, though some traces of them may have been found in some few localities even at that time. Wernz remarks that no vestige of any other than the first kind of affinity can be discerned in the canonical discipline enforced before the eleventh and twelfth centuries.

354. The second kind of affinity established a bond of relationship between the man and the *affines* (by the first kind of affinity) of the woman, and *vice versa.* Thus if a man contracted marriage with a widow, the *affines* of the woman by the first marriage became related to the man by the second kind of affinity, and *vice versa.* The third kind of affinity arose between the man and the *affines* related to the woman by the second kind of affinity.[416] There was yet a fourth kind of affinity resulting from generation rather than from carnal intercourse, affecting the children born of a second marriage (*soboles ex secundis nuptiis*). The

[414] ESMEIN, *op. cit.,* vol. I, pp. 377 ff.; WERNZ, *op. cit., loc cit.;* FREISEN, *op. cit.,* pp. 449 ff.; SANCHEZ, *loc. cit.,* lib. VII, disp. LXV, n. 8; and disp. LXVII, n. 3.

[415] C. 12, 21, 22, C. XXXV, q. 2 and 3.

[416] SANTI-LEITNER, *op. cit., h. t.,* n. 18; BURTSELL, in the *Catholic Encyclopedia,* art., *"Affinity";* GASPARRI, *op. cit.,* n. 689; BENEDICT XIV, *De Synodo Dioecesana,* lib. IX, c. XIII, n. 2.

widow who married remained affined to the relatives of her first husband even after his death, and transmitted this affinity to her second husband. Her children by the latter were forbidden to contract marriage with persons related to her deceased husband within the fourth degree.[417]

The tendency to give so wide a range to the impediment of affinity was checked by Innocent III, who in the fourth Lateran Council (1215) abolished the last named kinds of affinity. Thus only the first kind of affinity was retained, and that was restricted to the fourth degree. It could arise either from extra-matrimonial or from conjugal carnal intercourse.[418]

This impediment was submitted to another modification by the Fathers convened in the Council of Trent. As to licit affinity, the discipline of the Fourth Lateran Council was retained intact. The impediment of illicit affinity, arising from extra-matrimonial intercourse, was restricted to the second degree of the collateral line.[419]

The last stage of development is found in the new legislation in which this impediment, like the impediment of consanguinity, has been officially canonized. The impediment of affinity can no longer arise from two sources, namely, from licit and illicit carnal intercourse. In the new discipline the impediment of illicit affinity has been abrogated, and only that of licit affinity retained with a modification. This latter forbids marriage in all the degrees of lineal affinity, but the prohibition is restricted to the second degree of collateral affinity.[420]

417 C. 2, 3, 4, C. XXXV, q. 10; Esmein, *op. cit.*, vol. I, p. 381; De Smet, *op. cit.*, n. 307.

418 *Conc. Lateranense* IV, cap. 50, see Mansi, *op. cit.*, vol. XXII, col. 1035; C. 8, X, *de consanguinitate et affinitate*, IV. 14.

419 *De Reform. mat.*, sessio XXIV, cap. IV.

420 Cod. Iur. Can., Can. 1077.

3. Derivative Force of the Impediment.

355. It has been a much mooted question whether a marriage contracted in any degree of affinity is invalidated by virtue of natural law. No authors of note have ever claimed that natural law invalidates marriage between *affines* beyond the first degree of the direct line, whether the affinity is legitimate or illegitimate.

356. It is generally admitted that carnal intercourse, whether licit or illicit, establishes a natural bond between each of the parties and the blood-relatives of the other.[421] This natural bond arises even in infidelity, but it does not possess the force of invalidating a marriage between persons thus related.[422]

As far as lineal or collateral affinity arising in the first degree by means of extra-matrimonial carnal intercourse is concerned, the foregoing statement has never been questioned. In all such instances for just and grave reasons the Church has repeatedly granted a dispensation, which she could not presume to do, if she held that natural law invalidates such unions. The question is more difficult of solution as regards lineal affinity in the first degree arising from valid and consummated marriage. There are, however, enough convincing proofs to show that even in that degree the diriment impediment is not one of natural law but of ecclesiastical law.[423] The attitude of the Church in declining for a long time to dispense from licit lineal affinity in the first degree must be explained on the ground of inexpediency. Benedict XIV [424] reprimands

[421] D'Annibale, *op. cit.*, vol. I, n. 62; Wernz, *op. cit.*, *h. t.*, foot-note 43; Gasparri, *op. cit.*, n. 687; Schmalzgrüber, *op. cit.*, p. III, tit. XIV, nn. 87 sq.; Sanchez, *op. cit.*, lib. VII, disp. 65, nn. 1 sq.

[422] Wernz, *op. cit.*, n. 430.

[423] Giovine, *op. cit.*, §§305 and 306; Gasparri, *op. cit.*, n. 697; Feije, *op. cit.*, n. 379; Santi-Leitner, *op. cit.*, *h. t.*, nn. 25 ff.

[424] *De Synodo Dioecesana*, lib. IX, cap. XIII, n. 4.

the Synod of Lima (1583) for having prescribed separation in the case of converts who, while in infidelity, contracted marriage within the first degree of affinity. A contrary opinion would be equivalent to maintaining, against the teaching of approved authors, that natural law invalidates all marriages contracted in that degree. Therefore Benedict XIV emphasizes the fact that for very grave and urgent reasons the Church may certainly dispense in all such cases. The same truth is accentuated in his encyclical "*Aestas Anni.*"[425]

357. To refute further the false assumption of the Council of Lima one could adduce the decrees of the Councils of Agde (506),[426] Epaon (517)[427] and of Orleans III (538),[428] which distinctly state that marriages contracted in infidelity with stepmother and stepdaughter should not be dissolved.

On February 20, 1888, the Holy See gave an extraordinary faculty to Ordinaries *urgente mortis periculo.* They were authorized to dispense from all impediments from which the Church itself dispenses. From this faculty the impediment arising from the Holy Priesthood and from lineal affinity in the first degree *ex copula licita,* is withdrawn.[429] That the former is an impediment of merely ecclesiastical origin, no one will deny. Consequently, the latter is withdrawn from the faculty for the same reason. The new discipline *urgente mortis periculo* grants the same extensive faculties, exempting the same two impediments.[430]

The decree of the Holy Office issued on August 26, 1891, settles this question beyond all doubt. It stated expressly that affinity, contracted in infidelity, whether

[425] *Bull. Rom. Cont.*, vol. IV, App. altera ad tom., III, p. II, p. 473.
[426] MANSI, *op. cit.,* vol. VIII, col. 335, c. 61.
[427] MANSI, *op. cit.,* vol. VIII, col. 562, c. 30.
[428] MANSI, *op. cit.,* vol. IX, col. 14, c. 10.
[429] Litt. encycl. S. C. S. Off., 20 febr., 1888; new *Collectanea,* n. 1685.
[430] COD. IUR. CAN., Can. 1043; see this work, n. 151 ff.

it results from a licit or an illicit intercourse, should not be regarded as an impediment in the case of marriages entered into in infidelity.[431]

358. The statement contained in this decree is further corroborated by the fact that on December 2, 1911, the Sacred Penitentiaria has actually granted such a dispensation to parties whose request for such dispensation had been rejected by the Congregation of the Sacraments.[432] On another occasion, eight years before, the Roman Pontiff granted a similar dispensation by word of mouth.[433]

In view of these facts the statements of the canonists who maintained that the Roman Pontiff never dispenses in lineal affinity must be modified.[434]

359. Concerning the impediment of affinity as it exists in the Oriental Church the same thing is to be said as has been said of the impediment of consanguinity. The time, no doubt, is not far removed when its discipline will conform to that of the Occidental Church. Until then the past discipline of the Roman Catholic Church will obtain among the members of the Oriental Rite. Affinity will arise only from *copula perfecta* either from matrimonial or extra-conjugal intercourse, prohibiting and invalidating marriages in both cases in all the degrees of lineal affinity, and in collateral affinity to the fourth canonical or eighth Oriental degree (in case of legitimate affinity), and to the second canonical or fourth Oriental degree in case of

[431] "Affinitatem quae in infidelitate naturaliter contrahitur ex copula tum licita tum illicita non esse impedimentum pro matrimoniis quae in infidelitate ineuntur." (Instr. S. C. S. Off., 26 aug., 1891; new *Collectanea,* n. 1766.

[432] *Le Canoniste Contemporain,* vol. XXXV, 1912, pp. 659 ff.

[433] De Smet, *op. cit.,* n. 306; *Nouv. Rev. Théol.,* 1912, pp. 528 ff.; *Collat. Brug.,* 1912, pp. 674 ff.

[434] Perrone, *op. cit.,* vol. II, pp. 138 ff.; Schmalzgrüber, *op. cit.,* p. III, tit. XVI, n. 141; Wernz, *op. cit.,* n. 430; Gasparri, *op. cit.,* n. 703; Putzer, *op. cit.,* n. 220; Benedict XIV, quoted above; et alii.

illegitimate affinity.[435] The discipline prevailing among the Maronites extends this impediment to the seventh degree according to the civil computation.[436]

The Constitution of Benedict XIV, *"Etsi pastoralis,"* affecting the Italo-Greeks, prohibits marriage within the fourth degree of affinity according to the canonical computation.[437] With the consent of the Holy See a provincial Council[438] legislated that legitimate natural relationship will invalidate marriage up to the seventh degree (civil computation) in the first kind of affinity. As to the second kind of affinity (arising between the blood-relatives of the two consorts) it was decided that it must be retained wherever it is in force and it will invalidate marriages up to the seventh degree, *"ita tamen ut confusione nominum haud interveniente tum in septimo tum in sexto gradu impedimentum dirimens minime constituat."* At the same time the impediment arising from illicit affinity was restricted to the fourth degree.[439]

4. *Dispensation from the Impediment.*

360. As stated above the natural bond of affinity arising between two infidels does not possess an in-

[435] *Synodus Sciarfensis Syrorum,* Rome, 1896, art., XV, §8, n. 12; *Synodus Alexandrina Coptorum,* Romae, 1899, art. VIII, §5, n. 9. "Hinc affinitas semper aderit si facta fuerit conceptio (LEHMKUHL, *op. cit.,* vol. II, n. 998), vel eiamsi illa facta non fuerit si vir membro virili vas mulieris penetravit, et, rupto hymene, semen in vaginam deposuit." *Acta Sanctae Sedis,* vol. XXVII, pp. 339 ff.; WERNZ, *op. cit.,* n. 432; GASPARRI, *op. cit.,* nn. 686 and 687; DE SMET, *op. cit.,* n. 302; FEIJE, *op. cit.,* n. 370; DE BECKER, *op. cit.,* p. 185; MANSELLA, *op. cit.,* pp. 50 ff.

[436] *Synodus Mont. Lybani* (1736), in *Collect. Lac.,* vol. II, col. 161 sq.; ib., WERNZ, *op. cit.,* n. 442.

[437] BENEDICT XIV, 26 maii, 1742, *Bull. Rom. Cont.,* vol. I, p. 197, §8, n. 5.

[438] *Conc. Alba Iuliense* (1872), p. 96; ib., WERNZ, *op. cit.,* n. 442.

[439] PAPP-SZILÁGYI, *op. cit.,* pp. 44 ff.; ZHISHMAN, *loc. cit.,* pp. 290 ff.; MILASCH, Das Kirchenrecht der morgenländischen Kirche, p. 614. (Mostar, 1905); MANSELLA, op. cit., pp. 57 ff.

validating force. However, the individuality of the bond thus contracted, by virtue of ecclesiastical law, becomes endowed with a diriment force after the conversion of one or both parties in question.[440] The conversion, however, does not affect marriages contracted validly in infidelity. It extends only to prospective marriages, and to those invalidly contracted in infidelity, on account of an intervening impediment other than that of affinity. The impediment of affinity affects all baptized persons regardless of the sect in which the baptism was administered. The marriage of two infidels is invalid if the civil law should sanction the diriment force of the impediment of affinity. If two infidel *affines* should contract marriage invalidly, and only one of them should embrace the Catholic faith, not only the impediment of disparity of worship but also that of affinity would interfere with the validity of their marriage.

361. According to a principle formerly accepted, the Church, when dispensing from the impediment of disparity of worship, intended simultaneously to dispense from that of affinity, unless it should happen to be legitimate lineal affinity in the first degree, in which the Church has not dispensed until very recently. This principle is not in harmony with the new law, consequently it must be discarded. It may be said, however, that since the Church, owing to the relaxation of her discipline on this point, has already vouchsafed dispensations from the impediment arising from the first degree of legitimate lineal affinity, it probably will not decline to grant a similar favor in the future when the need of legitimating children already born of such union would make it imperative.

362. The dispensation granted in the past from

[440] Instr. S. C. S. Off., 26 aug., 1890 (ad Vic. Ap. Nankin.), new *Collectanea,* n. 1766.

illegitimate lineal affinity contained the conditional clause: Provided the intercourse with the mother of the prospective wife did not precede the birth of the latter.[441] This adjunct was intended to obviate the possibility of a man espousing his own natural daughter. While in the future such affinity will no longer arise from extra-matrimonial intercourse, it will be the duty of the parish priest to investigate carefully all such cases, if he should be aware of the illegitimate birth of the prospective spouse. If it should not be possible, physically speaking, that the woman in question could be the offspring of the man, the latter may marry her without dispensation. In all doubtful cases the advice of the Bishop should be asked.

In the past the impediment of affinity, as is seen from the foregoing exposition, could arise from two sources, namely, from a licit and an illicit intercourse. The new discipline deprives of its invalidating effect the impediment arising from illicit affinity. It may happen, however, that a person who contracted such an affinity while the old discipline was in force, after the promulgation of the new Code might intend to marry the person to whom he is thus related. In all such instances, since the marriage is not forbidden, the affinity which arose under the old discipline will be implicitly removed by the new.

Collateral affinity in the second degree is a minor impediment consequently, a dispensation once granted from it will be valid irrespective of an error, and regardless of obreption and subreption.[442] Since the impediment of collateral affinity is restricted to the second degree, whenever, in unequal line, one of the degrees falls below the second, the impediment ceases.

[441] De Smet, *op. cit.*, n. 306; Giovine, *op. cit.*, §307, n. 4; Wernz, *op. cit.*, n. 438.

[442] Cod. Iur. Can., Can. 1042, §2, n. 4.

Thus collateral affinity in which the third degree touches the first, does not constitute a matrimonial impediment.

5. *Penalty Attached to this Impediment.*

363. The censure the authors mention generally in connection with this impediment is to be interpreted by way of particular, namely, provincial or diocesan legislation. In the early discipline of the Church by virtue of general legislation a censure *latae sententiae non reservata* was incurred by persons who attempted marriage without dispensation with any one known to be related to them in a prohibited degree of consanguinity or affinity.[443] The Constitution of Gregory XIV, "*Sicut antiquus,*" issued on March 1, 1590,[444] instructs the Ordinaries that they should penalize with severe ecclesiastical censures persons who without the necessary dispensation attempt to contract marriage in the second degree of consanguinity or affinity. Though the Constitution of Pius IX, "*Apostolicae Sedis,*" issued on October 12, 1869, abolished the Clementine censure *ipso facto* incurred, it did not prohibit the infliction of one *ferendae sententiae* for the same transgression.

364. The new legislation declares *infames* all persons guilty of incest.[445] This infamy is called *infamia iuris,* for it is attached to certain determined acts,[446] as in this case to a sin against the sixth commandment with one's blood-relative or affinis.[447] The consequences

[443] C. un. *de consanguinitate et affinitate,* in *Clem.;* ib., PUTZER, *op. cit.,* n. 222; HOLLWECK, *Kirchliche Strafgesetze,* p. 267, §§169 ff.; SCHMALZGRÜBER, *op. cit.,* p. III, tit. XIV, nn. 115 ff.; WERNZ, *op. cit.,* n. 439.

[444] *Freib. Kirchenlex.,* ed. 2, vol. II, col. 1493; ib., PUTZER, *op. cit., ut supra.*

[445] COD. IUR. CAN., Can. 2357.

[446] *Op. cit.,* Can. 2293, §2.

[447] C. 2, 4, X, *de eo, qui cognovit consanguineam uxoris suae vel sponsae,* IV. 13.

of this infamy are manifold. It communicates irregularity. It renders one incompetent to obtain any ecclesiastical benefices, pensions, offices or dignities. It incapacitates one for performing legitimate ecclesiastical acts [448] and for exercising any ecclesiastical right or function.[449] This kind of infamy is not removed without a special dispensation granted by the Holy See.[450]

365. Affinity, as established by the new law being a public impediment by its very nature may be exposed by any person, like the impediment of consanguinity. Therefore, in this respect, the same principles are to be applied to both impediments.[451]

366. An adulterous intercourse with a blood-relative of one's true consort establishes an affinity between husband and wife, but the affinity thus occasioned does not invalidate the marriage.[452] The contrary opinion was held for a while which permitted the innocent party to remarry, but the guilty consort as well as his accomplice, if single, had to remain single all their life.[453] Though to adulterous incest for a century was attributed the force of dissolving marriage, such an effect was always denied to adultery committed with a non-consanguineous relative of the other consort.[454] It must, however, be borne in mind that this discipline was localized and was never approved by the universal legislation of the Church.[455] Even

[448] See this work, n. 270.

[449] COD. IUR. CAN., Can. 2294.

[450] *Op. cit.*, Can. 2295.

[451] See this work, n. 343 ff.; ST. THOMAS, *Suppl.* III, p., q. LV, a. X and XI, c.

[452] ST. THOMAS, *op. cit.*, q. LV, a. VI, c.; again, *op. cit.*, q. L, a. I, ad 7.

[453] *Conc. Vermer.* (753), c. 2, 10, 11, 12, 18; c. 21, 24, C. XXXII, q. 7; c. 30, C. XXVII, q. 2; ESMEIN, *op. cit.*, vol. I, p. 382; c. 19, C. XXII, q. 7.

[454] C. 22, C. XXXII, q. 2.

[455] HEFELE, *Histoire des Conciles,* t. III, 2me partie, p. 920, Paris, 1910.

the provincial councils held in the ninth century failed to approve it.[456] Furthermore, the Decretals of Gregory IX insist emphatically on the absolute indissolubility of a consummated Christian marriage, even if one of the consorts should happen to be guilty of incestuous adultery.

367. As a penalty for such crime the former discipline deprived the guilty party of the right *petendi debitum conjugale,* though he is was not freed from the obligation *reddendi debitum* when the innocent party demanded it. In order that such a right may be lost on the part of the offender, *incestus adulterinus debuit esse formalis, consummatus, non tantum inchoatus, neque vi vel metu gravi extortus.* Furthermore, the incest had to be committed with a person related to the other consort within the first or the second degree of consanguinity.[457] The affinity was not contracted, nor was the penalty incurred, in the case of *incestus adulterinus patratus cum propriis consanguineis.* The new law states distinctly that all penalties whether spiritual or temporal, medicinal or so-called vindictive, whether *latãe* or *ferendae sententiae,* are abrogated unless they are expressly mentioned in the new Code.[458] Since the loss of the *ius petendi debitum* was a temporal penalty occasioned in consequence of a specified moral offence, and since the Code fails to refer to it, the conclusion is forced on us that such a penalty is no longer incurred.

368. The reader's attention has already been called to the relaxation of the discipline of the Church as re-

[456] C. 1, 6, X, *de eo, qui cognovit consanguineam uxoris suae vel sponsae,* IV, 13; the statutes of the provincial councils held in the ninth century, see HEFELE, *op. cit., loc cit.*

[457] *Conc. Trid., De Reformatione matrimonii,* c. IV; WERNZ, *op. cit.,* n. 441.

[458] COD. IUR. CAN., Can. 16, n. 5; for former discipline consult GIOVINE. *op. cit.,* §302; FEIJE, *op. cit.,* n. 383; PUTZER, *op. cit.,* n. 124, p. 161.

gards the impediment of affinity. It was owing to this tendency to leniency that the two dispensations referred to above in the first degree of lineal affinity were made possible. Thus the prediction of Gasparri that the Church will never dispense in such affinity has failed.[459]

In the past it was against the practice of the Sacred Congregation to grant a dispensation in any degree of licit lineal affinity.[460] Such dispensations will naturally be rendered more obtainable in the future.

As to collateral affinity the Church never declined to dispense, even in the first degree, though a grave cause was required in case a widow wished to marry the brother of her deceased husband. The cause had to be even more grave in case the widow had offspring by her former husband. The instruction contained in the encyclical of Gregory XVI, issued on May 22, 1836, may be applied also to cases of collateral affinity. Since by nature the bond of consanguinity is stronger than that of affinity, the causes for granting a dispensation from the latter impediment suffice even if they should be less grave than those required for dispensation from the impediment of consanguinity.

6. *Civil Legislation.*

369. The present legislation of the Church conforms to the Roman and the Civil Law inasmuch as it requires a valid marriage for the contraction of affinity. In the eyes of the Civil Law, as a rule, the bond of affinity retains its force though the marriage which occasioned it should be annulled by judicial process (divorce). This bond, however, is dissolved if the marriage should be declared null and void from the

[459] GASPARRI, *op. cit.*, n. 703.
[460] AVANZANI, *Acta Santae Sedis*, vol. II, 127.

very beginning, having been originally unlawful on account of some civil prohibition.

The Code of Napoleon (art. 161) bases the impediment of affinity on valid marriage regardless of its consummation.[461] It prohibits marriage in every degree of the direct line and in the first degree of the collateral line (art. 162). Dispensation can be granted only by the supreme ruler.[462]

The Code of Italy in this respect conforms to the Code of Napoleon. After repeated introduction and rejection the English Parliament finally adopted in 1906 the "Colonial Marriage Act" by virtue of which marriages with a deceased wife's sister were permitted for the colonies. In 1907 the same enactment was extended to England itself under the title "Deceased Wife's Sister Marriage Act."[463]

The law of Germany (§§1310 and 1327) in case of lineal affinity prohibits marriage between one consort and the descendant of the other consort, and between the ascendant and the consort of the descendant. The statute fails to distinguish between licit and illicit affinity.[464]

In France all the degrees of lineal affinity but only the first degree of collateral affinity, constitute an impediment to marriage (art. 161 and 162).

In Spain this impediment may arise from either licit or illicit affinity (art. 84). It prohibits marriage in all the degrees of the direct line and in collateral affinity it forbids marriage up to the second or fourth degree (civil computation), according as it arises from a conjugal or extra-matrimonial intercourse.

[461] De Smet, *op. cit.*, n. 307, Scholion II.

[462] Le Congrès national, Loi du 28 fev., 1831, article unique.

[463] *Encyclopaedia Britanica* (eleventh edition), art., "*Marriage*" (England).

[464] Lehr, *Traité Elementaire de Droit Civil Germanique*, p. 263, Paris, 1892.

370. Some Civil Codes impose a severe penalty on those who in bad faith attempt marriage, though related in lineal affinity or consanguinity. Thus, for instance, the criminal Code of Germany (§173) penalizes such crime with an incarceration lasting two years, and the Italian criminal Code (art. 337) imposes the same penalty lasting from eighteen months to five years.

The prohibition of marriage with a deceased wife's sister has been abolished in most of the States of North America. An exception to this is the State of Virginia,[465] where such a marriage is absolutely void.[466] The statutes of the different states qualify as "void" those marriages that are contracted within the prohibited degrees of consanguinity and affinity. The courts, however, by repeated decisions attribute to the term "void" the meaning "voidable."

XI. The Impediment of Public Propriety.

(Canon 1078.)

371. In the former discipline the consent given in a ratified marriage (whether valid or invalid), or in valid espousals, produced a bond of quasi-affinity between each of the parties and the blood-relatives of the other, just as carnal intercourse is instrumental in inducing real affinity.

It is a difficult task to trace the origin of this impediment with certainty. Though no uniformity prevails on this point among the authors, the opinion of those who hold Roman law responsible for its introduction has as yet not been disproved. The Roman law emphasized a Christian principle when it established the legal rule that in marriage one should not

[465] BURTSELL, in the *Catholic Encyclopedia*, art., *"Affinity."*

[466] KELLY *v.* SCOTT, 5 Gratt. (Va.), 479; ib., KEESER, *The Law of Marriage and Divorce*, chap. III, §25, p. 17, Boston, 1906.

consider only what is lawful but also what is becoming.[467] This rule explains the prohibition directed against marriages violating public propriety, as, for example, those between father and the betrothed of his son, and *vice versa;* between mother and the betrothed of her daughter;[468] between a concubine and the relatives of the man.[469]

372. Owing to the close resemblance existing between the Church and the Roman law on this point there is nothing more natural than to look to the latter for the vestiges of this ecclesiastical impediment. Another difficulty which is awaiting solution is the determination of the particular period in which this impediment was adopted by the Church. Writers of the ninth century like Benedict the Levite, Hinkmar, and pseudo-Isidore fail even to allude to it. A decretal attributed to Pope Benedict positively rejects it,[470] while, on the other hand, other contemporary decrees, which Gasparri brands as apocryphal, speak of it as if it were the universal law of the Church.[471] For a long time the impediment of public propriety was enveloped in obscurity and several legislative measures enacted by different Pontiffs were required before its identity as an impediment distinct from affinity was clearly established.

The legislation of Alexander III (1159-1181) does not shed sufficient light to remove all doubts surrounding this impediment.[472] Innocent III in the Fourth Lateran Council (1215) lifted the prohibition whereby the offspring of a second marriage was barred from contracting marriage with the relatives of the first hus-

[467] L. 42 ff., *De ritu nuptiarum;* DE SMET, *op. cit.*, n. 308; GASPARRI, *op. cit.*, n. 706; WERNZ, *op. cit.*, n. 448.

[468] L. 12, §1 and §2; l. 14 ff., *De ritu nuptiarum.*

[469] L. 7, *De gradib. et affin.*

[470] C. 18, C. XXVII, q. 2.

[471] C. 11, 14, 15, C. XXVII, q. 2.

[472] C. 4, 5, 6, X, *de desponsatione impuberum*, IV, 2.

band,[473] and restricted the impediment to the fourth degree, just as was the case with the impediments of consanguinity and affinity. The suggestion made by the Fathers convened at the Second Council of Lyons (1274) relative to the limitation of this impediment to nearer degrees was not acted upon. With the decree of Boniface VIII the impediment began to assume a more definite form.[474] It was enacted that conditional and indeterminate espousals whose invalidity results from lack of consent cannot give rise to it. Finally the Council of Trent limited to the first degree the impediment arising from betrothment and decreed that only valid espousals can give rise to it.[475]

373. The Council of Trent did not concern itself about this impediment as it arises from a ratified marriage. Therefore until the promulgation of the new discipline one had to be guided by the law handed down in the Decretals, especially through the enactments of Boniface VIII. The terms in which the law of that Pontiff is couched occasioned a lively controversy. The decree states that the impediment of public propriety arises from marriage (even if not consummated) whether valid or invalid, provided the invalidity was not caused through want of consent. It would be to no purpose to give a detailed account of this controversy, for it is a subject of the past [476] with no bearing on the present discipline.

374. The change which the concept of affinity underwent in the present legislation [477] necessitated a change also in the impediment of public propriety. According to the new law the impediment of public

[473] C. 8, X, *de consanguinitate et affinitate,* IV, 14.

[474] C. un., *de sponsalibus et matrimoniis,* IV, 1 and 2, in VI°.

[475] Sess. XXIV, cap. III.

[476] WERNZ, *op. cit.,* n. 453, note 46; DE SMET, *op. cit.,* n. 311; GASPARRI, *op. cit.,* n. 722 ff.; D'ANNIBALE, vol. III, n. 434; FEIJE, *op. cit.,* n. 400 ff.

[477] COD. IUR. CAN., Can. 97, §1.

propriety arises from invalid marriage whether consummated or not, and from public or notorious concubinage; and it annuls marriage in the first and in the second degree of the direct line betwen the man and the blood-relatives of the woman, and *vice versa.*[478]

The new law specifies two causes which are instrumental in inducing this impediment, namely, invalid marriage and public or notorious concubinage. A few words must be said on each. The espousals do not give rise even to an impedient impediment, while the ratified marriage occasions the impediment of affinity.

375. 1. Invalid marriage whether consummated or non-consummated is the first cause giving rise to the impediment of public propriety. The words *"ex matrimonio invalido"* are to be interpreted in their fullest sense, so as to comprehend even a putative marriage which otherwise produces the same effects as the valid marriage. In order that the impediment may arise by virtue of this first cause it is necessary that the parties in question actually attempt to contract marriage, and that their contract have the appearance of marriage (*species vel figura matrimonii*) in a very wide sense of the term. It is immaterial whether the attempt was made before a civil magistrate, or before the minister of a religious sect. On this ground the impediment would arise even in the case of a common law marriage if the civil law in the locality in which it took place sanctions such marriages by attributing to them all the effects of a matrimonial contract and they are regarded as means whereby licit marriage relations may be established between a man and a woman.

Since the law does not specify any particular cause of nullity we are free to conclude that it does not matter whether the invalidity of the marriage was occa-

[478] *Op. cit.,* Can. 1078.

sioned by the non-observance of the proper form or by the presence of a diriment impediment. Even if the marriage is contracted *in facie ecclesiae,* unless it is objectively valid, it will give rise to an impediment of public propriety and not to that of affinity.

376. 2. Public or notorious concubinage is the second cause giving rise to the impediment of public propriety. The question might be asked: When is concubinage public or notorious? The new law legislates [479] that an offence is public when it is already divulged among the people or when circumstances are such that they induce one to conclude prudently and necessarily that the fact will easily be published. The offence is notorious by notoriety of law when a competent judge in his final sentence pronounces the delinquent guilty of it, or when the delinquent by confession of guilt admits the offence either in writing or by word of mouth, whether such confession be spontaneous or the result of inquiry by the judge.[480] An offence is notorious by notoriety of fact if it is publicly known and committed under such circumstances that no recourse to subterfuge can conceal it, and it cannot be excused by the voice of the law.

This impediment will occasion more doubts than perhaps any other. Public concubinage in this connection is not to be interpreted as referring to occasional extra-matrimonial intercourses. Thus, for instance, frequent visits paid to a house of ill fame would not constitute a sufficient ground to induce the impediment of public propriety even if the illicit relations should be limited to one and the same person. The concubinage presupposed by this law must result from a life which may be called a quasi-matrimonial cohabitation. Stress must be laid on the fact that the illicitness of

[479] Cod. Iur. Can., Can. 2197.
[480] *Op. cit.,* Can. 1750.

the carnal relations is supposed to be publicly known. A man and a woman having extra-matrimonial relations would not contract the impediment should they be publicly reputed as husband and wife.

377. The impediment of public propriety is computed like the impediment of affinity. It arises between the man and the lineal blood-relatives of the woman in the first and the second degree, and *vice versa.* Therefore the man could marry the collateral blood-relatives (the sister, for instance) of the woman with whom he contracted an invalid marriage, or with whom he lived in public or notorious concubinage, and *vice versa.* The impediment would assert itself should a man intend to marry the daughter or the granddaughter, or the mother or the grandmother of such a woman.

378. Since the impediment is of ecclesiastical origin it does not affect infidels in the absence of a similar civil impediment. The question might arise: How are we to decide the question when the man belongs under the jurisdiction of the Church and the woman is an infidel? The strict interpretation of the law would permit a conclusion militating against the spirit of the Church. Since the infidel woman is not affected directly by the impediment it would seem that she may contract marriage with the baptized son of the baptized man with whom she entered into an invalid marriage, or with whom she lives in public or notorious concubinage. Such a marriage would be against the spirit of the Church, but no impediment would stand in its way unless we are to conclude that the baptized person transmits or communicates his inability to all his baptized blood-relatives affected by this law. But such a conclusion is not warranted by the wording of the canon. No one would deny that she could marry the unbaptized son of such a man. In that case neither the son nor the woman (both being infidels) would come under the jurisdiction of the Church, therefore the impediment would not bind. The same conclusion is to be drawn when an infidel man is similarly correlated with the unbaptized or the baptized blood-relatives of the baptized woman with whom he lives in public or notorious concubinage or with whom he contracted an invalid marriage.

The new law bars from all legitimate ecclesiastical acts all persons guilty of public concubinage and the penalty remains in force until they show a sign of true repentance and of amendment.[481]

XII. The Impediment of Spiritual Relationship.
(Canon 1079.)

379. Spiritual relationship is a supernatural bond which, by virtue of ecclesiastical law, establishes a connection between certain persons through the reception or the administration of the sacraments of Baptism and of Confirmation. In the present discipline both these sacraments are instrumental in giving rise to spiritual relationship, but only that relationship has the force of a diriment impediment which is associated with the sacrament of Baptism.

The impediment of Spiritual Relationship passed through several stages of development in the course of its history. Its cause is to be sought in the bond which springs up between the minister of the baptism and the person baptized. This spiritual paternity and sonship, notions as old as Christianity,[482] were gradually extended to all persons who were actively connected with the administration of the sacrament of Baptism. Such persons were the godfathers and the godmothers

[481] Cod. Iur. Can., Can. 2357, §2; see this work, n. 270.

[482] I. Of St. Peter, V. 13; II *Timothy,* II, 1; *Titus,* I. 4; *Philemon,* I, 10 ff.

(*levantes, susceptores vel tenentes*) and also persons who instructed the catechumens in Christian Doctrine as a preparatory step to their reception of the sacrament of Baptism, and testified to the worthiness of the candidate (*offerentes*).[483] In the early ages the two sacraments, namely, Baptism and Confirmation, were conferred at the same time. The fact that the same persons were acting as sponsors at both sacraments dispensed with the necessity of introducing a distinct impediment of spiritual relationship associated with the sacrament of Confirmation.[484] Such provision became necessary when by virtue of custom a period of time was permitted to elapse between the administrations of the two sacraments, for in many cases the sponsors chosen for baptism were different from those at confirmation.

380. In the early ages of Christianity the impediment of spiritual relationship would have served no purpose, for the children were carried to the baptismal font either by their own parents or, on account of propriety, by persons who were of the same sex as the *baptizandus*. When this discipline was changed a praiseworthy custom gave rise to the impediment of spiritual relationship.[485]

The first law prohibiting marriage between the godfather and his god-child dates from the time of Emperor Justinian.[486] Though this civil law as such did not oblige the baptized, it nevertheless reflects the spirit of the age and leads one to believe that even at that early period Canon law accepted such an impediment and the purpose of this civil law was to aid its

[483] TERTULLIAN, *De bapt.*, c. XVIII; DIONYSIUS AREOP., *De hierarchia eccl.*, cap. VII, §11; see MIGNE, *P. G.*, vol. III, col. 567 ff.

[484] LAURIN, *Arch. f. k. K.*, t. XV, p. 220 ff., 239, 253, 259 ff.

[485] ESMEIN, *op. cit.*, vol. I, p. 362; WERNZ, *op. cit.*, n. 485; LAURIN, *op. cit.*, *loc. cit.*, p. 220; FREISEN, *Geschichte des canonischen Eherechts bis zum Verfall des Glossenlitteratur*, p. 508 (Paderborn, 1893).

[486] L. 26, Cod. *de nupt.*, V, 4.

enforcement.[487] The synod of Trullo (692) in its LIII chapter not only canonized this law of the Emperor, but extended the prohibition to marriages between the godfather and the natural mother of the baptized child. After this legislation, by degrees the impediment continued to widen its scope, weaving a net of spiritual relationship around paternity, compaternity, direct[488] and indirect,[489] and even around fraternity.[490] But even then it failed to reach its furthest limits. It was extended to the confessor and his penitent rendering incestuous all carnal relations between them.[491]

When it became customary to select several sponsors for Baptism and different sponsors for the sacrament of Confirmation a wide circle of persons became affected by this impediment. The Council of Rome (721), which was probably the first to legislate on this point in the Occidental Church, drew up a law which failed to remedy this undesirable tendency. It reads: Him who enters into marriage with one related to him by the bond of commaternity, let him be anathema. The same prohibition is emphasized by other Councils held in various places and at different periods. Canons legislating on spiritual relationship as a distinct impediment arising through the sacrament of Confirmation did not appear until the eighth and the ninth century.[492]

381. The Gratian collection incorporated the vari-

[487] BENEDICT XIV, *De Synodo Dioecesana*, lib. IX, cap. X, n. 6; GASPARRI, *op. cit.*, n. 734.

[488] Relationship between the sponsors and the natural parents of the child.

[489] Relationship between the baptized child and the husband or the wife of the sponsor.

[490] Relationship between the baptized child and the natural children of the godparents.

[491] C. 8, 9, 10, C. XXX, q. 1.

[492] Cap. I, *Synod. Gener. in reg. Franc.* (752), HEFELE, *op. cit.*, vol. III, n. 591; Cap. XV, *Conc. Comp.* (757).

ous decrees touching on this impediment,[493] but several official decisions coming from the supreme legislative authority of the Church were necessary before the numerous doubts arising in relation to this impediment were solved. These decrees are embodied in the official decretals of Gregory IX [494] and Boniface VIII.[495]

The Council of Trent was the first to attempt to narrow the compass of the impediment. It abrogated the spiritual relationship arising *ex catechismo* and through fraternity and spiritual affinity. The limits of the impediment were clearly defined, namely, it arose (1) between the minister of the sacraments of Baptism and of Confirmation and the sponsors on one side, and the recipient of the two sacraments on the other; (2) between the natural parents, whether legitimate or illegitimate, of the recipient of the two sacraments on one side and the minister and the sponsors on the other.[496]

Several Fathers of the Vatican Council were in favor of depriving this impediment of its diriment force, but their suggestion was disregarded. According to the present discipline both sacraments, namely, Baptism [497] and Confirmation,[498] give birth to spiritual relationship, but only the relationship associated with the sacrament of Baptism has the force of annulling marriage.[499] It constitutes a diriment impediment between the recipient of the sacrament of Baptism on one side, and the minister of the sacrament and the godparent on the other.

382. Since it is the spiritual bond that constitutes

[493] C. 1, 2, 3, 4, 5, 7, C. XXX, q. 3; c. 1, 2, 3, 4, 5, 6, C. XXX, q. 4; c. 4, C. XXX, q. 1.

[494] C. 2, 4, 5, 6, 8, X, *de cognatione spirituali*, IV, 12.

[495] C. 1, 2, 3, *de cognatione spirituali*, IV, 3, in VI°.

[496] Sessio XXIV, *De reform. matrim.*, cap. II.

[497] COD. IUR. CAN., Can. 768.

[498] *Op. cit.*, Can. 797.

[499] *Op. cit.*, Can. 1079.

the source of this impediment, no impediment will arise unless such a relationship is actually begotten between the recipient and the minister of the sacrament of Baptism, and between the recipient and the godparent. The existence of such relationship presupposes the objective validity of baptism and the competence of the godparent.

383. In order that one may validly act as godparent the following conditions are required by the new law: (1) He must be baptized. He must have reached the age of discretion and must have the intention of assuming the responsibilities attached to such an office; (2) He must not profess membership in a heretical or a schismatical sect, nor should he be excommunicated by a declaratory or condemnatory sentence, nor declared infamous by infamy of law, nor should he be a cleric deposed or degraded; (3) He should not be the father or the mother or the spouse of the recipient of Baptism; (4) He should be designated either by the natural parents, or by the guardians of the *baptizandus,* or, in their absence, by the minister; (5) In the act of baptism he should physically touch or hold, personally or by procurator, the person to be baptized, or should receive the same immediately from the sacred font or from the hands of the minister.[500] These conditions are *ad validitatem.* Should any of them be violated, or disregarded or omitted, no spiritual relationship would result from the administration of baptism. The law very wisely eliminates all possibility of spiritual relationship between the parents of a child baptized by its father or mother. The relationship being non-existent, the *debitum coniugale* would in no way be affected by such an act.

384. It is immaterial whether the baptism is solemn or private, spiritual relationship arises in both, for

[500] *Op. cit.,* Can. 765.

the spiritual bond owes its origin exclusively to spiritual regeneration.[501] A godparent should be chosen even in private baptism. Should such a baptism be administered without a godparent, his presence is required when the ceremonies are supplied, in which case no spiritual relationship is contracted.[502]

When baptism is repeated conditionally, the same godparent should be selected that assisted at the first conditional administration of baptism. Unless this is done, no spiritual relationship results from either conditional administration of the sacrament.[503] A baptism whose validity is doubtful can give rise only to a doubtful impediment of marriage.

385. If the marriage is contracted without a dispensation *ad cautelam* from a doubtful impediment of spiritual relationship and subsequently the absolute validity of the baptism is established, in our estimation, marriage contracted with such an impediment should be regarded as invalid, unless the Church tacitly intends to dispense in all such cases, which intention is not intimated by any official decisions. Wernz,[504] and Gasparri[505] subscribe to the contrary opinion. In this Gasparri is consistent (he applies the same principle in all similar cases throughout his work), but Wernz may be accused of inconsistency. He maintains that marriage contracted with a doubtful impediment of disparity of worship should be regarded as invalid if subsequently the invalidity of the doubtful baptism (which is the cause of the doubtful impediment) is ascertained with moral certainty.[506] It

[501] S. C. C., 5 mart., 1678.

[502] Cod. Iur. Can., Can. 762, §2; S. C. de Prop. Fide, instr. (ad Ep. Scodren.), 11 sept., 1779, n. 4.

[503] Cod. Iur, Can., Can. 763, §2.

[504] *Op. cit.*, n. 489.

[505] *Op. cit.*, n. 737.

[506] *Op. cit.*, n. 507; Gasparri in conformity with his principle upholds the validity of such marriage, see his work, n. 598.

is hard to see how the subsequent solution of such a doubt would produce so different an effect when in both instances the doubt concerns an impediment of marriage whose objective validity depends on whether at the time the contract was made the parties in question were free or not. Furthermore, our contention is corroborated by the principle adopted by the new law. It states distinctly that the validity of a marriage contracted without a dispensation from a doubtful impediment of disparity of worship is to be upheld only till such a time as it is proved beyond all doubt that one of the parties is baptized and the other unbaptized.[507] There is nothing militating against the application of the same principle to a marriage contracted with a doubtful impediment of spiritual relationship. Such marriage should be upheld until it is proved that a relationship was actually begotten by the act of baptism.[508] This once established, the disqualifying force of the impediment should be permitted to take effect from the time the contract was made, which owing to the inability of the contracting parties resulted in an invalid marriage, because the impediment has a retroactive force.

386. The impediment of spiritual relationship is of ecclesiastical origin and can be contracted only by baptized persons. Infidels can in no way be affected by it, not even indirectly, for the contracting of spiritual relationship, as has been already stated, presupposes baptism as a *conditio sine qua non.* In the new legislation the impediment of spiritual relationship will not be multiplied.

387. The Church always required a very grave reason before it dispensed from the impediment of spir-

[507] COD. IUR. CAN., Can. 1070, §2.
[508] *Op. cit.,* Can. 1014.

itual relationship arising through paternity.[509] The faculties given to the Bishops on February 20, 1888, to dispense *concubinarios in periculo mortis constitutos,* did not reserve this impediment. The same extensive faculty is granted to the Bishops and the priests by virtue of canons 1043 and 1044 in behalf of persons who are in danger of death and whose matters of conscience need to be adjusted, and should the case permit, their children legitimated.[510]

XIII. The Impediment of Legal Relationship. (Canon 1080.)

388. The change introduced by the new law in this impediment dispels many doubts and dispenses us from the necessity of devoting much space to the presentation of its history. We advise the reader to consult another part of this work,[511] as well as several other authors.[512]

Adoption is a legal act establishing relations of parenthood and filiation recognized by law between persons not so related by nature. The bond or connection of persons arising from adoption constitutes legal relationship. Cases of adoption were not uncommon even among the Israelites[513] and among the old Germanic races.[514] But it was nowhere so strictly regulated by laws as among the Greeks and the Romans.

Roman law did not as a rule permit adoption unless the adopter was childless and of such age as to pre-

[509] GASPARRI, *op. cit.*, n. 750: WERNZ, *op. cit.*, n. 495.

[510] See this work, n. 151 ff.

[511] See this work, n. 185 ff.

[512] ESMEIN, *op. cit.*, vol. I, p. 357 ff.; LAURIN, *loc. cit.*, t. XIX, p. 193 ff.; GASPARRI, *op. cit.*, n. 751 ff.; WERNZ, *op. cit.*, n. 469; DE BECKER, *op. cit.*, p. 199 ff.; FEIJE, *op. cit.*, n. 428 ff.; DE SMET, *op. cit.*, n. 319 ff.; SANTI-LEITNER, *op. cit.*, vol. IV, tit. XII, p. 234 ff.

[513] *Gen.* XLVIII, 5; *Exod.* II, 10; *Esther*, II, 7, 15.

[514] BENEDICT XIV, *De synodo dioecesana*, lib. IX, cap. X, n. 3; HOLTZENDORFF, *Encyklop. d. Rechtswissensch.*, p. I, p. 259.

clude reasonable expectation of any children being begotten by him. The maxim *"adoptio imitatur naturam"* required of the adoptive father to be at least eighteen years older than the adopted child. The words *alieni iuris* and *sui iuris* played an important rôle, for they determined the two species of adoption accepted by the Roman law. Persons who were still under the *patria potestas* were called *alieni iuris,* while those who were their own masters were called *sui iuris.*[515]

The adoption was either solemn or simple. The solemn adoption, otherwise called *adrogation,* consisted in a legal enactment issued generally by the head of the state[516] by virtue of which an individual who was *sui iuris* passed into the family of the adopter with all the privileges of a legitimate and natural offspring including the right to inheritance whether the adopter died intestate or not.[517] The simple adoption was a legal enactment effected by the authority of the judge or of a competent magistrate whereby relations of paternity and filiation were established between a person not yet of full age (*nondum sui iuris*) and the adoptive father, but in such a way that the former did not pass into the family of the latter, nor was he constituted a necessary heir, though he succeeded his adoptive father if he died intestate.

The adoption was perfect (*plena*) when the adopted person was transferred into the family of the adopter as was generally the case in all solemn adoptions or adrogations, and also in simple adoptions when the adopter was a lineal blood-relative in the ascendant line of the adopted. In every other instance the adoption was imperfect or *minus plena.*

[515] L. 1, 2, D. *De adopt.*, I, 7.
[516] L. 6, C, *De adopt.*, VIII, 48.
[517] Inst. III, 10, *de acquisitione per arrogationem.*

389. The authors are unanimous in maintaining that the impediment of legal relationship constituted a diriment impediment of marriage in the Roman law, but it is a controverted opinion whether such an effect followed only from the perfect or also from the imperfect adoption.[518] In the old law this question was of vital consequence, for on its solution depended whether the impediment existed or not in countries in which imperfect adoption was in vogue. The Holy See was consulted about certain countries and declared the impediment non-existent in Bulgaria[519] and in Tonkin while its presence was upheld for Austria, though the civil laws of that country do not invest the adoption with the force of a diriment matrimonial impediment.[520] From this it would seem that for the past discipline one should be guided by the opinion which denies to the imperfect adoption the power to induce the impediment of legal relationship. It is precisely owing to the imperfect adoption prevailing in countries above-mentioned that the Holy See did not admit the presence of the impediment.

390. The legal kinship sprang from its resemblance to natural relationship. Its purpose was to protect and safeguard the morals of the adopted as well as of those who by residing under the same roof contracted a certain propinquity which on the ground of public decency and propriety militated against their entering into marriage.[521] The intimacy begotten by adoption became recognized by the Church as an impediment to marriage on three grounds, namely, (1) on the ground

[518] WERNZ, *op. cit.*, n. 469, note 32; GASPARRI, *op. cit.*, n. 755; BENEDICT XIV, *De Synodo Dioecesana*, lib. IX, cap. X, n. 5; D'ANNIBALE, *op. cit.*, vol. I, n. 65; DE SMET, *op. cit.*, n. 320; BURTSELL, in the *Catholic Encyclopedia*, art., *"Adoption," (Canonical)*; SANCHEZ, *op. cit.*, lib. VII, disp. LXIII, n. 16; DE ANGELIS, *h. t.*, n. 1.

[519] S. C. S. Off., 16 apr., 1761.

[520] DE BECKER, *op. cit.*, p. 204; GASPARRI, *op. cit.*, n. 761 ff.

[521] ST. THOMAS, *suppl. IIIae, p.*, q. LVII, a. 2.

of paternity (in the direct line) between the adopter and the adopted as well as his descendants who were under his control at the time of the adoption; [522] (2) on the ground of fraternity (in the transverse line) between the adopted and the legitimate natural offspring (*nondum sui iuris*) living under the control of the adopter; [523] (3) on the ground of legal affinity, between the adopter's wife and the adopted, and between the wife of the adopted and the adopter.[524] The impediment arising from the bond of paternity and of legal affinity continued even after the dissolution of the adoption. The impediment to which the tie of fraternity gave rise ceased after the adoption was dissolved, or after the children affected by it either became of age or were emancipated.

391. Pope Nicholas (858-867) not only admits the existence of the impediment but comments upon it very favorably. His remarks were subsequently inserted in the Gratian collection.[525] The other proofs showing the early introduction of the impediment consist in the fact that it was recognized by such early authors as Roland,[526] Peter Lombard,[527] and Bernardus Papiensis.[528] The Decretals of Gregory IX devote only nine lines to this impediment [529] and the Council of Trent, as well as that of the Vatican, declined to sanction the suggestions of the convened Fathers to modify its scope.

392. The present discipline legislates definitely and its tenor makes the question of perfect and imperfect

[522] BENEDICT XIV, *De Synodo Dioecesana, loc. cit.*, n. 4; §§1, 10; *Inst. de nupt.*, I, 10; L. 55, D. *de ritu nupt.*, XXIII, 2.

[523] §§2, 3, 4, *Inst. de nupt.;* L. 3, 17, D. *de ritu nupt.*

[524] L. 14, D. *de ritu nupt.;* L. 23, D. *de ritu nupt.;* L. 4, §10, *de grad. et affin.*, XXXVIII, 10; S. C. C., *Hortana*, 25 sept., 1734.

[525] C. 1, C. XXX, q. 3.

[526] *Summa Magistri Rolandi*, p. 146 (Ed. Thaner.).

[527] Lib. IV, *Sent.*, dist. XLII.

[528] *Summa de matrimonio*, p. 298.

[529] Cap. un. X, *de cognatione legali*, IV, 12.

adoption entirely inconsequential. It reads: Persons who by virtue of civil law are rendered incapable of contracting marriage on account of legal relationship arising from adoption, are disqualified also by canon law from entering into a valid wedlock.[530] Thus the Church law contains an explicit canonization of the civil law of every country.[531] The tenor of the civil law will therefore decide not only the impedient or the diriment force of the impediment but also its scope, namely, the number of individuals who will be affected by it.

393. Though the principle is clear, its application will not be void of difficulties. In countries where the civil impediment of legal relationship is not recognized, the canonical impediment will be non-existent. Some uncertainties will be caused by the fact that the civil Codes are not sufficiently definite in determining the force and the scope of the civil impediment of legal relationship. The canonists of the respective countries will be expected to solve such doubts and to submit the result of their investigation to the Holy See for final decision. Until such conclusions are reached we can say tentatively that in the United States of North America the impediment will be unrecognized, for the civil law does not admit its existence. As regards the Code of Napoleon (art. 348), which is the official Code of Belgium and France, the impediment arising on the ground of legal fraternity in the transverse line is not confined to the adopted and the adopter's legitimate natural offspring. Its scope is extended even to the various children adopted by one and the same person.[532] Other civil Codes as, for example, the Code of Germany,[533] restrict the impediment to legal paternity.

[530] Cod. Iur. Can., Can. 1080.
[531] *Op. cit.*, Can. 1059.
[532] De Smet, *op. cit.*, n. 322, not 2.
[533] §§1311, 1762, 1763; Hollweck, *op. cit.*, p. 104, note 3.

And again in other countries the impediment arising from the direct line on the ground of legal paternity is dissolved by the dissolution of the bond of adoption,[534] while in others it remains in full force even after such dissolution. All these regulations will react on canon law which will conform to the civil law of every country in all its particulars.

394. According to the foregoing principles the impediment of legal relationship will not be in force in those countries of Europe which are in the state of formation, having repudiated the Code of the nation to which they were formerly allied. For such countries the existence or the non-existence of the impediment will depend on the subsequent legislation incorporated in their new civil Codes bearing the official sanction of the representatives of the government and promulgated as the law of the land.

395. To dispense from the impediment arising in the direct line a grave reason was always required, but even a slight cause is sufficient to justify the granting of a dispensation from this impediment as occasioned by legal affinity. In the transverse line the dispensation is hardly ever asked and very seldom granted for the bond of adoption suffers an automatic severance by the fact that the children became of age or are emancipated. To avoid all friction between the Church and the state law in connection with future dispensations, the Church will probably demand that the parties in question should first procure a civil dispensation from the impediment of legal adoption. The civil Codes as a rule hold out the prospect of such a dispensation. The power to grant it is generally vested in the supreme civil ruler. Should the civil authority deny it in the case of two baptized individuals, the Church strictly speaking has the right to grant it notwithstand-

[534] WERNZ, *op. cit.*, n. 480.

ing such refusal. Should there be grave reason justifying and demanding an ecclesiastical dispensation, recourse could be had to a marriage of conscience, if some evil is feared from the revelation of a marriage entered into under such circumstances.[535]

[535] Cod. Iur. Can., Can. 1106; see this work, n. 61 ff.

CHAPTER VII.

MATRIMONIAL CONSENT.

(Canon 1081—Canon 1093.)

I. Matrimonial Consent in General.

396. Consent referred to contracts in general is a deliberate act of the will which results in an agreement of two or more individuals regarding a well-defined object and including within its compass all things inseparable from the essence thereof.[1] Consent is therefore the vitalizing factor which legalizes all transactions. The properly manifested consent of parties juridically competent constitutes marriage. This consent cannot be supplied by any human power.[2] Matrimonial consent is an act of the will whereby the two parties mutually transfer and accept the right over the body, which right is perpetual and exclusive and its purpose is acts in themselves suitable for the generation of offspring.[3] When both parties are competent and the proper consent is given in the sense indicated by the foregoing canon the individual union called marriage springs into being and constitutes the man and the woman as one principle of legitimate procreation.

By declaring that *consensus* (when given under the

[1] GASPARRI, *op. cit.*, n. 771; D'ANNIBALE, vol. II, n. 4, 11.

[2] C. un., C. XXX, q. 2; c. 14, 23-26, 31, X, *de sponsalibus et matrimoniis.* IV. 1; LEO XIII, decr. *"Consensus mutuus,"* 15 febr., 1892; S. C. C., *Mutinen.*, 19 aug., 1724; S. C. de Prop. Fide (C. P. pro Sin.-Tunkin. Occident.), 5 apr., 1785.

[3] COD. IUR. CAN., Can. 1081.

circumstances specified above) *facit matrimonium* the new law settles the much-mooted question of the *copula* theory. One is no longer permitted to advocate the opinion which holds that the conjugal act is an indispensable requisite to marriage in the sense that marriage is an incomplete contract not invested with sacramental character until such an act takes place. This opinion was defended by Gratian[4] and the school of Bologna in opposition to Peter Lombard[5] and the school of Paris. Magister Rolandus, afterwards Alexander III, contributed to the solution of the controversy by propounding a mixed theory whereby it was admitted that *copula,* though it does not pertain to the essence of Christian marriage, is an integrant thereof endowing it with an accidental perfection and with absolute indissolubility.[6]

397. Marriage is a natural contract, hence its essence is to be determined on the ground of natural law. The marriage contract is vitiated whenever a circumstance connected either with the contracting parties or with their consent militates against its essence. Since the matrimonial consent cannot be supplied by any human power[7] we are to conclude that the consent must be:

1. Free and deliberate. Violence or coaction depriving the contracting parties of their freedom to dissent would result in an invalid consent. In order that the contract be vitiated and rendered null and void the fear need not necessarily be absolute, relative fear suffices as long as the person in question laboring

[4] C. 1-51, C. XXVII, q. 2.

[5] Lib. IV, *Sent.*, dist. XXVII.

[6] Esmein, *op. cit.*, vol. I, p. 117 ff.; Wernz, *op. cit.*, n. 36; Gasparri, *op. cit.*, n. 770; De Smet, *op. cit.*, n. 60.

[7] Sanchez agitates the question whether God by His absolute power could cause marriage to exist without the consent of the contracting parties. The conclusion is to be negative. (*Op. cit.*, lib. II, disp., XXVI.)

under its influence is coerced to feign a consent outwardly which inwardly does not exist.[8]

2. Internal, namely, actuated by the will. A feigned fictitious or an interpretative consent in the absence of matrimonial intent cannot give rise to a valid marriage.[9]

3. Personal, for no power except the individual will of the contracting parties can bring about the legitimate mutual transfer of the dominion over their bodies.

4. Outwardly manifested or external, for a reciprocal transfer of the bodies cannot be understood by both unless such intention is manifested by unmistakable signs.

5. Legitimate, presupposing that the person who gives the consent is competent or capable. Against the legitimate consent militate the natural and the positive law when for certain reasons they disqualify some persons from entering into valid wedlock.

6. Absolute or, if conditional, the condition must be such that it is not incompatible with the essence and integrity of the marriage contract.

7. Simultaneous, if not physically, at least morally so. It suffices that the consent of one party be given during the virtual continuance of the other party's consent.

II. Causes Militating Against Matrimonial Consent.

398. In order that the matrimonial consent may possess the characteristics specified above certain conditions are required on the part of the will and on the part of the intellect of the contracting parties. Causes militating against consent on the part of the intellect

[8] *Acta Apostolicae Sedis,* vol. II, p. 348.

[9] S. C. C., *Parisien.,* 7 iul., 1 sept., 1883; 7 mart., 1885; *Acta Sanctae Sedis,* vol. XXIII, p. 14 ff.; MASILIEN., 1 iun., 1911; *Acta Apostolicae Sedis,* vol. III, p. 525 ff.

are: (1) Want of proper discretion; and (2) Error. Those opposing it on the part of the will are: (1) Simulation; (2) Coercion or fear; (3) Condition. A few words must be said on each of these causes.

A. Causes Opposing Marriage on the Part of the Intellect.

1. Want of Proper Discretion.

399. In order that matrimonial consent may be present it is required that the contracting parties be not ignorant of the fact that marriage is a permanent state betwen a man and a woman for the purpose of procreating children.[10] This ignorance is not presumed after they reached the age of puberty.[11] Parties who are lacking in this minimum of the required knowledge cannot contract validly. This is a requirement of the natural law, its scope must therefore be extended to the unbaptized. Besides this required knowledge the baptized persons must be guided also by the ecclesiastical law prescribing a certain age.

400. The age of puberty for a male child is reached after the completion of fourteen years and for a female child of twelve years.[12] After that age the sufficient knowledge required for matrimonial contract is presumed, though the impediment of age would interfere with its validity unless the former completed his sixteenth and the latter her fourteenth year.[13] The knowledge required by the foregoing canon need not be so precise as to extend to all particulars or factors connected with the purpose of marriage. Even a confused knowledge has the force of inducing a valid consent provided its giver is aware of the permanent bond and

[10] S. C. C., *Ventimilien.*, 19 maii, 18 aug., 1888.
[11] Cod. Iur. Can., Can. 1082.
[12] *Op. cit.*, Can. 88, §2.
[13] *Op. cit.*, Can. 1067.

is ready to embrace all the conditions marriage implies. Thus, for instance, the validity of the consent would not be questioned should a person express willingness to comply with the primary end of marriage without being enlightened as to the nature of the act of procreation. Should lack of sufficient knowledge be pleaded against the validity of marriage the cause of nullity would have to be proved, for the contrary is presumed if the party in question was in possession of the age of puberty at the time the contract was made.

401. Persons incapable of giving valid consent are: (1) Those laboring under dementia or monomania; (2) Those who are born deaf, dumb and blind; (3) Those who are in a state of inebriety.[14] Even civil law disqualifies these three classes of persons from making a binding contract. Should the person mentally deranged enjoy some lucid intervals, marriage contracted during one of them would be valid but illicit.[15] In doubt whether the marriage was contracted during lucid intervals or in a state in which the faculty of coherent thought was wanting, the latter is to be presumed.[16]

Persons who are deaf, mute and blind from their nativity are generally classed among infants and for that reason are barred from marriage.[17] It is a controverted point whether the same inability is to be predicated of persons born deaf and dumb. If the instruction they had received renders them capable of discerning a formal violation of the moral law and of realizing the duties and the responsibilities attached to the marriage contract, it would seem that they could

[14] D'Annibale, vol. I, n. 31, and vol. II, n. 409.

[15] Gasparri, *op. cit.*, n. 779.

[16] Schmalzgrueber, *op. cit.*, IV, I, n. 14; Sanchez, *op. cit.*, lib. I, disp. VIII, n. 18.

[17] Sanchez, *op. cit.*, lib. I, disp. VIII, n. 13; St. Alphonsus, lib. VI, n. 303; D'Annibale, vol. I, n. 30.

give a valid consent. The testimony of men who observed the physical, mental and moral status of deafmutes favors the assumption that such an instruction is a possibility. Therefore, it would seem that they should not be barred from marriage as a class on the ground of natural law, but that their individual fitness should be the deciding factor. Innocent III distinctly states that the deaf and the dumb are capable of contracting marriage, but it is not clear whether he contemplates cases where the two classes are taken separately or a case where both deafness and muteness occur in the same individual.[18] Deafness, muteness and blindness when viewed separately, whether they are congenital or adventitious, do not disqualify one from marriage.[19]

A person in the state of inebriety depriving him of all use of his mental faculties [20] is regarded as incapable of giving a valid matrimonial consent.[21] The same is to be said of individuals found in the state of stupor, of delirium or of somnambulism.[22]

2. *Error.*

402. Error is a discrepancy between what is thought to be true and what is actually true. It implies not only a lack of information but also a positive element of mistaken judgment, in other words misapprehension. Gratian [23] distinguishes various kinds of error which can be reduced to error of fact (*error facti*) and error of law (*error iuris*). Error of fact relates either to the physical person who is the second party to the contemplated contract (*error substantialis*), or to his

[18] C. 23, 25, X, *de sponsalibus et matrimoniis,* IV, 1.
[19] WERNZ, *op. cit.,* n. 41.
[20] COD. IUR. CAN., Can. 2201, §3.
[21] GASPARRI, *op. cit.,* n. 781.
[22] DE LUGO, *De Sacramentis in genere,* VIII, n. 100 ff.
[23] C. XXIX, q. 1; PETRI LOMBARDI, *Sent.,* lib. IV, dist. XXX.

qualities (*error accidentalis*). Error of law concerns the principal object of marriage (*ius in corpus*), or its essential properties (*unitas, perpetuitas, indissolubilitas*).[24]

Error may be concomitant or antecedent. The concomitant error has no real effect on the consent, inasmuch as it would not have influenced the contracting party to desist from marriage, even if the error had been detected before the contract had been made. Not so with antecedent error, which presupposes that the consent would have been withdrawn had the error been discovered in time.

403. The new law legislating on the error of fact says: Error about the person nullifies marriage. Error regarding the quality of the person, even if it should be the cause of the contract, invalidates marriage only, (1) when the error about the quality amounts to an error about the person; (2) when a free person contracts marriage with a person whom he presumes to be free, while she is in a state of servitude strictly so called.[25]

404. Substantial error, or error about the person, whether it is antecedent or concomitant, vincible or invincible, nullifies marriages not only by virtue of special ecclesiastical legislation but also by virtue of natural law. Therefore the invalidating effect is not to be confined to marriages contracted by baptized persons but ought to be extended also to those entered into by the unbaptized. A classical example of such error is found in the Old Covenant where reference is made to the marriage of Jacob with Lia, whom Jacob erroneously thought to be Rachel.[26] The matrimonial contract presupposes a consent given to a determined

[24] Wernz, *op. cit.*, n. 223; Gasparri, *op. cit.*, n. 783; De Smet, *op. cit.*, n. 259; D'Annibale, vol. III, n. 444.

[25] Cod. Iur. Can., Can. 1083.

[26] *Genesis* XIX, 24.

person whom each of the contracting parties has in mind. If Charles intended to marry Agnes, but by mistake he is united to Cecilia whom he erroneously thinks to be Agnes, his consent is really given to the latter; consequently no marriage exists between him and Cecilia. Some authors maintain the result would be the same should Charles say: "I would want to marry this woman even if she were not Agnes." In that case, they say, the words "I would want to" express an interpretative will which *de facto* does not exist, and in reality his consent is directed toward the absent Agnes and not toward the woman who is actually present.[27] The contrary opinion, it would seem, has a more solid basis.

405. Accidental error affecting only the quality of the person does not, as a rule, invalidate marriage, though the erring person may suffer grave injury.[28] It is immaterial whether such an error is vincible or invincible, concomitant or antecedent, or whether the person is led into it without any deception or duplicity, or through imposture or fraud.[29] In the latter case the damage may have to be repaired, if it be possible, but the contract is not rescindable. The explanation lies in the fact that the consent tends principally towards the identity of the person and not toward one of his qualities.[30] A different judgment would have to be rendered if it were clear that the main object of the contract was a particular quality of a person, which character is specified as a *conditio sine qua non.*[31] Of this we shall treat more extensively later.[32]

[27] ST. THOMAS, *suppl.* IIIae, p., q. LI, art., land 2; SCHMALZGRÜBER, lib. IV, tit. I, n. 439; SANCHEZ, lib. VII, disp. XVIII, n. 11; GASPARRI, *op. cit.*, n. 784.

[28] ALPHONSUS, lib. VI, n. 1012; SCAVINI, *op. cit.*, III, n. 842.

[29] D'ANNIBALE, vol. III, n. 444; SANCHEZ, lib. VII, disp. XCII, n. 4.

[30] WERNZ, *op. cit.*, n. 227; SANTI-LEITNER, lib. IV, tit. I, n. 135; S. C. C., *Frisingen.*, 7 et 28 aug., 1745; *Romana*, 9 aug., 1817, 27 maii, 1820.

[31] COD. IUR. CAN., Can. 104.

[32] See this work, n. 433 ff.

Accidental error which affects the quality of the person annuls marriage whenever it is equivalent to a substantial error, namely, when it amounts to an error about the person. Thus, for instance, should Charles wish to enter into marriage with the oldest daughter of Cecilia, his marriage would be invalid should he contract with Agnes whom he mistakenly regards as such daughter; for his consent in this case is reserved to the daughter who is actually the oldest. Should no such limitation be placed on his intention but should his consent be given to the person present, then the contract would stand, and in case of doubt the presumption is always in favor of its validity.

406. Another instance in which accidental error annuls marriage is the case in which one erroneously believes that the person whom he is about to marry is free, while in reality she is laboring under servitude strictly so called.[33] In the former discipline error as to the servile condition of a contracting party was regarded as a diriment impediment of marriage.[34] The nullifying force of that impediment was acquired by virtue of ecclesiastical, not of natural, law.[35] Therefore the marriage entered into by two infidels, unless the civil law disqualifies the slave from contracting with a free person, is valid.[36] The marriage would be valid should a free person contract with another free person whom he mistakenly believes to be a slave; or should a slave contract with another slave whom he erroneously considers to be free. Only a baptized person can benefit by the nullifying force of error. Should a baptized person marry an infidel of whose servile condition he is ignorant, the contract would be null and

[33] C. XXIX, q. 1; c. 4, C. XXIX, q. 2; c. 2, 4, X, *de coniugio servorum,* IV, 9; S. C. C., *Frisingen.*, 7 et 28 aug., 1745.

[34] ESMEIN, *op. cit.*, vol. I, p. 317 ff.; FEIJE, *op. cit.*, n. 120.

[35] WERNZ, *op. cit.*, n. 242; GASPARRI, *op. cit.*, n. 639.

[36] SANCHEZ, *op. cit.*, lib. VII, disp. XVII, n. 9.

void. The contrary would be true if an infidel should marry a baptized person under the same condition. The Church law in contradistinction to the Roman law[37] always upheld the validity of a marriage between a bondwoman and a free man, or between a bondman and a free woman; provided the fact of serfdom was known to the free party at the time the contract was made. The state of slavery must be interpreted in the sense in which it was understood among the Romans or in which it prevails in our own times mostly among the untutored races.

407. The error would be deprived of its nullifying force, should the liberation from bondage occur simultaneously with the act of marriage. The contrary would be true, should the slavery continue after the marriage, even if for only a short time. The subsequent emancipation granted to the slave, even if it should take place before the other party becomes aware of his error, does not affect the objective invalidity of the contract. To validate such marriages the renewal of consent is necessary, though in some cases it might be advisable to have recourse to *sanatio in radice*. The declaration of nullity should emanate from a competent ecclesiastical tribunal. The burden of proof as regards the presence of error relative to servile condition devolves on the free person. The contract must be upheld should the bondman or the bondwoman succeed in proving that his or her condition of servility was known to the other party.[38] So much as regards error of fact.

408. The new Code legislating on the error of law says: Simple error as regards the unity or the indissolubility or the sacramental character of marriage, even if it should give cause for the contract, fails to

[37] L. 2, C. *de incestis nuptiis.*
[38] Feije, *op. cit.*, n. 123.

vitiate the matrimonial consent.[39] This canon rejects the opinion that persons entertaining a mistaken idea about the properties of marriage cannot enter into valid wedlock. The words *"simplex error"* characterize the misleading notions generally diffused in our times among infidels, heretics and schismatics. Such errors regard the practice of polyandry and polygyny, the rejection of the sacramental character of marriage, and the belief that certain circumstances warrant an absolute dissolution of the matrimonial bond. Such theoretical errors, the new law states, are not absolutely incompatible with valid matrimonial consent[40] as long as the persons laboring under them have the general intention to contract real marriage as it was instituted by God, and do not exclude any of its properties by a positive act of the will.[41] It is generally agreed, says Benedict XIV, that a person cannot wish a contract unless he wishes also its essence.[42] In order that a substantial constituent element of a contract may not be tacitly included, it must be positively excluded. This exclusion is not presumed and it is difficult to advance convincing proofs to show that it was present.

409. The knowledge of, or the belief in, the nullity of a marriage does not necessarily exclude the marriage consent.[43] The words *"consensum matrimonialem necessario non excludit"* cannot be overemphasized. Consent depends entirely on the frame of the mind. If the person firmly believes in the invalidity of the marriage he is about to attempt, but for the sake of endowing his invalid contract with legal sanction,

[39] COD. IUR. CAN., Can. 1084.

[40] S. C. S. Off., instr. (ad. Vic. Ap. Oceaniae Central.), 18 dec., 1872; (ad Vic. Ap. Iaponiae Merid.), 4 febr., 1891. See the new *Collectanea* under numbers 1327, 1392, 1746.

[41] GASPARRI, *op. cit.*, n. 792; WERNZ, *op. cit.*, n. 228.

[42] *De Synodo Dioecesana*, lib. XII, c. XII, n. 8.

[43] COD. IUR. CAN., Can. 1085.

submits to the formality of a civil ceremony, his frame of mind would hardly favor the necessary matrimonial consent. Should he be mistaken, and should the supposed obstacle militating against the validity of his marriage have no foundation in fact, the marriage would be invalid and its invalidation would necessitate a renewal of consent. To exemplify this canon we could take the case of a baptized non-Catholic who, being ignorant of the new law of the Church, believes that the impediment of disparity of worship exists between him and the unbaptized party with whom he intends to contract marriage. Being influenced by this wrong belief he does not attach any value to his matrimonial consent, nor does he give it, but goes through the civil ceremony merely to comply with the requirements of civil law. Though the stated impediment according to the new law would not exist in this case, the marriage would be invalid, for the true consent was wanting. But, on the other hand, if he intended to give the matrimonial consent in spite of his false notion as to the presence of such an impediment, his wrong conviction would not affect the contemplated marriage, which would be objectively valid, for the proper consent was given and the supposed impediment was absent.[44]

B. Causes Militating Against Matrimonial Consent on the Part of the Will.

1. Simulation.

410. The internal consent of the will is always presumed to correspond with the words spoken or the signs exhibited at the celebration of marriage. But, should one of the contracting parties, or both, by a positive act of the will, exclude either the marriage

[44] S. C. de Prop. Fide, instr. (ad Vic. Ap. Constantinop.), 1 oct., 1785; (C. P. Yaffnae), 23 aug., 1852, ad 7.

itself or all right to conjugal act, or any essential property of marriage, the contract would be invalid.[45]

It has already been stated that matrimonial consent must be internal, for without it no valid marriage can be conceived. To inform the other contracting party of such internal consent, the necessity of its external manifestation is a foregone conclusion. The new law insists that this be done by word of mouth, nor can any other mode be adopted if the parties enjoy the gift of speech.[46] Since in a matter of so grave importance as marriage serious reflection is taken for granted, the recognized standard adopted by all nations gauges the sentiments of the inward man by the words or signs outwardly expressed.[47] If the two are in conformity the consent is full; if they differ, it is fictitious, or feigned. In this last case the party would be guilty of simulation, which consists in an outward display of consent inwardly not existing.

411. Simulation may arise in three different ways: (1) Want of internal consent to contract;[48] (2) Intention to contract but not to oblige oneself; (3) Intention to contract and to oblige oneself, but not to fulfill the assumed obligation.

A contract entered into with a want of intention is vitiated at its very base, consequently its invalidity must be apparent to all. In the second instance one intends to contract marriage but declines to transfer the right of ownership over his body to the other party, or to accept the same right over the body of the prospective consort, or positively excludes the perpetual or exclusive character of that right. In this

[45] Cod. Iur. Can., Can. 1086.
[46] *Op. cit.*, Can. 1088, §2.
[47] S. C. C., *Avenionen.*, 23 iun., 1907; S. C. de Prop. Fide, instr. (ad Vic. Ap. Constantinop.), 1 oct., 1785.
[48] S. C. C., *Mutinen.*, 19 aug., 1724; 9 iun., 1725; *Parisien.*, 31 ian., 1891.

case the two acts of the will are exclusive of each other, for one wants the contract while the other excludes its essence. Should one be willing to assume the obligation, as in the third supposition, but be unwilling to fulfill it, he would sin gravely, but the contract would stand.[49]

412. These principles taken by themselves are sufficiently clear, but their application to concrete cases will not be void of insurmountable difficulties. In order that simulation, as expressed in the foregoing cases, may be invested with an invalidating force one must exclude the marriage itself or all right to the conjugal act "by a positive act of the will." The solution of all future pleadings for the nullity of marriages on the score of simulation will therefore hinge on these words of the new law. The contract would be invalid should one *positivo voluntatis actu* exclude one of the essential properties of marriage, such as its unity, indissolubility or sacramental character. This positive act of the will would practically have to amount to a *conditio sine qua non* or to a *conditio in pactum deducta.*[50]

413. Though simulation is very difficult to prove, its presence was discovered in several cases in which the Sacred Congregation decided in favor of the nullity of marriage.[51] In such trials the sworn testimony of the party supposedly guilty of simulation has only a slight juridical value. All sources calculated to shed light on, or to account for, such a frame of mind must be unearthed and consulted. An important rôle should be assigned to conjectures and to circumstances antecedent, concomitant, and subsequent to

[49] GASPARRI, *op. cit.*, n. 803.

[50] O'DONNELL, in the *Irish Ecclesiastical Record*, art., *Matrimonial consent in the New Code*, Oct. 18, 1918, p. 286.

[51] S. C. C., *Parisien.*, 7 mart., 1885, in the *Acta Sanctae Sedis*, vol. XVIII, p. 14; *Massilien.*, 1 iun., 1911, in the *Acta Apostolicae Sedis*. vol. III, p. 525.

marriage.[52] It is immaterial on which of the three grounds the invalidity of the marriage is contested (whether it be the exclusion of the marriage itself, or one of its essential properties, or of all right to conjugal act), it must be proved that the alleged reason did not result from a mere theoretical error, nor from an interpretative but a "positive act of the will." Failure to produce sufficient evidence to that effect would cause a verdict upholding the validity of marriage.

414. The application of the foregoing principles may cause various complications, not the least serious of which would be a conflict between the internal and the external forum. The nullity of the marriage may be unquestioned on the ground of the evidence presented to the internal forum, but the same evidence would prove inadequate for the external forum. To adjust the friction thus arising, practically the only remedy would be the validation of marriage, if the party originally guilty of simulation is willing to give the proper consent. Should he be unwilling to do so, or should he render the case still more complicated by contracting another marriage, the internal forum would be forced to admit the validity of his act (if the proper form was used), while the external forum would spurn it. The difficulty thus created would not be solved satisfactorily until enough evidence should be advanced to the external forum to prove the invalidity of the first marriage, or until the other party of the first contract should die. In this latter case the adjustment would be automatic.

2. *Coercion and Fear.*

415. The new Code legislates that marriage is in-

[52] SANCHEZ, *op. cit.*, lib. II, disp. XLV, n. 1 ff.; GASPARRI, *op. cit.*, n. 798.

valid when it is contracted under the influence of grave violence or fear extrinsically and unjustly caused, from which, in order to free oneself, the only alternative left is to select marriage. No other fear, even if it should give cause for the contract, brings with it the nullity of marriage.[53]

The terms coercion and fear are correlative, one applies to the external active agent (causing the violence), the other to the passive agent (suffering from violence).[54]

416. Violence in this connection is to be taken morally, in the sense that some external agent threatens some present or future physical or moral evil in order to extort consent.[55] A consent given under such circumstances is not considered altogether involuntary, but only *secundum quid,* inasmuch as the liberty of action is more or less interfered with. Therefore, we are not concerned here with an absolute or physical coercion which precludes all possibility of a human act, but with a conditional or moral violence with which the internal consent ratifying the external act is not essentially incompatible, though the liberty of action is impaired in a greater or less degree. Fear may be:

1. Extrinsic or intrinsic according as it originates from an external agent (as a man, or a shipwreck), or from an internal cause (as sickness).

2. Justly or unjustly caused, according as the agent against whom violence is employed is guilty or innocent.

3. Serious or trifling, according as it is liable to perturb even a steadfast man or only a man of weak will.

417. Special mention must be made of reverential

[53] COD. IUR. CAN., Can. 1087.
[54] SCHMALZGRÜBER, *op. cit.,* lib. IV, tit. I, n. 384.
[55] L. 1, 2, D. *quod metus causa.*

fear which exists between the superior and his subject. It has its source in the desire not to offend one's parents or superiors, in order to avoid incurring their indignation, wrath or displeasure. Mere reverential fear has not the force of invalidating marriage; it must be accompanied by, or based on, the fear of some impending danger or damage, as threats, blows, importunate, persistent entreaties, and the like. In the former discipline violence and fear constituted a matrimonial impediment in the strict sense of the term. The new law has very properly discontinued to class them among the impediments and treats them as conditions influencing consent. The earliest resemblance to this impediment is found in the penal laws of the Church enacted against persons guilty of the crime of abduction.[56] The Roman law rendered rescindable all matrimonial contracts entered into under the influence of fear and violence.[57] The fact that the disciplinary measures of the Church were sufficiently safeguarded by the Roman law relieved the Church from the necessity of legislating specifically on this point in the early ages. It was soon discovered, however, that the protection afforded by the Roman law was inadequate, for the doctrine of the indissolubility of the marriage tie militated against the rescindability of the contract. It was therefore necessary to declare invalid on the ground of Church law or of natural law a marriage entered into under such circumstances.[58]

418. Violence and fear were endowed with the force of annulling marriage even before the time of Gratian. This is evident from the epistle of Urban II.[59] The scope of the impediment was more clearly deter-

[56] Can. LXVII, *Apostol.;* Can. XXVII, *Concil. Chalcedon.* (451).

[57] L. 22, D. *de ritu nupt.*, XXIII, 1; L. 14, C. *de nupt.*, V, 4.

[58] C. 22, C. XXII, q. 4.

[59] C. 1, C. XXXI, q. 2; WERNZ, *op. cit.*, n. 262; DE BECKER, *op. cit.*, p. 62.

mined, and its nature more specifically defined by Alexander III (1159-1181).[60] The Council of Trent sanctions a species of this impediment when it decrees that no valid marriage can subsist between the abductor and the abducted until the latter is restored to a safe place not under the control of the former.[61] In addition the same Council anathematizes those feudal lords and civil magistrates who would presume to interfere with the liberty of their subjects, preventing them from contracting marriage freely.[62]

419. The new Code retains the former discipline, and while it clears several controverted points, it fails to settle the question whether the invalidating force of fear is to be attributed to natural or merely to ecclesiastical law. Both sides have their prominent adherents. Those who advocate the former opinion base their arguments on the grave duties and serious responsibilities attached to such a contract, as well as on the numerous evils which would inevitably result from unions entered into without free will.[63] The second opinion, which seems more likely, is based on the ground that a person under the influence of fear and violence is not placed in a position which precludes all possibility of giving a consent sufficient for other contracts, nor is there any particular reason why the matrimonial contract should be made an exception.[64] It is admitted by all that violence which precludes all possibility of a free human act vitiates the given consent on the ground of natural law.

[60] C. 15, X, *de sponsalibus et matrimoniis,* IV, 1.

[61] Sessio XXIV, *De reformatione matrimonii,* cap. VI.

[62] *Loc. cit.,* cap. IX and also can. IX.

[63] Wernz, *op. cit.,* n. 267; Reiffenstül, *op. cit.,* lib. I, *h. t.,* n. 47; St. Thomas, *Suppl.* IIIae, p., q. XLVII, a. 3; St. Alphonsus, *op. cit.,* lib. VI, n. 1054.

[64] Sanchez, *op. cit.,* lib IV, disp. XIV, n. 2; Gasparri, *op. cit.,* n. 811; Schmalzgrüber, *op. cit.,* lib. IV, I, n. 406; Santi-Leitner, vol. IV, tit. I, n. 148; Feije, *op. cit.,* n. 138 ff.

420. The new law states that marriage is invalid when contracted under the influence of a grave fear or violence unjustly caused by an external agent from which to liberate oneself one must consent to marriage. This canon implies four conditions which need a further elucidation.

I. The fear, in order that it may possess the effect indicated above, must be grave, namely, such as would affect even a steadfast man, or such as cannot easily be overcome.[65] It is immaterial whether the fear is absolutely or relatively grave. Though the external forum considers the objective gravity of the cause begetting fear, it does not disregard altogether the subjective state or disposition of the passive agent. The cardinal point on which the whole question hinges is the determination of the fact that the cause inspiring fear under the given circumstances was instrumental in extorting the consent of an individual who otherwise would have dissented. Therefore, if the threats are offered by one who is in a position to carry them out, or if they cannot be avoided, the fear would have a foundation.[66] Fear can be present even if the evil feared is directed against the parents or near kin of the contracting party.[67]

421. Reverential fear, such as described above, may, in exceptional cases and accidentally, constitute a fear invalidating marriage, namely, when one finds in it the element of extreme sensitiveness on the part of the passive agent and of extreme rigor on the part of the active agent. The fear of serious indignation of one's parents or lawful superiors, especially if com-

[65] C. 15, 28, X, *de sponsalibus et matrimoniis,* IV, 1; S. C. de Prop. Fide, 20 iun., 1883, in the new *Collectanea,* 1587, §36.

[66] *Acta Apostolicae Sedis,* vol. IV, p. 505; Causa *Tarvicin.*, 11 mart., 1912.

[67] De Smet, *op. cit.*, n. 266; Feije, *op. cit.*, n. 132.

bined with the fear of blows or other grave consequences, is generally estimated as sufficient to invalidate the prospective contract.[68]

422. II. The fear must be unjust. This element of fear presupposes an extrinsic and free agent. Not all the authors are in accord in determining when the fear is just. There are three things that ought to be taken into consideration, namely, (a) whether the person subjected to fear is bound to choose between marriage or some other obligation; (b) whether the active agent, be he a public or private person, has the right to exact marriage; (c) whether he has right to threaten and is likely to carry out his threats. Should the answer to these three questions be negative, the fear would be unjust. Should an individual be bound in conscience to marry for the sake of his honor, and should the person threatening him with fear have the right to insist on marriage, the fear would be just, provided an alternative between marriage or denunciation before the judge, or between marriage and dowry, were offered to the guilty party.[69] The fear would be unjust if to the passive agent were given the choice between marriage and death.[70]

423. III. The fear must be inflicted by an extrinsic free agent. It does not matter whether the agent is the other contracting party or a third party espousing his cause. Fear of disease, of eternal punishment, or of death is regarded as proceeding from an intrinsic

[68] GASPARRI, *op. cit.*, n. 816; WERNZ, *op. cit.*, n. 264; SANCHEZ, *op. cit.*, lib. IV, disp. XIV, n. 17; S. C. C., *Vesprimien.*, 2 iun., 1911, in the *Acta Apostolicae Sedis*, vol. IV, p. 108 ff.; *Parisien*, 1910, *loc. cit.*, vol. II, p. 348 ff.; *Lugdunen.*, 28 iun., 1912, *loc. cit.*, vol. IV, p. 646 ff.; *Tunkinen.*, 7 iul., 1911, *loc. cit.*, vol. III, p. 661 ff.

[69] *American Ecclesiastical Review*, 1913, p. 181 ff.; FEIJE, *op. cit.*, n. 133.

[70] S. C. C., *Vigilien.*, 13 iul., 27 sept., 1725; DE BECKER, *op. cit.*, p. 64; GASPARRI, *op. cit.*, n. 820; WERNZ, *op. cit.*, n. 265.

necessary cause, consequently it has no power of invalidating the contract.[71]

424. IV. The fear explained above, in order to have the force attributed to it, must be correlated to marriage. It is not necessary that the active agent demand marriage as a *conditio sine qua non.* It suffices that the passive agent should have no avenue of escape from the threatened evil except the choice of marriage. This opinion of some authors is formally adopted by the new Code.[72]

425. In the former discipline the right to impugn the validity of a marriage contracted under the impulse of fear or violence belonged to the passive agent exclusively.[73] The new law, by virtue of canon 1971, authorizes also the other consort to challenge the validity of his wedlock provided he was not instrumental in causing the fear or violence to which his marriage owes its nullity. The party whose consent was extorted by so illegal a means should avail himself of the first opportunity, when not impeded in his freedom of action, to place before the proper ecclesiastical tribunal the grounds on which he challenges the validity of his wedlock. Should he delay too long with such a step, and continue to cohabit in matrimonial relations with the other party, he would run the risk of forfeiting this right according to the tenor of the former discipline.[74]

426. The solution of the controversy whether fear interferes with the validity of the matrimonial contract on the ground of natural or of merely ecclesiastical

[71] SANCHEZ, *op. cit.,* lib. IV, disp. XII, n. 4; REIFFENSTÜL, I, XL, n. 26; ST. ALPHONSUS, *op. cit.,* lib. VI, n. 1049; GASPARRI, *op. cit.,* n. 819.

[72] SCHMALZGRÜBER, *op. cit.,* lib. IV, n. 398; DE LUGO, *De iustitia et iure,* XXII, n. 175 ff.; see also GASPARRI, *op. cit.,* n. 821; DE BECKER, *op. cit.,* p. 64; FEIJE, *op. cit.,* n. 134.

[73] SCHMALZGRÜBER, *op. cit., loc. cit.,* tit. I, n. 429;; WERNZ, *op. cit.,* n. 269; DE SMET, *op. cit.,* n. 268; FEIJE, *op. cit.,* n. 143.

[74] S. C. de prop. Fide, instr., 20 iun., 1883, n. 36, in the new *Collectanea,* n. 1587; c. 4, X, *qui matrimonium accusare possunt, vel contra illud testificari,* IV, 18; c. 21, X, *de sponsalibus et matrimoniis,* IV, 1.

law would decide the objective validity or invalidity of marriages entered into by infidels, under such impulse. Since the new law fails to commit itself in either way we are free to pronounce in favor of the validity of such marriages in countries in which no civil diriment impediment of fear is enforced. Should the validity of a marriage contracted between a baptized person and an infidel be questioned on the ground of grave fear, we are to consider whether the passive agent was baptized or unbaptized. In the first instance the marriage would be valid; the contrary would be true in the second instance.

427. The Church does not supply, by way of dispensation, the consent either withdrawn or suspended or not freely given. The fact that she never dispensed from the impediment of fear and violence is to be attributed partly to the doubt occasioned by the controversy whether the impediment is of natural or of ecclesiastical law, and partly to her desire to safeguard the liberty required by a matrimonial contract and the right of the person whose consent was extorted in so illegitimate a way.

428. It must be noted that the marriage is not invalidated unless the fear continues to the very moment of its celebration.[75] If this fact is proved the Church law invalidates the marriage even though the consent was actually given, provided the party chose marriage because it was the only expedient whereby he could disentangle himself from a serious difficulty.[76] Emphasis should be laid in this connection on the fact that the fear must be unjustly caused by an extrinsic agent. In some parts of the United States of North America there is a civil law in force which imposes the alternative of imprisonment or marriage on a man who

[75] Gasparri, *op. cit.*, n. 807.
[76] Lehmkuhl, *Theologia Moralis*, vol. II, n. 738.

acquired carnal knowledge of a woman either against her will or by seducing her with the prospect of wedlock. Should the woman's consent to marriage be obtained under those circumstances, the contract would be absolutely valid even if the man's consent was the result of fear and violence such as already described for it would be justly caused.[77]

429. The proper way to validate marriages which are invalid on the ground of fear and violence is by public renewal of consent, if the fear is a public fact; otherwise the renewal should take place secretly. Sometimes *sanatio in radice* is more feasible, provided the consent of both parties is present, of one by continuance and of the other by private renewal.

3. Condition.

430. Condition is a circumstance attached to an act, on which the validity of the act, as well as the consent, depends for an indefinite time.[78] The two general categories of condition are: Voiding and suspensive condition. In a contract entered into with a voiding condition the party is absolved from all assumed obligation as soon as the condition is verified. The contract made with a suspensive condition does not impose any obligation nor does it take effect until the actual fulfillment of the condition. The individuality of the marriage contract, or, more properly its character of indissolubility, is incompatible with a voiding condition.

431. The several classes of condition are:

1. Past, present, and future, according as the circumstance determining the validity of the act and the obligation following therefrom is past, present or future. A past or present condition is a condition

[77] GASPARRI, *op. cit.*, n. 820.

[78] D'ANNIBALE, vol. I, n. 41; GASPARRI, *op. cit.*, n. 47.

improperly so called, or only a relative condition. It has no influence on the contract objectively but only subjectively in so far as the parties are ignorant of certain qualities or circumstances which actually exist. Conditional contract, therefore, in the strict sense is one whose validity depends on some future event which is in the realm of the contingent but has not as yet taken place.

2. Possible or impossible. The first embraces a circumstance which in the natural order of things either already exists or is contingent. The impossible condition is one whose realization would require the intervention of divine power. The possible condition is subdivided into necessary and contingent condition. These terms are self-explanatory. The necessary condition whose verification is inevitable belongs to the same class as *conditio de presenti* or *de futuro*.[79]

3. Honest and immoral. Honest condition is one which does not militate against the natural or divine, positive or human law. Immoral condition is subversive of morality and good order.

4. Repugnant and non-repugnant to the substance of the contract. Three factors, namely, the good of the offspring (*bonum prolis*), the good of the faith (*bonum fidei*), the good of the sacrament (*bonum sacramenti*) are intimately related to the essence of the matrimonial contract. An express condition directed against any of these, as, for instance, "I will marry you if you will avoid or destroy all offspring, or if you will practice adultery for the sake of lucre, or until I find another person who is richer or who will appeal to me more" would render the contract null and void *ab initio*.[80]

432. In conformity with general principles condi-

[79] WERNZ, *op. cit.*, n. 293; GASPARRI, *op. cit.*, n. 844.

[80] SANTI-LEITNER, *lib.* IV, tit. V, n. 6; GASPARRI, *op. cit.*, n. 859 ff.; c. 7, X, *de conditionibus appositis in desponsatione vel in aliis contractibus*, IV, 5.

tional marriages were tolerated among the Romans, though an express text giving them positive approbation is wanting in the ancient Roman law.[81] The Gratian collection, on the ground of a decree drawn by the African Council, does not attribute any value to a condition under which marriage is contracted.[82] Contrary to this doctrine is the opinion incorporated in the Decretals of Gregory IX, attributed to Alexander III [83] and to Urban III,[84] in which a condition is invested with unmistakable legitimacy and value, though the subsequent consummation of marriage, should it take place before the verification of the condition, is interpretatively looked upon as a relinquishment of the proposed condition.[85] St. Thomas [86] and St. Bonaventure [87] gave a fairly precise exposition of the doctrine relative to conditional marriage contracts. The Council of Trent did not venture to introduce a change in the discipline theretofore accepted, nor was any other legislative measure enacted by the Church on this point until the new legislation recast the former law and gave it a more precise expression. The new law reads: A condition attached (to a matrimonial contract) and not revoked: (1) Is to be regarded as nonexistent if it concerns the future, whether it is necessary or impossible or immoral, but is not against the substance of marriage; (2) Should it be based on the future and militate against the substance of marriage, it would render the contract null and void; (3) Should it be directed to the future, involving something that is honest, it would suspend the validity of the mar-

[81] WERNZ, *op. cit.*, n. 294, note 7; FREISEN, *op. cit.*, p. 247 ff.

[82] C. 7, 8, C. XXVII, q. 2.

[83] C. 3, 4, X, *de conditionibus appositis in desponsatione, vel in aliis contractibus,* IV, 5.

[84] C. 4, X, *tit. cit.*, IV, 5.

[85] Innocent III, c. 6, X, *tit. cit.*, IV, 5.

[86] *Suppl.* IIIae, p., q. XLVII, a. 5.

[87] *Comment,* in lib. IV, *Sent.*, dist. XXVIII, q. 3.

riage; (4) Should it concern the past or the present the marriage would be valid or invalid according as the thing on which the condition is based exists or does not exist.

These four propositions containing the doctrine regarding "condition" in a nutshell, will be explained individually in the pages that follow.

433. I. Should one say: "I will marry you provided the sun will rise to-morrow," the condition would be vitiated by the fact that it is based on a future event whose occurrence in the natural order of things cannot be prevented (*conditio de eventu futuro necessario*). Such a condition would not suspend the validity of the marriage.[88] The same is to be said of an impossible condition as, for instance, "I will marry you if you will touch the heavens with your finger."[89] Should the future concern something immoral but not repugnant to the substance of marriage the condition would be void of force.[90] Such condition would be: "I will marry you if you will murder your brother." The reason why such conditions are not permitted to affect marriage is that it is generally taken for granted that they are not meant seriously. This supposition, however, is to be accepted only by a presumption of law (not *praesumptione iuris et de iure*), as admitting a proof to the contrary. If therefore in certain instances it can be proved that such conditions were actually suspensive of consent, or that they were meant as *conditiones sine quibus non* the objective validity of the marriage would depend on their verification. Under such circumstances an impossible condition would result in an invalid contract. A necessary condition would beget a contract valid from the very beginning.

[88] SANCHEZ, *op. cit.*, lib. V, disp. II, n. 3; GASPARRI, *op. cit.*, n. 843; DE LUGO, *De iustitia et iure*, disp. XXII, n. 336; WERNZ, *op. cit.*, n. 301.

[89] C. 7, X, *tit. cit.*, IV, 5; WERNZ, *op. cit.*, n. 300.

[90] C. 8, X, *de pactis*, I, 35.

Should the condition be immoral, the validity of the marriage would be suspended, without any obligation on the part of the other party to contribute his efforts toward aiding the fulfillment of such a condition. What is more, he must positively abstain from lending his aid, for such an act would involve him in sinfulness. Should the immoral condition be fulfilled, the contract would become valid automatically, provided in the meantime the consent of the conditioning party has not been revoked.[91]

It is easy to see how difficult it would be to advance convincing proofs in the external forum showing that any of these three species of condition was actually intended to suspend one's consent. Should the doubt remain after a careful inquiry the condition is to be treated as non-existent. In the internal forum the declaration of the individual constitutes all the evidence on which the question would have to be decided.

434. II. If the contract is conditioned on the future contrary to the substance of marriage, it is null and void. The nullity in such a case results by virtue of natural law, for nothing can exist when deprived of its essence. To the substance of the matrimonial contract belong the marital right of each contracting party over the body of the other, the essential properties of marriage (unity, indissolubility and sacramental dignity), the good of the offspring and the good of the faith. Accordingly, the marriage would be invalid if it should be entered into without transferring the right of ownership over the body to the other consort for the sake of procreating offspring, or should a condition be directed against having any children, or should a limit be placed on their number in the sense that after a

[91] De Lugo, *op. cit., loc. cit.*, n. 340; Reiffenstül, *h. t.*, n. 42; Gasparri, *op. cit.*, n. 853; Sanchez, lib. V, disp. III, n. 15.

specified number has been reached the *ius in corpus* will be revoked.[92]

435. Should the right to the body be transferred, but by mutual understanding a restraint placed on its use, such a pre-matrimonial agreement, tending to cultivate chastity, would not annul the marriage contract, for the transfer of the right and its actual use are two distinct things, the former pertaining to the essence of marriage, but not so the latter.

436. Since the procreation of offspring is the primary end of marriage by virtue of natural law, any condition interfering with that end would invalidate the contract, whether it be a demand to renounce the *ius in corpus,* or to resort to preventives making the attainment of the primary end impossible, as for instance, the practice of onanism, the procuring of abortion, etc. The same is to be said of a condition involving the positive exclusion of the reception of the sacrament. To entertain a hope of absolute separation (namely, the dissolution of the matrimonial bond *quoad vinculum*) for any causes, or to reserve the right to have relations with others besides the legitimate wife, would also invalidate the contract, provided these conditions were not merely interpretative but actual accessories (*conditiones in pactum deductae*) placed in the contract by one or both of the contracting parties.[93] Marriages contracted outside the Catholic Church, though they are generally entered into with this theoretical error of seeking an absolute dissolution of the matrimonial bond in case of adultery, are valid if the condition is *in mente tantum;* the contrary is true should it be *in pactum deducta.*[94]

[92] C. 7, X, *de conditionibus appositis in desponsatione, vel aliis contractibus,* IV, 5; GASPARRI, *op. cit.*, n. 856; SANTI-LEITNER, lib. IV, tit. V, n. 19.

[93] BENEDICTUS XIV, *De Synodo Dioecesana,* lib. XIII, cap. XXII, n. 9 ff.

[94] SANTI-LEITNER, lib. IV, tit. V, n. 24.

437. If the condition concerns a future event and something that is honest, the validity of the marriage is suspended. Such a condition would be: "If my father will consent." In this case the ascertainment of the father's consent or dissent will decide the objective validity of the marriage thus contracted.[95] Should he decline to consent, no marriage would exist between the two parties.

The question might arise whether contracts of this nature, entered into under similar conditions, as, for instance, "I will marry you provided my dying mother will be spared to life," become *ipso facto* validated by the realization of the condition, or whether a renewal of consent is necessary. Theologians espouse both sides of the question. St. Thomas with the majority of canonists maintains [96] that such a marriage is valid as soon as the condition is verified.[97]

438. This teaching was confirmed by the decision of the Sacred Congregation of the Council. It bases its decrees on the theory that in such conditional marriages the presence of the pastor and of the witnesses, as well as the consent, virtually perseveres (unless the consent be expressly revoked) up to the time the condition is fulfilled.[98] Hence the renewal of consent can be dispensed with, unless, as some authors maintain, the marriage was entered into under the condition "If the Holy See will dispense." [99] In that case we uphold the opinion that the consent must be renewed at the time the parties are benefited by the dispensation. The prospective consorts under those circumstances were rendered incapable of giving the proper consent and

[95] C. 5, X, *de conditionibus appositis in desponsatione, vel in aliis contractibus,* IV, 5.

[96] *Suppl.* IIIae, p., q. XLVII, a. 5, c.

[97] FAGNANUS, *Commentarium,* ad c. 5, X, *de conditionibus,* etc., n. 4 ff.

[98] SANTI-LEITNER, lib. IV, tit. V, n. 12.

[99] FEIJE, *op. cit.,* n. 647; WERNZ, *op. cit.,* n. 297.

of placing the condition *de futuro* by the fact that they were laboring under an impediment.[100]

439. A conditional marriage contracted with another person while the condition of the first marriage was pending, would be valid, provided no undispensed impediment interfered, for such an act would indicate an explicit recession from the conditional consent previously given. Should also the second marriage be conditional then that marriage would be valid whose condition is verified first, provided the consent given to that particular marriage was not expressly revoked in the meantime. Should the realization of the conditions specified in two conditional marriages be simultaneous, neither of them would be valid, unless sufficient evidence can be advanced in the external forum to prove that the party in question revoked his or her consent to the first conditional marriage before the fulfillment of the specified condition.[101] A free *copula* intervening by mutual agreement between parties bound by a conditional contract, should be interpreted, *praesumptione iuris,* as implying a recession from the placed condition.[102]

440. In all conditional contracts it is tacitly understood that should the consent be withdrawn before the condition is actually fulfilled (an act not entirely void of sinfulness if unexcused by a just cause) its subsequent fulfillment would fail to validate such a contract. If the fact of conditional marriage is public, the external forum may demand convincing proofs as to the actual fulfillment or non-fulfillment of the proposed condition. The parties are not free to desist from the conditional marriage until the occurrence of the event

[100] De Lugo, *De Sacramentis, in genere,* VIII, n. 98.

[101] Sanchez, *loc. cit.,* disp. VIII, n. 12; Gasparri, *op. cit.,* n. 845; Wernz, *op. cit.,* n. 298.

[102] Wernz, *loc. cit.,* Fagnanus, *op. cit., loc. cit.,* n. 21; Gasparri, *op. cit.,* n. 847.

calculated to decide the validity or the invalidity of the contract. Should they disregard this law their action would be valid but sinful.

441. The canonists raise the question: "When do the parties to a conditional marriage contract receive the sacrament of matrimony?" The conferring of the sacrament, it is generally answered, begins at the time when the parties manifest their consent, and its administration is completed after the consent takes full effect, which, in conditional marriages, does not happen until the condition is verified.

442. IV. The foregoing principles will guide the reader in those conditional contracts which are entered into *cum conditione de praeterito* or *de presenti.* They are to be declared valid or invalid according as the specified condition actually exists or does not exist. Such conditions would be: "I will marry you if your father was a nobleman"; or, "If your mother is dead"; or, "If your dowry is of a certain specified sum," etc. In default of the verification of any of the foregoing specified conditions, when they are *in pactum deductae* as *conditiones sine quibus non,* the contract would not stand.

III. Manifestation of Consent.

443. This subject has already received partial treatment in another part of the book.[103] The new Code legislates that the contracting of a valid marriage necessitates the presence of the parties either in person or by proxy. The parties should express their consent by word of mouth, nor are they permitted to resort to equivalent signs when endowed with the faculty of speech.[104]

[103] See this work, n. 22 ff.

[104] Cod. Iur. Can., Can. 1088.

The sense of this canon needs no commentary. By implication it is probably intended to abolish the contracting of marriages by letter. Such abolition could be effected only by virtue of a special ecclesiastical law, for natural law does not militate against such marriages. Therefore, marriages entered into by letter, provided the contracting parties are not bound by the Catholic form of marriage, are valid. Though the contracting parties are forbidden to make use of signs expressive of matrimonial consent when they enjoy the gift of speech, such signs, though gravely sinful, would nevertheless result in a valid marriage, provided they are unmistakably translated by the other party as conveying a matrimonial intent.[105]

444. In regard to marriages contracted by proxy or by interpreter the new law introduces several substantial innovations, and casts the ancient discipline in unequivocal words. It states that the diocesan statutes on this point must be observed and that the procurator, in order to contract the contemplated marriage validly, must have a special mandate to contract with a specified person. This mandate should be signed by the authorizer and by the parish priest, or by the Ordinary of the place in which the mandate is issued, or by a priest delegated by either, or by at least two witnesses. Should the *mandans* be unable to write, the document must take cognizance of that fact and an additional witness should sign it to that effect, otherwise the mandate is without force. If the principal revoked the commission or became demented before the time when the proxy contracted marriage in his name, the contract was invalid, though neither the procurator nor the other contracting party was aware of the revocation or the dementia. In order that the marriage may

[105] C. 25, X, *de sponsalibus et matrimoniis,* IV, 1.

be valid the procurator must in person perform the service committed to his care.[106]

445. The ancient discipline of the Church relative to the rights and duties of the procurator finds a thorough exposition in the Decretals of Boniface VIII.[107] The foregoing canon introduces several important changes. These changes have already been explained under number 22 and following.

As a supplement we might add that the *mandans* need not be apprised of the day and the hour in which the proxy will interview the intended spouse. The validity of the marriage would not be suspended should the contract be made while the *mandans* is in the state of insobriety or of sleep. Nothing but his insanity would have such an effect.[108]

The requirements specified in the foregoing canon are so important that failure to comply with them would result in an invalid contract. The same is to be said should the proxy disregard the fulfillment of a certain condition which the *mandans* specified as a *conditio sine qua non.*[109]

446. Marriage may be contracted also through an interpreter.[110] Some authors denied that such marriages could be valid, though the Church has acted on the contrary principle.[111] An interpreter will become more of a necessity by virtue of the fact that the new law insists on the manifestation of the consent by word of mouth. A graver cause is required for a marriage by proxy than for one through an interpreter. As long as the interpreter is reliable and the parties are

[106] COD. IUR. CAN., Can. 1089.

[107] C. 1-9, *de procuratoribus,* in VI°.

[108] This opinion must be accepted against that of SANCHEZ. Consult his work, lib. II, disp. XI, n. 12.

[109] GASPARRI, *op. cit.*, n. 838.

[110] COD. IUR. CAN., Can. 1090.

[111] BENEDICTUS XIV, *De Synodo Dioecesana,* lib. XIII, cap. XXIII, n. 9.

unable to communicate with the priest witnessing their marriage in a tongue known to him, the services of an interpreter may be justly employed.

447. The pastor should not assist at a marriage contracted by proxy or by interpreter, unless there is a just cause and not the slightest doubt can be entertained as to the authenticity of the mandate or the trustworthiness of the interpreter. If time allow, he should secure the permission of the Ordinary.[112]

This canon mentions some of the precautions which must be taken in order to lessen the possibility of error or fraud. To resort to so exceptional a way of contracting marriage, the presence of a just cause and the permission of the Bishop are required.

448. Marriage by proxy or through an interpreter is a real sacrament if entered into by persons who are baptized. Therefore on the part of the contracting parties it is required that they be in the state of grace. The state of mortal sin on the part of the procurator or interpreter would not involve an additional guilt.[113]

449. Although the marriage should be contracted invalidly owing to the presence of an impediment, the consent originally given is presumed to persevere unless its revocation is manifest.[114]

This canon retains the ancient discipline, and the law it promulgates is of vital importance in the validation of marriages. The consent once given but ineffective on account of the presence of an impediment becomes a factor by means of which a marriage can be validated. The revocation of the consent is a fact which must be proved in the external forum, otherwise its continuance is presumed. Separation or divorce would

[112] Cod. Iur. Can., Can. 1091.

[113] Sanchez, *op. cit.*, lib. II, disp. XI, n. 29; Gasparri, *op. cit.*, n. 740; St. Alphonsus, lib. VI, n. 884; Salmaticenses, *De Matrimonio*, c. III, p. 1, n. 10; and p. III, dub. 4, n. 89, 92.

[114] Cod. Iur. Can., Can. 1093.

indicate a revocation of consent. Though the consent may persevere, it does not produce its effect by the mere fact that the inability of the parties was lifted by a dispensation from the impediment interfering with the validity of their wedlock. In all such cases in addition to the dispensation a renewal of consent must also take place. Should such a renewal be impracticable or impossible, as is sometimes the case, then a *sanatio in radice* would validate the marriage in its very root and would effect the automatic legitimation of such offspring as do not stand in need of a special mandate of the Roman Pontiff to that effect.[115] To apply a *sanatio in radice* no formality whatsoever is required and even the presence of the contracting parties may be dispensed with.

[115] See this work, n. 173 ff.

CHAPTER VIII.

THE FORM OF MARRIAGE.
(Canon 1094—Canon 1103.)

I. About the Form of Marriage in General.

450. The history of the form of marriage is somewhat involved and the scope and purpose of this work will be served sufficiently by the presentation of a few leading historical facts.

The Council of Trent declared [1] that the Church always discountenanced clandestine marriages on account of the evils which they occasioned. As early as the second century St. Ignatius of Antioch inculcates the necessity of apprising the Bishop of one's intention to enter into marriage.[2] It is the testimony of Tertullian that clandestine marriages in the early ages of Christianity were looked upon as sinful unions.[3] The Church was always conscious of the sacredness of marriage and it guarded solicitously the right to marriage which every man inherits by virtue of natural law. To prove these statements sufficient evidence could be advanced from the writings of the early Fathers and the enactments of the various Councils.[4] The different rites and ceremonies for whose introduction local cus-

[1] Sessio XXIV, *De reformatione matriomonii,* cap. I.

[2] ST. IGNATII, *Epist. ad Polycarpum,* cap. V.

[3] *De pudicitia,* cap. IV, see MIGNE, *P. L.,* vol. II, col. 987; also vol. I, col. 1302.

[4] ST. AMBROSII, *epist.* XIX, ad *Vigilium,* cap. VII; see MIGNE, *P. L.,* vol. II. col. 984; c. 5, 6, XXVII, q. 2; c. 4, 5, 6, C. XXX, q. 5; c. 17, C. XXVIII, q. 1; c. 4, C. XXXI, q. 2.

toms or universal legislation of the Church were responsible, serve the purpose of enhancing the solemnity of the celebration of marriage and of emphasizing its sacred character.[5]

451. Notwithstanding the strict vigilance exercised and the severe condemnation hurled by the Church against clandestine marriages, the evils assumed proportions so alarming that they necessitated the intervention of the Fathers convened at the Fourth Lateran Council (1215), whose well-known decree prescribes at least one public announcement of every marriage to be contracted.

Up to the time of the Council of Trent the redressive measures taken by the Church with the intention of checking the tendency to contract marriages secretly, were not sufficiently rigorous owing to the fact that the validity of such wedlocks was accepted. As a last resort the Holy See was constrained to have recourse to the most powerful weapon at its command, namely, to promulgate the decree *"Tametsi"* and to declare null and void all marriages except those contracted in the presence of the proper pastor and at least two witnesses.[6] Though this decree, more than any other factor, contributed to the abolition of clandestine marriages, it failed to eliminate them altogether. Some of the existing abuses remained unremedied owing to the fact that those places in which the decree was unpublished were exempted from the obligation of submitting to the law it enforced. Besides this effect, many hardships were created in places benefited by its actual publication. At the root of these perplexities lay the difficulty encountered in the attempt to determine in every individual case the identity of the *parochus proprius.* Prompted by the desire to simplify the dis-

[5] WERNZ, *op. cit.*, n. 154.

[6] Decr., *De Reformatione matrimonii*, sess. XXIV, cap. I.

cipline and to reduce the number of invalid marriages, the Holy See, yielding to the entreaties coming from the Hierarchy of the universal Church, deemed it necessary to modify the Tridentine law. The result was the promulgation of the decree *"Ne temere"* which became operative on the Easter of 1908.[7] The wisdom and circumspection with which this decree was formulated and its adaptability to modern times and needs, are evidenced by the fact that it was incorporated into the new Code in its entirety with only a few changes of minor importance.

II. The Form of Marriage in the Present Legislation.

452. As regards the form of marriage, the new law decrees that only those marriages are valid which are contracted before the pastor, or the Ordinary of the place, or a priest delegated by either, and at least two witnesses; due regard being paid to the rules expressed in the canons on the subject and to the exceptions contained in Canons 1098 and 1099.[8]

1. Qualifications of the Witnesses, the Pastor and the Ordinary of the Place Relative to Valid Assistance at Marriages.

453. The new law does not require any special qualifications for persons who are to be the witnesses of a marriage. The natural inference is that any person enjoying the use of reason may fill that office, whether a man or a woman, religious or lay, Catholic or non-Catholic, even if excommunicated or interdicted. Individuals belonging to the last three classes may not be tolerated unless no scandal is feared and the permission of the Ordinary is obtained.[9] It is not abso-

[7] Pius X, S. C. C., 2 aug., 1907.
[8] Cod. Iur. Can., Can. 1094.
[9] S. C. S. Off., 19 aug., 1891.

lutely necessary that the witnesses be asked and designated for that special purpose. It suffices that they be physically and morally present, cognizant of the fact that a marriage is being contracted, and capable of testifying to it.[10] They should, however, be sufficiently determined owing to the necessity of recording their names in the Matrimonial Register. The assistance of the Ordinary or of the pastor and that of the two witnesses must be simultaneous and complete. They must all witness the same marriage, and attest to the consent elicited by the same bride and bridegroom.

454. The wording of the decree presupposes that their presence is physical. The requirements of the law would not be fully satisfied if they could not be seen or heard except by means of a telescope, or a telephone.[11]

Violence and fear employed against the witnesses in order to coerce them to bear testimony to the marriage, would not militate against their valid assistance. The contrary would be true, as we shall see later, should violence and fear be used in order to compel the pastor or the Ordinary to render his assistance to the marriage.

455. The pastor and the Ordinary of the place may assist validly at marriage: (1) Only from the day on which they have taken canonical possession of their benefice in accordance with the rules laid down in canons 334, §3, and 1444, §1, or on which they began to exercise the functions of their office, unless by sentence they have been excommunicated, or interdicted or suspended from office, or declared such; (2) Within the limits of their territory, in which they may assist validly at the marriages of their subjects as well as of

[10] S. C. de Prop. Fide, instr. (ad Vic. Ap. Tunkin.), 2 iul., 1827.

[11] WOUTERS, *Commentarius in decretum "Ne temere,"* p. 39 (Amstelodami, 1910).

non-subjects; (3) Provided they are not constrained either by force or by grave fear to ask and to receive the consent of the contracting parties.[12]

456. According to the definition of the new law a pastor is a priest, or a moral person to whom a parish is entrusted with the care of souls under the jurisdiction of the local Ordinary. As regards pastoral rights and obligations, to pastors are equal, and by law are so regarded, the quasi-pastors to whose care a quasi-parish [13] is committed, and parochial vicars if vested with full pastoral rights. Military chaplains, whether minor or major, must be guided by the special legislation of the Holy See.[14]

457. Under the term Ordinary are included, besides the Roman Pontiff, each for his own territory, the residential Bishop, Abbot or *Praelatus nullius* and their Vicar General, Administrator, Vicar and Prefect Apostolic, and all those who on the vacancy of such offices become their successors either by law or by approved custom.[15]

458. Neither the Bishop nor the pastor is authorized to witness a marriage validly within his own territory unless he has *de facto* taken canonical possession of his benefice. This presupposes either an official installation or an inception of the performance of the functions inherent in such offices. The residential Bishops take canonical possession of their diocese as soon as either in person or by proxy they present the Apostolic letters to the Chapter of the Cathedral, in the presence of the Secretary of the Chapter, or the chancellor of the Curia, whose office it is to record it

[12] COD. IUR. CAN., Can. 1095.

[13] Parts of Vicariates Apostolic, or Apostolic Prefectures to which a particular rector has been assigned (COD. IUR. CAN., Can. 216, §3).

[14] *Op. cit.,* Can. 451.

[15] *Op. cit.,* Can. 198.

among official acts.[16] Where the Cathedral Chapter is wanting, as in the United States of North America, the document of appointment is generally presented to the Diocesan Consultors who, in view of canon 427 of the new law take the place of the Cathedral Chapter.

459. The pastor does not obtain jurisdiction over the souls of his parish until he takes formal possession of it.[17] The tenor of the local law or legitimate customs will guide him in the mode of taking canonical possession of his benefice, unless by virtue of just cause the Ordinary should dispense him from the formalities connected with an official installation. In such a case the dispensation would be equivalent to taking possession.[18] Should no rites or ceremonies be in vogue on such occasions, the moment the pastor begins to exercise the functions of his pastoral office he is regarded as having taken formal possession of the benefice to which he was assigned.

460. In accordance with the foregoing principles the Roman Pontiff, by virtue of his general jurisdiction, could either in person or through a delegate witness the marriage of any of his subjects in any part of the world. The Ordinaries whose names were given above may do likewise within the limits of the territory over which they have jurisdiction. The pastor has the same right over those who reside within the limits of his parish.[19]

461. This power of the Bishops and pastors ceases by the loss of their office,[20] and is suspended after a sentence has been pronounced which is followed by a legitimate appeal. The loss of a benefice may

[16] *Op. cit.*, Can. 334, §3.
[17] Cod. Iur. Can., Can. 461.
[18] *Op. cit.*, Can. 1444, §1.
[19] McNicholas, *The new legislation on engagements and marriage*, p. 23, Philadelphia, 1908.
[20] Cod. Iur. Can., Can. 208.

be effected in six different ways, namely, by privation,[21] by removal,[22] by transfer,[23] by reduction to the state of the laity,[24] by dismissal,[25] and by exchange of offices.[26] Besides the foregoing six causes Bishops and pastors are deprived of their jurisdiction and the right to witness marriages validly within the limits of their territory by the fact that a declaratory or a condemnatory sentence was fulminated against them with the effect of excommunication,[27] or interdict,[28] or suspension from office.[29]

With this explanation in our possession we shall proceed to interpret individually the three propositions mentioned under number 455 of this work.

462. A. The clause of the first proposition would not be verified should a Bishop or a pastor incur a secret or even a public excommunication *latae sententiae,* or should either of them commit a crime which would *ipso facto* deprive him of his office or place him under interdict. It is necessary that a special condemnatory or declaratory sentence, emanating from a competent ecclesiastical superior, should declare him excommunicated or suspended from office or placed under interdict. As regards suspension, it must be borne in mind that suspension from order, or from benefice, or from jurisdiction does not disqualify the Bishop or the pastor from assisting at marriage validly, for such assistance does not involve an act of jurisdiction. Since the judicial sentence must always contain the name of the guilty party,[30] it is obvious that

[21] *Op. cit.,* Can. 2299, §§1, 3.
[22] *Op. cit.,* Can. 183, §1.
[23] *Op. cit.,* Can. 1421, 1422, 1426, 1428, §§2, 3.
[24] *Op. cit.,* Can. 211, §1, 213, 214, 2305, §1.
[25] *Op. cit.,* Can. 1484 ff.
[26] *Op. cit.,* Can. 1487 ff.
[27] *Op. cit.,* Can. 2257, 2258, 2264.
[28] *Op. cit.,* Can. 2268, 2275.
[29] *Op. cit.,* Can. 2324, 2342, n. 1, 2347, n. 2.
[30] *Op. cit.,* Can. 1874.

the one against whom any of the above-mentioned censures was fulminated becomes *nominatim* excommunicated or interdicted, or suspended, as the case may be.

463. B. The most significant deviation from the Tridentine discipline is contained in the second point of the foregoing canon. The new law declares that the Bishop and the pastor may assist validly at those marriages which are contracted within the limits of their respective territory. Within these limits their assistance is valid regardless of whether the parties in question are their subjects or not. Outside those limits they have no competency even over their own subjects, unless they have received proper delegation.[31]

464. This law, which is identical with the one promulgated in the decree *"Ne temere,"* gave rise to several doubts submitted to the Holy See for solution. Their solution, published by the Sacred Congregation of the Council on February 1, 1908, is here given.

Dubium VII. To what territory is confined the competence over their subjects of the military chaplains, and of those pastors to whom no particular territory, not even jointly with another pastor, is assigned, but who exercise direct jurisdiction over certain persons or families, in the sense that they follow those people wherever they choose to establish a home? The response was: As regards military chaplains and other pastors referred to above nothing has been changed. The inference is that pastors of the class mentioned above can assist validly everywhere at the marriages of their subjects, but they would need to be delegated by the pastor or the Ordinary, if they intended to join in marriage those who are not their subjects, even if

[31] De Smet, *op. cit.*, n. 64; Wouters, *op. cit.*, p. 42; Leitner, *Die Verlobungs und Eheschliessungsform nach dem Decrete "Ne temere,"* p. 34 (Regensburg, 1910).

the ceremony were to take place in their own church or military chapel.

Dubium VIII. In what place and how are those pastors to assist at marriages who, not possessing territory exclusively their own, hold territory in common with another pastor or other pastors? The Sacred Congregation of the Council responded: Affirmatively in the territory which they share in common with others.

Dubium IX. In what place and how is a pastor who has jurisdiction over some persons or families residing in the territory of another pastor to assist at the marriages of his subjects? The answer was: Anywhere within the mentioned territory. This decision was rendered after a consultation with the Roman Pontiff. Subsequently it was decided, for a particular case in the East Indies, that the valid assistance is reserved to the personal pastor to the exclusion of the territorial pastor (the delegation not being presumed).[32]

Dubium X. May the chaplains or rectors of pious places exempted from parochial jurisdiction, validly assist at marriage without the delegation of the pastor or the Ordinary? Affirmatively, for persons committed to their care in places where they exercise jurisdiction, provided it is clear that they were invested with full pastoral rights. Such places are hospitals, seminaries, Catholic Universities, orphanages, etc. Should the rector or chaplain of such places be invested with only partial jurisdiction not including marriages, delegation from the pastor or the Ordinary would be required for such functions.[33]

The foregoing declarations provide an answer for those pastors who do not possess a territory exclu-

[32] S. C. de Sacramentis, 2 iun., 1910, in the *Acta Apostolicae Sedis*, 1910, p. 447.

[33] GENNARI, *Breve Commento della nuova legge sugli sponsali e sul matrimonio*, p. 29 (Roma, 1908).

sively their own but hold certain territories in common with other pastors, or who exercise care over certain persons or families.

465. Canon 209 legislates that in positive or probable doubt (*sive iuris sive facti*) the Church supplies the necessary jurisdiction for the external as well as the internal forum. By virtue of this law a putative pastor, one who is mistakenly regarded as the pastor of the place, would assist validly at marriage; nor would such marriages be in need of being validated *ad cautelam* as was the custom according to the former discipline.[34] The foregoing canon must not be interpreted in the sense that a valid assistance could be rendered even by a pastor who is called *intrusus,* namely, who without the consent of the legitimate superior, by usurped authority was placed in the pastoral office.[35]

466. C. The valid assistance of the Bishop and the pastor demands that they should not be constrained either by violence or grave fear to ask and receive the consent of the contracting parties. This is a signal departure from the Tridentine law which accepted as valid even unwilling or coerced assistance. The decree *"Ne temere"* introduced this particular article by the words *"dummodo invitati et rogati"* (*sint Episcopi vel parochi*). These words were subsequently expounded as being verified even in the case of an interpretive or implicit invitation to witness the proposed marriage.[36] The new law discards them as inconsequential but retains the rest of the article unchanged. The words *"requirant et excipiant consensum"* indicate an active and not a merely passive assistance. The decree is to be interpreted in the sense that an

[34] S. C. C., *Caesaraugust.*, 10 mart., 1770; NOLDIN, *Summa Theologiae Moralis,* vol. III, n. 643 (Oeniponte, 1914).

[35] Pius VI, ad Apiscopos Galliae, 26 sept., 1791.

[36] S. C. C., 28 mart., 1909, *Romana et aliarum,* n. 4.

active assistance, but only as far as the asking and receiving of consent, is prescribed even for mixed marriages.

467. One is said to ask and receive the consent of another under coercion if one acts against one's own express will. One does it under the influence of grave fear, if it is done voluntarily though under intimidation resulting from grave fear, whether justly or unjustly caused.[37] The fear in this connection denotes the fear of a grave injury threatened by an extrinsic agent or by a free cause. It is immaterial whether the fear is occasioned by the other contracting party, or by one who espoused his or her cause.

This fear, in order to prevent the validity of the contract, must be caused with the intention of extorting assistance at marriage. Some maintain that a fear justly caused does not militate against the validity of marriage.[38] Others contend that such an effect follows only when the fear is just not only *quoad substantiam* but also *quoad modum*.[39] A third class of authors teaches that fear, whether justly or unjustly caused, always renders the assistance at marriage invalid.[40] This opinion is the most probable, for the new law fails to distinguish between fear justly and unjustly caused, and such a distinction was rejected by the Sacred Congregation.[41] In default of a specific law to the contrary, fraud and deceit as regards assistance at marriages do not affect the objective validity of the contract.

[37] Noldin, *op. cit.*, vol. III, n. 644.
[38] Noldin, *op. cit.*, *loc. cit.*
[39] De Becker, *Legislatio nova de forma substantiali quoad sponsalia et matrimonium*, p. 27 (Lovanni, 1908).
[40] Wouters, *op. cit.*, p. 44; Besson, *De la publicité des fiançailles et du mariage dans la nouvelle législation. N. R. Théol.*, t. XL (1908), p. 34; Choupin, *Les fiançailles et le mariage*, n. 31 (Paris, 1911).
[41] *Acta Santae Sedis*, vol. XL, p. 338.

2. *Authorization to Assist at Marriages.*

468. The pastor and the Bishop of the place who are qualified to assist validly at marriage may authorize another priest to witness the nuptials validly within the limits of their territory.[42] Permission to assist at marriage granted in accordance with this canon must be given expressly to a determined priest for a specified marriage, all general delegations being excluded, save in the case of assistant vicars (*vicarii cooperatores*) with regard to the parish to which they are assigned. Otherwise the delegation remains inoperative. The pastor or the Ordinary of the place should not grant such a permission unless all the conditions prescribed by law to ascertain the free state of the contracting parties have been complied with.[43]

It has already been stated that a priest *delegated* by the pastor, or the Ordinary may assist validly provided the marriage is contracted within the limits of their respective territory.[44] This authorization must be express, a presumed permission would be void of all force.[45] In order that such a delegation may be operative it must proceed from a pastor, or an Ordinary who is qualified to assist validly at the nuptials in question. These qualifications have already been explained.[46] Therefore a pastor or an Ordinary against whom a condemnatory or a declaratory sentence of excommunication or interdict or suspension from office has been fulminated is disqualified from communicat-

[42] Cod. Iur. Can., Can. 1095, §2.
[43] *Op. cit.*, Can. 1096.
[44] See this work, n. 452 ff.
[45] Wernz, *op. cit.*, n. 180; Gasparri, *op. cit.*, n. 946; S. C. C. *Parisien.*, 14 dec., 1889, in the *Acta Sanctae Sedis*, vol. XXII, p. 477 ff.; 22 iun., 1581.
[46] See this work, n. 455 ff.; Gennari, *op. cit.*, p. 58; Wouters, *op. cit.*, p. 58.

ing valid delegation, for no one can transfer to another a right not possessed by him.[47]

469. In the former discipline a universal as well as a particular delegation was permitted. It was immaterial whether the authorization was extended to all marriages, or whether it was limited to certain determined ones to be contracted within the territory of the delegator. A very important change is introduced by the new law in this respect. In the future only the assistant priests will be authorized to receive a general delegation, in the sense that they may witness any and all marriages that may take place in the parish of the delegator. Such a delegation would hold good only for the period of their assistantship. Outside that period the former assistants or any other priests may receive only particular delegation, namely, a determined priest for a specified marriage. Such delegation would not be sufficiently specific were it to include all the marriages that might take place in the parish, let us suppose, within the coming week. What has been said about presumed delegation applies also to tacit delegation. It would seem that the new law demands that the delegator should designate the contracting parties by name.

470. The delegation may be conferred either by word of mouth or by writing, and even by a telephone or telegram.[48] The last two methods are not to be encouraged, for the reason that generally there is no necessity of resorting to so extraordinary a measure and in case of extreme necessity (*urgente mortis periculo*) no special delegation is needed should all avenues of communication with the proper superior be closed, except the two referred to above.[49]

[47] *De regulis iuris*, Reg. LXXIX, in VI°.
[48] McNicholas, *op. cit.*, p. 26.
[49] See this work, n. 151 ff.

471. The determination of the delegated priest does not necessarily have to be by name, it would suffice if such terms were used as would equivalently establish his identity, as, for instance, the pastor of St. Peter's Church, Westernport, Maryland.

A delegation extorted by fear or fraud is regarded by canonists as valid to all intents and purposes.[50]

472. The wording of the new law clearly indicates that for matrimonial purposes general delegations have fallen into desuetude. Even a Bishop can no longer authorize a determined priest to assist validly at all marriages to be contracted within the limits of his diocese, nor can a pastor do the same for his own parish, except in the one case stated above, when, namely, the priest to be delegated is an assistant in the strict sense of the term appointed to the parish by the legitimate ecclesiastical superior.

473. What is to be said of the general custom established in the archdiocese of Baltimore in the United States of North America whereby the pastor undertakes to marry in any part of the diocese a person who rents a pew in his church without residing within the limits of his Parish? Such means would contribute to the acquisition of a proper pastor, but the new law does not condition the validity of the contract on the assistance of the proper pastor (by virtue of domicile or quasi-domicile), but of the pastor of the place where the marriage is solemnized. The assistance of a pastor whom one acquires in the way indicated above would be valid only if such parties were placed under his jurisdiction with the understanding, or by virtue of a special ruling, of the Ordinary, as is the case with national churches. In want of such arrangement with the Ordinary of the diocese a pastor could not assist

[50] St. Alphonsus, lib. VI, n. 1088; Sanchez, lib. III, disp. XXXIX, n. 13; Schmalzgrüber, IV, III, n. 208 ff.; Gasparri, *op. cit.*, n. 942.

validly at the marriage of such pewholders except within the limits of his parish, unless he is delegated by the pastor of the place in which the marriage is to be solemnized.

474. Formerly it was generally understood that a priest who was nominally excommunicated or suspended from office could not assist at marriages validly though he possessed the authorization of the Bishop or the pastor.[51] The new law does not legislate on this point specifically. The fact that a pastor who is excommunicated or interdicted or suspended from office may not assist validly at marriages contracted within the limits of his parish, or delegate another priest to do so, does not *ipso facto* deprive him of the possibility of assisting validly (though illicitly) at marriages contracted outside the limits of his parish, when he receives a special authorization from the proper source. Unless the Holy See should legislate otherwise, assistance at such marriages cannot be deprived of its validity.

475. Closely allied to delegation is subdelegation. Delegation may be particular or universal. The former implies delegation for a certain marriage or for a specified number of marriages; the latter for all marriages that may be contracted within the limits of the parish. A priest invested with particular delegation cannot subdelegate unless such a faculty was expressly granted to him by an authorized agent for each individual case.[52] Since general delegation in the new law must be limited to assistant priests, it is to be inferred that, without a special permission granted by the delegator, no one may presume to subdelegate of his own accord except the assistant priest who enjoys

[51] GENNARI, *op. cit.*, p. 34.

[52] GASPARRI, *op. cit.*, n. 945; WERNZ, *op. cit.*, n. 180; WOUTERS, *op. cit.*, p. 58 ff.

the privilege of special delegation from the pastor, or from the Ordinary. Such delegation must be limited to the parish to which the assistant is legitimately appointed with the duty to aid the pastor to take care of souls.

476. It must be borne in mind that the person delegated, as well as the delegator, must possess the Order of the Priesthood. The new law does not permit deacons to be assigned to a parish with the title of pastor,[53] consequently, they cannot witness marriages validly. As a matter of advisability the pastor should invest at least one of his assistants with universal delegation *ad omnia negotia matrimonialia.*

477. The delegated priest in order to assist validly must witness the marriage within the territory over which the delegator has jurisdiction, and must not be coerced by force or grave fear. These propositions have already been explained.[54]

Even if the pastor should intend to delegate someone to witness a certain marriage, it is incumbent on him to perform all the transactions preliminary to such contract, and calculated to ascertain the free state of the contracting parties, such as the examination of the parties, publication of banns, etc. He should not shift the burden of this obligation on another without a just cause.[55] Should he neglect this duty the delegated priest would assist illicitly unless his act was preceded by compliance with this law.

3. *Requirements for Licit Assistance at Marriage.*

478. The pastor and the Ordinary of the place may assist licitly at marriage, provided: (1) By due process of law they have ascertained the free state of the con-

[53] Cod. Iur. Can., Can. 451, §1.
[54] See this work, n. 466 ff.
[55] Gennari, *op. cit.*, p. 34.

tracting parties: (2) They have concluded that one of the contracting parties has a domicile or a quasi-domicile or a one month's residence or, if there is a question of a *vagus,* actual residence, in the place in which the marriage is to be contracted; (3) Should the conditions mentioned in number 2 be unfulfilled, they have obtained permission from one who is the pastor or the Ordinary of either of the contracting parties by virtue of domicile or quasi-domicile or one month's residence; unless there is question of *vagi* who are in the act of traveling and who do not possess anywhere a place of residence, or a grave necessity intervenes excusing from the asking of permission.[56]

479. A. The ascertainment of each party's freedom to marry is the first step the pastor will take. The mode of procedure in this initiatory act has already been clearly outlined.[57] In other words he must make sure that they are immune from all impediments whether diriment or impedient, public or occult, especially from that of *ligamen.* This process consists in the examination of the contracting parties [58] and also of two competent witnesses,[59] should doubt arise as to the presence of an impediment. This investigation should be followed by the proclamation of the banns.[60] The domicile or the quasi-domicile of the prospective consorts will be the deciding factor as regards the pastor by whom this proclamation is to be made.[61]

480. The pastor will not neglect to exact the baptismal certificate of the Catholic party and also of the non-Catholic baptized party should the marriage be contracted with a dispensation from the impediment of

[56] COD. IUR. CAN., Can. 1097, §1.
[57] See this work, n. 97 ff.
[58] COD. IUR. CAN., Can. 1020.
[59] *Op. cit.,* Can. 1031.
[60] WOUTERS, *op. cit.,* p. 50; GENNARI, *op. cit.,* p. 30.
[61] COD. IUR. CAN., Can. 1023.

mixed religion.[62] The marriages of *vagi* should be referred to the Ordinary or to the priest delegated by him for such cases, and the pastor should abide by their instructions as regards the preliminaries of marriage.[63]

481. B. Another important question which the pastor must solve with certainty before he lends his assistance to a marriage is that of the domicile or quasi-domicile or one month's residence. Should a case involve a marriage to be contracted by a *vagus* the priest would face the necessity of ascertaining such person's actual residence in his parish.

482. The question of domicile and quasi-domicile plays so important a rôle in connection with marriage that a familiarity with at least the leading factors connected with them is an indispensable requisite for the pastor.

Neither the modern civil law nor the ecclesiastical law has an independent or original theory for the determination of one's domicile. They both draw on Roman law in this respect. The notion of domicile according to Roman law may be defined as: Dwelling in a place with the intention of remaining there permanently, provided no unforeseen circumstance shall interfere.[64] Thus the juridical element constitutive of domicile is the intention to take up a permanent abode in a place. A domicile is not acquired unless the material element (actual residence) is combined with the mental element (intention to remain indefinitely).[65] Even when a domicile or a quasi-domicile is presumed (*praesumptione iuris tantum*), the presumption yields to certainty should it be subsequently ascertained that

[62] *Op. cit.*, Can. 1021.
[63] Cod. Iur. Can., Can. 1032.
[64] L. 7, C. *de incolis*.
[65] Cod. Iur. Can., Can. 92.

the person by a positive act of the will excluded the intention of acquiring a domicile or a quasi-domicile.

A domicile is acquired by a residence in a parish or a quasi-parish or at least in a diocese, or in a vicariate or prefecture apostolic. Should an individual have resided for ten years in a place the acquisition of a domicile would be presumed (*praesumptione iuris et de iure*).[66]

483. Quasi-domicile is acquired by an actual residence in a place combined with the intention of remaining there for at least the greater part of the year. According to an instruction issued for the United States of North America and for England the intention to reside in a place until the completion of six months, or an actual residence for that length of time would be sufficient to constitute a quasi-domicile.[67] A domicile or quasi-domicile in a parish or quasi-parish is called parochial; in a diocese, a vicariate or a prefecture, but not in a parish or quasi-parish, it is called diocesan.[68]

484. In contradistinction to English law[69] the canonists, as a rule, admit the possibility of acquiring more than one domicile or quasi-domicile.[70] This is to be determined not so much by the length of time which one allots to one's residence as by the intention with which one takes up an abode. The time need not be divided equally with mathematical precision between the different places.[71]

[66] INNOCENTIUS XII, const. "*Spiculatores,*" 4 nov., 1694; l. 2, C. *de incolis.*

[67] S. C. C. Off., litt. encycl. (ad Ep. Angliae et Statuum Foeder. Americae Septentrion.), 7 iun., 1867; 9 nov., 1898; in the new *Collectanea*, n. 1305.

[68] COD. IUR. CAN., Can. 92, §3.

[69] WESTLAKE, in the *Encyclopaedia Britannica* (eleventh edition), art., "*Domicile.*"

[70] GASPARRI, *op. cit.*, n. 918; VLAMING, *Praelectiones de iure matrimonii*, n. 460 (Warmundae, 1896, 1902); BOUDINHON, in the *Le Canoniste Contemporain*, 1899, p. 273; WERNZ, *op. cit.*, n. 177 ff.

[71] VLAMING, *op. cit.. loc. cit.;* WOUTERS, *op. cit.*, p. 109; SANCHEZ, *op. cit.*, lib. III, disp. XXIV, n. 3.

485. A wife not separated legitimately from her husband retains the domicile of her husband; a demented person that of his guardian, and a minor retains the domicile of him who exercises tutelage over him.[72] Persons residing on the bordering line of two parishes have their domicile or quasi-domicile in the parish to which the principal door of their home leads. A minor after the completion of his seventh year and a wife not legitimately separated from her husband may acquire a proper quasi-domicile.[73] The latter may even acquire a domicile provided she is legitimately separated.[74] Children acquire a domicile in the parish within whose limits their parents or tutors reside. Soldiers are not classed as *vagi,* though they may not be assigned to a permanent post; for, should they reside in a place for a longer term than the greater part of the year, they would acquire a quasi-domicile, and unless they renounce such an intention they retain the legal domicile of their parents. Orphans and foundlings acquire a domicile or quasi-domicile in the orphanage to whose care they are entrusted. Persons incarcerated for life or for an indefinite period acquire domicile in the prison to which they are confined. Should their imprisonment last only six months they would acquire a quasi-domicile. In order that an indisposed person may acquire a quasi-domicile in a hospital, it is necessary that his ailment should detain him there for the greater part of the year. Servants, as a rule, do not lose the domicile of their parents, and may acquire also a quasi-domicile in the place where their masters reside. Young men and women availing themselves of a college education acquire a quasi-

[72] C 3, *de sepulturis,* III, 12 in VI°; S. C. S. Off., 30 iun., 1892; S. C. C., *Romana seu Tusculana,* 27 apr., 1720; S. C. de Prop. Fide, instr. a. 1883, n. 2; Cod. Iur. Can., Can. 93.

[73] S. C. C., *Caietana et Terracinen.,* 31 ian., 21 febr., 1835.

[74] Cod. Iur. Can., Can. 93.

domicile in the place where their college is situated, though they do not lose their paternal legal domicile.[75] A domicile or quasi-domicile is forfeited by the act of departure from the place with no intention of returning.[76]

486. For all legal effects, as a general rule, the act of establishing a home in a place with the intention of remaining there permanently (domicile) or for the greater part of the year (quasi-domicile) bestows on one from the first day of residence the prerogatives of a domicile or quasi-domicile. If the intention of an individual to establish such a residence is clearly manifested by his actions, the pastor of the place, *per se,* could witness his marriage licitly even from the very first day of his residence. This gives rise to a possibility of acting *in fraudem legis,* or to abuses against which the pastor must guard. If there is a well-founded doubt as to the sincerity of the person's intention, he should be compelled to wait until he establishes at least one month's residence which, *in ordine ad matrimonium,* is likened to a quasi-domicile.

Chaplains of colleges, educational institutes, hospitals, orphan asylums, and prisons are not competent to assist validly at the marriages of those who acquired a domicile, or quasi-domicile, or one month's residence in such places, unless they are invested with the full power of a pastor, or possess a particular delegation given to them by the pastor or the Ordinary.

487. As regards valid assistance in the case of one month's residence it must be borne in mind that after

[75] For a more complete exposition of this doctrine the reader should consult other authors. For instance, LAURIN, in the *Archiv für kath. Kirchenrecht,* t. XXVI, p. 165 ff.; BOUDINHON, in the *Catholic Encyclopedia,* art., *"Domicile"*; WERNZ, *op. cit.,* n. 177 ff.; GASPARRI, *op. cit.,* n. 916 ff.; BINDERS, *Praktisches Handbuch des katholischen Eherechts,* p. 150 ff (Freiburg, im Bresgau, 1891).

[76] COD. IUR. CAN., Can. 95.

the expiration of the month, namely, of thirty days, the pastor would assist not only validly but also licitly even if from the very first day the party did not intend to prolong his stay beyond that period of time.

The month's residence does not require an uninterrupted stay for thirty consecutive days. The intention to establish a home for a month in a certain locality would be sufficient though the person's avocation in life might necessitate an arrangement whereby he would be constrained to spend his days in another place, provided he should return to his abode at night. The marriage ceremony under such circumstances, if witnessed by the pastor or the Ordinary of the place or a priest delegated by either, may be performed lawfully in the morning of the thirtieth day.[77]

By actually residing or intending to continue to reside within the limits of a determined diocese but not within the confines of a particular parish, one could acquire a diocesan but not a parochial domicile or quasi-domicile. Such individuals, the new law states, may be married by the pastor in whose parish they actually reside at the time the marriage is to be contracted.[78] In this respect such persons are likened to *vagi,*[79] but while the pastor's assistance at the marriage of the latter must be preceded by the permission of the Ordinary, or of the priest delegated for such cases, he may assist at the wedlock of the former without the asking of such permission.[80]

488. *Vagi* are persons without a domicile or quasi-domicile or one month's residence.[81] Any pastor in whose diocese they tarry *hic et nunc* has the right to

[77] S. C. C., 28 mart., 1908, *Romana et aliarum* ad 4; ib., GENNARI, *op. cit.,* p. 31.

[78] DE SMET, *op. cit.,* n. 72.

[79] COD. IUR. CAN., Can. 94, §3.

[80] *Op. cit.* Can. 94, §2.

[81] *Op. cit.,* Can. 1032.

assist at their marriage not only validly but also licitly. It is presumed that his assistance was preceded by permission granted by the legitimate authority appointed to exercise vigilance over such marriages. Should one of the contracting parties have a domicile or a quasi-domicile or one month's residence and should the other party have none, the marriage should be contracted in the parish of the former, regardless of whether it is the prospective husband or wife that is without a legal home.

489. C. Should the bride or the bridegroom have a domicile or a quasi-domicile or one month's residence in a different place from the one in which they wish to contract marriage, the pastor of the parish where they wish to get married would have to ask permission of the pastor or the Ordinary of the place where at least one of them has a legal home. In such cases, since the pastor of the bride has the first right to witness the marriage, his permisison should be asked in preference to the other pastors'. The pastor of the place where she has her one month's residence has the least claim of the three to witness such marriage.

The permission of which this canon speaks is required only for the lawfulness of the assistance, and the law permits the pastor to dispense himself from this requirement when grave necessity so demands.[82] The pastor himself is the judge whether in a certain case the necessity is sufficiently grave to justify his non-compliance with the foregoing rule. Such necessity would arise if the marriage is urgent and the time to be consumed by asking permission cannot be spared, or if there is a well-grounded fear that unless they are

[82] GREGORIUS XVI, ep. *"Accepimus,"* febr., 1836; S. C. S. Off. (Vic. Ap. Sandwic.), 11 dec., 1850, ad 25-27; S. C. de Sacramentis, *Romana et aliarum,* 13 mart., 1910, ad 5; S. C. C., decr. *"Ne temere,"* 2 aug., 1907, art. V, §3.

married immediately the parties will attempt marriage before a state official or a minister of a religious sect, or will live in concubinage.[83] A notable financial loss, scandal, or defamation of character threatening the prospective consorts would also be considered a sufficiently grave reason. Since there is question here of mere permission, not of delegation, a tacit or presumed permission would suffice for a licit assistance.

490. From the application of the foregoing principles the reader is to conclude that in case each of the contracting parties has a domicile and a quasi-domicile and also a month's residence, the marriage is to be contracted in the domicile of the bride, though it may be contracted in any of the other places. If the bride has at least one month's residence in a place she is entitled to contract marriage in it though the bridegroom may have a domicile (in another place). If the bride and the bridegroom reside in different parishes, the former having only a one month's residence while the latter has a domicile, the bridegroom's domicile yields to the one month's residence of the bride, because by virtue of general custom marriages are contracted in the home parish of the bride and to act contrary to such a custom would entail inconvenience and probably even unpleasant comment. In the same case McNicholas maintains [84] that the marriage should be contracted in the parish where the future husband has his domicile. This is true should the bride so desire, but we believe that the spirit of the law gives her the first choice.

491. The new law says: In every case the general rule shall be that the nuptials be witnessed by the pastor of the bride, unless a just cause excuses; the marriages of Catholics who belong to different rites, are to be contracted according to the rite of the bridegroom

[83] McNicholas. *op. cit.*, p. 37; Gennari, *op. cit.*, p. 31.
[84] *Op. cit.*, p. 38.

and before his pastor, unless some particular law ordains otherwise. A pastor who assists at marriage without permission, as required by law, should not appropriate the stole-fee but should deliver it to the proper pastor of the contracting parties.[85]

By virtue of this canon the parish of the bride always takes precedence over the parish of the bridegroom. There may be many just causes which would justify the solemnization of the marriage in the parish church of the bridegroom in preference to that of the bride. Among such reasons one could enumerate the following: (1) The intention to establish a home in the parish where the prospective husband has a domicile; (2) Saving of considerable expense; (3) Avoiding some inconvenience; (4) Forestalling an expected humiliation, etc. The fact that the prospective husband is a very prominent member in his own parish, and that his staunch faith and well-known generosity have won for him the particular friendship of his pastor may also be reputed among just causes.

492. The foregoing canon contains something exceptional in the fact that it is one of the very few which legislate for the Oriental rite. The new law gives to the woman, whose rite is different from that of the man, liberty to follow the rite of the husband both in entering into marriage and while the marriage endures.[86] After the marriage is dissolved she is free to return to her native rite, unless a particular law ordains otherwise.[87] Should the two contracting parties belong to different rites of the Oriental Church, the marriage must, as a general rule, take place before the pastor of the man and according to his rite. This gen-

[85] Cod. Iur. Can., Can. 1097, §§2, 3.

[86] Cod. Iur. Can., Can. 98, §4.

[87] Benedictus XIV, const. *"Etsi pastoralis,"* 26 maii, 1742, §VIII, n. 9; Leo XIII, litt. ap. *"Orientalium,"* 30 nov., 1894, n. VIII; S. C. de Prop. Fide (*C. G.*), decr. 19 maii, 1759.

eral legislation is not meant to abrogate those particular laws which were promulgated on this discipline for certain places. Thus, for instance, the Ruthenians in the United States of North America must contract marriage according to the rite of the bride and in presence of her pastor.[88]

493. The specific punishment meted out to pastors who disregard the prescriptions regulating licit assistance at marriages, is the necessity of returning the matrimonial stole-fees to the pastor whose permission they have failed to obtain, in case they witnessed the marriage of parties neither of whom had a domicile, or a quasi-domicile or at least one month's residence within the limits of their parish. The pastor in question may appropriate such fees only on condition that there was some grave necessity for his assistance at the marriage and time did not permit the obtaining of permission from the *parochus contrahentium.*

494. The pastor of the bride is one to whom the law concedes the right to perform the marriage ceremony and who is to be benefited by the stole-fees. Therefore should the contracting parties belong to different parishes and should each of them have a domicile as well as a month's residence, the pastor in the case of an unauthorized assistance should return the perquisites to the pastor who is the bride's *parochus proprius* by virtue of her domicile.[89] Should he decline to accept the fees they belong to the pastor of the place in which she has a one month's residence. A pastor in whose parish the bridegroom has a domicile or a quasi-domicile or a one-month's residence would satisfy the

[88] S. C. de Prop. Fide, decr. *"Cum Episcopo,"* 17 aug., 1914; this new law was enforced in Canada five years before the promulgation of the new Code. (S. C. de Prop. Fide, decr. *"Fidelibus Ruthenis,"* 18 aug., 1913.)

[89] Gennari, *op. cit.*, p. 40; Wouters, *op. cit.*, p. 83; McNicholas, *op. cit.*, p. 46.

requirements of the new law for a valid and licit assistance at his marriage. Therefore the surrendering of the emolument would not apply in such a case even if he should witness the marriage *sine iusta causa.*[90]

4. Causes Justifying the Non-observance of the Foregoing Law.

495. Provided the parties are unable without grave inconvenience to resort to a pastor or an Ordinary or a priest delegated by either who would assist at their marriage in accordance with the rule laid down in canon 1095 and 1096: (1) Their marriage contracted in danger of death in presence of merely two witnesses would be valid and licit, and also outside such danger provided it is prudently foreseen that such state of affairs will last for a month; (2) In both cases, if another priest who can be present should be nigh, he should be called and should assist at the marriage together with the witnesses, without prejudice to the validity of the marriage if contracted solely in the presence of the latter.[91]

The foregoing canon states the conditions which must be verified before one is dispensed from the necessity of complying with the form of marriage prescribed by the Church and explained above. When such conditions are present one is authorized to contract a valid and licit marriage in the presence of two witnesses only. In order that one may avail oneself of so exceptional a privilege, it is necessary that: (1) The circumstances make it impossible to have access to the pastor or the Ordinary of the place or a priest delegated by either; (2) The danger of death threaten the contracting parties or one of them.

[90] LEITNER, *op. cit.*, p. 57.
[91] COD. IUR. CAN., Can. 1098.

496. The law does not leave us in doubt as to the main condition under which one is entitled to the foregoing privilege, but it fails to specify the cause from which this danger must result. Therefore any cause which would threaten one with the danger of death, such as sickness, a shipwreck, a fairly serious operation, the necessity of confronting the line of the enemy in wartime, etc., would be regarded as cases for which this law means to legislate. Since the canon with which we are concerned leaves the danger of death unqualified, it need not be imminent as required in the decree *"Ne temere,"* nor urgent as exacted by canon 1043. There must, however, be a well-founded fear or probability which would induce one to expect death. When such circumstances are complied with the inability of securing the services of one's pastor or the Ordinary or a priest delegated by either, marriage may be contracted in the presence of two witnesses only. This inability need not be absolute. A relative inability, in the sense that the death feared is liable to occur before any of the above-named priests is accessible, suffices.

497. The same canon provides also for cases in which the danger of death is not threatening but in which there is a reasonable probability that neither the pastor nor the Ordinary nor a priest delegated by either can be had for a month. The decree *"Ne temere"* connected this inability to secure the services of a qualified priest for the period of a month with the word "region." The result was that the term *"regio"* led many theologians to believe that the law legislated for general inability,[92] and only for certain regions suffering from scarcity of priests. Only a few advocated the theory that even an individual impossibility to procure a competent priest is included within the scope of the law. The present canon discards the word

[92] S. C. de Sacramentis, 31 ian., 1916.

"regio"[93] and retains the rest of the old law unchanged, namely, *"si haberi vel adiri nequeat sine gravi incommodo parochus vel Ordinarius vel sacerdos delegatus."* Therefore, in the new discipline the foregoing privilege may be used regardless of whether the impossibility be physical or moral. Physical impossibility would involve a case in which a priest of any of the three classes mentioned would not be accessible with any effort or cost. Moral impossibility pertains to the overcoming of grave difficulty militating against his presence. Such a hardship may affect either the contracting parties or the priest. Both hypotheses would justify a marriage contracted in the presence of two witnesses only. The same is to be said when the difficulty to procure a proper priest is personal (limited to the persons in question), or local (affecting a certain class of people residing in the same locality), particular or general.[94]

The privilege is not to be extended to a case in which the parties would experience grave difficulty in securing the services of their pastor or the Ordinary of the place or a priest delegated by either, but no hardship would be encountered by them in resorting to another pastor. By virtue of a special decision of the Sacred Congregation the foregoing privilege could be invoked even by persons who *in fraudem legis* repaired to a locality in which they would labor under a physical or moral inability to secure a competent priest to witness their marriage.[95]

498. On January 31, 1916, the Sacred Congregation of the Sacraments decided that the Holy See should be consulted in every case individually should in certain

[93] S. C. de Sacramentis, decr. 10 mart., 1910, in the *Acta Apostolicae Sedis*, vol. II, n. 5, p. 193 ff.

[94] WOUTERS, *op. cit.*, p. 78 ff.

[95] S. C. de Sacramentis, 13 mart., 1910; SABETTI-BARRET, *op. cit.*, n. 912, p. 18; WOUTERS, *op. cit.*, *loc. cit.*

localities the law of the state demand the celebration of civil marriage before the religious ceremony is performed. Exception was made for the danger of death, which case is provided for by canon 1043 of the new law.[96] If, outside such danger, time would not permit a recourse to the Holy See and the assistance of a priest could not be secured, owing to the penalty with which the civil law threatens the priest who would dare to disregard such legislation, the tenor of the present canon permits the parties to avail themselves of the privilege it confers. The same is to be said when a country, as is the case in some parts of the United States of North America, enforces a law against miscegenation, prohibiting marriages between the white and the black race in order to obviate their amalgamation. A priest presuming to witness such marriages would be regarded as a transgressor, and would become liable to severe penalty. Such circumstances would induce a moral inability on the part of the contracting parties to secure a competent priest to witness their marriage and would authorize them to benefit by the law promulgated in canon 1098.

499. The canon does not require any particular reason for marriage in order that the law it contains may become operative. Therefore, provided the other conditions can be established in the case, no other reason need be had than the wish of the parties to enter into wedlock.

500. The witnesses mentioned in this canon need not possess any other qualifications than those required by natural law. The office could be filled validly whether they are men or women, religious or lay, Catholic or non-Catholic, even if excommunicated or interdicted. The last three classes could not be employed licitly unless others could not be secured without grave

[96] See this work, n. 151 ff.

inconvenience. Any witness would be qualified provided he (a) enjoys the use of reason, (b) takes cognizance of the parties' intention to contract marriage, (c) is capable of giving testimony to that effect.

The same canon says that outside the danger of death nothing but a reasonable certainty as regards the inability to procure a competent priest for a month *(eam rerum conditionem esse per mensem duraturam)* would justify one's entering into marriage before two witnesses only. The month in this connection consists of thirty days. The decree *"Ne temere"* exacted a wait of full thirty days before the parties were permitted to avail themselves of the privilege it extended. This delay of thirty days is not required by the new law. The parties may profit by the exemption from the general law even on the first or the second day if they foresee that for thirty days to come they will be unable to contract marriage according to the prescribed form.

501. Whether the marriage for which this canon legislates is contracted in danger of death or outside such danger, should a priest chance to be near he must be asked to assist together with two witnesses. The words *"alius sacerdos"* permit the inference that the obligation to request the presence of a priest would not be removed even if the parties were constrained to use the services of one who is excommunicated or interdicted or suspended. It must be borne in mind that his presence is not required *ad validitatem matrimonii contrahendi* but only *ad eius liceitatem.* Should he decline to accede to their wishes their marriage, contracted in the presence of two witnesses only, would be not only valid but also licit.

5. *Persons Affected by the Catholic Form of Marriage.*

502. The form of marriage prescribed by the Church binds: (1) All individuals baptized in the Catholic Church or converted to it from heresy or schism though either the former or the latter may have subsequently fallen away from it, whenever they contract marriage among themselves; (2) All persons referred to above when they enter into wedlock with non-Catholics, whether baptized or unbaptized, even after they have obtained a dispensation from the impediment of mixed religion or of disparity of worship; (3) Orientals if they contract with persons of the Latin rite, subject to this form.[97]

The foregoing canon brings us to the discussion of the nature and meaning of Catholic baptism. This question has already received an extensive treatment in this work in connection with the impediment of disparity of worship, which in the future will exist only between a person baptized in the Catholic Church and one unbaptized.[98] The conclusions reached from the discussion of the meaning of the terms *"in Catholica Ecclesia baptizati"* would impose the observance of the prescribed form of marriage on all persons:

1. Who are the offspring of Catholic parents and in their infancy were baptized in the Catholic Church;

2. Who as adults received Catholic baptism but subsequently relapsed into their former heresy or lost all faith;

3. Who were born of non-Catholic parents and in their infancy (whether in urgent necessity or outside such necessity) were baptized in the faith, provided from their childhood they have not been reared in heresy or schism or infidelity or brought up without any religious training whatsoever.

4. Who were baptized validly outside the Catholic Church and admitted into its membership by profession of faith and absolution from heresy.

[97] Cod. Iur. Can., Can. 1099, §1.
[98] See this work, n. 222 ff.

5. Children of Catholic parents who after their Catholic baptism fell away from the faith either in their infancy or in their adult age.

503. All persons belonging to the foregoing five classes whenever they contract marriage among themselves are bound by the prescribed form. The same is to be said when they contemplate a mixed marriage with a non-Catholic, whether baptized or unbaptized, even when a dispensation has been obtained from the impediment of mixed religion or of disparity of worship.

The above-explained form of marriage is extended to the whole world with the exception of Germany and Hungary. The former's exemption was granted by the Papal Constitution *"Provida"* issued on January 18, 1906, the latter's exemption was granted by a decree of the Sacred Congregation of the Council, dated February 27, 1909. In these two countries mixed marriages did not have to conform to the general law as embodied in the decree *"Ne temere."* [99] In order that the exemption may have its force it was decided that the marriages must be contracted by the natives of Germany and in German territory, or in the case of Hungarians by the natives of Hungary and on the soil of that nation.[100] Therefore a native of Germany could not be benefited by this exemption if he should intend to contract marriage with a subject of Hungary regardless of the territory in which the marriage was to be solemnized. Thus, unlike the decree *"Tametsi,"* the *communicatio privilegiorum* was excluded. This particular legislation is not *ipso facto* abolished by the general law promulgated in the new Code, though many difficulties are placed in the way of its operation by the

[99] De Smet, *op. cit.*, n. 72 ff.; Leitner, *op. cit.*, p. 68 ff.; Sabetti-Barrett, n. 913 (ed. XXV).

[100] S. C. C., *Romana et aliarum*, 1 febr., 28 mart., 1908.

fact that the present limits of the two countries are far from being well determined.

504. Whenever the Orientals contract marriages with any of the above classified persons the validity or invalidity of their marriage depends on their adherence or non-adherence to the form prescribed for the Latin rite. Therefore, should the forms of marriage enforced by the two rites differ, a marriage contracted between a Catholic of the Latin rite and one of the Oriental rite would be invalid if celebrated according to the latter rite.

505. Non-Catholics whether they are baptized or unbaptized are nowhere bound by the Catholic form of marriage, provided they contract among themselves. The same is to be said of a person born of non-Catholic parents but baptized in the Catholic Church, provided that from his very infancy he was brought up in heresy or infidelity or without any religious training whatsoever, whenever he contracts marriage with a non-Catholic.[101]

The first of the two classes of persons expressly exempted from the Catholic form of marriage will cause no difficulty. Individuals belonging to the second class, when they contract marriage with an unbaptized person, are not exempted from the impediment of disparity of worship but only from the Catholic form of marriage. The terms *"ab infantili aetate"* are to be applied to a child before he has completed his seventh year.[102] If at any time before that age the teachings of the Catholic Church were not inculcated on the child, but, on the contrary, he was reared from infancy in an atmosphere of heresy or schism or infidelity or irreligion, the Catholic form of marriage would not be obligatory on him as long as the other party to the con-

[101] COD. IUR. CAN., Can. 1099, §2.
[102] *Op. cit.*, Can. 88, §3.

tract is a non-Catholic. Should he intend to enter into marriage with a Catholic, a dispensation from the impediment of mixed religion would have to be obtained in view of the fact that, though baptized in the Catholic Church, he is an adherent of a heretical sect or an unbeliever.

Even if such a person should profess infidelity he would not be an infidel in the strict sense of the term, for it implies the non-reception of baptism. Therefore, even in that hypothesis the impediment of disparity of worship would not arise between him and the Catholic party. Nor would an impediment of unworthiness arise between them for the reason that it presupposes a public rejection of the Catholic faith.[103]

On the supposition that such a child was reared in the Catholic faith up to the completion of his seventh year and after that age fell away from the Church, the law of exemption from the Catholic form of marriage could not be invoked in his favor.

6. Rites to be Observed in the Celebration of Marriage.

506. Outside the case of necessity the celebration of marriage must conform to the rites prescribed by rituals bearing the approbation of the Church or received by laudable customs.[104]

The ceremonies usually connected with the celebration of marriage consist in: (1) Mutual declaration of intention on the part of both contracting parties; (2) Sanction and blessing of the union imparted by the assisting priest; (3) Blessing of the ring; (4) The placing of the ring on the bride's finger by the bridegroom; (5) Prayer offered up by the assisting priest in behalf

[103] COD. IUR. CAN., Can. 1065, §1.
[104] *Op. cit.*, Can. 1100.

of the spouses; (6) Celebration of the nuptial Mass *(Missa pro Sponso et Sponsa)* at which the solemn nuptial blessing is imparted with prayers contained in the Missal; (7) Short exhortation.

507. The pastor should take care that the spouses receive the solemn blessing, which may be imparted even after they have lived in matrimony a long time, but only during the Mass (attention being paid to special rubrics) and outside the forbidden time. Such a blessing may not be given except by a priest who is authorized to assist at the marriage validly and licitly or by one whom he commissions.[105]

The solemn nuptial blessing, whenever the parties are entitled to it, should not be omitted. It is immaterial how long the contracting parties have lived in married life, the blessing may be imparted at any time and it is the wish of the Church that it be not postponed without reason.[106]

508. In imparting this blessing, (a) the special rubrics regulating it should not be disregarded, (b) it should not be given in forbidden times; (c) the officiating priest should be one who is authorized to assist validly and licitly at the marriage in question, or one deputed by him.

The forbidden time during which the new law prohibits the solemn blessing of the nuptials runs from the first Sunday of Advent to the feast of the Nativity inclusively, and from Ash Wednesday to the Resurrection Sunday inclusively.[107]

The Mass *"Pro Sponso et Sponsa"* may be celebrated any day except a double of the first or the second class, except Sundays and other holy days of obligation, except the vigil of Pentecost and the entire

[105] *Op. cit.,* Can. 1101.
[106] S. C. S. Off., 31 aug., 1881.
[107] Cod. Iur. Can., Can. 1108.

octaves of the Epiphany, Pentecost and Corpus Christi. In parish churches where only one Mass is celebrated the Missa *pro Sponso et Sponsa* may not be said on Rogation days.[108] On feasts which do not permit the celebration of *"Missa pro Sponso et Sponsa"* the prayer of that Mass may be inserted in the Mass of the day by way of commemoration but not *sub eadem conclusione.* This prayer should be said after the prayers prescribed by the rubrics, but it takes precedence of an *oratio imperata.* The prayers containing the nuptial blessing should be borrowed from the *"Missa pro Sponso et Sponsa"* and inserted in their proper places in the Mass of the day.

509. If a locality is placed under a general interdict, unless the decree ordains otherwise, no solemn nuptial blessing can be imparted in it until the interdict is lifted.[109] Should the interdict be fulminated against only certain specified churches, the privilege to bless the nuptials would thereby be withdrawn from them.[110]

510. A woman who received the nuptial blessing at her first marriage may not be benefited by it when she contracts marriage the second time.[111]

The blessing in question should be given either by the pastor or the Ordinary of the place or a priest deputed by either.[112] Compliance with this law is only *ad liceitatem benedictionis.* Needless to say that the

[108] S. C. R., July 3, 1869, D. 3208 (5439). WAPELHORST, p. 487, n. 299. (Ed. 9th, 1915.)

[109] COD. IUR. CAN., Can. 2271, n. 2.

[110] *Op. cit.*, Can. 2272, §3, n. 2.

[111] *Op. cit.*, Can. 1143; c. 1, 3, X, *de secundis nuptiis,* IV, 21; INNOCENTIUS IV, ep. *"Sub catholicae,"* 6 mart., 1254, §3, n. 21; BENEDICTUS XIV, const. *"Etsi pastoralis,"* 26 mart., 1742, §VIII, n. 4.

[112] *Conc. Trid.*, sessio XXIV, *De reformatione matrimonii,* cap. I; LEO X (*in Conc. Lateranen. V*), const. *"Dum intra,"* 19 dec., 1516, §13; S. C. S. Off., instr. (ad Praef. Mission. Martinicae, etc.), 6 iul., 1817; S. C. de Prop. Fide, decr. 6 oct., 1863.

priest selected as a substitute must be one whose right to celebrate Mass has not been withdrawn.

511. In marriages between a Catholic and a non-Catholic the asking of the consent must comply with the prescription of canon 1095, §1, n. 3, but all sacred rites must be barred. Should it be foreseen that this prohibition would occasion greater evils, the Ordinary may permit some of the customary ecclesiastical ceremonies, but the celebration of Mass must always be excluded.[113]

The assistance of the priest at marriages may be either active or merely passive.[114] Passive assistance implies the mere presence of the officiating priest and excludes any active part in the ceremony, even the asking of the consent. The new law prescribes that even in mixed marriages the consent of the contracting parties must be asked and received by the witnessing priest, but *ad validitatem* it is furthermore required that neither violence nor fear should coerce him to engage in that work.[115]

His active participation in the ceremony, however, must be limited to the asking and receiving of consent, and, as a general rule, all sacred rites are forbidden. This question has already received full treatment in connection with the impediment of mixed religion.[116] The ritual approved for the United States of North America, besides the asking and receiving of the consent, permits a declaration to be made by the assisting priest as to the state of marriage begotten by the given consent and the placing of the unblessed ring on the finger of the bride by the bridegroom.

512. The prohibition as to the employment of sacred

[113] Cod. Iur. Can., Can. 1102.

[114] See this work, n. 266.

[115] S. C. C., decr. *"Ne temere,"* 2 aug., 1907, art. IV, §3; art. XI, §2; *Romana et aliarum*, 27 iul., 1908, ad III.

[116] See this work, n. 196 ff.

rites is only relative not absolute. Should the avoidance of greater evils make it advisable or necessary that certain sacred rites be permitted, the Ordinary is expressly authorized to show some leniency, provided the Mass does not become a part of the nuptial ceremonies.[117]

7. *Registration of Marriage.*

513. After the marriage has been celebrated the pastor or the priest who is acting as such should record as soon as possible in the Matrimonial Register the names of the consorts and the witnesses, the place and date of the celebrated marriage and all other information as required by the ritual books or by the order of the Ordinary. This obligation devolves on the pastor even if another priest delegated by him or by the Ordinary assisted at the marriage.

Moreover, in conformity with canon 1070, §2, the pastor should note also in the Baptismal Record that the consorts on such a day contracted marriage in his parish. If a contracting party was baptized elsewhere, the pastor who witnessed the marriage should either personally or through the Episcopal Curia transmit a notice to the pastor of the place where the party in question was baptized in order that the marriage may be inscribed in the Baptismal Record.

Whenever a marriage is celebrated according to the provisions of canon 1098, the priest, if one assisted at it, otherwise the witnesses are obliged jointly with the contracting parties to see to it that the contracted wedlock be entered in the prescribed books as soon as possible.[118]

[117] GREGORIUS XVI, ep. *"Non sine gravi,"* 23 maii, 1846; S. C. S. Off. (Quebec), 10 sept., 1820; S. C. de Prop. Fide, instr. (ad Ep. Graeco-Rumen.), a. 1858; litt. encycl., 11 mart., 1868.

[118] COD. IUR. CAN., Can. 1103.

514. The legislation embodied in the foregoing canon needs little commentary. The Church insisted repeatedly on the observance of the same law. The Council of Trent thought it necessary to exhort the pastors to procure a register in which to enter the names of the consorts and of the witnesses, and the place and date of the contracted wedlock.[119] A similar instance is found in many other ecclesiastical sources.[120]

The enforcement of the same discipline was made not only more rigorous but also more specific and better adapted to the needs of modern times by the promulgation of the decree *"Ne temere."*[121] The law of that decree is identical with the one incorporated in the new Code. The purpose of the law is important, hence it is generally conceded that it obliges under pain of mortal sin.[122]

515. The word *"statim"* of the decree *"Ne temere"* was replaced by the term *"quamprimum."* The commentators of the decree *"Ne temere"* contended that the spirit of the law required that the pastor should record the marriage within two or three days after it was contracted. While the word *"quamprimum"* does not imply the same necessity of speedy compliance with the law as the term *"statim"* implies, nevertheless it would seem that a delay of four or five days should not be exceeded.

This obligation rests with the pastor of the place (or his substitute) where the marriage was contracted. The recording is not to be made by the Ordinary or by the personal pastor who might have assisted at the

[119] Sessio XXIV, *De reformatione matrimonii*, cap. I.

[120] BENEDICTUS XIV, const. *"Satis Vobis,"* 27 nov., 1741; S. C. de Prop. Fide, instr. (ad Vic. Ap. Indiar. Orient.), 8 sept., 1869, n. 21; *Rituale Rom.*, tit. VII, c. 2; *Ritus celebrandi matrimonii sacramentum;* c. 5, *Forma describendi coniugatos.*

[121] S. C. C., 2 aug., 1907, art. IX, §1.

[122] GENNARI, *op. cit.*, p. 39; WOUTERS, *op. cit.*, p. 81; S. C. de Sacr., 6 mart., 1911.

marriage. This duty incumbent on the pastor of the place would be fulfilled if another priest should be authorized by him, for the words "*manu sua*" are not contained in the new law.[123]

516. The marriage register should contain (a) the names of the contracting parties; (b) the place and the date of marriage; (c) information relative to proclamation of banns; (d) dispensation from the impediment if granted in the external forum; (e) the fact of delegation if the pastor did not assist in person; (f) validation of marriage if it took place in the external forum; and finally (g) the name of the assisting priest and of the two witnesses.[124]

517. The pastor should record the fact of marriage also in the Baptismal Register if one or both parties were baptized in his parish. In case they were baptized elsewhere the pastor of the place where they were baptized must be notified of the marriage. The notification must be sent by the local pastor either personally or through the Diocesan Curia.

When marriage is contracted in presence of two witnesses only, whether it be in danger of death or outside such danger, the same information must be imparted to the pastor in whose territory the marriage took place. The duty to impart this information devolves on the assisting priest, or, if no priest was present, on the witnesses and the contracting parties conjointly (*in solidum*). They are all equally bound by the obligation until it is satisfied.[125] The others are not freed until it is certain that one of them complied with the law. The pastor is to see to it that the marriage will not pass unrecorded in the proper Baptismal and Matrimonial Registers.

[123] WOUTERS, *op. cit., loc. cit.;* LEITNER, *op. cit.*, p. 54.

[124] GENNARI, *op. cit.*, p. 38; MCNICHOLAS, *op. cit.*, p. 41.

[125] S. C. de Prop. Fide, 23 iun., 1830.

CHAPTER IX.

Marriage of Conscience.

(Canon 1104—Canon 1107.)

518. Marriage of conscience is a union contracted with a special permission of the Ordinary by means of the proper form but without the proclamation of the banns and with an obligation to secrecy imposed on the contracting parties, on all who witness it, as well as on the Ordinary. No substantial change has been introduced on this point by the new law. In its essentials it conforms to the principles enunciated by Benedict XIV.[1] The reader is referred to another part of this work in which this question has already received a partial treatment.[2]

519. As regards the licitness of the marriage of conscience the new Code says: Only for a very grave and very urgent reason, and by the Ordinary alone, to the exclusion of the Vicar General unless he has a special mandate, may it be permitted that a marriage of conscience be contracted, namely, that a wedlock be entered into without the proclamation of the banns and in secret, according to the canons that follow.[3]

The witnessing of the marriage of conscience is one of the extremely few ecclesiastical functions in which the Vicar General may not engage unless he has a very special mandate from the Ordinary. The lead-

[1] Const. *"Satis Vobis,"* 27 nov., 1741.

[2] See this work, n. 61 ff.

[3] Cod. Iur. Can., Can. 1104; Leo XIII, litt. *"Il divisamento,"* 8 febr., 1893; S. C. de Prop. Fide, instr. a. 1785.

ing factors connected with a marriage of conscience are: (1) A very grave and very urgent cause; (2) Permission of the Bishop or the Vicar General, if the latter has a special authorization; (3) Dispensation from the proclamation of the banns; (4) Absolute secrecy. For reasons justifying a marriage of conscience consult this work under number 62.

520. As regards the secrecy to be observed in connection with the marriage of conscience the new law legislates thus: Permission to celebrate a marriage of conscience brings with it the promise and the grave obligation to observe secrecy on the part of the assisting priest, the witnesses, the Ordinary and his successor, and even on the part of each of the contracting parties unless the other party consents to its divulgence.[4]

521. The secrecy to which are pledged all those who witness such a marriage as well as the Ordinary and his successor is a very grave matter and therefore its intentional revelation on their part involves them in mortal sin. Even one of the consorts is not free to reveal the secret without the express permission of the other party. A presumed or a tacit permission would not absolve him from observing secrecy, nor would it excuse him from mortal sin in case he intentionally communicated the secret to others. The witnesses are always obliged to keep the secret and only an extremely grave reason would free them of its observance. Should a grave danger threaten, or should the manifestation of the secret become necessary for a very serious reason, if time permits they ought to have recourse to the Ordinary, who would either absolve them from secrecy, or would himself reveal the fact of marriage under such circumstances.

522. Conditions which would justify the divulgence

[4] Cod. Iur. Can., Can. 1105.

of the secret on the part of the Ordinary are clearly specified in the new law and have already been explained in this work.[5]

523. Another factor contributing to the secrecy of the marriage of conscience is its mode of registration. The new law does not permit the entering of such a marriage in the usual Marriage and Baptismal Registers. It should be recorded in a special book to be kept in the secret archives of the Diocesan Curia.[6] This depository for secret documents should be so constructed as not to be removable; in other words, it ought to be a vault or a safe built into the wall. The door of this vault should be provided with two different locks to be opened with different keys, of which one should be kept by the Bishop or the Apostolic Administrator, and the other by the Vicar General or, in his default, by the Chancery.[7]

[5] See this work, n. 61; COD. IUR. CAN., Can. 1106; BENEDICTUS XIV, *const. cit.*, §9, 11-13.
[6] *Op. cit.*, Can. 1107.
[7] *Op. cit.*, Can. 379.

CHAPTER X.

Time and Place of Marriage.
(Canon 1108—Canon 1109.)

I. The Time of Marriage.

524. Marriage may be contracted on any day of the year.[1] The solemn blessing of the nuptials is forbidden from the first Sunday of Advent to Christmas Day inclusively, and from Ash Wednesday to Easter Sunday inclusively.[2] The Ordinaries of places, however, heeding the liturgical laws, may permit the solemn nuptial blessing even on the above-mentioned days provided there is a just cause, and provided they admonish the spouses to abstain from too much display.[3]

As regards the time at which marriage may be contracted the new law does not introduce any change from the former discipline.[4] While the general law permits marriages on any day of the ecclesiastical year a particular custom in vogue in a certain locality may prohibit them at certain times.[5] This conclusion

[1] C. 4, X, *de feriis,* II, 9; S. C. C., *Arianen.,* mense maii, 1587; *Bosnen.,* 2 dec., 1644; S. R. C., *Montis Albani,* 14 aug., 1858.

[2] C. 8-10, C. XXXIII, q. 4; *Conc. Trident.,* sessio XXIV, *De reformatione matrimonii,* cap. X; Benedictus XIV, ep. encyc. *"Inter omnigenas,"* 2 febr., 1744, §16; S. C. S. Off., 31 aug., 1881.

[3] Cod. Iur. Can., Can. 1109.

[4] Benedictus XIV, *Inst. Ecc.,* n. 80.

[5] Gasparri, *op. cit.,* n. 1028; Schmalzgrüber, *op. cit.,* IV, XVI, n. 34; Reiffenstül, IV, XVI, n. 12; Sanchez, *op. cit.,* lib. VII, disp. VII, n. 14.

is justified by the decision rendered by the Sacred Congregation of Propaganda.[6]

525. A departure of signal consequence from the former discipline is noted in the new legislation with regard to the nuptial blessing. In the past for a just reason the Ordinary could permit the celebration of the Mass even in forbidden times, but it was not within his power to authorize the nuptial blessing on those days.[7] The period of forbidden time in the ante-Tridentine discipline comprehended almost twice as many days as it did subsequently.[8] The present legislation has reduced it to still fewer days, and limited the period to the two main seasons of penance, namely, Advent and Lent. The forbidden time runs from the midnight of the first Sunday of Advent to the midnight of the Feast of the Nativity, and from the midnight of Ash Wednesday to the midnight of Easter Sunday.

526. The forbidden time is a period during which the solemn nuptial blessing should not be given. The prohibition contained in the new Code is not absolute, as it was in the past, but only relative, obliging the priest and the Ordinary under pain of mortal sin, unless there is a just cause to dispense from the general law. As regards the justness of the cause the judgment must always proceed from the Ordinary, nor may a pastor assume the right to render a decision in the matter and to act on his own initiative without consulting the Ordinary of the place.

The insistence that marriages contracted by Catholics should be accompanied by the solemn nuptial blessing shows the ardent desire of the Church to benefit her members by the graces it imparts, for the

[6] S. C. de Prop. Fide, 5 iul., 1841.

[7] Feije, *op. cit.*, n. 553; Carrière, *op. cit.*, n. 921; Gasparri, *op. cit.*, n. 1029; Wernz, *op. cit.*, n. 549.

[8] Conc. Trident., *tit. cit.*, *loc. cit.*

precise purpose of this blessing is to give that particular supernatural aid of which the newly wedded stand most in need. It is for this reason that the new law does not require a grave cause; even a just cause would warrant the decision of the Ordinary to impart the solemn blessing in forbidden time. Such *iusta causa* would be present whenever the parties cannot, without inconvenience or scandal, postpone their nuptials till the end of the prohibited period. If the favor of having their nuptials blessed is granted to them, the assisting priest must observe the liturgical laws relating to the nuptial blessing, and the parties should be forewarned not to indulge in a display of worldliness and frivolity which would be in conflict with the spirit of the holy season.

527. Should the Ordinary permit the nuptial blessing in forbidden time the commemoration of the *nupturientium* may be made *sub unica conclusione* with the prayer of the feast on Christmas Day, and on Resurrection Sunday. The Congregation of Rites decreed that by "the nuptial blessing" are meant the special prayers found in the Missal and said during the Mass over the *nupturientes* kneeling at the altar. According to canon 1108 the Ordinary for a just cause may permit that nuptial blessing in the closed, or forbidden time, but with the restriction *"Salvis legibus liturgicis."* In other words, the nuptial blessing thus permitted may be given with the *Missa pro Sponso et Sponsa,* if the liturgical laws permit that Mass on a certain day; otherwise the blessing would have to be given with the Mass of the day.[9] Should the Ordinary of the place *ex iusta causa* permit the solemn nuptial blessing in forbidden time, the votive Mass for the spouses may be said any day, excepting the Sundays and the holy days of obligation of the first and second

[9] D. A., May 9, 1893, D. 3798. See this work, n. 525.

class, the privileged octaves of the first and second order, the privileged ferias, and the vigil of the Nativity.[10]

II. The Place of Marriage.

528. Marriage contracted by Catholics should be celebrated in the parish church; it may, however, be solemnized in another church or oratory either public or semi-public, if the permission of the Ordinary, or of the pastor be obtained. The Ordinaries of places, in extraordinary cases and in presence of a just and reasonable cause may grant permission to celebrate marriage even in private houses; but they should not permit such celebration in the churches or oratories of a seminary or of religious women, unless there is an urgent necessity and only after all proper precautions have been taken. Marriages betwen a Catholic and a non-Catholic should be celebrated outside the church (*extra ecclesiam*). If in the prudent judgment of the Ordinary this rule cannot be observed without the danger of greater evils resulting, it is left to his discretion to dispense from this law, due regard being paid to canon 1102, §2.[11]

Since marriage is a sacred thing one would naturally infer that whenever possible it should be solemnized in a sacred place. The Roman Ritual insists that the church is the proper place for the celebration of marriage.[12] The present law contains probably the first formal injunction that the *parish church* is the only place in which marriages between Catholics may be contracted without any special permission. Should the parties wish to contract in another church or in a public or semi-public oratory, it is in the power of the

[10] S. C. R., 14 iun., 1918. See *Acta Apostolicae Sedis*, vol. X, n. 8; p. 332.

[11] Cod. Iur. Can., Can. 1109.

[12] *Rituale Rom.*, tit. VII, c. 1, *de sacramento matrimonii*, n. 18.

Ordinary of the place, or of the pastor to accede to their wishes.

529. A public oratory is a place devoted to divine worship and erected for the convenience of a college or of some individuals with the understanding that all the faithful may frequent the divine services held therein. A semi-public oratory is erected for the convenience of a community, or of a particular class of the faithful; entrance being barred to all others.[13]

No one but the Ordinary or his superior may permit the celebration of marriage in private houses or domestic chapels. Oratories of that nature are constructed for the convenience of a family or of a private individual.[14] The Ordinary would act illicitly should he, in the absence of a just and reasonable cause, permit a marriage to take place in them.[15] Such a just cause would present itself if one of the parties to the contract should be a member or a near relative of the family or the person who is the owner of the oratory. Only urgent necessity would justify the Ordinary to permit the celebration of marriage in the oratories of a seminary or of a convent, and such permission must be preceded by the taking of all necessary precautionary measures to obviate scandal.

530. The new law does not introduce any change as regards mixed marriages contracted with a dispensation from the impediment of mixed religion or of disparity of worship. They are not to be solemnized within the church.[16] The terms *"extra ecclesiam"* permit the inference that their celebration in the sacristy or in a private oratory is not forbidden.[17] Should the avoidance of greater evils necessitate per-

[13] COD. IUR. CAN., Can. 1188, §2, n. 1, 2.
[14] *Op. cit.*, Can. 1188, §2.
[15] S. C. R., *Barcinonen.*, 31 aug., 1872; *Rituale Rom.*, *tit. cit.*, n. 16.
[16] S. C. S. Off., instr. (ad Archiep. Corcyren.), 3 ian., 1871, n. 3.
[17] See this work, n. 196 ff.

mission for their celebration in the church, the Ordinary would be at liberty to show leniency, but under no circumstances is he allowed to extend the privilege of a Mass to parties entering into a mixed marriage.[18]

[18] S. C. S. Off., instr. 15 nov., 1858; 29 nov., 1899. COD. IUR. CAN., Can. 1102, §2.

CHAPTER XI.

The Effects of Marriage.
(Canon 1110—Canon 1117.)

I. The Matrimonial Bond.

531. A valid marriage begets between the consorts a bond perpetual and exclusive by its very nature, and in addition the Christian marriage confers grace, provided the consorts do not place an obstacle in its way.[1]

The purpose of the foregoing canon is to emphasize the three properties of marriage, namely, its indissolubility, its unity and its sacramental character. The first two belong to all marriages, whether Christian or non-Christian, the third exclusively to Christian marriage. An explanation of these properties has already been submitted, and the scope of this work does not require their more lengthy presentation.[2] The legitimate marriage, which springs from mere natural contract, is endowed with only a relative indissolubility. Absolute indissolubility can be attributed only to consummated Christian marriages, and to those contracted in infidelity and consummated after the conversion of the parties.

532. In favor of the unity of Christian marriage plead: (1) The fundamental principles of natural law;[3] (2) The Sacred Scriptures;[4] (3) The testimony

[1] Cod. Iur. Can., Can. 1110.
[2] See this work under numbers 11-18; 36-45.
[3] See this work, n. 36 ff.
[4] *Matt.* V, 32; XIX, 9; *Mark* X, 11; *Luke* XIV, 18.

handed down in the writings of the early Fathers of the Church;[5] (4) The legislation of the Councils;[6] and (5) the official declarations proceeding from the lips of supreme ecclesiastical legislators.[7]

533. As regards the indissolubility of the marriage bond it is the teaching of theologians founded on repeated legislation of the Church that marriage is dissoluble only extrinsically, but not intrinsically. In other words, the consent of the parties, from which the matrimonial bond takes its rise, has not the power to annihilate what it created. Such dissolution of the marriage bond can be effected only by higher authority in the case where certain conditions specified by divine law are verified, or in a case in which the Church, by virtue of her divine commission, has the power to dissolve the *vinculum.*[8] The indissolubility of the matrimonial bond can be established: (1) From the principles of natural law;[9] (2) From the Sacred Scriptures;[10] and (3) From ecclesiastical legislation.[11]

II. Effects of Marriage as to the Consorts and Their Children.

534. Both consorts from the very beginning of

[5] ATHENAGORAS, *Legatio pro Christianis*, n. 33; MIGNE, *P. G.*, vol. VI, col. 967; ST. THEOPHILUS ANTIOCH., *Ad Autolycum*, lib. III, n. 15; MIGNE, *loc. cit.*, vol. VI, col. 1142; CLEMENS ALEX., *Stromatum*, lib. III, c. XII; MIGNE, *loc. cit.*, vol. VIII, col. 1183; ST. AMBROSIUS, *De Abraham*, lib. I, c. VII; MIGNE, *P. L.*, vol. XIV, col. 442.

[6] *Conc. Lugdun. II*, DENZINGER, *op. cit.*, n. 388; *Conc. Trid.*, sessio XXIV, can. 2; DENZINGER, *op. cit.*, n. 848.

[7] NICHOLAUS I, *Ad Consulta Bulgarorum*, c. LI, MIGNE, *P. L.*, vol. 119, col. 999; INNOCENTIUS, III, c. 8. X, *de divortiis*, IV. 19.

[8] PESCH, *Praelectiones Dogmaticae*, vol. VII, n. 763 (Friburgi Brisgoviae, 1897).

[9] See this work, n. 41 ff.

[10] *Matt.* XIX, 6; *I Cor.* VII, 10; *Rom.* VII, 2, 3.

[11] NICHOLAUS, *Ep. ad Adon. Vien.*. n. 1; MANSI, t. XV, col. 343; INNOCENTIUS III, c. 7, X, *de divortiis*, IV, 19; *Conc. Trident.*, sessio XXIV, *de sacramento matrimonii*, can. V-VIII; ALPHONSUS, *op. cit.*, lib. VI, n. 956.

their marriage have an equal right and duty as regards the proper acts of conjugal life.[12]

The statement of this canon simply emphasizes a doctrine clearly set forth in the Sacred Scripture.[13] The *ius ad copulam* (or rather the making use of that right) may sometimes be forfeited either temporarily or permanently. This would happen: (1) If one of the consorts should be bound by a vow of chastity taken before or after marriage;[14] (2) If the conjugal act would seriously jeopardize the health of one or both spouses;[15] (3) In the case of supervening impotency, whether it be temporal or perpetual;[16] and (4) If a well-grounded doubt should arise as to the validity of the marriage.

535. With regard to canonical effects the wife becomes a participant in the state of her husband, unless a special law ordains otherwise.[17] This presumed equality ceases by an ante-nuptial agreement made by the contracting parties, as is the case in morganatic marriages. The husband is the head of the family, to him all its members owe submission and obedience, and he in turn should show them paternal affection, cherish them with solicitude and protect them. The fidelity which the two consorts owe to each other must in all respects be reciprocal.

536. As regards the obligation of parents the new law says: Parents are bound by a very grave obligation to cherish to the best of their ability the religious, moral, physical and civil education of their offspring and also to provide for their temporal welfare.[18]

[12] COD. IUR. CAN., Can. 1111.

[13] *I Cor.* VII, 3, 4.

[14] ST. ALPHONSUS, *op. cit.*, lib. VI, n. 944.

[15] ALEXANDER III, c. 1, X, *de coniugio leprosorum*, IV, 8; ST. THOMAS, 4 *Sent.*, dist. XXXII, q. un. a 1, ad 4.

[16] ST. ALPHONSUS, *op. cit.*, lib. VI, n. 933-954.

[17] COD. IUR. CAN., Can. 1112; c. 3, *de sepulturis*, III, 12, in VI°; see this work, n. 60.

[18] COD. IUR. CAN., Can. 1113.

The duties inculcated in this canon flow from natural law. The obligation of the parents is not satisfied unless they exert every effort to instill into the heart of their child those principles of right and wrong without which he cannot attain his supernatural destiny, and without which he is not qualified for the field of moral endeavor or to become a useful member of the community. To promote these ends the parents are obliged to impart religious and moral education to their children, and their attention must be extended also to their physical and moral training. Not only the many lofty motives inculcated by Christianity, but also the animal creation should serve as an incentive to the parents in their task of providing for their children those temporal necessities which are indispensable for their existence. This duty does not cease until the child reaches an age at which he is able to secure such temporalities by his own efforts.[19]

537. Those children are legitimate who are conceived in, or born of, a valid or putative wedlock, unless the parents, at the time the child was conceived, were forbidden to use the contracted marriage, because solemn religious profession or the reception of Holy Orders had supervened.[20]

The first effect of the conjugal bond is the establishment of a distinct family under the supervision and guardianship of the husband and wife and of a union which in sacredness excels even the one existing between them and their parents, for "a man shall leave father and mother, and shall cleave to his wife: and they shall be two in one flesh."[21] This union begets a particular relationship between the husband and the blood-relatives of the wife, and *vice versa;* and between their children and their blood-relatives.[22]

[19] See this work, n. 30, 42.
[20] *Op. cit.,* Can. 1114.
[21] *Gen.* II, 24.
[22] De Smet, *op. cit.,* n. 162.

The conjugal bond constitutes the two contracting parties a principle of legitimate generation and invests their offspring with all the prerogatives of legal and canonical legitimacy. In conformity with the ancient discipline the offspring of a putative marriage is made equal in all things to one born of a valid marriage. Putative marriage is a wedlock contracted in good faith by at least one of the contracting parties. It remains putative until both consorts become certain of its invalidity.[23] In the strict sense only those children are legitimate whose parents are validly married. By a signal concession, which is based on the good faith of the putative husband and wife, the church does not discriminate against the offspring born of such a union.

538. The use of marriage is forbidden to consorts who entered into marriage and one of whom subsequently took a solemn vow of chastity or received Holy Orders. The legitimacy or illegitimacy of their offspring would depend on whether it was conceived before such a step was taken by one or both of its parents, or afterwards.[24] On the latter supposition, children of such unions are sacrilegious, and their legitimation can be effected only by a special mandate procured from the Holy See.

539. Should there be a doubt as to the father of the child, the new law states that the father of the child is he whom the valid marriage indicates, unless the contrary is proved by evident arguments. Children born at least six months after the marriage, or within ten months from the day the conjugal life was discontinued are presumed legitimate.[25]

The first part of the foregoing canon is taken *ver-*

[23] Cod. Iur. Can., Can. 1015; see this work, n. 54.

[24] C. 1, 2, 14, X, *de filiis presbyterorum ordinandis vel non,* I, 17; c. 2, 4, 8, 10, 11, 13-15, X, *qui filii sint legitimi* IV, 17.

[25] Cod. Iur. Can., Can. 1115.

batim from the Roman law.[26] The declaration that the legitimate husband of the wife is not the father of the child to which she gave birth, would not be accepted by an ecclesiastical court, unless supported by irrefutable, conclusive proofs.[27] The fact that the mother was guilty of adultery, even after her admission of such moral offence, would not clearly indicate the illegitimacy of her offspring. On the contrary, even under such circumstances, the child has the right to vindicate legitimacy for himself if at least six months elapsed between the celebration of his parents' marriage and his birth; or not a longer period than ten months elapsed between the discontinuance of his parents' matrimonial cohabitation and his birth. Thus a child is endowed with a presumptive legitimacy if in the first instance 180, and in the second 300 days passed between the periods indicated. This presumption is only presumption of law, which is equivalent to giving the child the benefit of the doubt, therefore convincing proofs to the contrary would disestablish it.[28]

540. The last two canons of this chapter are devoted to legislation relative to illegitimate offspring. The child becomes legitimate, says the new Code, by the subsequent marriage of the parents, whether such a marriage be real or only putative, newly contracted, or validated, even if non-consummated, provided the parents were competent to contract marriage at the time the child was conceived, or during the period of the mother's pregnancy, or at the time of the child's birth.[29]

One of the canonical effects of the revalidation of

[26] L 5 ff., *De in ius voc.*

[27] L. 6, §1, *De iis qui sui.*

[28] GASPARRI, *op. cit.*, n. 1069; DE LUGO, *De iustitia et iure*, XIII, n. 26; ST. ALPHONSUS, lib. III, n. 654, 924; REIFFENSTÜL, IV, XVII, n. 24; SCHMALZGRÜBER, IV, XVII, n. 40.

[29] COD. IUR. CAN., Can. 1116.

marriage is the automatic legitimation of the offspring.[30] The law embodied in this canon introduces no innovation, on the contrary, it approves the opinion generally advocated by the leading canonists of the past.[31] There are two main classes of children, namely, spurious and natural. The former are subdivided into adulterine, sacrilegious, incestuous and nefarious.[32] An automatic legitimation by way of validating the marriage can be effected only in the case of natural children, namely, offspring whose parents were free to marry either at the time the child was conceived, or during the period the mother was with child, or at the time the child was born. In all such cases by a fiction of the law the effects of a validated marriage retroact to the time the illegitimate child was born.

541. Even if there was an obstacle in the way of the parents' marriage at the time the child was conceived, but this obstacle was removed either during the period of gestation, or at the birth of the child, the subsequent marriage will not be hindered in effecting the legitimation of such offspring. To exemplify, let us suppose that A. (married) acquired carnal knowledge of B. (single) during the lifetime of his wife. After the death of his wife, but before a child is born as the result of his sinful act, he marries B. As long as there was no impediment between A. and B. at the time of the child's birth, the subsequent marriage would effect its legitimation.

The same would be true if the two contracted marriage in good faith and it was subsequently discovered that they were laboring under a diriment impediment. The effect would be the same whether the natural

[30] C. 1, 6, X, *qui filii sint legitimi,* IV, 17.

[31] REIFFENSTÜL, IV, XVII, n. 30; DE ANGELIS, I, XVII, n. 4; SCHMALZGRÜBER, IV, XVII, n. 65 ff.

[32] For the definition of the foregoing terms consult this work under n. 173.

parents entered into marriage before the child was born, or after its birth, as long as in any of the three periods indicated above they were free to enter into wedlock. Even if the parents contracted an invalid marriage in bad faith, the illegitimate offspring of such union may be legitimated by the validation of their marriage, provided the other conditions are the same as stated above.[33]

542. Children whose parents are unknown, as, for instance, foundlings, according to the common opinion are to be reputed as legitimate, for the child is always entitled to the benefit of the doubt.[34]

The legitimation of the child in canonical discipline has far-reaching consequences. The law says: Children legitimated by subsequent marriage are likened to legitimate children as regards all canonical effects, unless the law expressly ordains otherwise.[35] The new law rules that only legitimate children may register in a Seminary for the purpose of pursuing theological studies,[36] but it removes the blemish of irregularity *ex defectu* from a child that was legitimated.[37] Illegitimate children though legitimated by subsequent marriage may not be elevated to the dignity of the Cardinalate,[38] of the Episcopate,[39] of Abbot or of Prelate *nullius*.[40] Outside these few exceptions the canon law does not discriminate between a legitimate child and one who was legitimated by subsequent marriage. It must be borne in mind that an illegitimate child can be legitimated only under the condition that his natural

[33] Benedictus XIV, ep. *"Redditae Nobis,"* §38, 5 dec., 1744.
[34] Benedictus XIV, *loc. cit.*, §4.
[35] Cod. Iur. Can., Can. 1117.
[36] *Op. cit.*, Can. 1363, §1.
[37] *Op. cit.*, Can. 984.
[38] *Op. cit.*, Can. 232, §2, n. 1; Sixtus V, const. *"Postquam,"* dec., 1586, §12.
[39] *Op. cit.*, Can. 331, §1, n. 1.
[40] *Op. cit.*, Can. 320, §2.

mother enteres into marriage with his natural father. Marriage between a natural mother and an adoptive father would fail to produce a similar effect.

CHAPTER XII.

The Separation of Consorts.
(Canon 1118—Canon 1132.)

I. Dissolution of the Bond.

1. Absolute Indissolubility.

543. A valid marriage ratified and consummated cannot be dissolved by any human power, or any cause except death.[1]

This canon, more emphatically than some others,[2] defends the absolute indissolubility of the ratified and consummated Christian marriage. It distinctly proclaims that no power on earth can dissolve the bond begotten by such marriage, nor can any cause except death be instrumental in producing the same effect.

Theologians discuss the question whether God by His absolute power can effect the dissolution of such a bond. The answer to this question must be affirmative, but it is clear that such a revelation has never been made nor has God authorized any institution, not even the Catholic Church, to dissolve under any circumstances or for any reasons the bond of such a union.[3]

544. The proposition announced in this canon can be defended by means of every source the Church has

[1] Cod. Iur. Can., Can. 1118.

[2] *Op. cit.*, Can. 1013, §2; Can. 1110.

[3] Pesch, *op. cit.*, vol. VII, n. 818 ff.; Tanner, *De matrimonio*, disp. VIII, q. 5, dub. 3; Palmieri, *De matrimonio*, p. 202 ff.

at her disposal. As has already been stated, natural law endows marriage with a relative indissolubility.[4] This relative indissolubility becomes absolute if two Christians contract and consummate marriage, for the matrimonial bond that springs up between them is invested with sacramental character. The decrees of the various Councils,[5] the pronouncements of the Roman Pontiffs,[6] and the testimony of the Fathers of the Church and the ecclesiastical writers[7] vindicate the absolute indissolubility of the matrimonial bond between baptized persons when strengthened by the fact of consummation. The ruling of the supreme ecclesiastical authority in the case of Lothaire, Philip Augustus of France and Henry VIII of England can be advanced as incontestable historical facts attesting the tenacious adherence of the Church to the doctrine contained in the canon with which this chapter begins.

545. The foregoing testimony gathered from various ecclesiastical sources is endowed with still greater force by the authority of the Sacred Scripture.[8] There are only two passages in Holy Writ which can be advanced as seemingly militating against the teaching of the Church on this point. These are found in

[4] See this work, n. 41 ff.

[5] Can. VIII, IX, *Council of Elvira* (300); Can. VIII, the *XI Synod of Carthage* (407); Can. VI, *Council of Angers* (435); Can. XII, *Council of Nantes* (about 685); Can. X, *Council of Hereford* (673); Decree of the Armenians, *Council of Florence;* Can. VII, *Council of Trent,* sess. XXIV.

[6] INNOCENT I (401-407) to *Exuperius, Probus* and *Victricius* (HARDOUIN, I, col. 1005, c. 6; col. 1008; col. 1002); ZACHARY (741-752), *op. cit.,* col. 1902; STEPHEN II (754), *op. cit.,* vol. III, col. 1987-1988; ALEXANDER III, c. 7, X, *de conversione coniugatorum,* III, 21; INNOCENT III, c. 7, X, *de divortiis,* IV, 19; LEO XIII, encycl. *"Arcanum."*

[7] ORIGIN, *Comment. in Matth.,* t. XIV, n. 23, MIGNE, vol. XIII, col. 1246; ST. ASTERIUS AMASENUS, *Homelia in locum Evang. sec. Matth.,* MIGNE, *P. G.,* vol. XL, col. 227; ST. AUGUSTINE, *De coniugiis adulterinis,* MIGNE, *P. L.,* vol. XL, col. 483 ff.; PERRONE, *op. cit.,* vol. III, p. 219-352; ROSKOVÁNY, *Suppl. et collect. monumentorum,* vol. I, p. 457 ff.; PALMIERI, *op. cit.,* p. 141 ff.

[8] *Mark* X, 11; *Luke* XVI, 18.

Matthew V, 32,[9] and XIX, 9.[10] Should these passages be interpreted in the sense in which they are understood by some of our dissentient brethren, there would be a positive contradiction in the Sacred Scripture, for the parallel passages of St. Mark [11] and St. Luke [12] teach just the contrary. Since we cannot claim the inspiration of the Holy Ghost for contradictory statements there must be a clue whereby the two above-quoted texts of St. Matthew can be reconciled with the statements of the other Evangelists.

546. St. Matthew quotes our Lord as stating that from the beginning of creation man was not permitted to put away his wife.[13] Such permission was granted by Moses "by reason of the hardness of your heart," said Christ to His Jewish hearers.[14] After these words the Master announced His doctrine on marriage, which was to be the law of the New Covenant. If we consult the parallel passages of the other Evangelists we must conclude that Christ restored marriage to its pristine ideality, namely, to an indissoluble bond correlated with monogyny and monandry. It was in this sense that His words were interpreted by His hearers, for on the contrary supposition the New Testament would have introduced no change, and the displeasure expressed by the disciples at the hearing of Christ's new doctrine would have been entirely out of place.[15]

[9] "But I say to you, that whosoever shall put away his wife, excepting for the cause of fornication, maketh her commit adultery: and he that shall marry her that is put away committeth adultery."

[10] "And I say to you, that whosoever shall put away his wife, except it be for fornication, maketh her commit adultery: and he that shall marry her that is put away committeth adultery."

[11] "Whosoever shall put away his wife and marry another, committeth adultery against her. And if the wife shall put away her husband, and be married to another, she committeth adultery. (*Mark* X, 11-12.)

[12] "Every one that putteth away his wife, and marrieth another, committeth adultery, and he that marrieth her that is put away from her husband, committeth adultery." (*Luke* XVI, 18.)

[13] *Matt.* XIX, 8.

[14] *Matt., loc. cit.,* and V, 31.

[15] *Matt.* XIX, 10.

Should it be asserted that adultery *ipso facto* dissolves the matrimonial bond, such teaching would prove a very potent incentive to sin. Furthermore, such an admission would give rise to a new difficulty irreconcilable with St. Matthew. How are we to expound the words: "And he that shall marry her that is put away, committeth adultery," if the moral offence involved in such a crime effects an automatic dissolution of the matrimonial bond?

The words "maketh her to commit adultery" can be interpreted, without taking undue liberty with the sacred text, as conveying the meaning that he who puts away his wife, unless she is guilty of fornication, exposes her to the danger of committing adultery, and by contributing to that danger "maketh her commit adultery"; in other words, should she commit such a moral offence God would look upon him as sharing her guilt. Should he put her away because she was guilty of adultery, he would not be responsible in the sight of God for the adultery she might commit.

The second text taken from St. Matthew can also be explained in a sense not disagreeing with the other scriptural passages. The sentence, as some exegetes maintain, is to be considered elliptical, and the ellipsis must be supplied thus: He who shall put away his wife (which is lawful only in the case of fornication) and shall marry another, committeth adultery. This would be equivalent to saying that in the case of fornication the man is justified in putting away his wife; in other words, a separation is warranted; but, St. Paul adds, "if she depart, let her remain unmarried or be reconciled with her husband." [16]

Another interpretation suggests that in this second passage Christ stigmatizes as adulterous the man who would put away his wife and marry another, but He

[16] *I Cor.* VIII, 11.

refrains from pronouncing a judgment upon a man who would put away his wife because she is guilty of fornication. Such a suspended judgment would have to be supplied from other passages of Holy Writ, as, for instance, those of St. Mark, St. Luke and St. Paul, quoted above in foot-notes 11, 12 and 16.

2. *Relative Indissolubility.*

547. Absolute indissolubility, as explained above, can be attributed only to ratified and consummated marriages. A non-consummated marriage, the new Code says, between two baptized individuals, or between a baptized and an unbaptized person is dissolved by the very act of making a solemn religious profession, or by means of dispensation granted for a just cause by the Apostolic See at the request of both parties, or of either party even if the other is unwilling.[17]

The two different ways whereby a non-consummated marriage can be dissolved are: (1) Religious profession; (2) Papal dispensation. The new law does not discriminate in this respect between a marriage in which both parties are baptized, and another in which one of the consorts is unbaptized.

In the course of the serious controversy, already referred to in this work, between Peter Lombard with the school of Paris on one side, and Gratian with the school of Bologna on the other, Alexander III cut the Gordian knot by declaring officially that a ratified and non-consummated marriage is a perfect contract and a real sacrament, but that the fact of non-consummation makes it dissoluble by religious profession and by Papal dispensation.[18]

[17] Cod. Iur. Can., Can. 1119.

[18] C. 2, 7, X, *de conversione coniugatorum*, III, 32; Esmein, *op. cit.*, vol. I, p. 124 ff.

A. Religious Profession.

548. Besides Alexander III, Innocent III also advocated the opinion that a non-consummated marriage is dissolved by religious profession.[19] This doctrine was subsequently incorporated into the official acts of the Council of Trent.[20] The doctrine being thus determined as a dogma of faith, it is inconsequential whether it follows by virtue of natural or of ecclesiastical law,[21] though we do not join the ranks of those who advocate the former opinion.

The ratified marriage is dissolved as soon as one of the contracting parties takes a solemn vow of religion, even if the other party should object to such a step.[22] The conditions necessary to constitute a solemn vow are discussed in this work in connection with the diriment impediment of solemn religious profession.[23]

When a solemn religious profession is made validly and the vow of chastity is taken according to the form prescribed by the new law, the bond of a ratified and non-consummated marriage, *a fortiori,* of a legitimate non-consummated marriage becomes *ipso facto* dissolved.

The power of the solemn religious profession to dissolve the matrimonial bond must not be limited to marriages contracted originally by two baptized persons or by a baptized and an unbaptized individual. The effect would be the same even if the marriage was contracted by two infidels who after the consummation of their wedlock became converts, or by two infidels one of whom, after the marriage was consummated in

[19] C. 14, X, *tit. cit.,* III, 32.
[20] Sessio XXIV, *De sacramento matrimonii,* can. VI.
[21] GASPARRI, *op. cit.,* n. 1082; WERNZ, *op. cit.,* n. 698; LEHMKUHL, *op. cit.,* vol. II, n. 703; SCHMALZGRÜBER, lib. IV, tit. VI, n. 54.
[22] PESCH, vol. VII, n. 804 ff., where he enumerates several Saints whose marriage was dissolved owing to such a profession.
[23] See this work, n. 288.

infidelity, received baptism in a non-Catholic sect and before a new consummation of the marriage embraced the true faith, and subsequently made a solemn religious profession. Both these hypotheses presuppose that after the conversion the marriage was not consummated. Thus the new Code terminates a long-standing controversy and endows the solemn religious profession with the power to dissolve automatically the matrimonial bond arising from the foregoing four kinds of marriage.

Should the conversion be followed by a new consummation of marriage, whether due to an accident, or to violence, or even if unintentional, the vow would become divested of its nullifying force and the party remaining in the world would lose his privilege to remarriage and would have to live a celibate life.[24]

549. The simple vow of chastity taken by the Scholastics of the Society of Jesus invests one with the religious status and constitutes a diriment impediment, but it does not possess the effect [25] proper only to a solemn religious vow strictly so called.

The marriage of two infidels who become converted to the faith without consummating their marriage either in infidelity or subsequently to their conversion, becomes ratified to all intents and purposes. Without any renewal of consent it becomes a sacrament, and the matrimonial bond would be dissolved should one of them embrace the religious state. It must be borne in mind that the reception of Sacred Orders does not produce the effect attributed to solemn religious profession.

B. Papal Dispensation.

550. The new law states distinctly that a papal dispensation granted *ex iusta causa* dissolves a non-con-

[24] Wernz, op. cit., n. 698; Rosset, *op. cit.*, I, n. 684 ff.
[25] Benedictus XIV, *De Synodo Dioecesana,* lib. XIII, cap. XII, n. 9 ff.

summated marriage, between two baptized persons or between a baptized and an unbaptized person. Thus the new law terminates a long-standing controversy and clearly vindicates the right of the Roman Pontiff to dissolve such marriages provided there is a just cause. In the absence of such a cause the Holy See could not put into operation such privilege, for the power invoked by it in the contemplated cases is the result of delegation embodied in divine commission.[26]

Examples in which a dispensation from a ratified and non-consummated marriage was granted are not infrequent.[27] Among the causes justifying such a dispensation should be enumerated: (1) The well-founded fear of great future scandal or of dissension among consanguineous persons; (2) The well-founded suspicion of impotency combined with the danger of incontinence; (3) A supervening contagious disease; (4) The danger of perversion in case the Catholic contracted marriage with one who is a serious menace to his faith; (5) The attempting of another marriage from which, though it is invalid, there is no avenue of escape; (6) Mutual consent of the two parties to separate, provided there is a good cause.[28]

551. Besides the presence of a just cause [29] for separation, the fact of the non-consummation of the marriage must also be ascertained beyond all doubt. The new law rules that this be done by means of *inspectio corporis per peritos facienda* [30] and by the testimony of seven witnesses (*testes qui septimae manus audiunt*) adduced by each contracting party.[31] The evidence

[26] WERNZ, *op. cit.*, n. 699; GASPARRI, *op. cit.*, n. 1081; SCHMALZGRÜBER, lib. IV, tit. XIX, n. 5; SANCHEZ, *op. cit.*, lib. II, disp. XV, n. 6.

[27] SCHMALZGRÜBER, *loc. cit.*, n. 46; PERRONE, vol. III, p. 509 ff.; PESCH, vol. VII, n. 811 ff.

[28] DE JUSTIS, II, X, n. 21-34; SANCHEZ, lib. II, disp. XVI; SCHMALZGRÜBER, *loc. cit.*, n. 53 ff.

[29] COD. IUR. CAN., Can. 1973.

[30] *Op. cit.*, Can. 1976.

[31] *Op. cit.*, Can. 1975.

thus collected must be submitted to the Sacred Congregation of the Sacraments [32] and the matrimonial process must be regulated by rules laid down in the new Code.[33]

552. The question might arise what competence may the Roman Pontiff claim over marriages contracted and consummated in infidelity? It is manifest that as long as the consorts remain unbaptized they are in no way subject to his jurisdiction. If one or both of them should become converted their marriage would be subject to the regulation of the Church. Under the scope of the new law must be included also the marriage of persons who previously to their conversion contracted and consummated their marriage in infidelity. In the past there was a controversy among theologians as to whether such a marriage could be dissolved as *ratum non-consummatum,* it being supposed that after their conversion it was not consummated. The affirmative side of the question was defended by the majority of canonists,[34] though the negative side was not without advocates whose opinions have great weight.[35] The arguments of the affirmative side are based on the historical fact that dissolution of such marriages was actually effected by the Roman Pontiffs,[36] and on the principle that *ab esse ad posse valet illatio,* provided the axiom is applied to the Roman Pontiff. The bond of a marriage contracted and consummated in infidelity is assuredly stronger when it becomes also ratified

[32] *Op. cit.,* Can. 1962.

[33] See lib. IV, tit. XX, Canon 1960—Canon 1992.

[34] GASPARRI, *op. cit.,* n. 1108 ff.; ST. ALPHONSUS, lib. VI, n. 956; GURY-BALLERINI, tom. II, n. 759, 789; SANCHEZ, lib. II, disp. XVII, n. 62; WERNZ, *op. cit.,* n. 699; DE SMET, *op. cit.,* n. 188; D'ANNIBALE, vol. III, n. 470.

[35] BENEDICTUS XIV, *De Synodo Dioecesana,* lib. VI, cap. IV, n. 5, and lib. XIII, cap. XXI, n. 4; and also *Quaest. Can.,* 546; FEIJE, *op. cit.,* n. 602; SCHMALZGRÜBER, *h. t.,* n. 58 ff.; ROSSET, *op. cit.,* n. 647.

[36] PIUS V, decr., 2 aug., 1571; GREGORIUS XIII, decr., 25 ian., 1585.

after the conversion of the consorts than a mere non-consummated ratified marriage.[37]

Furthermore, the new law conditions the power of the Roman Pontiff to dissolve such marriages on the presence of a just cause. If such cause is required for the dissolution of a mere ratified marriage *a fortiori* would there be an additional reason to exact the same requirement in the case of a ratified marriage contracted and consummated in infidelity. Moreover, it would be an easier task to find a sufficiently just cause in the former case than in the case of persons who already lived in matrimonial relations for some time and who probably became parents of several children. But even in such case the presence of a just cause being presupposed the Roman Pontiff may dissolve their bond, for his right to do so is supported not only by the practice of the Holy See but also by the new law.[38] It is seriously questionable whether the Roman Pontiff could, arbitrarily and without just cause, annul such marriages.

The pages that follow treat on the dissolution of a marriage legitimate and consummated, namely, contracted and consummated in infidelity between persons of whom one becomes a convert.

C. *Pauline Privilege.*

553. The Pauline Privilege is a special concession by virtue of which, on the ground of the words of St. Paul,[39] a converted infidel, whose consort remains in

[37] WERNZ expressly denies that solemn religious profession could dissolve the bond of such a marriage. See his work, n. 799.

[38] Such is the first impression conveyed by Canon 1119. Since it has not been explained yet by any canonist, we have no authority to quote in its support.

[39] "If any brother hath a wife that believeth not, and she consent to dwell with him, let him not put her away. And if any woman hath a

infidelity and declines to cohabit with him or will not do so without offering an insult to the Creator (*sine contumelia Creatoris*), may contract another marriage, whereby his first marriage, though it be consummated, becomes *ipso facto* dissolved. This privilege does not obtain in a marriage between a baptized and an unbaptized person contracted with dispensation from the impediment of disparity of worship.[40] A correct interpretation of the Pauline Privilege is given by Innocent III in the Decretals of Gregory IX.[41]

The Pauline Privilege is of divine origin,[42] promulgated by the Apostle of the Gentiles to favor the faith. It is natural that a married infidel would have been reluctant to embrace the true faith if he foresaw that subsequently to his conversion he would have to live a life of continence owing to the fact that his consort, remaining in infidelity, would very likely refuse to cohabit with him peaceably.

554. It is morally certain that St. Paul, in the text quoted in the foot-note number 39, contemplates the case of two infidels who contracted marriage in infidelity and one of whom subsequently became a convert to the faith. Such is the interpretation of all reliable exegetes and it is, moreover, confirmed by the practice of the Church, for she never dissolves wedlock entered into by a Catholic and an infidel when the proper dis-

husband that believeth not, and he consent to dwell with her, let her not put away her husband. For the unbelieving husband is sanctified by the believing wife: and the unbelieving wife is sanctified by the believing husband: otherwise your children should be unclean, but now they are holy. *But if the unbeliever depart, let him depart. For a brother or sister is not under servitude in such cases. But God hath called us in peace.*" (*I Cor.* VII, 12-15.)

[40] Cod. Iur. Can., Can. 1120.

[41] C. 7, X, *de divortiis,* IV, 19.

[42] S. C. S. Off., decr. 11, iul., 1886; Benedictus XIV, *De Synodo Dioecesana*, lib. VI, cap. IV, n. 3; Cornely, *Comment. in I, Cor.*, p. 179 ff.; St. Alphonsus, *op. cit.*, lib. VI, n. 955; Sanchez, *op. cit.*, lib. VII, disp. LXXIV, n. 4.

pensation has been obtained.[43] This fact is emphasized also by the new law.[44]

St. Paul states expressly that if the unconverted consort wishes to cohabit peaceably the converted party should "not put her away." The context leads one to believe that this is only a personal advice, for he introduces this statement with the words: "For the rest I speak, not the Lord." If, therefore, a converted consort leaves the unconverted spouse who is willing to cohabit peaceably, by virtue of Pauline Privilege such a marriage would not be dissolved *quoad vinculum,* but only a separation *a toro et mensa* would be effected.[45]

555. In order that the Pauline Privilege may be invoked the conversion of one of the infidels is a *conditio sine qua non.* Conversion here implies the reception of baptism, even if it should be in a heretical or schismatic sect.[46] Should a convert to a heretical or schismatic sect make use of the Pauline Privilege by marrying a person who professes membership in the same sect, his marriage would be valid, but illicit for the reason that St. Paul promulgated that privilege in order to benefit converts to the true faith. The words of the Apostle clearly indicate that only a convert may resort to the privilege, a catechumen would not be permitted to avail himself of it.[47]

The words *"if the unbeliever departs, let him de-*

[43] S. C. Inq., 11 aug., 1759; see PERRONE, *op. cit.*, vol. II, p. 323.

[44] COD. IUR. CAN., Can., 1120, §2.

[45] ST. THOMAS, *Suppl. IIIae, p.*, q. LIX, art., V, c.; LOMBARDUS, 4, *Sent.*, dist. XXXIX; SCHMALZGRÜBER, *De divortiis*, n. 35; ST. AUGUSTINUS, MIGNE, *P. L.*, Vol. XL, col. 469.

[46] PALMIERI, *op. cit.*, th. XXVII; LEHMKUHL, t. II, n. 705; PERRONE, vol. II, p. 319; BALLERINI, *Opus Morale*, vol. VI, n. 718 ff.; ST. THOMAS, *Suppl. IIIae, p.*, q. LIX, art. 4; *Archiv f. k. K.*, vol. XLVI, p. 402; WERNZ, *op. cit.*, n. 702.

[47] S. C. de Prop. Fide, 16 ian., 1803; in the *Collectanea*, n. 1379; an infidel should not be taken into the Church unless he consents to retain his consort, provided the latter is disposed to cohabit with him peaceably. (S. C. S. Off., 13 apr., 1908.)

part'' are not to be interpreted only in the sense of physical departure. There meaning is to be extended so as to comprise also moral departure which would take place should the infidel party refuse to cohabit peaceably with the converted spouse, or should it (without such refusal) be clear that no such cohabitation can be established without the offering of insult to the Creator.

The departure of the infidel consort need not necessarily be effected by hatred of religion, nor does it have to be a *discessus malitiosus*. It suffices that the infidel consort is actually, whether willingly or by abduction, separated from the converted spouse and fails to return after the interpellations are duly made.[48] Should the deserting consort subsequently embrace the true faith, the other consort could not invoke the Pauline Privilege in his favor unless his second marriage preceded the conversion of his consort.[49] The converted party would not forfeit his right to another marriage even if the other consort should express a willingness to embrace the true faith, provided she refused to extend to him the privilege of community of bed and board.[50]

556. It is immaterial by what motive the infidel party was actuated in his refusal; provided it was not occasioned by an overt act performed by the converted party after the reception of baptism, and in itself sufficient to offer the infidel consort a reasonable and just cause for the discontinuance of cohabitation.[51] If an infidel party should repudiate a legitimate consort on

[48] S. C. Inq., 22 nov., 1871, and 8 iul., 1891; see *Collectanea*, n. 1356 and 1362; D'ANNIBALE, vol. III, n. 475, note 13; SANCHEZ, lib. VII, disp. LXXIV, n. 15 ff.

[49] S. C. S. Off., 11, 20 iun., 1866, 18 maii, 1892; see *Collectanea*, nn. 1353, 1354, and 2185; INNOCENT III, c. 8, X, *de divortiis*, IV, 19.

[50] S. C. S. Off., 8 iul., 1891; see *Collectanea*, n. 1362.

[51] S. C. S. Off., 5 aug., 1759; see *Collectanea*, n. 1312; 26 apr., 1899, see new *Collectanea*, n. 2044.

the ground of adultery committed before conversion, and such guilty party after becoming a convert should invite the innocent infidel party to cohabitation, the latter's refusal would justify the converted consort's entrance into another marriage.[52] But such entrance into marriage would not be justified should the converted party be guilty of adultery after his or her conversion.[53]

The words "*contumelia Creatoris*" are verified when the intention on the part of the unconverted consort to jeopardize the faith of the converted spouse is manifested, whether it be by an attempt to prevail upon her to renounce her faith,[54] or to participate with him in acts that are sinful.[55] An insult to the Creator would be offered if the infidel party should refuse to discontinue the practice of concubinage or should decline to bring up the offspring in the Catholic faith.[56]

The right of the converted party to resort to the Pauline Privilege would not be lost even if the infidel consort should be willing to comply with all the conditions required by law, but is so situated, even if through no fault of her own, that a restoration of conjugal relationship is a practical impossibility. This condition would be verified if the unconverted party were held in captivity or sequestration,[57] or even if she were sold by her own husband, provided the sale had taken place before his conversion.[58] Should the converted party after the reception of baptism place an act which would make the re-establishment of marital relations impossible he would forfeit his right to the Pauline Privilege.

The converted party may not presume to benefit by

[52] S. C. de Prop. Fide, 30 ian., 1807; see *Collectanea,* n. 1332.
[53] S. C. de Prop. Fide, 16 ian., 1797; see *Collectanea,* n. 1318.
[54] S. C. S. Off., 29 nov., 1882; see *Collectanea,* n. 1358.
[55] S. C. de Prop. Fide, 5 mart., 1816; see *Collectanea,* n. 1323.
[56] S. C. S. Off., 11 iul., 1886; see *Collectanea,* n. 1353.
[57] S. C. S. Off., 12 iun., 1850; see *Collectanea,* n. 1339.
[58] S. C. S. Off., 8 iul., 1891; see *Collectanea,* n. 1362.

the Pauline Privilege if the state implied by the words "*contumelia Creatoris*" is caused, not by the other consort, but by her kin.[59]

557. The marriage contracted in infidelity is not dissolved by the fact of conversion or reception of baptism.[60] It remains valid until the infidel party becomes guilty of physical or moral desertion and the converted party, having complied with the conditions prescribed by law, contracts another marriage.

The converted party by virtue of the Pauline Privilege would not be at liberty to contract another marriage validly if the infidel party should consent to cohabit peaceably and should be willing to subscribe to all conditions required by law, but be unwilling to be converted. Such liberty on the part of the converted party is nowhere intimated in the Pauline Privilege, nor is it in harmony with the former discipline of the Church or the teaching of theologians.[61] To maintain that the Church promulgated a general law by which the converted spouse was constrained to discontinue his cohabitation with the infidel spouse, is to advocate an opinion irreconcilable with the present discipline. Wernz remarks that such a law would of itself contain an implicit permission for the converted party to enter into another marriage, but it can nowhere be shown that such a law has ever been enforced except in cases in which the promise of the infidel party to cohabit peaceably proved fictitious. This opinion is in perfect accord with the views advanced by the medieval canonists.[62]

[59] S. C. de Prop. Fide, 5 mart., 1816; see *Collectanea*, n. 1323.

[60] "Cum per sacramentum baptismi non solvantur coniugia, sed crimina dimittantur." (INNOCENTIUS III, c. 8, X, *de divortiis*, IV, 19.

[61] WERNZ, *op. cit.*, n. 702, note 63; PESCH, vol. VII, n. 788; SCHMALZGRÜBER, *De divortiis*, n. 35; ST. THOMAS, *Suppl. IIIae, p.*, q. LIX, a. 5; ROSSET, *op. cit.*, n. 604 ff.

[62] S. C. Inq., 28 nov., 1894; see *Acta Sanctae Sedis*, vol. XXIX, p. 564; ROSSET, *op. cit.*, n. 607 and 611.

It is therefore the second marriage bond contracted in Christianity that dissolves the one contracted in infidelity. After the converted consort enters into a second marriage, owing to the absolute dissolution of the former *vinculum,* the infidel party is also free to contract another marriage, but not until then. This statement would apply even if such infidel party should attempt marriage after becoming a convert.[63]

558. In doubtful marriages contracted between an infidel and a person doubtfully baptized, or between two infidels, the doubt must be settled favorably to the faith. In this connection one must bear in mind that a marriage between an infidel and a doubtfully baptized individual is to be considered invalid,[64] and that such a baptism is subject to the principal of presumption.[65] Should the conversion of one consort be followed by the conversion of the other, provided their marriage contracted in infidelity was valid, the spouse converted first should re-establish conjugal life with the other.[66] Such an obligation may be urged only *ex caritate,* it is a point of controversy whether it binds also *ex iustitia.* Needless to say that no such obligation can be imposed if the spouse converted first has already remarried, or made a solemn religious profession, or received Holy Orders. Nor can the second convert be forced to return to the first if the latter after his conversion was guilty of an act which justified the former in discontinuing community of bed and board even while yet an infidel. It is advisable that in case dissensions are feared cohabitation should not be urged, but rather separation *a toro et mensa* should willingly be granted.

[63] S. C. Inq., 16 sept., 1824; 15 sept., 1858; see *Collectanea,* n. 1328 and 1349; SCHMALZGRÜBER, *h. t.,* n. 28 ff.; BENEDICTUS XIV, *Quaest. canon.,* 546, n. 12.

[64] S. C. Inq., 5 iul., 1853.

[65] See this work, n. 238.

[66] FEIJE, *op. cit.,* n. 499; S. C. Inq., 11 iul., 1866, ad 8.

559. As long as the converted party, whom the infidel party has deserted without reason, remains celibate, the infidel party cannot validly enter into another marriage. The same would hold good even if the converted party under such circumstances would embrace the religious state or receive Holy Orders. With regard to Holy Orders all theologians agree, but they are not in agreement as regards the effect the solemn profession has on such marriage. No doubt can be entertained should there be question of a marriage which was not consummated either before or after the baptism of one or both consorts. In that case the dissolution of such a matrimonial bond would be effected by the very act of either party taking the solemn vow.[67] But the contemplated cases presuppose two things, namely, (a) a marriage consummated in infidelity; (b) departure of the infidel party without a reason. Should such a marriage be dissolved by the solemn religious profession of the converted party, and should the infidel be at liberty to marry another, such liberty would be equivalent to catering to the contumacious infidel party.[68] Since we cannot suppose that the Church or the Roman Pontiff would wish to offer to the unconverted party an incentive to sin, we are constrained to adhere to the opinion that such solemn religious profession, under the given circumstances, does not effect an absolute dissolution of the matrimonial bond.

560. The perusal of the foregoing statements ought to make it clear that the converted party after the reception of baptism may not depart from the other consort without warning "*quasi insalutato hospite.*" To prevent such an action the present discipline, as well as the former, prescribed interpellations to be made by the converted party. The new law says: Before the

[67] COD. IUR. CAN., Can. 1119.
[68] WERNZ, *op. cit.*, n. 702, note 71.

converted and baptized consort may contract a new marriage validly, he is obliged, the provision made in canon 1125 being observed, to interpellate the infidel party as to whether she is willing: (1) To be converted and to receive baptism;[69] (2) At least to cohabit peaceably without offering insult to the Creator. These interpellations must always be made unless the Holy See declares otherwise.[70]

The foregoing canon settles the question whether the interpellation is necessary *ad validitatem secundi matrimonii* in the case of a convert whose first marriage was consummated in infidelity. Ballerini maintains that interpellation is prescribed for the purpose of ascertaining the will of the unconverted consort, but that the validity of the second marriage depends exclusively on the objective willingness or unwillingness of the infidel party to cohabit with the converted spouse *sine contumelia Creatoris.*[71] This opinion can no longer be advocated, for even the former discipline inculcated the necessity of interpellation as a duty originating from divine precept,[72] and insisted on it even if the infidel party publicly repudiated the converted consort.[73]

561. The two questions which form the matter of the interpellation are proposed by the converted consort to the infidel party in order to ascertain whether there is a sufficient reason for the contracting of a second marriage. A negative answer to the first question would not authorize such a step, unless the answer to

[69] S. C. de Prop. Fide, 16 ian., 1797; see *Collectanea,* n. 1318, 1323, 1361.

[70] Cod. Iur. Can., Can. 1121.

[71] Gury-Ballerini, vol. II, n. 579, foot-note; Perrone, vol. II, p. 323; for the criticism of the opinion of D'Annibale and Scherer, see Wernz, *op. cit.,* n. 703, note 72.

[72] S. C. Inq., 12 iun., 1850; see *Collectanea,* n. 1339; Feije, *op. cit.,* n. 487 ff.; Putzer, *op. cit.,* n. 200.

[73] S. C. de Prop. Fide, 5 mart., 1810; see *Collectanea,* n. 1323.

the second question be also negative. Should the first question be answered affirmatively and the second negatively, the converted spouse would be justified in entering into another marriage, provided it should take place before the conversion of the other party. A negative answer to the first question and an affirmative answer to the second would necessitate the re-establishment of conjugal life, provided the answer was not feigned.

562. By a special concession of the Holy See the interpellation may be dispensed with either *in toto,* in which case such a dispensation amounts to a dissolution of the former marriage bond, or *in parte,* namely, from the first or the second question. By virtue of special faculties granted to missionaries in infidel countries, a converted polygamist may be dispensed from the necessity of interpellating his first and only legitimate wife in infidelity as to whether she wishes to cohabit with him peaceably or not. A negative answer given to the first part of the interpellations, namely, a disinclination to become a convert, is in itself a justifying reason for the baptized consort to enter into a second marriage with any of his pseudo-wives, provided the one he selects embraces the true faith.[74]

In practice the new law establishes the rule that the interpellation is always required for the validity of the second marriage, even if the futility of such an act is clearly foreseen, unless the Roman Pontiff dispenses from it. Of the dispensation we shall treat later.

563. The manner of making these interpellations is clearly stated in the new Code: Interpellations, as a rule, should be made in at least a summary or extra-judicial form by the authority of the converted consort's Ordinary, who is also to grant, at the request of the infidel consort, a time for deliberation with the

[74] PUTZER, *op. cit.*, n. 128; FEIJE, *op. cit.*, n. 481; *Coll. Miss.*, n. 942, 948.

warning that after the futile expiration of the allotted period a negative answer will be presumed. Even private interpellations made on the initiative of the converted consort are valid, and also licit, if the foregoing form cannot be observed; in such a case, evidence that the interpellations have been made must be presented to the external forum and must be confirmed by the testimony of two witnesses or by any other legitimate juridical process.[75]

For the lawfulness of the interpellations it is required that they be made after the reception of baptism, though their validity would not be impaired should they be made before the reception of that sacrament. The course generally to be observed is the same as that prescribed for any other juridical process, though it would sufficiently serve the purpose if it were informal, consisting of merely summary proceedings instituted by the converted party's Bishop or his delegate.[76] The infidel party must be summoned by the ecclesiastical court by letter in order that in the presence of an authorized judge he may give an oral answer to the two questions forming the burden of the interpellations. The letter should not be lacking in the formalities required of an official document. The name of the summoned, of the summoner and of the judge should be inserted in it; and it should give concise information as to the nature of the cause to be handled. The place and date at which the summons was served, and at which the cited person is to appear must be clearly stated. The questions are to be asked in the presence of the judge who represents the converted party and of two sworn witnesses.[77] If a negative an-

[75] COD. IUR. CAN., Can. 1122.

[76] S. C. S. Off., 11 iul., 1886; WERNZ, *op. cit.*, n. 703; GASPARRI, *op. cit.*, n. 1089; S. C. de Prop. Fide, 21 iul., 1821.

[77] PUTZER, *op. cit.*, n. 129; ZITELLI, *op. cit.*, p. 122; MANSELLA, *op. cit.*, p. 430.

swer is given to the first question, the party should be asked whether he or she consents at least to peaceable cohabitation, which is the minimum requirement the law exacts. After a negative answer to this question the judge should pronounce the sentence which will declare the converted party free to choose whether he will contract another marriage or embrace the religious state or remain celibate. If the infidel party consents to peaceable cohabitation, the first marriage retains its force without any necessity of renewing the consent. The adjudicated case should be recorded and after the document has been signed by two witnesses and countersigned by the judge it should be placed in the archives of the Episcopal Curia for future reference, should any occasion require such reference.[78]

564. The interpellation once made need not be repeated, no matter how long a time may elapse before the converted party decides to take another consort, provided the conversion of the other party does not precede such a step.

The law concedes to the infidel consort the right to ask for time for deliberation.[79] No one but the Ordinary is authorized by law to refuse or to grant such a wish. Charity and justice demand that this right be not denied to the infidel party unless the delay occasioned by the granting of the request would seriously jeopardize the faith and the morals of the converted spouse. Should the wish be granted, the case does not become adjudicated until the time allotted to the infidel party for reflection has expired. Should the infidel consort neglect to declare his intention before the expiration of the allotted time, his neglect would be construed as a tacit unwillingness to subscribe even to the mini-

[78] *Conc. Plen. Baltim. III*, p. 287, §45.
[79] S. C. de Prop. Fide, 27 iul., 1820; S. C. S. Off., 12 iun., 1850.

mum requirement, namely, to live peaceably and *sine contumelia Creatoris* with the baptized spouse.[80]

565. The foregoing juridical process may not always be feasible, and may even be impossible, when, for instance, the cited unconverted party declines to respond to the summons. In such a case it will suffice that the converted party either in person or by proxy interview the unconverted consort in the presence of two witnesses and ask an answer to the two questions explained above. The answer must be communicated to the Ordinary or his delegate and after the converted spouse and the two witnesses have confirmed it by their oath it will constitute full proof justifying a declaration favoring a continuance of cohabitation or a separation with the privilege of remarrying, as the case may warrant. The infidel party may declare his intention by letter, provided it is corroborated by trustworthy witnesses. If the interpellation is made privately, namely, without any witnesses, and the baptized consort communicates a negative answer to the external forum, such evidence would influence the ecclesiastical court to decide in favor of the discontinuance of cohabitation but not in favor of remarriage.

566. If the interpellation by virtue of a declaration proceeding from the Holy See may be omitted, or if the infidel, either expressly or tacitly, had given a negative answer, the baptized consort has the right to enter into new wedlock with a Catholic party, unless subsequently to his baptism he gave to the infidel party just cause for departure.[81]

The Roman Pontiff is authorized to dispense from the necessity of interpellating, that is to say, he may permit the converted party to contract a new marriage

[80] Reg. 25, *R. I.*, in VI°; c. 10, C. XXVIII, q. 1; S. C. S. Off., instr. (ad Superior. Mission. Peguan.), 11 iun., 1760.

[81] COD. IUR. CAN., Can. 1123.

with another person without any warning whatsoever being given to the infidel party.[82] Having the power to dispense from the interpellations *in toto, a fortiori* has he the power to dispense *in parte* from them, namely, from the first or the second part of the interpellations taken separately.[83] But this extraordinary faculty cannot be resorted to without a just cause. In the former discipline the dispensation had to be renewed if the converted party had failed to contract marriage within a year after the granting of the dispensation.[84] Since the new Code does not require such a renewal, it would seem that a dispensation once obtained would not have to be renewed, but would hold good until used (the same as with the *interpellationes viva voce peractae*) provided in the interim the infidel party be not converted.

567. The Roman Pontiff would be justified in granting a dispensation from the interpellation whenever: (1) The polygynous convert does not recollect which of his infidel wives was the first and legitimate one;[85] (2) The infidel party's place of residence is not known; (3) The infidel party resides in distant regions to which safe access is barred;[86] (4) It is feared that the interpellations will be instrumental in causing serious molestations and persecutions to the converted party or to the Christians residing in that locality;[87] (5) There is a serious doubt whether the polygynous

[82] GREGORIUS *XIII*, const. *"Populis,"* 25 ian., 1585; BENEDICTUS XIV, const. *"In suprema,"* 16 ian., 1745; S. C. Inq., 16 aug., 1895; in *Acta Sanctae Sedis*, vol. XXIX, p. 564 ff.; S. C. de Prop. Fide, 3 ian., 1777; FEIJE, *op. cit.*, n. 488; GASPARRI, *op. cit.*, n. 1094 ff.; PUTZER, *op. cit.*, n. 130.

[83] S. C. Inq., 5 aug., 1759; 4 iul., 1855; 20 iun., 1866; S. C. de Prop. Fide, 26 sept., 1837.

[84] S. C. de Prop. Fide, 26 iun., 1820.

[85] PAULUS III, const. *"Altitudo,"* 1 iun., 1537.

[86] GREGORIUS XIII, const. *"Populis,"* 25 ian., 1585; S. C. Inq., 29 nov., 1882.

[87] S. C. Inq., 23 nov., 1769.

neophyte has actually given proper matrimonial consent to any of his infidel wives;[88] (6) The first legitimate wife is not known and it is difficult to locate her;[89] (7) The infidel consort fails to intimate her intention after the expiration of the stipulated time; (8) There is a well-founded belief that the promises of the infidel party were fictitious.

568. If the Holy See should dispense from the necessity of interpellating, or if the infidel party should respond negatively to both or only the second question, (even if in this hypothesis an affirmative answer were given to the first question) the converted party would be free to contract a second marriage. The new Code states the condition on which this freedom is based, namely, provided the selected consort is a Catholic. It is understood that marriage would be valid and also licit even if a dispensation from the impediment of mixed religion or from disparity of worship should have to be obtained, the other consort being a non-Catholic. Such a dispensation, however, is very seldom given for the reason that the second marriage in the case would not be altogether *in favorem fidei.*

569. If after the reception of baptism the converted consort was guilty of an offense justifying the desertion by the infidel party, the baptized spouse would not be free to contract a second marriage. Such a just cause of desertion would be adultery committed after baptism. The same moral offense, if committed before baptism, would not be a just cause, for such guilt is washed away by the reception of the sacrament.

570. Dispensation from interpellation has the effect of upholding the validity of the second marriage even

[88] S. C. Inq., 8 iun., 1836; 18 maii, 1892.

[89] PIUS V, const. "*Romani Pontificis,*" 2 aug., 1571; S. C. Inq., 22 nov., 1872.

if the subsequent investigation should disclose the fact that the infidel consort was prevented from declaring his or her mind, or even if he had embraced the true faith at the very time the second marriage was contracted.[90]

The question might be asked: How can such a juridical effect be attributed to such a dispensation? It is certain that the Pauline Privilege does not *in se* justify such far-reaching results. In answering the proposed question the authors are divided. Some maintain that such a dispensation is a mere extensive interpretation of the Pauline Privilege which the Roman Pontiff has the right to give by virtue of his supreme ecclesiastical power. Others contend that he actually dispenses. The two opinions are seemingly in conflict, but if followed to their final analysis they agree, for both admit the absolute dissolution of the first matrimonial bond and the validity of the second marriage.

571. It is evident that a dispensation from the interpellation may be given not only by the Head of the Church but also by his delegate. Needless to say that in both cases the validity of the dispensation depends on the presence of a just cause.[91]

The authors are unanimous in maintaining that the supreme ecclesiastical legislator has the power to dissolve marriages contracted in infidelity but not consummated either before or after the reception of baptism, regardless of whether both consorts have become converts to the faith or only one of them. This right can be claimed on the ground that the bond of such marriages is not firmer than that of a ratified marriage. If the Roman Pontiff may dissolve the marriage bond in the case of a non-consummated Christian

[90] Gregorius XIII, const. *"Populis,"* 25 ian., 1585; Benedictus XIV, const. *"In suprema catholicae,"* 16 ian., 1745; *Synodus Dioecesana*, lib. XIII, cap. XXI, n. 5.

[91] Wernz, *op. cit.*, n. 704.

marriage, *a fortiori* may he dissolve that bond in the proposed case. The authors agree that the Visible Head of the Church would exceed his power should he attempt to dissolve the marriage of two infidels while they remain in infidelity, or after their conversion and subsequent consummation of the marriage.

572. Formerly it was a controverted question whether the Roman Pontiff has the power to dissolve a marriage contracted and consummated in infidelity, but unconsummated after the conversion of both consorts or of one of them. Several authors deny him such a right,[92] others again vindicate it.[93] Though such marriages are consummated in infidelity, provided no new consummation took place after the conversion of one party or of both of them, they are to be regarded as non-consummated marriages between two baptized persons or between a baptized and an unbaptized individual. But the new law states that the Holy See has a right to dissolve such bonds provided there is a just cause.

It cannot be denied that such marriages have actually been dissolved by virtue of special papal decrees, and since so far-reaching a right is not to be sought in the *Casus Apostoli* it must be concluded that it is derived from the plentitude of pontifical power.[94]

573. The converted consort does not lose the right to contract a new marriage with a Catholic, and may resort to it, even if marital relations with the infidel party were re-established after the reception of baptism, provided the infidel party, having changed his

[92] Feije, *op. cit.*, n. 602; Pontius, IX, II; Schmalzgrüber, IV, IX, n. 60; Vasquez, *De matr. disp.*, II, cap. VI, n. 58; Benedictus XIV, *Quaest. Can.*, q. 546; *De Synodo Dioecesana*, lib. VI, cap. IV, n. 5; lib. XIII, cap. XXI, n. 4.

[93] Gasparri, *op. cit.*, n. 1108; Navarrus, *Consil.*, lib. III, *De convers. infid.*, Consil. III, n. 13 (Venetiis, 1621); Sanchez. lib. II, disp. XVII; St. Alphonsus, lib. VI, n. 956; Scavini, III, n. 983 et alii.

[94] Wernz, *op. cit.*, n. 705; Gasparri, *op. cit.*, n. 1109.

or her mind, subsequently deserts the converted party without just cause or does not continue to cohabit peaceably without offering insult to the Creator.[95]

This law is based on the Pauline Privilege. After the conversion of one of the infidel consorts matrimonial relations should be restored provided the other consort, though remaining in infidelity, promises to cohabit peaceably. This is a *conditio sine qua non* of the re-establishment of former marital relations. Should the infidel party prove untrue to the promise the converted party's right to another marriage would revive, even if after baptism the marriage contracted in infidelity had again been consummated. In order that such a right may assert itself, it is required that the converted spouse should not have given a just cause for the departure of the infidel consort. The new Code states furthermore that the other party to the second marriage must be a Catholic, but this is not required *ad validitatem* provided the proper dispensation has been obtained.

574. Things referring to marriage in the Constitutions of Paul III *"Altitudo"* issued on June 1, 1537; of Pius V, *"Romani Pontificis,"* on August 2, 1571; and of Gregory XIII, *"Populis,"* on January 25, 1585, though intended for particular places are to be extended also to other regions provided the circumstances are the same.[96]

The three foregoing Constitutions contain the most important legislation regarding the extensive interpretion of the Pauline Privilege. In the former discipline it was questionable whether these decrees were to be applied to all places or only to those places for whose special benefit they were issued.[97] The new law dispels

[95] Cod. Iur. Can., Can. 1124.
[96] Cod. Iur. Can., Can. 1125.
[97] Wernz, *op. cit.*, n. 705.

all doubt on this subject by declaring that they are not conditioned on territory but only on circumstances. Should the conditions which they relate be present in all parts of the world, the law they enforce would be operative everywhere.

575. The Constitution of Paul III,[98] among other things, says: Whereas the inhabitants of the Western and the Southern Indies, though unacquainted with divine law, have rooted out from their hearts and minds the errors that heretofore guided them and wish to embrace the truth and the unity of the Catholic Church; and, whereas, they desire and intend to live according to the teachings of that same Church, the following is decreed by us as regards their marriages: Those who according to their custom have practiced polygyny before their conversion and do not recollect who their first wife was, may select after their conversion to the faith one of their former wives and according to the law enter with her into marriage. Those who remember whom they have married first should retain her and dismiss all others. Furthermore, until the Holy See ordains otherwise, a relationship in the third degree of consanguinity or affinity should not be regarded as an obstacle to their marriage.

576. The Constitution of Pius V is more comprehensive. Because, it says, the Indians, while they remain in infidelity, practice polygyny and repudiate their wives even for the most trifling reasons, it was permitted by the missionaries that those who receive baptism may remain with the wife who simultaneously becomes a convert with the husband. Since it happens very frequently that such a wife is not always the one they have married first, the Bishops and the priests were tormented by grave scruples, thinking that no

[98] This Constitution as well as the other two that follow can be found in the supplement of the new Code under DOCUMENTA VI, VII, VIII.

valid marriage was contracted under the circumstances. Since it would be most cruel to separate the Indians from the wives who have become converted with them, and since it would be a difficult task to locate the first wife, therefore we decree, *by the plenitude of our apostolic power,* that the Indians who were thus baptized or are to be baptized in the future may remain with the wives who have become baptized or shall become baptized with them, and should dismiss all the others. By virtue of the tenor of this letter we declare such marriages valid.

577. The Constitution of Gregory XIII is the most extensive of the three. It is of frequent occurrence, he says, that many infidels of both sexes, but especially men, after having contracted a marriage according to pagan rites in Angola, Ethiopia, Brazil or some other part of the Indies, are captured by their enemies and transferred to regions very distant from their country and their wives. After their conversion the long intervening distance renders impossible the interpellation of their former infidel consorts as to whether they are willing to cohabit with them *sine contumelia Creatoris.* Whereas marriages contracted by infidels are not so ratified that they could not be dissolved if necessity so demands (*ut necessitate suadente dissolvi non possint*) we give permission to the Ordinaries, the parish priests, and the missionaries of the Society of Jesus to dispense the converted inhabitants of those places so that if they should had married before their conversion they may solemnize marriage (*in facie Ecclesiae*) with any Christian, even if he be of another rite, without requiring the consent of their living consort, and without being constrained to await her answer. We furthermore decree that after they have consummated such marriages they may remain in them licitly, provided it has been ascertained, at least by a summary extra-judicial process, that the absent consort could not be legitimately warned or that she failed to intimate her will within the specified time. Such marriages should never be rescinded but must be regarded as valid and firm and the children born of them as legitimate even if subsequently it should be learned that the first infidel consorts were justly prevented from declaring their will or at the time of the contracted marriage had already embraced the true faith.

The decree of Gregory XIII shows clearly that the Roman Pontiff exercised a power which far exceeds the limits of the Pauline Privilege, and which presupposes the objective dissolution of the matrimonial bond begotten by ratified marriages consummated before conversion but not after.

578. As regards the automatic dissolution of the marriage bond by virtue of Pauline Privilege the new law says: The bond of the first wedlock entered into in infidelity is dissolved only at the time when the converted party actually contracts a new and valid marriage.[99]

This canon does not introduce any new teaching. It has always been believed that the bond contracted in infidelity is not dissolved either by the reception of baptism or by mutual consent, or by the refusal of the infidel party to consent to peaceable cohabitation. It is the second marriage which causes an absolute severance of the bond of the first and sets free the infidel consort.[100] It must be borne in mind that such an effect follows only upon a validly contracted second marriage, which in turn presupposes that the converted party has the right to enter into another wedlock.[101]

[99] Cod. Iur. Can., Can. 1126.

[100] Benedictus XIV, ep. *"Postremo mense,"* 28 febr., 1747, §LVII; const. *"Apostolici missionarii,"* 16 sept., 1747.

[101] S. C. S. Off. (Cochinchin.), 1 aug., 1759, ad 2, 5; (Natal), 11 iul., 1866; S. C. C., *Florentina,* 27 iul., 1726, 29 mart., 1727.

579. In doubtful matters the privilege of the faith is favored by the law.[102]

By the privilege of the faith to which the foregoing canon refers is to be understood the freedom of the converted party to enter into another marriage. In all doubtful matters connected with the Pauline Privilege the convert is to be favored. If the validity of the first marriage is questioned, or if it is doubtful whether the conditions prescribed for the application of the Pauline Privilege are present, the converted consort should not be prevented from contracting another marriage. The same is to be said when a doubt is entertained as to whether the act committed by the converted consort after the reception of baptism was a sufficient or an insufficient cause for the departure of the unbaptized consort.[103]

II. Separation from Bed, Board and Dwelling.
(Canon 1128—Canon 1132.)

580. The first chapter of this article treated of the absolute indissolubility of a ratified and consummated marriage as well as of the conditions which justify the absolute dissolution of the matrimonial bond contracted in infidelity. This article does not concern itself with the *vinculum,* it merely states the causes which justify the separation of the husband from the wife, or *vice versa,* without the matrimonial bond being broken.

The community of bed, board and dwelling place is required by the very nature of marriage, but, since it pertains only to the integrity of marriage and not directly *ad substantiam,* the consorts are excused from it

[102] Cod. Iur. Can., Can. 1127.

[103] S. C. S. Off., instr. (ad Ep. S. Alberti), 9 dec., 1874, n. 13, 18 maii, 1892, ad 1, 2; 19 apr., 1899; instr. (ad Archiep. Quebecen.), 16 sept., 1824, ad 1.

whenever there is a just cause.[104] This has been the discipline of the Church from the time of the Apostles.[105] Such a just cause very often arises by force of circumstances under which the husband or the wife lives and to which they both become reconciled. In other cases certain reasons justify the violent severance of the bond which united the two contracting parties in a community of bed, board, and dwelling place, the matrimonial *vinculum* continuing undissolved. The Church has always claimed the right to grant to her members a separation from bed and board whenever there is a just cause; and when her practice was attacked by the self-constituted pseudo-reformers she has anathematized them in the Council of Trent.[106]

581. The just causes of separation may be twofold, namely, intrinsic and extrinsic to marriage. The new Code legislating on the former says: On account of adultery committed by one consort, the other consort, though the bond remains, has the right to discontinue the community of life even permanently, unless he consented to the crime or was its contributory cause, or condoned it expressly or tacitly, or committed the same crime himself. By a tacit condonation is understood a spontaneous intercourse with marital affection that the innocent consort had with the other after he became certain of the crime of adultery. The tacit condonation is presumed unless within six months he had banished or deserted the adulterous consort or made a legitimate accusation.[107]

Adultery taken by itself has always been considered a just cause for separation. It intrinsically antagon-

[104] Cod. Iur. Can., Can. 1128.

[105] *Matt.* V, 31, 32; XIX, 9; I *Cor.* VII, 11, 12.

[106] Sessio XXIV, *De sacramento matrimonii,* can. VIII; Eugenius IV (in Conc. Florent.), const. *"Exultate Deo,"* 27 nov., 1439, §16; Benedictus XIV, ep. *"Nuper ad nos,"* 16 mart., 1743.

[107] Cod. Iur. Can., Can. 1129.

izes the unity of marriage, and it is the only cause mentioned expressly in the Sacred Scripture.[108] The Gratian collection contains several ecclesiastical enactments handed down from the early ages of Christianity which forbid the Christian consort even to cohabit with the spouse guilty of adultery.[109] The right to separation belongs to the innocent consort by virtue of divine, natural [110] and positive law.[111]

582. In order that adultery may be a just cause for separation, it must be:

1. Formal, not merely material. The consort must be guilty of adultery in fact.[112] Should he erroneously believe that his relationship was with someone else while in reality it was with his own wife, the act, though sinful, would not constitute a sufficient cause for separation.

2. Committed with full consent of the will. Therefore adultery to which one was coerced by violence or fear, would not suffice.[113] The same is to be said should the act be committed in the state of unconsciousness or semi-consciousness, provided the guilty party did not resort to such a state for the express purpose of being exonerated from the consequences which such an act entails.

3. Morally certain. A mere circumstantial evidence would not suffice to pronounce the consort guilty of adultery unless several other indications should point to the moral offense and should justify the presumption that it was actually committed.[114]

[108] *Matt.* V, 19.

[109] C. 4, C. XXX, q. 5; c. 2, C. XXXII, q. 1; c. 18, 19, 21, 22, C. XXXII, q. 5; c. 1, C. XXXII, q. 6; c. 1-8, 10, 17, C. XXXII, q. 7.

[110] SANCHEZ, *op. cit.*, lib. X, disp. III, n. 4; WERNZ, *op. cit.*, n. 707.

[111] C. 9, X, *de sponsalibus et matrimoniis*, IV, 1; c. 19, X, *de conversione coniugatorum*, III, 32.

[112] C. 6, X, *de eo qui cognovit consanguineam uxoris suae vel sponsae*, IV, 13.

[113] C, 3-6, C. XXXII, q. 5.

[114] C. 12, X, *de praesumptionibus*, II, 23; NOLDIN, vol. III, n. 666.

4. Consummated, and not merely begun, namely, the union must be such that it is in itself fitted for procreation.[115] In doubt such a consummation may be presumed.

5. Against the will of the consort. In other words, the other spouse should not give his tacit consent by neglecting to take some means of preventing the crime, when he is in a position easily to do so. Therefore if the other consort either consented to the crime, or was its instrumental cause, or its instigator, he would forfeit the right to separation.[116]

6. One-sided, not counteracted by a similar guilt of the other consort. If the guilt of one consort was known to the other, and this other committed a similar offense in secret, the party whose crime is secret would have no right to separation in the eyes of the internal forum, though the external forum would grant such a right merely on the ground of lack of information.[117]

7. Uncondoned, namely, neither an express nor a tacit act on the part of the innocent consort should indicate that he has pardoned the crime and is reconciled. If the innocent spouse, notwithstanding the fact that the moral offense of the guilty consort was known to her, continues to cohabit with him in marital relations, her conduct would be interpreted as a tacit condonation. A tacit forgiveness is presumed if the innocent spouse refrains from dismissing or abandoning the guilty consort, or from duly denouncing him within six months after the crime became known to her.[118]

583. The common opinion, says Gasparri, permits the innocent consort to separate from her spouse even

[115] Gasparri, *op. cit.*, n. 1112; Wernz, *op. cit.*, n. 707.

[116] C. 6, X, *de eo qui cognovit consanguineam uxoris suae vel sponsae*, IV, 13.

[117] C. 6, 7, X, *de adulteriis et stupro,* V, 16; Morino, *Theologia Moralis,* vol. II, n. 812 (Neapoli, 1912); St. Alphonsus, lib. VI, n. 966.

[118] Sanchez, lib. X, disp. IV, n. 19; Schmalzgrüber, *h. t.*, n. 108; Reiffenstül, *h. t.*, n. 71.

for the crime of sodomy or bestiality.[119] While it must be admitted that such an act implies *divisionem carnis cum alio,* it is not adultery in the strict sense of the term. Therefore, since the new law is to be interpreted strictly, and since it makes no specific mention of them, it would seem that such an opinion can no longer be advocated.

584. The innocent consort, after he has departed lawfully, whether as the result of a judge's sentence or by his own authority, is never again bound to admit the adulterous consort to a community of life, though he may do so; or he may recall her unless with his consent she embraced a state incompatible with marriage.[120]

The innocent consort lawfully separated is never obliged *ex iustitia* to re-establish conjugal cohabitation with the adulterous spouse. Her right, however, to recall him remains intact, and sometimes *ex caritate,* or in order to avert some serious public danger, she might be advised to take back the reformed consort. Moreover, such an obligation could even be imposed on her if the crime of the guilty consort was counterbalanced by her commission of a similar moral offense.[121] The right of the innocent consort to recall the guilty one to cohabitation would be forfeited if with her consent the adulterous spouse had embraced the religious state either by the reception of Holy Orders or by solemn religious profession.[122]

585. Adultery is the only intrinsic cause justifying a perpetual separation. For a temporary separation *a toro, mensa et cohabitatione* even extrinsic causes would suffice. Of these the new Code says: If one of

[119] CONSCI, *De separatione tori coniugalis,* II, XIII, n. 25; SANCHEZ, *loc. cit.,* n. 3 ff.; WERNZ, *op. cit.,* n. 708; GASPARRI, *op. cit.,* n. 1112.

[120] COD. IUR. CAN., Can. 1130.

[121] C. 3, X, *de adulteriis et stupro,* V, 16.

[122] GASPARRI, *op. cit.,* n. 1114; ST. ALPHONSUS, lib. VI, n. 967.

the consorts affiliates himself with a non-Catholic sect; if he rears the child in a non-Catholic spirit; if he leads a criminal and scandalous life; if he occasions grave danger to the soul or body of the other consort: if his cruelty renders a community of life very difficult; these and other causes of a similar nature are just causes for the departure of the other spouse by the authority of the Ordinary of the place, or even by private authority, provided the causes are evident and there is danger in delay. In all these cases, the cause of separation having ceased, the community of life should be restored. If the separation was declared by the Ordinary for a certain or indefinite time the innocent consort is not obliged to conjugal relations, except by a decree of the Ordinary, or after the expiration of the specified time.[123]

No serious difficulty will be experienced as regards the foregoing causes of separation. It must be borne in mind that these causes are not *taxative propositae* and there are many others that would justify the same course. The law makes a wise provision by referring the aggrieved consort to the Ordinary of the place, who is to decide whether his grievances would justify a separation. On his own private authority the offended party may effect such a separation, but only on condition that the cause is self-evident, and that there is danger in delaying until the case is laid before the Ordinary. Even in such cases the innocent party, after having withdrawn from the guilty consort, should submit his complaints to the ecclesiastical superior in order to have his act officially ratified by the Church.

586. The apostasy of which the foregoing canon speaks must consist in a public enrollment of the consort in a heretical or schismatic or infidel sect. Apostasy must not be confounded with affiliation with a for-

[123] Cod. Iur. Can., Can. 1131.

bidden society or with indifference displayed toward one's faith. The non-Catholic education of the offspring must be actual and continued. If the child were at liberty to receive both Catholic and non-Catholic education, no just cause for separation would be afforded. Criminal and scandalous living, whether public or known only to some of the immediate members of the family, would also be a sufficient cause for separation. Such living would be verified in case of sodomy, or bestiality, or addiction to acts redounding to the disgrace of the family, or occasioning serious danger of civil penalty. By grave spiritual danger is understood an endeavor on the part of the consort to induce the other spouse to grave sin, like adultery, onanism, abuse of the marriage rights, theft, etc. To the grave corporal danger would contribute causes like fatal contagious disease, insanity, etc. The term cruel treatment could be applied to very frequent and serious dissensions, and to the avarice of the husband denying to the wife the necessary victuals or remedies in time of sickness.[124] To these could be added the intolerable prodigality of the consort, an uncalled for desertion, avidity of the husband menacing the private fortune of the wife, etc. Whatever may be the nature of the cause for separation the consorts should not seek it at the hands of the civil court, without having first consulted the proper ecclesiastical authority.[125] The causes are not to be judged objectively only. The subjective disposition of the aggrieved consort must also be taken into consideration.[126]

587. It must be noted that by mutual consent the

[124] Gasparri, *op. cit.*, n. 1117 ff.; Consci, *op. cit.*, II, V, n. 1; Sanchez, lib. X, disp. XVII; Reiffenstül, IV, VIII, n. 81; St. Alphonsus, lib. VI, n. 971; Wernz, *op. cit.*, n. 713; Breitenbach, *Die Trennung von Tisch und Bett*, pp. 26, 27 (Luzern, 1908).

[125] *Conc. Plen. Baltimorense*, III, n. 126.

[126] Noldin, *op. cit.*, vol. III, n. 669.

consorts are at liberty to separate for a time for any just cause, or even for no cause whatever, provided the danger of incontinence is absent.

588. After a separation has been effected on account of the guilt of one of the consorts, the children are to be reared by the innocent spouse, or, should one of the parties be a non-Catholic, by the Catholic consort, unless in both cases for the welfare of the children the Bishop ordains otherwise, having always at heart their Catholic education.[127]

If the presence of a cause for separation is established with certainty in a particular instance, the innocent consort is always to be entrusted with the care of rearing the children. In case the other consort is non-Catholic, the Catholic spouse, notwithstanding his guilt, should get the preference as regards supervision over the offspring, for it is naturally supposed that their rearing in the faith will thus be in safer hands. Should this supposition fall before a contrary probability, the Ordinary may rule that the children be committed to the solicitude of the innocent non-Catholic spouse. In taking this step the Bishop must be actuated exclusively by the spiritual and temporal welfare of the children, always permitting the former to predominate.[128]

[127] COD. IUR. CAN., Can. 1132.

[128] ST. ALPHONSUS, lib. VI, n. 976; SANCHEZ, lib. III, disp. XX; GASPARRI, *op. cit.*, n. 1119; WERNZ, *op. cit.*, n. 714; *Acta Sanctae Sedis,* vol. II, p. 138; c. 2, X, *de conversione infidelium,* III, 33; BENEDICTUS XIV, const. *"Probe,"* 15 dec., 1751, §18.

CHAPTER XIII.

The Validation of Marriage.

I. Simple Validation.

(Canon 1133—Canon 1137.)

589. To validate marriage is equivalent to contracting it anew. The new law classifies the invalid marriages into three categories, namely, according as their invalidity resulted: (1) From a diriment impediment; (2) From lack of consent; or (3) From lack of the proper form. The effects of a validated marriage when correlated with illegitimate offspring have already been explained in another part of this book.[1]

1. Marriage Invalid on Account of Impediment.

For the validation of a marriage whose invalidity is owing to the presence of a diriment impediment, it is required that the impediment cease or be dispensed from, and that the consent be renewed at least by the spouse who is aware of the impediment. The ecclesiastical law requires the renewal of consent for validity, notwithstanding the fact that in the beginning both consorts have given consent and that their consent was not revoked subsequently.[2]

Some impediments cease without the necessity of having recourse to a dispensation, as, for instance, the impediment of age, of abduction, of ligamen, of dis-

[1] See this work, n. 540 ff.

[2] Cod. Iur. Can., Can. 1133.

parity of worship, etc. Other impediments require the intervention of an authorized dispenser, such as that of affinity, consanguinity, spiritual relationship, etc. It is immaterial to which of the two classes of impediments the marriage owes it invalidity; in both hypotheses, besides requiring that the impediment either cease automatically or be lifted, the ecclesiastical law prescribes also a renewal of consent as a *conditio sine qua non* for the validation of the marriage.

590. This renewal of consent must be a new act of the will consenting to the marriage which, it has been discovered, was invalid from the very beginning.[3]

The required renewal of consent is not imposed by virtue of natural law, for if it were so imposed the Church could not validate marriages by means of a *sanatio in radice,* as this act implies a dispensation from the necessity of renewing the consent. Ordinarily, therefore, the ecclesiastical law requires that the parties whose marriage is invalid on account of an impediment should not only be freed from the impediment (either by its automatic cessation or by dispensation), but should also renew their consent, thus to validate their marriage by a new act of the will.[4] This duty will devolve on them even if their original consent perseveres. By insisting that the renewal of consent must be a "*novus voluntatis actus*" the new law implicitly presupposes that the nullity of the first consent is known to one party or to both.

591. Should the impediment be public, the consent is to be renewed by both parties in the form prescribed by law. Should it be occult but known to both parties, it will suffice if both renew their consent privately and

[3] Cod. Iur. Can., Can. 1134.

[4] S. C. S. Off., 8 iun., 1836; (Cochinchin. Occident.), 12 iun., 1850, ad 2.

secretly. Should it be occult and unknown to one party, it will suffice if only the consort who is aware of the impediment renew his or her consent privately and secretly, provided the other party's consent perseveres.[5]

As regards the first part no doubt can be entertained. A marriage whose nullity is of public knowledge requires a public validation for various reasons, such as the avoidance of scandal, the protection of the good name of the parties and of the offspring, and the sanctity of the sacrament. Such validation implies the employment of the proper form of marriage prescribed by canon 1094, and explained under number 452 and following. The indispensable condition of such form is the presence of an authorized priest or the Ordinary of the place and two witnesses. A marriage thus validated will be accepted by both forums.

592. Since the public validation of marriage is always connected with more or less inconvenience and very frequently the good name of the reputed consorts and their offspring is at stake, the Church permits a private and secret validation provided the impediment is occult, namely, no one but the contracting parties having any knowledge of it. The words *"privatim et secreto"* relieve the consorts of the obligation of renewing their consent by having recourse to the form mentioned above.

Even this requirement is modified should the presence of an impediment be known only to one of the reputed consorts. In that hypothesis, should it be advisable to leave the other spouse in good faith, as is generally the case, the renewal of consent need not be reciprocal. Such was the principle on which the Sacred Penitentiaria has acted for a long time before the promulgation of the new Code. This mode of renew-

[5] COD. IUR. CAN., Can. 1135.

ing consent presupposes that the consent of the other party, who is ignorant of the impediment, perseveres. The authors suggest various ways to facilitate the renewal of consent under such circumstances.[6] These ways are very seldom practicable for they are liable to arouse suspicion in the unsuspecting consort. Therefore the new law legislates wisely when it says: "*Satis est ut sola pars impedimenti conscia consensum privatim et secreto renovet.*" Such a private and secret renewal of consent would be effected by the conjugal act performed with matrimonial intent, with the consort whose consent perseveres.[7]

2. *Marriage Invalid for Want of Consent.*

593. A marriage whose invalidity is owing to want of consent is validated if the party who has failed to consent gives his consent, provided the consent given by the other party perseveres. If the want of consent was merely internal, it suffices that the party who did not consent should consent internally. If the want of consent was external also, it is required that the consent be manifested externally also, either according to the form prescribed by law, if the want of consent was public, or in some other private or secret way, if it was occult.[8]

The foregoing canon treats of the hypothesis from which want of consent may result. Consent, being the essence of marriage, begets the marriage contract and without it no contract can exist, for no power can supply a consent that is wanting. For this reason the law of the Church insists that a marriage null for want of consent cannot be validated unless the party who

[6] WERNZ, *op. cit.*, n. 651; NOLDIN, vol. III, n. 659; DE SMET, *op. cit.*, n. 410.

[7] C. 7, X, *de eo, qui duxit in matrimonium quam polluit per adulterium*, IV, 7; S. C. S. Off., 12 ian., 1769, II, 5.

[8] COD. IUR. CAN., Can. 1136.

withheld his consent at the time the marriage took place should ratify it subsequently by actually and freely consenting to it.[9] Until this is done the marriage is invalid, and even if it should be done the marriage would be null unless the other party's consent perseveres.[10] If the consent was given only externally, as, for instance, on account of fear or violence, or fictitiously, or erroneously, in all these suppositions the marriage would be invalid for want of internal consent. In that case the validation of marriage would require an internal renewal of consent, on the part of the consort who had failed to consent internally at the time the marriage was solemnized. If the want of internal consent can be traced to both parties, then both have to give such a consent. If the proper consent given by one party *ab initio* perseveres unrevoked and the other party consented only externally, the marriage cannot be validated, unless the latter supplies the necessary internal consent as a minimum requirement. In this case the new law does not demand that the party who is in good faith should be informed of the nullity of marriage.[11]

It is to be noted that the consent is not regarded as withheld unless such an intention is manifested by a positive act of the will. An interpretative withholding of consent has no force in the eyes of the ecclesiastical tribunal.[12]

594. Should the want of consent be external its renewal will depend on whether it is a public or an occult fact. In the former case the consent cannot be supplied except by resorting to the prescribed form of

[9] WERNZ, *op. cit.*, n. 648; GASPARRI, *op. cit.*, n. 1145.

[10] C. 2, 4, X, *de coniugio servorum*, IV, 9; S. C. S. Off., instr. (ad Vic. Ap. Oceaniae), 6 apr., 1843; S. C. C., *Vigilien.*, 23 iun., 13 iul., 22 sept., 1725.

[11] C. 21, 30, X, *de sponsalibus et matrimoniis*, IV, 1; FEIJE, *op. cit.*, n. 760; GASPARRI, *op. cit.*, n. 1142.

[12] NOLDIN, *op. cit.*, vol. III, n. 657.

marriage. If the want of external consent is occult it may be supplied privately and secretly regardless of whether both or only one party has failed to give the proper consent.[13]

3. *Marriages Invalid for Want of Proper Form.*

595. A marriage whose nullity is owing to the lack of proper form, in order to become valid, must be contracted by means of the prescribed form.[14]

The general law contained in the foregoing canon is not to be interpreted in the sense that it brooks no exceptions. The requirement is only relatively necessary, for in certain instances the Church dispenses from the necessity of having recourse to the proper form. The insistence on this form can be gathered from the various decisions of the Holy See.[15] If the lack of proper consent is a public fact the renewal of consent must also be public, namely, it must take place in the presence of the authorized priest or the Ordinary of the place and two witnesses. Should it be an occult fact, the same mode should be used, but the renewal of consent may take place secretly. In the former instance the proclamation of banns should precede such a marriage, unless for a just cause a dispensation be obtained. Such a dispensation should always be granted if the fact of the lack of the proper form is occult.

Not infrequently it happens that the renewal of consent by any of the preceding modes is either impracticable or even impossible. The *sanatio in radice* provides for such cases, to whose consideration will be devoted the pages that follow.

[13] S. C. S. Off., instr. (ad Vic. Ap. Oceaniae), 6 apr., 1843.
[14] Cod. Iur. Can., Can. 1137.
[15] S. C. C., 2 aug., 1907; *Poloniae,* 13 nov., 1638; Secret. Status, instr. 27 mart., 1830.

II. Sanatio in Radice.

596. The *sanatio* of marriage *in radice* is its validation, carrying with it, besides dispensation from, or cessation of, an impediment, dispensation from the law requiring a renewal of consent, and (by a fiction of the law) a retroaction to the past, as regards canonical effects. The validation takes place from the moment the favor is granted, the retroaction goes back to the very beginning of the marriage, unless the law expressly ordains otherwise. Dispensation from the law requiring the renewal of consent may be granted whether only one of the parties or both are unaware of the impediment.[16]

This mode of validating a marriage was resorted to first by Boniface VIII (1301), and the principle on which such a validation is founded was clearly defined by Clement V.[17] Gregory XIII, Clement XI and Clement XII, made use of the *sanatio in radice* and toward the end of the eighteenth century such favors were extended not only to individuals but even to whole dioceses and extensive territories.[18]

1. The Nature of a Sanatio in Radice.

597. The main difference between a simple dispensation and a *sanatio in radice* consists in the mode whereby a marriage which is invalid *ab initio* is validated. In the first instance the renewal of consent is necessary. Whether such renewal should be required of both parties or only of one, whether it should be private or public, external or internal, will depend entirely on whether only one or both parties withheld their consent at the time the marriage was celebrated, whether the withholding of their consent was a public

[16] Cod. Iur. Can., Can. 1138.
[17] C. un. *de immunitate ecclesiarum*, III, 17, in *Clem.*
[18] Wernz, *op. cit.*, n. 654; Perrone, *op. cit.*, vol. II, p. 167 ff.

or an occult act, and whether their consent was given internally but not externally, or *vice versa.*

A renewal of consent prescribed for only one consort presupposes the continuance of the other party's consent. On the strength of this continued consent the marriage can be validated by means of *sanatio in radice* without the renewal of such unrevoked consent. In the case of a simple dispensation the Church does not go any further than to remove the obstacle which stands in the way of the validity of the marriage. In the second instance besides lifting the impediment the Church automatically confirms the continued consent, endows it with a retroactive force, and invests it with such juridical and canonical effects that the vitiated acts which it begot formerly become *ipso facto* ratified.

598. By the concession of a *sanatio in radice* the marriage becomes valid *ex nunc,* namely, from the moment the grace is conceded. The canonical effects of such validation begin *ex tunc,* namely, with the time the marriage was contracted. The most important of these effects is the legitimation of offspring. All children are *ipso facto* legitimated except those stigmatized as adulterine and sacrilegious.[10] These effects are the natural consequences of a *sanatio in radice* unless a provision in the rescript ordains otherwise in particular instances.

Every *sanatio in radice* carries with it a dispensation from the necessity of renewing the consent, for such necessity is prescribed only by ecclesiastical and not by natural law. The *sanatio in radice,* however, and the renewal of consent are not mutually exclusive and the Church very frequently gives the former with an insistence on the latter as a matter of penalty, in the case, for instance, where one or both parties were in bad faith when they attempted marriage. Should

[10] See this work, n. 173.

such a condition be contained in the rescript its fulfillment would be required *ad validitatem.*[20]

599. Dispensation from the renewal of consent may be given without the knowledge of both or of either of the contracting parties.[21] Should such a dispensation be granted the objective validity of the marriage would depend on the answer one could give to the question: Does the presumed or alleged consent of the two consorts actually persevere or not?

2. Conditions Under Which a Sanatio in Radice is Granted.

600. Any marriage entered into by both parties with a consent naturally sufficient but juridically ineffective on account of a diriment impediment of ecclesiastical law or on account of the want of the legitimate form, may be validated in the root provided the consent perseveres. A marriage contracted with an impediment of natural or divine law, even if later the impediment should have ceased, the Church does not validate *in radice,* not even from the moment when the impediment disappeared.[22]

On the strength of this canon the conditions under which a *sanatio in radice* is possible are:

1. A consent naturally sufficient but juridically ineffective. This consent, as has already been explained, must be free, deliberate, internal, personal, outwardly manifested, legitimate, absolute, and mutually simultaneous.[23] Should the consent be lacking in any characteristics necessary to the validity of marriage, no *sanatio in radice* should be resorted to. The *sanatio*

[20] NOLDIN, vol. III, n. 662; BENEDICTUS XIV, *De Synodo Dioecesana,* lib. XIII, cap. XXI, n. 7; LEHMKUHL, *op. cit.*, vol. II, n. 828.

[21] S. C. S. Off. (Iaponiae), 11 mart., 1868; instr. (ad Ep. S. Adalberti), 9 dec., 1874; 22 aug., 1906, ad 4; Secret. Status, instr. 27 mart., 1830.

[22] COD. IUR. CAN., Can. 1139.

[23] See this work, n. 397.

in radice could be applied if both parties give their consent in good faith and with the firm conviction that their marriage is valid; or give the proper consent even if they were morally certain of the invalidity of their marriage. The new law distinctly states that the knowledge of the objective invalidity of a marriage can co-exist with the giving of a consent naturally sufficient to constitute marriage.[24] The possibility of a *sanatio in radice* would therefore depend exclusively on whether a natural marital consent was actually given and continues unrevoked, or whether it was not given. A *sanatio in radice* would be given even in case one of the consorts cannot be induced to renew his consent but there is no reason to fear that his consent was withheld *ab initio* or, if given at that time, was afterwards revoked.[25]

2. The lack of effectiveness of the consent must be due to the presence of a diriment impediment of ecclesiastical law, or to the non-compliance with the proper form of marriage. Any impediment of ecclesiastical origin can be lifted by a *sanatio in radice,* and in case the proper form was disregarded the same dispensation can supply it. Marriages null on account of an impediment whose nature or origin is a matter of controversy cannot be validated by a *sanatio in radice,* such would be the invalid marriage of persons related beyond the first degree of lineal or in the first degree of collateral consanguinity.

3. Another requisite without which the marriage cannot be validated in *radice* is the presumed perseverance of the consent given at the time the invalid marriage was contracted.[26] Under ordinary circumstances

[24] COD. IUR. CAN., Can. 1085.

[25] FEIJE, *op. cit.,* n. 767.

[26] S. C. S. Off. (Iaponiae), 11 mart., 1868; 12 apr., 1899; 26 aug., 1906, ad 3; S. C. de Prop. Fide, litt. (ad Coadiut. Superior. Mission. in ora Coromandel), 5 iul., 1788.

the continuance of such consent is presumed (*praesumptione iuris tantum*). Its revocation would have to result from a positive act of the will, an interpretative act of the will would not suffice. Actions from which the discontinuance of the consent could legitimately be inferred are, a civil divorce, a *separatio a toro et mensa,* etc. It is not required that the consent originally given should persevere morally; its virtual continuance suffices. Such continuance would be implied in continued cohabitation under the same roof and in conjugal relations. The invalid marriage of deceased persons can be validated by means of *sanatio in radice* but only *secundum quid,* namely, it may be endowed with juridical effects, such as the legitimation of children.[27] Such a validation presupposes the virtual perseverance of the consent to the moment of death. If it had been revoked before that time the *sanatio in radice* would be void of all objective juridical value.

4. *Sanatio in radice* is not applied to invalid marriages attempted by parties laboring under an impediment of natural or divine law, no matter whether they were in good or in bad faith. The Church does not validate such marriages, not even from the moment the impediment has ceased.[28]

As regards the first proposition it is clear that the Church has not the power to validate a marriage whose invalidity results from a higher law, like that of natural or divine law. After the impediment has ceased, provided the consent of the parties persevered, strictly speaking the Church could apply a *sanatio in radice* but only back to the time at which the impediment disappeared. As a matter of fact the Church has actually

[27] WERNZ, *op. cit.*, n. 656; GASPARRI, *op. cit.*, n. 1151; GIOVINE, *op. cit.*, p. 602.

[28] S. C. S. Off., 8 mart., 1900; 2 mart., 1904.

done this in a case in which the impediment of *ligamen* (which was the cause of the nullity of the marriage) came to an end [29] after the death of the first husband. Such a dispensation would be a *sanatio in radice impropria* or *relativa,* for the period preceding the cessation of the impediment would in no way be affected by it, nor would the children born during that time be legitimated. In this case the words *sanatio ex tunc* are to be applied to the moment the impediment of natural or divine law has ceased. Formerly a *sanatio* under such circumstances was very seldom granted and the new law inaugurated a ruling which intimates that the Church does not intend to make use of her power to validate in this way a marriage entered into with such an impediment. Should only an ecclesiastical impediment interfere with the validity of the marriage at the time it was attempted, and should the impediment of perpetual and incurable impotency arise subsequently to the birth of a child, such a marriage could be validated but only *secundum quid,* namely, as regards its effects (legitimation of children) up to the inception of the impediment of natural law. Such *sanatio* would legitimate the offspring but would fail to validate the marriage for the future, because the contracting parties were laboring under an inability to contract it. Feije advocates the absolute validation even of such future marriage but forbids its use.[30]

This case must not be confounded with another in which a mere concubinage on which the impediment of impotency supervened was followed by an attempted marriage. Under such circumstances the remedy of a *sanatio in radice* could not be applied because the marital and conjugal consent, given in the invalid marriage, was preceded by an impediment of natural law.[31]

[29] S. Poenitentiaria, 25 apr., 1890.
[30] *Op. cit.*, n. 769; SABETTI-BARRETT, n. 932.
[31] S. C. S. Off., 18 mart., 1900.

5. The authors generally demand a proportionately grave cause for a recourse to *sanatio in radice.* They hold that in the absence of such grave cause recourse to *sanatio in radice* would be inexcusable. Such grave causes are: (1) If one consort cannot be induced to renew his consent and yet wishes to live in marriage; (2) If only one spouse is conscious of the impediment whose existence could not be revealed to the other without grave inconvenience; (3) If both parties are in good faith and cannot be apprised of the nullity of their marriage; (4) If a number of marriages is to be validated and recourse to the *sanatio in radice* would be the most practical method.[32]

601. Should one or both parties fail to give the consent the marriage cannot be validated *in radice,* whether the consent was wanting from the very beginning, or whether it was given in the beginning but revoked subsequently. Should the consent be wanting in the beginning but given later, the marriage can be validated *in radice* from the moment the consent was given.[33]

If the consent is given at the beginning of an attempted marriage and it perseveres, the marriage can be validated *in radice.* If at the beginning the consent was wanting but it was given later, the marriage can be validated from the time the consent was given. If it was given at the beginning but subsequently revoked, the validation of marriage is an impossibility. If the marriage was attempted and from the very beginning an impediment of natural or divine law interfered with its validity, it cannot be validated *in radice,* except from the time the impediment has ceased. But the Church does not intend to extend the favor of a *sanatio* under such circumstances. Should

[32] Noldin, vol. III, n. 663; Wernz, *op. cit.,* n. 659, note 35.
[33] Cod. Iur. Can., Can. 1140.

such an impediment arise after a certain period of cohabitation with matrimonial consent, the marriage could be validated as regards its effects up to the end of that period. If a marriage was null *ab initio* (on account of an impediment of ecclesiastical law) and then an impediment of natural or divine law supervened, a *convalidatio matrimonii secundum quid* can be effected up to the period at which the impediment of natural law arose. This kind of validation would have the effect of legitimating the offspring born of such union during the period referred to above, but it would be void of all subsequent effects.

602. The granting of a *sanatio in radice* may be a public or an occult act. If it is a public act the *sanatio* should be applied publicly. If it is an occult act it is to be applied in the tribunal of penance, though no special formalities are prescribed by law. Should the impediment for which an occult *sanatio* was granted become public, a public dispensation must also be obtained. An occult *sanatio* should be procured and executed secretly by the confessor. He is to have direct recourse to the Sacred Penitentiaria. His petition should contain full information as to the consent of the parties, namely, whether it was given *ab initio* and is unrevoked; whether in the beginning it was denied but supplied subsequently; whether it was given in good or bad faith. The petition must reveal also the causes which actuated the petitioner, as well as the name and the correct address of the confessor. It is generally suggested that the confessor should apply the *sanatio in radice* in the tribunal of penance after the sacramental absolution and before the prayer *"Passio Domini."* [34]

[34] The form usually suggested runs thus: Ego auctoritate Apostolica mihi concessa matrimonium a te contractum cum N. in radice eius sano et prolem susceptam legitimam declaro. In nomine Patris, etc.

603. *Sanatio in radice* can be conceded only by the Apostolic See.[35]

The purpose of this canon is not to derogate from the principle which holds that personal juridical rights are communicable.[36] It is a well-known fact that the Holy See not only may but actually does delegate the power to dispense by means of *sanatio in radice.* The Sacred Consistorial Congregation decreed that the Bishops of America should enjoy the faculty of dispensing from any minor impediment mentioned in canon 1042 and also of granting a *sanatio in radice* for marriages whose invalidity resulted from the presence of an impediment therein mentioned. This faculty is to last for five years from the date of concession.[37] The same faculty authorized the Bishops to dispense for five years even from the impediments of major grade, whether public, or occult, or even multiple, provided they originate from ecclesiastical law (with the exception of the impediments arising from the Order of the Holy Priesthood and from lineal affinity when the marriage had been consummated), and provided the petition is sent to the Holy See and urgent necessity for dispensing arises before the answer is received. This last condition (*si petitio dispensationis ad S. Sedem missa sit et urgens necessitas dispensandi supervenerit, pendente recursu*) was subsequently suspended *for the duration of the war.* The present faculties of the Bishops extend over all impedient and diriment impediments of ecclesiastical law (excepting the two mentioned above) and they may also grant a *sanatio in radice* to validate a marriage whose invaliditv was caused by the presence of a diriment impediment

[35] Cod. Iur. Can., Can. 1141.

[36] "Potest quis per alium, quod potest facere per seipsum." (Reg. LXVIII, *R. I.*, in VI°.)

[37] S. C. Consistorialis, 25 apr., 1918. See, *Acta Apostolicae Sedis,* vol. X, n. 5, p. 190-192.

from which they have power to dispense, whether it be of minor or of major grade.[38]

In a subsequent decree the same Congregation has granted a concession by virtue of which these faculties are to remain in force for the period of six full months following upon the signing of the peace terms by the nations presently at war.[39]

[38] Sacra Congregatio Consistorialis, 2 aug., 1918. See *Acta Apostolicae Sedis,* vol. X, n. 9; p. 363 and 364.

[39] S. C. C., 4 mart., 1919; in the *Acta Apostolicae Sedis,* vol. XI, p. 120; ib., "*Monitore Ecclesiastico,*" ser. IV, vol. I, p. 106.

CHAPTER XIV.

About Second Nuptials.

(Canon 1142—Canon 1143.)

604. Though chaste widowhood is more honorable, yet second and further nuptials are valid and licit, the prescription of canon 1069, §2, being observed.[1]

The clause of the foregoing canon refers to the impediment of *ligamen* of which the new law says: Though the first marriage was null or dissolved for whatever cause, another should not be contracted until the nullity or dissolution of the first is legitimately and beyond all doubt ascertained. This provision makes it clear that successive polygyny or polyandry is permitted but only on condition that the first marriage has been legitimately dissolved, either by the death of the first consort or by a declaration of nullity proceeding from the supreme ecclesiastical legislator.

605. The law expressed in this canon conforms to the general law of the Church promulgated by St. Paul.[2] Hermas (first or second century) testifies that such was the law of the Church in the early ages of Christianity.[3] Similar testimony is proffered by Clement of Alexandria, Origen, Epiphanius and others.[4] The condemnation hurled by the Council of Nice

[1] Cod. Iur. Can., Can. 1142.

[2] "But I say to the unmarried, and to the widows: It is good for them if they continue even as I. But if they do not contain themselves, let them marry, for it is better to marry than to be burnt." (I. *Cor.* VII, 8, 10.)

[3] Hermas, lib. II, *Mandat. IV,* n. 4.

[4] Wernz, *op. cit.,* n. 719.

against the Montanists and Novatians is another evidence we can adduce to corroborate the foregoing contention.[5] The bitter vituperation set in motion by the ecclesiastical writers of the early centuries against those who entered into second nuptials does not warrant any further conclusion than that the Church discountenanced such a step and that it was generally looked upon with disfavor.

606. The Oriental Church took more drastic measures to suppress the tendency to contract second nuptials and went so far as to brand them with the stigma of unlawfulness, but not with that of invalidity.[6] Whatever punishments were meted out in the penitential books to those who indulged in successive polygyny or polyandry, fell into desuetude in the time of Gratian,[7] Roland[8] and Bernardus Papiensis.[9]

The legal infamy with which the Roman law branded those widows who entered into second nuptials before at least one year elapsed after the death of their first husband,[10] was not generally approved by the Church. The forty-fourth canon of the Council of Paris (829) permits a widow to enter into second nuptials thirty days after her first husband's death, and in the twelfth century all vestige of such a stigma was removed.[11]

607. As regards the nuptial blessing the new law rules: A woman to whom the solemn blessing was once imparted is not permitted to receive it again in the following nuptials.[12]

Whether in the new law the second nuptials will re-

[5] Can. VII, *Conc. Nicaenum.*

[6] ZHISMAN, *op. cit.*, p. 435; FREISEN, *op. cit.*, p. 669.

[7] Dict. Grat., post c. 7, C. XXXI, q. 1.

[8] Magister *Rolandus, Summa*, p. 155.

[9] *Summa*, p. 194.

[10] L. 11, §1 sq. D. *de his, qui not. inf.*, III, 2; L. 2, Cod. *de sec. nupt.*, V. 9.

[11] URBAN III, c. 4, X, *de secundis nuptiis*, IV, 21; INNOCENT III, c. 5, X, *tit. cit.*, IV, 21.

[12] COD. IUR. CAN., Can. 1143.

ceive the solemn blessing or not will depend on whether the prospective wife received such a blessing before or not. If she was never married, or if at her first marriage the blessing was omitted, or if the first marriage was invalid, she is entitled to a solemn blessing on the occasion of her second nuptials. If at her first marriage the blessing is given, she cannot receive that blessing at her second marriage. Therefore a man who enters into wedlock with a widow whose first nuptials were blessed would not have the right to receive the blessing on the ground that this is his first marriage.[13] But, on the other hand, a widow whose first nuptials were not blessed would be entitled to have her second nuptials blessed even if the widower whom she marries had received a solemn blessing at his first marriage. In the former case the *Missa pro Sponso et Sponsa* could not be celebrated.[14] In the latter case that Mass would be proper.[15]

608. It must be noted, finally, that the Church does not encourage the second nuptials though they are not branded as invalid or illicit. This conclusion is based on the new law by virtue of which among *irregulares ex defectu* are classed all persons who may be characterized as bigamists, in the sense that they have contracted two or more valid marriages successively.[16]

[13] BENEDICTUS XIV, const. *"Etsi pastoralis,"* 26 maii., 1741; §VII, n. 4; RITUALE ROMANUM, tit. VII, c. 1, *de sacramento matrimonii*, n. 15; S. C. C., *Mileten.*, mense febr., 1590, ad 6; S. R. C., *Aquen.*, 3 mart., 1761, ad 1; decr. gen. 30 iun., 1896, n. VI.

[14] S. R. C., 3 mart., 1761.

[15] GASPARRI, *op. cit.*, n. 1042.

[16] COD. IUR. CAN., Can. 984, n. 4.

INDEX.

References contained in this Index allude to numbers placed at the beginning of paragraphs.

D.

BIBLIOGRAPHY.

The following are the most important works consulted in the preparation of this treatise:

A. Sources.

Acta Apostolicae Sedis. Roma, 1909-1919.
Acta et Decreta Conc. Plen. Americae Latinae (1899). Romae, 1900.
Acta et Decreta Conc. Plen. Quebecensis I (1909). Quebec, 1912.
Acta Sanctae Sedis. Roma, 1865-1906.
Analecta Ecclesiastica. Roma, 1893-1908.
Analecta Iuris Pontificii. Roma, 1855-1888.
Bullarii Romani Cont. Prati, 1845.
Codex Iuris Canonici Pii X Pontificis Maximi, Benedicti XV Auctoritate Promulgatus. Romae, 1917.
Collectanea S. Cong. de Prop. Fide. Roma, 1843.
Collectio Omnium Conclusionum et Resolutionum S. Concilii Tridentini. Romae, 1879.
Corpus Iuris Canonici (Richter). Lipsiae, 1839.
Decreta Conc. Plen. Baltimorensis II (1866). Baltimorae, 1868.
Decreta Conc. Plen. Baltimorensis III (1884). Baltimorae, 1886.
Decretales Gregorii Papae IX. Romae, 1582.
Decretum Gratiani. Roma, 1582.
Mansi, *Amplissima Coll. Concil.* Paris and Leipzig, 1901-1913.
Synodus Alexandrina Coptorum (Cairi in Aegypto, 1898). Romae, 1899.
Synodus Sciarfensis Syrorum (in Monte Libano, 1888). Romae, 1896.

B. Books Containing General Information.

Aichner, *Compendium Iuris Ecclesiastici.* Brixinae, 1887.
Alphonsus, *Theologia Moralis.* Ratisbonae, 1846.
American Ecclesiastical Review, *The New Canon Law in its Practical Aspects.* Philadelphia, 1918.
André-Wagner, *Dictionnaire de Droit Canonique.* Paris, 1901.
Antonelli, *Disciplina Medicinalis in usum Confessariorum et Curiarum Ecclesiasticarum.* Romae, 1905.
Arner, *Consanguineous Marriages in the American Population.* (A Doctorate Dissertation.) Columbia University, 1908.
Augustinus, *De Civitate Dei.* Lipsiae, 1867.
Bachofen, *Das Mutterrecht.* Stuttgart, 1861.
Baruffaldo, *Ad Rituale Romanum Commentaria.* Florentiae, 1847.
Benedict XIV, *Bullarii Romani Cont.* (4 vols.). Prati, 1845.
Benedict XIV, *De Synodo Dioecesana.* Parmae, 1764.
Capelmann, *Medicina Pastoralis.* Aquisgrani, 1890.
Cappello, *De Curia Romana.* Romae, 1913.
Castelein, *Droit Naturel. (Droit Domestique).* Namur, 1903.

Catholic Encyclopedia, Art. *"Marriage," "Consanguinity," "Affinity,"* etc.

Cathrein, *Moralphilosophie.* Freiburg, 1904.

Cronin, *Science of Ethics.* New York, 1917.

D'Annibale, *Summa Theologiae Moralis.* Romae, 1891.

De Angelis, *Praelectiones Iuris Canonici.* Romae, 1872.

De Luca, *Summa Praelectionum in Libros Decretalium.* Prati, 1904.

Devine, *The Law of Christian Marriage According to the Teaching and Discipline of the Catholic Church.* London, 1909.

Encyclopaedia Britannica (Eleventh Edition), Art., *"Marriage," "Insanity* (Consanguinity)," etc.

Encyclopédie, La Grande. Art., *"Consanguinité," "Mariage,"* etc. Paris.

Eschbach, *Casus de Feminea Impotentia.* Romae, 1899.

Eschbach, *Disputationes Physiologico-theologicae.* Romae, 1901.

Fagnanus, *Ius Canonicum, sive Commentaria absolutissima in Quinque Libros Decretales.* Coloniae, 1676-1682.

Ferraris, *Prompta Bibliotheca.* Romae, 1899.

Ferreres, *Institutiones Canonicae.* Barcinone, 1917.

Gennari, *Quistioni Canoniche.* Romae, 1908.

Gennari-Boudinhon, *Consultations de Morale, de Droit Canonique, et de Liturgie.* Paris, 1907.

Giraldi, *Expositio Iuris Pontificii.* Romae, 1829.

Hergenröther-Hollweck, *Lehrbuch des katholischen Kirchenrechts.* Freiburg I. B., 1905.

Lega, *Praelectiones de Iudiciis Ecclesiasticis.* Romae, 1905.

Martène, *De Antiquis Ecclesiae Ritibus.* Rotomagi, 1700.

McLennan, *Studies in Ancient History.* London, 1886.

Meyer, *Institutiones Iuris Naturalis.* Friburgi Brisgoviae, 1900.

Micheletti, *Ius Piamum.* Augustae Taurinorum, 1914.

Milasch, *Das Kirchenrecht der morgenländischen Kirche.* Mostar, 1905.

Morgan, *Ancient Society.* London, 1877.

Ojetti, *Synopsis Rerum Moralium et Iuris Pontificii.* Romae, 1911.

Paoli, *Etude sur les origines et la nature du mariage civil, mis en regard de la doctrine catholique.* Paris, 1890.

Papp-Szilágyi, *Enchiridion Iuris Ecclesiae Orientalis Catholicae.* Magno Varadini, 1862.

Pourrat, *La Théologie Sacramentaire.* Paris, 1909.

Probst, *Sacramente und Sacramentalien in den drei ersten christlichen Jahrhunderten.* Tübingen, 1872.

Reiffenstühl, *Ius Canonicum Universum.* Venetiis, 1726.

Sägmüller, *Lehrbuch des katholischen Kirchenrechts.* Friburgi Br., 1909.

Salmanticenses, *Cursus Theologiae Moralis. Tractatus de Matrimonio.* Lugduni, 1879.

Sanford, *Pastoral Medicine.* New York, 1905.

Santi-Leitner, *Praelectiones Iuris Canonici.* Ratisbonae, 1904.

Schmalzgrüber, *Ius Ecclesiasticum Universum.* Romae, 1845.

Schmidt, *Thesaurus Iuris Ecclesiastici.* Heidelbergae, 1772.

Schöpf, *Handbuch des katholischen Kirchenrechts.* Schaffhausen, 1863.

Schüch, *Handbuch der Pastoraltheologie.* Innsbruck, 1910.

Sebastianelli, *Praelectiones Iuris Canonici.* Romae, 1905.

SILBERNAGEL, *Verfassung und gegenwärtiger Bestand sämtlicher Kirchen des Orients.* Regensburg, 1904.
SMITH, *Elements of Ecclesiastical Law.* New York, 1878.
SOUARN, *Memento de Théologie Morale* (A l'usage des Missionaires). Paris, 1907.
SURBLED, *La Morale dans ses Rapports avec la Médecine et l'Hygiène.* Paris, 1896.
TAUNTON, *The Law of the Church.* London, 1906.
THEINER, *Acta Genuina SS. Oecum. Conc. Tridentini.* Zagrabiae (Crotiae).
THOMAS, *Summa Divi Thomae Aquinatis.* Romae, 1894.
TOPAI, *De Necessitate uteri in generatione et in Matrimonio.* Romae, 1903.
VACANT-MANGENOT, *Dictionnaire de Théologie Catholique.* Art., "*Disparité de Culte,*" "*Parenté Naturelle,*" "*Affinité,*" etc. Paris, 1903.
VECCHIOTTI, *Institutiones Canonicae.* Augustae Taurinorum, 1905.
VERING, *Lehrbuch des katholischen, orientalischen und protestantischen Kirchenrechts.* Freiburg, i. B., 1893.
VON SCHERER, *Handbuch des Kirchenrechts.* Graz, 1898.
WERNZ, *Ius Decretalium.* Romae, 1905.
WETZER-WELTE'S KIRCHENLEXIKON. Art., "*Ehe,*" "*Verwandtschaft,*" etc. Freiburg i. B., 1882.
ZHISMAN, *Das Eherecht der Orientalischen Kirche.* Wien, 1864.
ZITELLI, *Apparatus Iuris Ecclesiastici.* Ratisbonae, 1903.

C. BOOKS CONTAINING PARTICULAR INFORMATION.

ALLÈGRE, *Impedimentorum Matrimoniorum Synopsis.* Paris, 1889.
AVOGARDO, *Teorica dell' istituzione del Matrimonio.* Torino, 1861.
AYRINHAC, *Marriage Legislation in the New Code of Canon Law.* New York, 1919.
BANGEN, *Instructio Practica de Sponsalibus et Matrimonio.* Monasterii, 1858.
BASDEVANT, *Des Rapports de l'Eglise et de l'Etat dans la Législation du Mariage.* Paris, 1900.
BASSIBEY, *Le Mariage devant les Tribunaux ecclésiastiques.* Paris, 1899.
BINDERS, *Handbuch des kath. Eherechts.* Freiburg im Bresgau, 1891.
BINGHAM, *Christian Marriage.* New York, 1900.
BISHOP, *Marriage, Divorce and Separation.* Chicago, 1892.
BOUDINHON, *Le Mariage et les Fiançailles.* Paris, 1908.
BURTSELL, in the *Catholic Encyclopedia.* Art., "*Consanguinity,*" "*Affinity.*"
CARRIÈRE, *Praelectiones Teologicae de Matrimonio.* Parisiis, 1837.
CREAGH, *A Commentary on the Decree "Ne Temere."* Baltimore, 1908.
CRITCHLOW, *The Forms of Betrothal.* Baltimore, 1903.
CRONIN, *The new matrimonial legislation.* London, 1909.
DANIEL, *Le Mariage Chrétien et le Code Napoléon.* Paris, 1870.
DE BECKER, *De Sponsalibus et Matrimonio.* Bruxellis, 1896.
DE JUSTIS, *De Dispensationibus Matrimonialibus.* Lucae, 1691.
DE SMET, *De Sponsalibus et Matrimonio.* Brugis, 1909.
DESMOND, *The Church and the Law.* Chicago, 1898.

DEVAS, *Studies in Family Life.* London, 1886.
DEVINE, *The Law of Christian Marriage.* New York, 1908.
ESMEIN, *Le Mariage en Droit Canonique.* Paris, 1891.
EVERSLEY, *The Law and Domestic Relations.* London, 1906.
FAHRNER, *Geschichte der Ehescheidung im kanonischen Recht.* Freiburg, 1903.
FEIJE, *De Impedimentis et Dispensationibus Matrimonialibus.* Lovanii, 1874.
FERRERES, *Los Esponsales y el Matrimonio.* Madrid, 1909.
FREISEN, *Geschichte des kanonischen Eherechts bis zum Verfall der Glossenlitteratur.* Paderborn, 1893.
FUNK, *Cölibat und Priesterehe im christlichen Alterthum.* Kirchengeschichtliche Abhandlungen und Untersuchungen. Paderborn, 1897.
GASPARRI, *Tractatus Canonicus De Matrimonio.* Paris, 1891.
GEARY, *Marriage and Family Relations.* London, 1892.
GENESTAL, *Histoire de la légitimation des enfants naturels en droit canonique.* Paris, 1905.
GENICOT, *Theologiae Moralis Institutiones* (vol. II. *De Matrimonio,* pp. 486-636). Lovanii, 1905.
GIOVINE, *De Dispensationibus Matrimonialibus Consultationes Canonicae.* Neapoli, 1863.
GIRAUD-TEULON, *Les Origines du Mariage et de la Famille.* Paris, 1884.
HEINER, *Grundriss des katholischen Eherechts.* Münster i. W., 1905.
HEISS, *De Matrimonio Tractatus Quinque.* Monachii, 1861.
HEUSER, *De Potestate statuendi impedimenta dirimentia, pro fidelium matrimoniis soli Ecclesiae propria.* Lovanii, 1853.
HILLING, *Die Römische Curie.* Paderborn, 1906.
HOLLWECK, *Die Kirchlichen Strafgesetze.* Mainz, 1899.
HOLLWECK, *Das Civileherecht des Bürgerlichen Gesetzbuchs, dargestellt im Lichte des kanonischen Eherechts.* Mainz, 1900.
HUSSAREK VON HEINLEIN, *Die bedingte Eheschliessung.* Wien, 1892.
HUTH, *The Marriage of Near-Kin considered with respect to law of nations, the results of experience and the teachings of biology.* London, 1875.
JODER, *Formulaire Matrimoniale.* Paris, 1891.
LECLERCQ, *La Législation conciliaire relative au célibat ecclésiastique,* in the *Dictionnaire d'Archéologie chrétienne.* 1910.
LEFEBVRE, *Leçons d'introduction générale à l'histoire du droit matrimonial français.* Paris, 1900.
LEHMKUHL, *Teologia Moralis* (vol. II, *De Matrimonio,* pp. 480-634). Friburgi Brisgoviae, 1910.
LEHR, *Le Mariage, le Divorce et la Séparation de corps dans les principaux pays civilisés.* Paris, 1899.
LEITNER, *Die tridentinische Eheschliessungsform nach der Konstitution Pius X. "Provida."* Regensburg, 1906.
LEMAIRE, *Le Mariage Civil.* Paris, 1901.
LEO XIII, Encyclical *"Arcanum Divinae"* (February 10, 1880), *Leonis XIII, Acta,* vol. II, pp. 10-40. Romae, 1882.
LEROY, *La Religion des Primitifs.* Paris, 1909.
LUCKOCK, *The History of Marriage, Jewish and Christian, in relation to Divorce and certain forbidden degrees.* London, 1895.
MATHARAN, *Casus de Matrimonio.* Paris, 1893.

MANSELLA, *De Impedimentis Matrimonium dirimentibus ac de Processu Iudiciali.* Romae, 1881.
MAZZEI, *De Matrimonio Conscientiae.* Romae, 1766.
MCLENNAN, *Exogamy and Endogamy.* In the *Fortnightly Review*, vol. XXI, p. 884 ff.
MCNICHOLAS, *The new legislation on engagements and marriage.* Philadelphia, 1908.
MELODY, *Marriage and Near Kin.* In the *Catholic University Bulletin* (January, 1903, pp. 40-60). Washington, D. C.
MEYNIAL, *Le Mariage après les invasions.* Paris, 1898.
MIFSUD, *La Deroga all' impedimento de clandestinità.* Roma, 1891.
MOY, *Das Eherecht der Christen in der morgenländischen und abendländischen Kirche bis zur Zeit Karls des Grossen.* Regensburg, 1833.
MURRAY, *The Law relating to the Property of married Persons.* Glasgow, 1892.
NEUSTADT, *Kritische Studien zum Familienrecht des bürgerlichen Gesetzbuchs.* Berlin, 1907.
NOLDIN, *Summa Theologiae Moralis* (vol. III, *De Matrimonio*, pp. 572-786). Oeniponte, 1912.
OJETTI, *De Romana Curia.* Romae, 1910.
OJETTI, *Ius Antepianum et Pianum ex decreto "Ne Temere."* Romae, 1908.
ORTOLAN, *Disparité de culte.* In the *Dictionnaire de Théologie Catholique.* Paris, 1903.
PALMIERI, *Tractatus de Matrimonio Christiano.* Romae, 1880.
PERRONE, *De Matrimonio Christiano.* Leodii, 1861.
PLANCHARD, *Dispenses Matrimoniales.* Angoulême, 1882.
POMPEN, *Tractatus de Dispensationibus et de revalidatione Matrimonii.* Amstelodami, 1897.
PUTZER, *Commentarium in Facultates Apostolicas.* Neo-Eboraci, 1893.
ROSKOVÁNY, *Supplementa ad Collectiones monumentorum et Litteraturae de Matrimonio.* Nitriae, 1887.
ROSSET, *De Sacramento Matrimonii, tractatus dogmaticus, moralis, canonicus, liturgicus et indiciarius.* Parisiis, 1895-1896.
ROSSI, *de Consensu Matrimoniali.* Romae, 1911.
ROSSI, *De Impedimento Impotentiae.* Romae, 1910.
SABETTI-BARRETT, *Compendium Theologiae Moralis.* (*De Matrimonio*, pp. 796-970). Neo-Eboraci, 1916.
SANCHEZ, *Disputationum de Sancto Matrimonii Sacramento tomi tres.* Antverpiae, 1626.
SCHNITZER, *Katholisches Eherecht.* Freiburg i. Br., 1898.
SCHULTE, *Handbuch des katholischen Eherechts.* Giessen, 1855.
SLATER, *A Manual of Moral Theology. Marriage* (vol. II, pp. 251-366). New York, 1908.
SLATER, *The New Marriage Law.* In the *Month*, 1908, pp. 337 ff.; and 633 ff.
STAPF, *Pastoralunterricht über die Ehe.* Frankfurt am Main, 1829.
THEOLOGIA MECHLINIENSIS, *Tractatus de Sponsalibus et Matrimonio.* Mechliniae, 1911.
THOMAE AB ARGENTINA Commentaria in Sententiis. (Lib. IV, Dist. XXVI-XLII). Venetiis, 1564.
THOMAS, *Summa Theologiae, De Sacramento Matrimonii* (Tertiae Partis Supplementum qq. XLI-LXVIII). Romae, 1894.

TOURNEAU, *The Evolution of Marriage and of the Family.* New York, 1891.
TRENTA, *La Nuova Disciplina sulla Celebrazione degli Sponsali e del Matrimonio.* Ascoli Piceno, 1909.
VAN DE BURGT, *Tractatus de dispensationibus matrimonialibus.* Sylvae-Ducis, 1865.
VAN DE BURGT-SCHAEPMAN, *Tractatus de Matrimonio.* Ultrajecti, 1908.
VECCHIOTTI, *De Matrimonio.* Augustae Taurinorum, 1905.
VENTURA, *Il Matrimonio Cristiano.* Napoli, 1859.
VERMEERSCH, *De Casu Apostoli.* Brugis, 1911.
VERMEERSCH, *De Forma Sponsalium ac Matrimonii.* Brugis, 1908.
WATKINS, *Holy Matrimony.* London, 1895.
WERNZ, *Ius Matrimoniale Ecclesiae Catholicae* (Lib. IV, Ius Decr.). Romae, 1904.
WESTERMARCK, *Geschichte der menschlichen Ehe.* Yena, 1893.
WOOD, *Marriage.* Manchester, 1887.
WOUTERS, *Commentarius in Decretum "Ne Temere."* Amstelodami, 1910.
ZIMMERMAN, *Der Priester-Cölibat.* Kempten, 1899.
ZITELLI, *De dispensationibus Matrimonialibus.* Romae, 1887.

Universitas Catholica Americae

Washingtonii, D. C.

S. Facultas Theologica

1918-1919

No. 6

TITULI

DEUS LUX MEA

TITULI

QUOS

AD DOCTORATUS GRADUM

IN

IURE CANONICO

Apud Universitatem Catholicam Americae

CONSEQUENDUM

PUBLICE PROPUGNABIT

JOSEPHUS JULIUS PETROVITS

SACERDOS DIOECESIS HARRISBURGENSIS

SACRAE THEOLOGIAE DOCTOR

ET

JURIS CANONICI LICENTIATUS

HORA X A. M. DIE XXXI. MAII A. D. MCMXIX

I. De rescriptis (Can. 36—Can. 62).
II. De privilegiis (Can. 63—Can. 79).
III. De dispensationibus in genere (Can. 80—Can. 86).
IV. De personis relate ad domicilium et quasi-domicilium (Can. 91—Can. 95).
V. De clericorum adscriptione alicui dioecesi (Can. 111—Can. 117).
VI. De electione Episcoporum in Statibus Foederatis Americae Septentrionalis.
VII. De potestate ordinaria et delegata (Can. 196—Can. 209).
VIII. De baptismo et de ministro et subiecto baptismi (Can. 737—Can. 754).
IX. De significatione verborum "Persona baptizata in Ecclesia catholica" relate ad impedimentum disparitatis cultus et formam matrimonii.
X. De ritibus et caeremoniis baptismi et de patrinis in baptismo adhibitis (Can. 755—Can. 769).
XI. De ministro, subiecto, tempore et loco confirmationis et de patrinis in confirmatione adhibitis (Can. 782—Can. 797).
XII. De ministro et subiecto sacrae communionis (Can. 845—Can. 866).
XIII. De reservatione peccatorum, de subiecto sacramenti poenitentiae et de loco ad confessiones audiendas (Can. 893—Can. 910).
XIV. De ministro, subiecto, ritibus et caeremoniis extremae unctionis (Can. 938—Can. 947).
XV. De iis quae sacrae ordinationi praeire debent (Can. 992—Can. 1001).
XVI. De natura matrimonii eiusque divisione (Can. 1012 et Can. 1015).
XVII. De finibus matrimonii eiusque essentialibus proprietatibus (Can. 1013).
XVIII. De competentia et differentia potestatis ecclesiasticae et civilis in rebus matrimonialibus (Can. 1016).
XIX. De sponsalibus (Can. 1017).

Vidit Sacra Facultas:
EDMUNDUS T. SHANAHAN, S. T. D., Ph. D., J. U. L., p. t., Decanus.

JOANNES I. RYAN, S. T. D., LL. D., p. t., a Secretis.

Vidit Rector Universitatis:
✠ THOMAS I. SHAHAN, S. T. D., J. U. L., LL.D.

www.ingramcontent.com/pod-product-compliance
Lightning Source LLC
LaVergne TN
LVHW050300080826
844660LV00012B/666

* 9 7 8 0 8 1 3 2 2 1 9 7 7 *